Virtualizing Oracle®
Databases on vSphere®

VMware Press is the official publisher of VMware books and training materials, which provide guidance on the critical topics facing today's technology professionals and students. Enterprises, as well as small- and medium-sized organizations, adopt virtualization as a more agile way of scaling IT to meet business needs. VMware Press provides proven, technically accurate information that will help them meet their goals for customizing, building, and maintaining their virtual environment.

With books, certification and study guides, video training, and learning tools produced by world-class architects and IT experts, VMware Press helps IT professionals master a diverse range of topics on virtualization and cloud computing and is the official source of reference materials for preparing for the VMware Certified Professional Examination.

VMware Press is also pleased to have localization partners that can publish its products into more than 42 languages, including, Chinese (Simplified), Chinese (Traditional), French, German, Greek, Hindi, Japanese, Korean, Polish, Russian, and Spanish.

For more information about VMware Press, please visit **vmwarepress.com**.

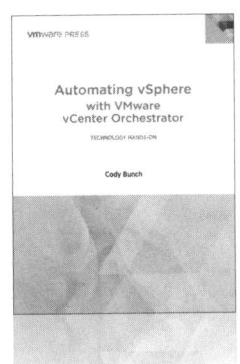
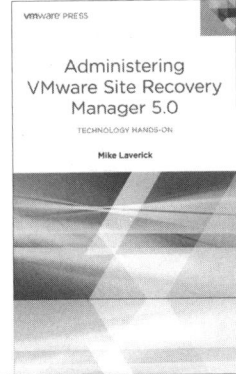

Virtualizing Oracle® Databases on vSphere®

Kannan Mani, Don Sullivan

vmware® PRESS

Upper Saddle River, NJ • Boston • Indianapolis • San Francisco
New York • Toronto • Montreal • London • Munich • Paris • Madrid
Capetown • Sydney • Tokyo • Singapore • Mexico City

Virtualizing Oracle® Databases on vSphere®

ISBN-10: 0-13-357018-5
ISBN-13: 978-0-13-357018-2

Library of Congress Control Number: 2014914987

Printed in the United States of America

First Printing: October 2014

Warning and Disclaimer

Special Sales

For information about buying this title in bulk quantities, or for special sales opportunities (which may include electronic versions; custom cover designs; and content particular to your business, training goals, marketing focus, or branding interests), please contact our corporate sales department at corpsales@pearsoned.com or (800) 382-3419.

For government sales inquiries, please contact governmentsales@pearsoned.com.

For questions about sales outside the U.S., please contact international@pearsoned.com.

VMWARE PRESS PROGRAM MANAGER
Dave Nelson

ASSOCIATE PUBLISHER
David Dusthimer

ACQUISITIONS EDITORS
Joan Murray
Mary Beth Ray

DEVELOPMENT EDITOR
Dan Young

TECHNICAL EDITORS
Greg Loughmiller
Marlin McNeil

MANAGING EDITOR
Sandra Schroeder

PROJECT EDITOR
Mandie Frank

COPY EDITOR
Keith Cline

PROOFREADER
Kathy Ruiz

INDEXER
Brad Herriman

DESIGNER
Chuti Prasertsith

COMPOSITOR
Bumpy Design

EDITORIAL ASSISTANT
Vanessa Evans

*This book is dedicated to my wife, Mohana, and my two sons,
Sricharan and Akshay, for their continued support in all ways,
and to my parents for their inspiration.
I also dedicate this book to the Oracle and VMware communities.*

—Kannan Mani

*The success of this book should be shared. First, Donald E. Sullivan,
my dad, who taught business computing before the first billionaires,
introduced me to computing many years ago.
My friend Ron Sparagoski taught me how to coach and how to lead.
Two of my professors at Arizona State University, Roger Eck and
Michael Goul, are responsible for my expertise in the subject of data.
My friend Jeff Francis worked tirelessly to help me understand
operating systems. My colleagues at Polyserve inspired me to
brave the world of the start-up, and Kannan Mani believed
in me enough to convince me to co-author this book.
And finally, my friend and mentor in all things Oracle, Scott Gossett.*

—Don Sullivan

Contents

Foreword   xv

Introduction   xix

About the Authors   xxiii

Acknowledgments   xxv

About the Reviewers   xxix

Chapter 1   Introduction to Oracle Databases on Virtual Infrastructure   1

Virtualization with ESXi and vSphere and the Software-Defined Datacenter   3

Virtualizing Oracle Databases on vSphere: Benefits and Examples   7

Oracle Databases and DBA Fundamentals   8

Understanding Oracle Database Architectures   11

Summary   12

Chapter 2   Virtualization and High-Performance Oracle Workloads   15

Virtualized Oracle Environments on vSphere Key Benefits   15

Consolidating Platforms to Reduce Datacenter Costs   17

Enhancing Database Availability and Cost-Effective Disaster Recovery   19

Provisioning Rapid and New Database Server Environments   21

Reducing Planned Downtime with Migration of Live Oracle Database Servers   22

Guaranteeing Resources in a Shared Environment   23

Achieving IT Compliance   24

Zeroing In on Key Trigger Events   24

Solving Oracle Database Deployment and Management Issues Using VMware   25

Implementing Dynamic Oracle Datacenter Resource Management   26

Minimizing Server Sprawl   27

Meeting SLA Demands for Database Performance, Availability, and Disaster Recovery   27

Supporting a Dynamic Business Environment   27

Minimizing License Costs   28

Maximizing Oracle Workloads and Sizing   28

Option 1: Sizing the Oracle DB Workload   30

Option 2: Sizing the Oracle DB Application Vendor Recommendations   32

Option 3: Sizing Oracle DB Server Vendor Guidelines   35

Testing the Limits: Performance Studies and Stress Tests   36

Summary   36

Chapter 3   Oracle Databases and Applications in Virtual Infrastructure: Architectural Concepts   37

VMware ESXi Hypervisor   38

Designing Databases on VMware   41

Designing for Scalability on Demand   42

Designing for High Availability   44

Maintaining Compliance   48

Consolidating Database Servers   48

Virtualizing Oracle RAC   51

Identifying Key Stakeholders   53

Summary   54

Chapter 4   Oracle on vSphere Best Practices   55

Implementing ESX Host Best Practices   57

Maximizing Performance Using BIOS Settings   58

Operating System Processes   59

Upgrading the Version of ESX/ESXi and vSphere   60

Maximizing Support for a Hardware-Assisted Memory Management Unit   61

Implementing Memory-Related Best Practices   61

Supporting Large Pages   64

Implementing Compute (vCPU)-Related Best Practices   65

Configuring Storage-Related Best Practices   68

Categorizing Storage Virtualization Technologies   71

Understanding Storage Protocol Capabilities   71

Understanding Database Layout Considerations   73

Comparing VMFS to RDM: Performance and Functionality   76

Networking Guidelines   78

Monitoring Performance on vSphere   79

Timekeeping in Virtual Machines   81

Summary   82

Chapter 5   Oracle Database High Availability: Planned and Unplanned Downtime   83

Protecting the Virtualized Environment with vSphere High Availability   84

Protecting Applications with vSphere and Symantec AppHA   86

Understanding Oracle RAC in Virtual Machines   88

Implementing Oracle RAC One Node   88

Implementing Multinode RAC   90

Deploying Oracle RAC on vSphere   92

Protecting Oracle Databases Against Downtime   98

Transitioning RAC Nodes Between Hosts Using VMware vMotion   100
To RAC or Not to RAC   103
Summary   104

Chapter 6   Performance Workload and Functional Stress Test Studies   105

Oracle Single-Instance Workload Study   106
Test Methodology   106
Test Result Details   109
Oracle RAC Workload Characterization Study   121
vMotion and VMware HA   121
Large-Scale Order Entry Benchmark Kit (Swingbench)   122
Architecture   123
Network Configuration   125
Oracle RAC Installation Overview   130
24-Hour Workload Test   131
Oracle RAC Node vMotion Test   132
Mega vMotion-RAC Functional Stress Test   135
Summary   139

Chapter 7   Support and Licensing   141

Contemplating Oracle Software Support and Licensing   141
Understanding Oracle Certification and Support for VMware Environments   143
Certification of Oracle on VMware vSphere   144
Licensing Oracle   147
Advising VMware Customers   149
Summary   154

Chapter 8   Performance Management and Monitoring   155

Performance Management Terminology   157
The Role of the DBA in Performance Management   158
Processing Power: CPU or vCPU   159
CPU Ready Time (%RDY)   162
Memory   164
System Huge Pages   167
Transparent Page Sharing   172
Non-Uniform Memory Access   172
Networking   175
Network Load Testing   176
Dropped Packets   177

Storage Configuration and Utilization   181

    SCSI Queues   182

    NFS Storage   185

    Storage Access Latency   187

    Spindle Busy Average   190

Understanding SCSI Queue Depth on an ESX/ESXi Host and Virtual Machine   191

    Storage Path Throughput   192

    Storage Benchmarking VMDK   193

    Benchmarking and Ongoing Maintenance   197

    Iometer   198

    Oracle ORION   203

Comparing Storage Types   219

    Block Alignment   220

    Using pvSCSI and LSI Controllers   222

    ASM Is Comparable to an LVM   225

Understanding the Oracle Enterprise Manager vCOPS Adapter   228

    Using Oracle Database Server Metrics   230

    Installing Oracle Enterprise Manager Adapter   232

    Validating the OEM Adapter   233

    Creating Oracle Database Custom Dashboard   233

    Configuring a Metric Graph (Rollover View) Widget   235

    Configuring a Generic Scoreboard Widget   235

    Finalizing the Oracle Database Dashboard   236

Summary   239

Chapter 9   Business Continuity and Disaster Recovery   241

VMware vCenter Site Recovery Manager   243

    vSphere Replication   245

    Storage Array-Based Replication   247

    Storage Replication Adapters   247

    Application-Based Replication   248

    Oracle Data Guard   248

    Repairing Logical Data Block Corruption with Oracle Data Guard   249

Combining vSphere Replication and Data Guard   250

    Testing SRM vSphere Replication   251

Using Storage Array-Based Replication with vSphere   253

Virtual Provisioning for Oracle ASM Disk Groups   255

Solution Findings   256

Creating a Disaster Recovery Plan   257

    Configure Connections   257

    Break the Connection   257

Export System Logs   257

Using Array-Based Replication   258

Summary   264

Chapter 10   Backup and Recovery   267

Backup and Recovery Principles   269

Backing Up Data Using In-Guest Software Solutions   270

Oracle Database Backup Methods   270

Classic Oracle Database Backups   270

Listing of Storage Vendor Backup Tools   272

Other Backup Tools   273

Storage Vendor Backup Solutions   273

Working with NetApp Backup Solutions   274

NetApp Backup and Restore Solution Overview   274

Integrating NetApp with vSphere   274

Working with NetApp Snapshot   275

Backing Up a Virtualized Oracle Database with NetApp Snapshot   275

Tools Available for Backups of Oracle Using NetApp   276

Step-by-Step Solution for Backing Up a Virtualized Oracle Database with NetApp Storage and NFS Datastores   277

Restoring a Database Using NetApp Snapshot   277

Backup and Restore Use Case with Snap Creator   278

EMC Avamar Backup and Restore Solution Overview   279

Backing Up the Oracle Database   280

Restoring the Oracle Database   281

VMware Data Protection Advanced   281

Comparing VMFS and RDM   282

Backups   283

Understand the Functionality of VMFS Versus RDMs   283

Oracle Data Guard for Backup   284

Oracle Database Backup Strategy Matrix   286

Summary   286

Chapter 11   Provisioning and Automation   289

Migrating Oracle Database from a Physical to Virtual Environment   291

Viewing Oracle Migration from a Physical to Virtual Solution   293

Facilitating Deployments   294

Understanding the Business Scenario   294

Lab Architecture   295

Migrating Oracle Database from Physical to Virtual   296

Configuring Application Blueprints Using vCAC   302

Building a Database-as-a-Service Platform   311

    Listing the Benefits of DBaaS   312

    Allocating Storage as Part of the DBaaS Paradigm   313

    Choosing the Components of a DBaaS Architecture   313

Summary   314

Chapter 12   Case Studies   317

Indiana University   318

American Tire Distributors   320

EMC Information Technology   321

Green Mountain Power   323

The Idaho Supreme Court   324

The University of British Columbia   326

VMware Information Technologies   327

So Many Others   330

Working with Events   330

Summary   332

Book Conclusion   332

Index   341

Foreword

One of my favorite quotes comes from motivational speaker and business leader Harvey Mackay. He recently wrote, "'Genius' is sometimes just not realizing that something is impossible." That most certainly is the story behind my success as one of the earliest people to virtualize Oracle databases on VMware vSphere. My first experience with this impressive combination of technology was virtualizing Oracle 10g on Linux using VMware ESX 2.5 for the production environment and VMware GSX Server for the non-production systems.

The system was SharePoint Portal Server in a medium server farm configuration, with an in-house application using custom Web Parts. SQL Server was used for the SharePoint database. For reasons tied to "developer preferences," Oracle 10g was used as the back-end database that the custom Web Parts used for their work. We loaded and tuned the systems following the spirit of much of the best practices we know and are now documented in this book today.

It worked. Flawlessly.

In fact, it worked so well that something as simple as a virtual machine (VM) snapshot on our GSX server systems literally saved the entire project one day from an overzealous developer who accidently trashed the entirety of the production and development code bases. A simple snapshot rollback saved both of them in a matter of minutes. Nobody questioned whether it would work. Nobody knew enough to question this. Nobody worried about licensing per se. Of course, this client's very deep pockets gave us "all you can eat" enterprise site licenses for everything, so we wouldn't have worried anyway. Nobody questioned whether anything we did was supported by the vendors. It was early enough in those days that the vendors provided support because they didn't know, or weren't concerned, about using a hypervisor to deploy their systems and applications on virtualized infrastructure.

A few years later, some vendors (arguably more for business as opposed to technical reasons) had begun to care. Once again, my new team and I were challenged to break a new set of rules—ironically with another division of the same client. This time, we deployed a production vSphere platform on converged infrastructure, complete with an iSCSI over lossless 10GbE SAN using jumbo frames (no Fibre Channel anywhere), disk-based backup, and offsite archive to Cloud storage. We deployed multiple three-node Oracle RAC 11.2.0.1 clusters with grid control (and later 11.2.0.2) running in a configuration where the individual RAC nodes were vMotion capable. All of that was running with VMware vSphere 4.0 (and later 4.0.1). This was the first known production system of its kind ever deployed for a client. While this configuration is considered routine today, back then vMotion capable Oracle RAC nodes were considered impossible.

But, for us, this was a non-negotiable client requirement. So that inevitable combination of 5% inspiration and 95% desperation drove us to ignore the idea of "impossible" and instead find a way to make it work. We broke all kinds of established rules along the way—and set industry firsts and new best practices in the process.

Again, it worked flawlessly, and even more impressive, it was easily fast enough to serve as a backup platform for the Oracle Exadata V2 system we had integrated into our overall solution. I'll never forget the phone calls I had with Kannan back then when we'd realized what we had just accomplished.

A short time later, we adapted what we learned with Oracle RAC on that fully converged architecture to create a configuration that enabled both RAC and SQL Server clusters to be virtualized and be vMotion capable on any supported vSphere configuration—not just native iSCSI storage. The way we did it is still considered ground breaking today all of these years later.

All throughout this engagement and others since, we fought through the mislaid perceptions and even outright objections to virtualizing Oracle databases being possible. We learned that it is tough for certain software vendors to argue against something being possible to do when faced with the direct evidence of it working perfectly right before their eyes. Amazingly, a few were not convinced even when faced with this evidence. We then learned the importance of negotiating our way through both the business and technology sides of the Oracle database virtualization proposition. That meant having sometimes-heated discussions about Oracle licensing and support with people who were part of the technical side as well as sales. Most amazing were the discussions where some clients were absolutely convinced of their (mis)perceptions of the capabilities of virtual infrastructure. One client I worked with actually considered licensing every single ESX server they had in their building, including production and development, for Oracle RAC—because they were concerned that it might someday run an Oracle database (even though Oracle had never been running or installed anywhere even close to the vast majority of those systems).

You, the reader of this book, have a distinct advantage over early adopters and those of us who learned these lessons the hard way. In this book, Don and Kannan have provided a treasure trove of information and time-saving tips to get the most out of your Oracle on vSphere deployments. As a part of that, they have included ways to overcome the most common issues (and several less-common ones), as well as organizational and even political objections you might encounter. It's all presented in an easy to understand and easy to use format by authors who, by the way, happen to be the foremost experts on the subject you can find anywhere today.

You'll learn about the four V's: viability, value, versatility, and vision. These four tenants cover the full spectrum of issues most everyone will face when virtualizing Oracle on vSphere. Building upon this foundation, the authors deliver a practical set of technical and business best practices for compute, networking, and storage topics, which are presented in detail. You'll learn how to plan for, install, and properly optimize Oracle and Oracle RAC from the leading technical minds on the subject. In addition, there are discussions and tips on how to plan for and properly license Oracle to fit your business needs to ensure that you get maximum value out of your investment. Most important, you'll learn how to get support for Oracle on your vSphere platform, and along the way, you'll see that Oracle on vSphere is arguably supported in a way that's even better than what is available when running Oracle on physical infrastructure alone.

If you're looking to get the most out of Oracle on vSphere, keep this book in an easy-to-reach, prominent place on your desk. You will want to come back to it again and again. Oracle and vSphere together make up one of the most powerful and compatible combinations of technology you can find anywhere. I never cease to be amazed at what we've been able to accomplish with these tools and, as they continue to mature, the future looks very bright. I look forward to seeing you on this incredible journey.

—Chris Williams,
Global Practice Director Data Center
Consulting, Dimension Data

Introduction

The idea of virtualization of infrastructure for all levels of workload is a settled concept in the information technology industry. Because the subject of this book is VMware, we will examine the various factors that have driven the industry toward this inevitable outcome from the perspective of VMware, but the concept of virtualization is a much older and broader concept than the company that has changed the world over the past decade, VMware. The term *virtual* as well as the basic concept of virtualization was probably first used by IBM in the 1960s, along with the concept of a hypervisor, which was derived from the technical concept of a supervisor.

As the decades have progressed, the term virtual has been used, and overused, and as so many other terms in this industry, the term has often been abused. But most significantly, the term has come to depict a true and comprehensive abstraction of the server from a physical resource to a logical resource. As the chapters in the book progress, we discuss the ideas of Type 1 and Type 2 hypervisors as well as paravirtualization versus non-paravirtualization, but regardless of the specific architectural precepts, the idea of true virtualization allows for ubiquitous resource abstraction and all the benefits that are implied therein.

There is a trend in the technology industry of various companies monopolizing or at least claiming certain cultural ownership over letters of the alphabet. Technology professionals can easily guess which companies effectively have laid claim over certain letters. Facebook has claimed the letter *F*, Google *G*, Oracle *O*, Apple *i*, and Twitter has the letter *t*. VMware can therefore claim the letter *v*, specifically in lowercase. Sticking with the theme and labeled with the letter *v*, it is useful to have the discussion about virtualization categorized with that same letter, four times. Viability, value, versatility, and vision constitute the most significant headings of any VMware discussion, especially a discussion focused on business-critical applications (BCAs). Most prominent among those BCA or Tier 1 (maybe even Tier 0) apps are SAP, Microsoft apps such as SQL Server and Exchange, and of course, Oracle.

As time progresses, it is impossible to ignore the pervasive trends in the industry. You may resist, but you will eventually have to at least adapt to and recognize those trends or have them render you obsolete. Years ago, database administrators (DBAs) were responsible for managing databases and only databases. As the more sophisticated relational database management systems (RDBMS) were developed, the role of the DBA was innately expanded. Oracle Parallel Server and subsequently Oracle Real Application Clusters (RAC) forced the database professional to become adept at managing certain network functions; otherwise, the RAC interconnect would not be defined adequately, and the ensuing instability would return unfavorable results. Automatic Storage

Management (ASM) forced the Oracle professional to become a storage administrator, because most professional storage administrators did not embrace the idea of managing an ASM instance. In this decade, we have observed the concepts of virtualization being imposed on the database professional. Reporters in the blogosphere, speakers at conferences, and frequent chat room residents readily use terms such as *vDBA* and *vRAC-DBA* to depict the new set of skills that this decade's database professional must possess or risk obsolescence.

Prerequisites

This book will enhance the overall work and academic experience of anyone on any level who considers themselves to be an Oracle professional. The deep technical considerations are appropriate for the DBAs as well as the developers in the audience, whereas the higher-level architectural concepts will help information architects of all disciplines to build out elegant and effective systems architectures. Management personnel will find this book invaluable with regard to the nontechnical areas, particularly the sections on licensing and support. They will also find the high-level technical explanations both revealing and confirming.

Anyone who has responsibility for any part of an application stack that includes Oracle software, from the most junior administrator to the seasoned veteran, will find something within these pages to enhance their overall effectiveness as an IT professional.

Who Should Read This Book

This work has been crafted to include subject matter that is pertinent to not only each level of an application stack but also to each professional discipline. Many technical books are crafted as technical manuals or as academic texts. This book, in part, is a compilation of stories and analogies taken from many conversations over many years and therefore, is written in a manner best suited to be used as the focus of dialogue of a group of disparate IT professionals loitering around someone's cube at the end of a day. It is written to be conversation starter, and it is written in a conversational style.

Book Overview

The topics this book covers vary from the deep minutia to elegant architecture and from the profoundly obvious to the subtle and elusive. This book is neither a textbook nor a technical manual; it is literary work. In the interest of that literary effort, we have made substantial use of allegories, metaphors, and analogies for the purpose of both attaining and maintaining the attention of the reader and creating indelible images that have some lasting effect. We have also endeavored to create a conversational tone, which is similar to the approach that we have both used at countless customer meetings, conference speaking sessions, and executive briefings over many years. Our intent is to use this literary work to bring to you, the reader, the essence and the substance of the conversations that we have had over many years. In respect of this effort, we have included web links to many of the documents that we cite so that the reader may immediately access pertinent details. The compilation of the graphs, tables, links, and lists is an essential element of philosophy that this book is based on.

The initial chapters (1–3) focus on the basic ideas of Oracle and vSphere, as well as Oracle on vSphere, and the various different roles involved with that effort. Small, medium, and high workloads are discussed as well as the respective architectures and architectural concepts that should be utilized to optimize the capabilities of the virtualized infrastructure.

Chapter 4 focuses on long-developed best practices for all high workloads, with particular focus on Oracle running on vSphere. Chapter 5 transitions into the realm of high availability and all the options available to meet the requirements of every service level agreement (SLA). Chapter 6 digs deeper into the technical details necessary to grasp when optimizing Oracle performance on vSphere. This subject includes each of the various methods of implementing Oracle, including Oracle RAC.

Chapter 7 takes a slight deviation from the technical to discuss the always-intense areas of Oracle Licensing and Support, with special emphasis on the specialized Oracle support team, which is part of VMware's Global Support Services.

The later chapters, beginning with Chapter 8, focus on performance monitoring and management as well as on infrastructure and application management, starting with vCenter Operations Management (vCOPS) and the Oracle Enterprise Manager (OEM) plug-in. A plethora of other tools and management methodologies are either introduced or discussed in detail in this chapter. Chapter 9 focuses on disaster recovery, discussing both VMware's Site Recovery Manager (SRM) and Oracle's Data Guard. Backup and recovery follows in Chapter 10, which covers concepts such as snapshots both from a vSphere and storage perspective. Major storage paradigms, such as Fibre Channel (FC) and network-attached storage (NAS), are given ample coverage.

Chapter 11 encapsulates the Oracle and business-critical applications discussion by transcending the application layer and focusing on the infrastructure management. Provisioning and automation are becoming more important aspects of systems management, and VMware has all the tools to accomplish these tasks and meet the requirements of the provisioning SLAs. vCenter Automation Center (VCAC), vFabric Application Director (vFAD), and vFabric Data Director will soon be coalesced into a single automation and provisioning system, but they are discussed here in terms of their individual functionality.

Finally, the success stories and many case studies are discussed in Chapter 12, "Case Studies." From the massive government institutions to the small start-ups, and from the largest universities to the smallest local school systems, customers are using vSphere as their platform of choice for business-critical and Tier 1/0 applications. ESXi is a hypervisor, but vSphere is a platform of virtualized hardware, and companies of all sizes and styles, and institutions of every possible configuration and purpose, are recognizing the viability and value of running Oracle on vSphere. Everyone who reads the following chapters will also come to recognize vSphere as the premier platform in existence to run Oracle.

About the Authors

 **Kannan Mani** (@kantwit) is currently a Staff Architect - Oracle Solutions for VMware. Kannan has been with VMware for more than 4 years, involved in developing and architecting business critical Oracle solutions on VMware platforms, and helping customers and partners successfully virtualize Oracle on VMware vSphere platform globally. Kannan was previously Reference Architecture Specialist at NetApp, where he architected and developed Oracle solutions on NetApp Storage. Prior to NetApp, Kannan was an Architecture Specialist at Unisys, where he led Oracle Center of Excellence. Kannan is the domain expert in Oracle technologies on various platforms (Storage and Virtualization) and published numerous customer-facing technical documents on Oracle and Database technologies. Kannan has over 17 years in the IT industry experience, and his expertise includes Oracle Real Application Clusters (RAC), Automatic Storage Management (ASM), clustering, customer relationship management (CRM), enterprise resource planning (ERP), business intelligence, performance and scalable enterprise architectures, benchmark and performance, technical solutions marketing and management, virtualization, and Cloud solutions. Kannan is a regular speaker at IOUG, VMworld, VMware Partner Exchange, Oracle Open World, EMC World, NetApp Insight, SNIA, and he is also an evangelist of Oracle technologies. Kannan has been recognized by Oracle as an Oracle ACE, and by VMware as CTO Ambassador and vExpert. Kannan holds a Master's degree in Computer Applications and a Master's degree in Business Administration focused on technology.

 **Don Sullivan**, an Oracle Certified Master, a vExpert, and a VMware CTO Ambassador joined VMware in June of 2010 as a Systems Engineer Database Specialist and Oracle Solution Architect for the entirety of the Americas. In that capacity, he has worked with numerous customers and partners focused on the proposition of running Oracle, SQL, and other high-workload systems on vSphere. Presently, the Product Line Marketing Manager for Business Critical Applications at VMware, Don is a frequent speaker at conferences focused on databases and virtualization.

After finishing his Master's thesis at Arizona State University in 1996, Don focused on logical database design with Sybase TxSql, and he moved to Denver to work as a contract DBA. Don subsequently worked for AT&T as a contract DBA with both Sybase and Oracle. In 1998, he joined Oracle and Oracle University and became a Senior Principal Instructor for Oracle University, focusing on server products. He taught all server-based classes for 6 years, which included all New Features classes, OPS/RAC, Backup & Recovery, Performance Tuning, SQL Tuning, Data Guard, and the Data Server Internals (DSI) classes from 7.3 through 10g. He is a co-author of the Oracle Certified Master Practicum, and he is an original Oracle Certified Master. He also co-authored a performance-tuning class text for MySQL. In 2004, he became a consultant with Oracle's Advanced Technology Services (ATS) and spent the next 18 months involved in a number of proofs of concept (POCs) and other post-sales engagements. In 2005, Don joined Polyserve Corporation as the primary customer-facing Oracle Solution Architect. Although his role was primarily pre-sales, he was involved with all Polyserve customers who had Oracle implementations at every step of their implementation, both pre- and post-sales. In 2007, Polyserve was acquired by HP, and he stayed with HP. In that capacity, Don spent the majority of 2009 through 2013 delivering seminars and workshops to large customer groups focused on Oracle over Network File System (NFS). In 2010, Don joined VMware as a customer-facing Systems Engineer Database Specialist with both Sales and later PSO. In addition, Don is also a project manager for many projects to include cross-corporate functional stress tests. Finally, Don manages the virtualizing applications sub-track at VMworld and VMware's series of select database workshops.

Acknowledgments

Any attempt at listing each and every individual or institution that has influenced our development in the subjects of computing, databases, Oracle, and virtualization (and thus the essence of this book) would prove embarrassingly inadequate. We will, however, endeavor to acknowledge those who directly contributed to the writing of this book by either providing material or explicitly helping us describe the many disparate yet interconnected technical concepts in these pages. Material contributions came in a number of forms. Some individuals contributed to the vast supply of VMware best practices and deployment guides as well as Knowledge Base articles. A few folks directly edited our work, whereas others simply helped us understand nuances of specific areas of technology that are necessary to recognize and discuss if one is to compose a comprehensive book on a subject as deep and broad as Oracle on vSphere.

We should start by recognizing a few companies other than VMware. Oracle, EMC, Cisco, NetApp, and Pure Storage all have many individuals who have significantly influenced our understanding of this technology. VMware has a series of elite Oracle implementation partner companies such as House of Brick, VLSS, Ntirety (now part of Hosting), Viscosity North American, the Yucca Group, and others. These partners work with us at conferences, on panels, and most importantly, with customers on a daily basis.

We will also mention some institutions of higher learning such as Stanford University whose land VMware lives upon but has also provided a number of the great minds that made and keep VMware a great pioneer in technology. Don graduated from both the University of Virginia and Arizona State University, and Kannan studied at Madras University and Walden University. Each of these institutions provided the intellectual framework for both of us on our individual journeys in computing.

Our formal editors from Pearson as and our individual tech editors, Greg Loughmiller and Marlin McNeil, spent significant time with us developing approaches to subtle concepts and composing each and every word. Marlin easily joined us on 25 conference calls, all of which lasted between 1 and 3 hours. Others who contributed to the editing include Mark Achtemichuk, who worked with us on the deep ideas of performance tuning and found the time despite the responsibilities of real life and the arrival of his second child, Luke Patrick. Mark helped us understand that this was an endeavor that needed to be complete and that we were the individuals that needed to complete it. Anoop Jalan stepped up to help us at a time when we were very uncertain as to where, when, or how we would finish. He provided both technical insights and a sense of calm encouragement that helped us attain a degree of serenity during that difficult time. Amanda Blevins has provided much support both professionally and personally over many years. Jonathan Nimer helped us describe the subtleties of the multifaceted requirements of running Oracle on vSphere with clarity. And Tracie Giovanni helped over multiple decades with the creation of a vast array of analogies, many of which are used in this book.

Todd Muirhead, Bob Goldsand, Mohan Potheri, and Vas Mitra all contributed mightily to the VMware SAP collateral, which was the source of our application examples. Avi Nayak contributed to the intellectual direction of our discussion on the subject of database-as-a-service (DBaaS). Jeff Browning referred to vSphere as a platform of virtualized hardware in many public forums and conferences years before the world accepted that profound notion. Shruti Bhat, Chris Rimer, Dave Welch, Will Monin, and the author of our Foreword, Chris Williams, collectively paved the path toward the messaging many years ago that still to this day defines the fundamental parameters of the Oracle on vSphere discussion. Sam Lucido, Darryl Smith, Jeff Szastak, and Mike Webster have all helped develop the industry accepted approaches and methodologies. Kevin Closson, one of the great authorities on Oracle performance, has been a remarkable and generous source of deep and true understanding and discovery for many years.

Jeremy Kuhnash should be acknowledged for his contributions in the area of automation and provisioning. Emad Benjamin is responsible for development of the majority of the Java content, and that underscores much of the application virtualization approach that we have espoused. K. Gopalakrishnan lent his experience around authoring Oracle books, and Sudhir Balasubramanian continuously contributes to all areas of Oracle-related customer-centric and academic-based activities that we engage in. Andy Nelson, through his calm and thoughtful approach to all things technical, has educated both of us in the area of disaster recovery concepts more than anyone.

Jeff Margolese, Scott Salyer, Mike Adams, Stephen Beck, Matt Stepanski, and John Steiner all provided leadership as well as tolerance of the time dedicated to writing this book. Mike Matthies led the Global Support Team that specializes in Oracle with the unambiguous and enthusiastic promise that all Oracle on vSphere-related problems would be addressed by his team and that the service requests would not be closed until resolution was achieved.

All these individuals, named and unnamed, have profoundly assisted us in developing this text which comprehensively covers everything from technical details to philosophical approaches. Maybe even more important, these individuals kept us from being skewered by audiences everywhere by noticing subtle errors and helping us write with a greater degree of linguistic clarity than we could have done alone.

Other contributors who may not even realize that they have implicitly contributed to the body of knowledge that has been drawn from to create this book include the testing teams from Principled Technologies, especially Corey Bunch, who successfully managed the tests and report generation that is often cited in this book. Also Tushar Patel helped complete the hardware configuration and generate the data for the original Oracle workload studies that we describe. Samir Shah for his contribution towards Oracle on VCE.

All the panelists on all the panels at VMworld and other events run over the years, including both customers as well as partners, have contributed enormously to the body of knowledge that made this book possible. Some of those panels and panelists are referenced in this book, and some of the actual panel discussions were videoed and are linked in the various chapters.

Overall, these small but impactful groups of Oracle and VMware professionals that have influenced and contributed to this book constitute a loosely connected team that has no restrictive boundaries to entry and extend well beyond the lawns of the VMware campus and past the temporary residences of our professional careers. The commonality that binds this group is our belief that the best approach for any twenty-first century company to implement their Oracle-based business-critical applications and respective databases is on VMware virtualized infrastructure with vSphere. The introduction of the new Independent Oracle Users Group (IOUG) VMware SIG at VMworld-US in San Francisco in August 2014 is indicative of the worldwide adoption of this approach. In closing, we believe that this book constitutes a triumph of the committed with both Oracle and VMware with their shared customers being the ultimate victors.

About the Reviewers

Greg Loughmiller is currently a member of NetApp's Enterprise Ecosystem Organization with a focus on Database Solutions and Architecture using NetApp Storage Systems. He works with the NetApp field community to assist with Solutions and deployments of Oracle databases in the Unix infrastructure space. He also provides assistance with customers for their Oracle deployments on NetApp storage. Prior to working in the Enterprise Ecosystem Organization, Greg was part of the NetApp Professional Services Organization, responsible for designing and implementation of Oracle solutions to meet the needs of those customers across the East Coast of the United States for five years. Greg has been part of organizations responsible for Oracle Database Architecture and deployments for 19+ years. Prior to joining NetApp in 2006, he spent 15 years with a wireless telecommunication provider. All of this time was in the Oracle RDBMS technology space, from Operations DBA, Management of Databases, to a Database Infrastructure Architect.

Marlin McNeil is Managing Partner and co-founder at the Yucca Group. There he champions virtualizing all kinds of Oracle on VMware and is helping clients establish innovative business practices through virtualizing their business-critical computing infrastructure. Formerly, he worked as Technical Services Director at Justice Systems, Inc. (1996–2011) and as an Analyst at RE/SPEC, Inc. (1991–1996) contracted to Sandia National Laboratories.

We Want to Hear from You!

As the reader of this book, *you* are our most important critic and commentator. We value your opinion and want to know what we're doing right, what we could do better, what areas you'd like to see us publish in, and any other words of wisdom you're willing to pass our way.

We welcome your comments. You can email or write to let us know what you did or didn't like about this book—as well as what we can do to make our books better.

Please note that we cannot help you with technical problems related to the topic of this book.

When you write, please be sure to include this book's title and author as well as your name and email address. We will carefully review your comments and share them with the author and editors who worked on the book.

Email: VMwarePress@vmware.com

Mail: VMware Press
         ATTN: Reader Feedback
         800 East 96th Street
         Indianapolis, IN 46240 USA

Reader Services

Visit our website at www.informit.com/title/9780133570182 and register this book for convenient access to any updates, downloads, or errata that might be available for this book.

## Chapter 1

Introduction to Oracle Databases on Virtual Infrastructure

Oracle databases and software run successfully on vSphere and provide significant scalability, availability, and performance benefits. In fact, virtualization quite simply makes Oracle better. What makes the transition smooth is that the Oracle database administrator's (DBA) skill set, deployment technique, and responsibilities do not change when transitioning from a physical to virtual environment. However, it is important that the DBA's scope of responsibility does increase in breadth.

In years past, the DBA's concerns moved into the nedtwork realm as Oracle introduced horizontal scalability with Oracle Cluster (later to become Oracle Parallel Server and finally Oracle Real Application Cluster [RAC]). Over the past decade, the focus of the DBA grew to include storage as Oracle introduced Automatic Storage Management (ASM), and thus, the DBA was confronted with a lack of willingness on the part of the storage administrator to manage the ASM instance. Similarly today, we see the realm of the DBA extend into the virtualization arena. Importantly, it is axiomatic that basic database administration skills do not change when virtualization is included in the stack. This is because ESXi does not alter the kernel of any guest operating system (OS). Likewise, it is equally important for the DBA to embrace the fact that the some components of the stack that affect the database have been extended into the virtualized infrastructure, such as networking, storage access, processing capability, and memory. Consequently, the areas of concern for the DBA have been extended, respectively.

Throughout this book, we maintain a conversational tone along with a thematic approach to the organization centered on the idea of the four V's. Often, it can be both entertaining and memorable to point out certain technology industry trends. The trend of the monopolization of specific letters by certain well-known companies is an example. We all know who dominates the use of the letter *f* or *t* or *i* or even *O*. Ironically, VMware prominently uses the uppercase letter *V* to begin the name VMware, and VMW is the acronym most often associated with VMware. However the main product vSphere begins with a lowercase *v*, and it is commonplace for the individual features to begin with the lowercase letter *v*. The thematic approach referred to earlier will be centered on that letter *V*, although no adherence to the case will be necessary.

The four V's are viability, value, versatility, and vision and are shown in Figure 1-1. The first step in any early implementation process is to convince the critical stakeholders such as the DBAs and information technology (IT) managers that virtualized infrastructure is a *viable* alternative to nonvirtualized infrastructure. Notice the subtlety in the reference to "nonvirtualized infrastructure" as opposed to the more common reference of "physical infrastructure." Subsequent to the viability concerns being satisfied, we move on to the *value* discussion. The value of vSphere as a platform of virtualized hardware for business-critical applications (BCAs) is discussed in great detail as the chapters of this book unfold. The discussion eventually leads to the *versatility* of vSphere and VMware broadly. VMW field personnel will proudly state to all prospective customers that "We are agnostic to both logical and physical architectures." And finally, no discussion on this subject is complete without acknowledgment of the future *vision* of vSphere's capabilities and VMware as a corporation. The choice of transitioning a company's entire IT architecture to this wonderful "Platform of Virtualized Hardware" is succinct in description, profound in consequence, but colossal in potential. Therefore, every potential stakeholder in the company should have an understanding of this vision.

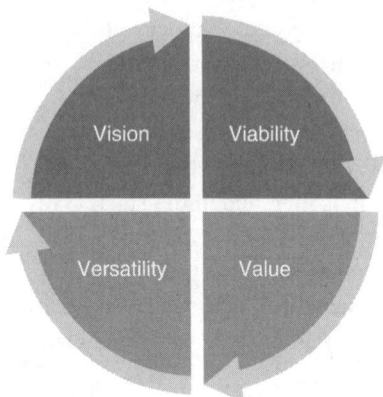

Figure 1-1 Four V's approach

Virtualization with ESXi and vSphere and the Software-Defined Datacenter

ESX or ESXi is the world's leading x86 hypervisor. Hypervisors were first introduced at IBM in the 1960s by abstracting the machine's supervisor state and allowing multiple virtual machines (VMs) to run simultaneously in separate VM contexts. A hypervisor, sometimes scientifically referred to as a virtual machine monitor (VMM), is software that allows for the creation, management, and runtime execution of independent VMs running their own guest operating systems. The physical machine that the hypervisor runs on is referred to as the host machine.

A number of hypervisor types exist. A Type 1 hypervisor, such as ESXi, runs on the bare metal of the computer. The VMs are created on the layer above ESXi and the guest OS runs within that second layer. ESXi has a minimal memory footprint (144M for vSphere version 5.x). A Type 2 hypervisor runs within a base OS, and therefore the guest operating systems run on the third layer above the hardware. See Figure 1-2.

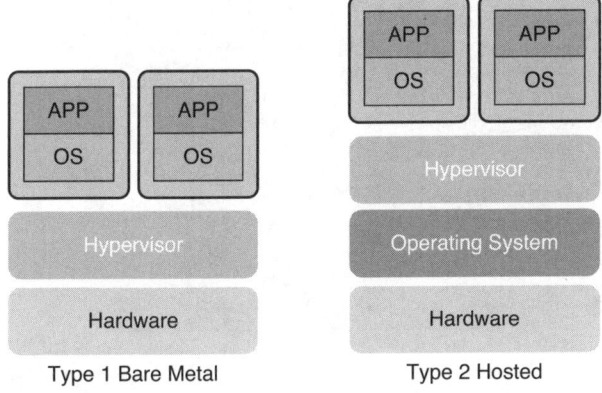

Type 1 Bare Metal   Type 2 Hosted

Figure 1-2 Type 1 and Type 2 hypervisor

It is also important to point out that ESXi is nonparavirtualized. Paravirtualization is discussed later in the book, but it is important to understand that this means that no guest OS kernel is altered and that there therefore exists a perfect state of abstraction between the guest OS and the hardware.

ESXi is a hypervisor, but vSphere is a "platform of virtualized hardware." It is logical hardware and should always be described and understood as such. And from this point on, we refer to virtualized hardware and nonvirtualized hardware.

The software-defined datacenter (SDDC) is a philosophy of architecture, not an actual product, although it does imply comprehensive full-stack virtualization. In a complete SDDC, all elements of the datacenter are virtualized. VMware has been very successful virtualizing the server components to include processing with virtual CPUs (vCPUs) and memory allocated to the VM (we avoid using the phrase *virtual memory* because it has other well-accepted connotations), but virtualization of the network and storage have been elusive. It is true that common terms such as virtual disk (VMDK), virtual network interface card (vNIC), and virtual distributed switch (vDS) all imply virtualization, but that is not the reality. An important attribute of true virtualization is abstraction. See Figure 1-3.

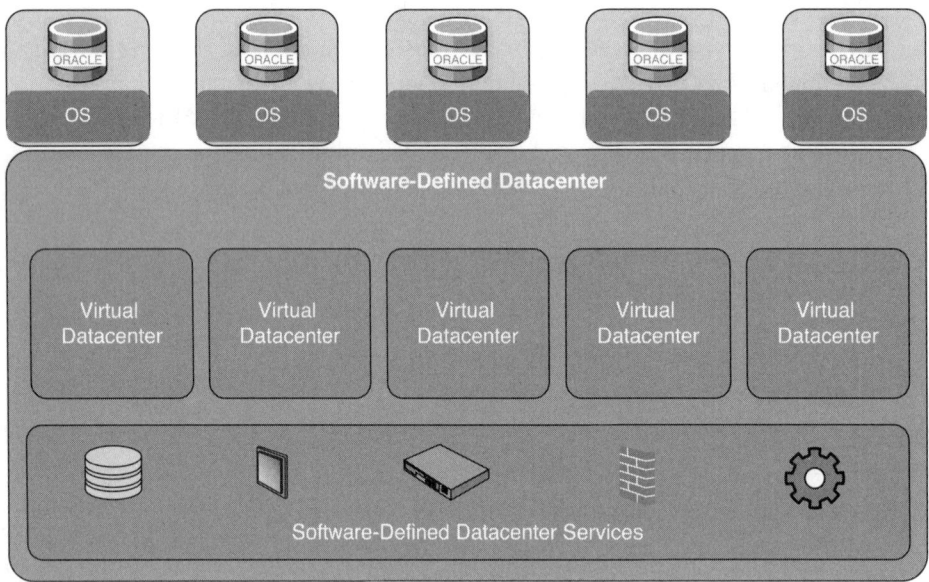

Figure 1-3 VMware SDDC (high level)

As VMware moves into the next phase of technology, the SDDC will include not only the virtualization of the server but also the virtualization of the network and storage. In 2012, VMware acquired Nicira Corporation, whose technology has led to the Network Virtualization and Security platform (NSX), which does meet anyone's strict definition of true network virtualization. Figure 1-4 shows vSphere with NSX incorporated. Subsequent chapters cover specific networking recommendations.

For more information on VMware NSX, refer to the link below.

www.vmware.com/products/nsx.

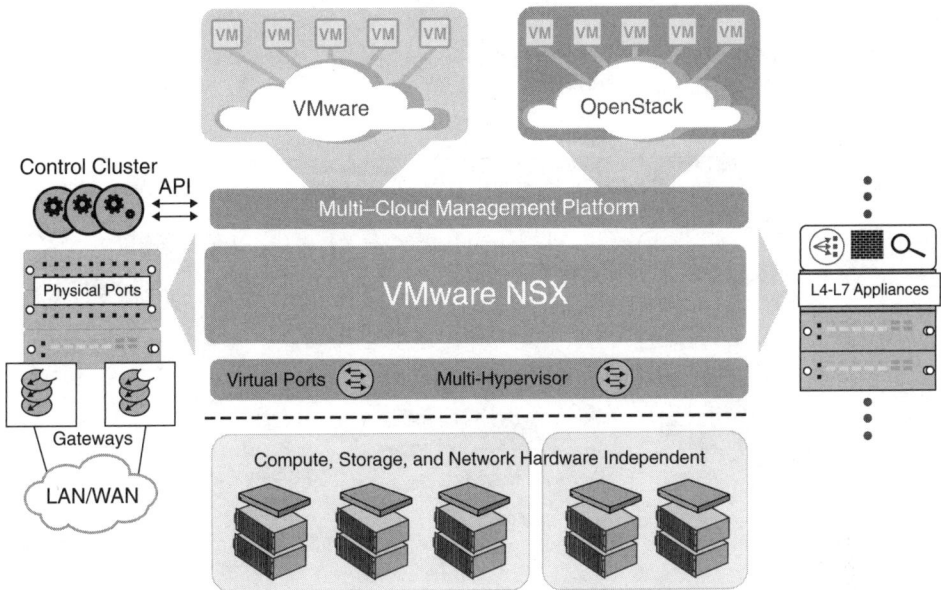

Figure 1-4 VMware NSX

Storage virtualization comes in many flavors. Often, the phrase is used to describe the storage paradigms used only with "stretch clusters," in which a single logical unit (LUN) of storage will exist in two different physical locations but synchronicity will be maintained through disk mirroring. Systems such as IBM SAN Volume Controller (SVC), shown in Figure 1-5, HP 3PAR Peer Persistence, and EMC VPLEX, shown in Figure 1-6 (formally Yotta-Yotta technology), correctly come to mind when the phrase *storage virtualization* is used. In the VMware context, we understand storage virtualization as an intrinsic part of the SDDC, and we include advanced VMware storage capabilities such as virtual storage-area network (vSAN), the soon-to-be released virtual volumes (vVols), and vFlashReadCache (vFRC) among others as the essential components of the storage virtualization paradigm.

For more information on HP 3PAR, refer to hp.com or to the link below.

www8.hp.com/us/en/products/storage-software/product-detail.
html?oid=5335710#!tab=features.

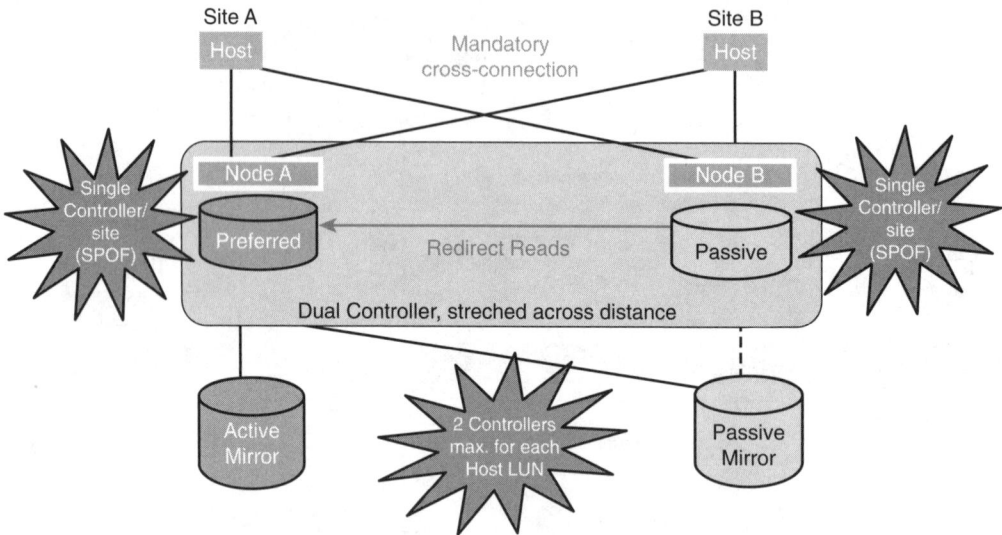

Figure 1-5 IBM SVC stretch cluster

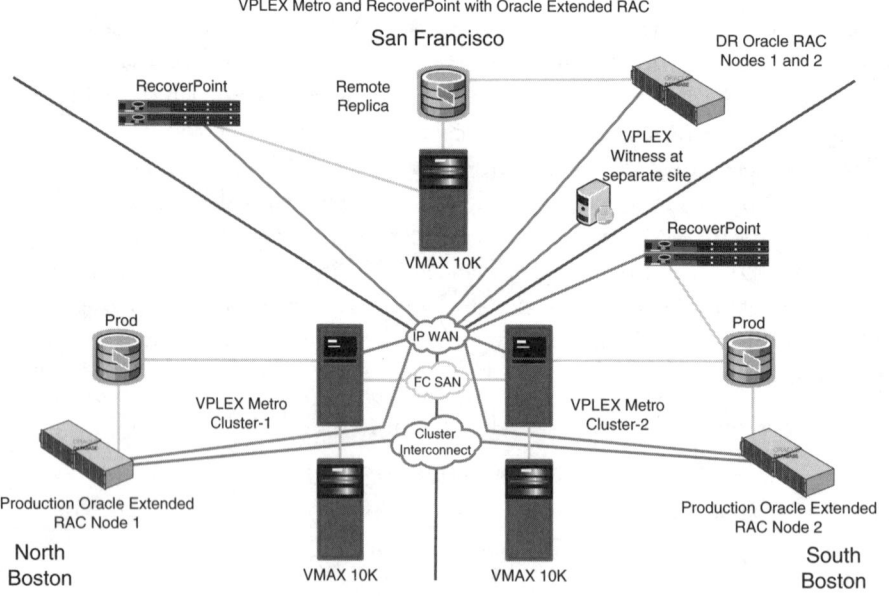

Figure 1-6 EMC VPLEX stretch cluster

Together, the tried-and-true virtualization of the server through vSphere when combined with the more recent ideas of network and storage virtualization constitute the SDDC VMware style. And throughout this book, we refer to each component of this evolutionary leap in datacenter design. Paul Maritz, the former CEO of VMware and present CEO of Pivotal Solutions, once referred to VMware as "the magic pixie dust that was changing the world." We agree, although we constantly have to point out to customers that despite the magical illusion presented by VMware products, the laws of physics still apply, and so each implementation must consider the limits of those pesky rules of Newton and Einstein otherwise risk disappointment. However, it is not overheated rhetoric to state that VMware is changing the world. For example, it would be difficult to find a single corporate entity that has facilitated more reduction in power consumption throughout its customer base. More importantly, the name VMware itself implies a tectonic-like shift in the world of technology. Computing started with hardware, and then intrepid minds developed software to effectively use that hardware; but to comprehensively tie software to hardware, the world needed VMware.

For more information on EMC VPLEX stretch clusters, refer to the link below.

www.emc.com/storage/vplex/vplex.htm.

Virtualizing Oracle Databases on vSphere: Benefits and Examples

There are many benefits to virtualizing infrastructure for Oracle databases on vSphere. Among those are the reduction of the number of physical systems your organization requires and the more efficient use of existing systems. However, the most important benefits are the resource management capabilities innate in vSphere and the features that facilitate the guarantee of adherence to service level agreements (SLAs) such as availability, disaster recovery, performance, security, and provisioning. This section describes these benefits and then illustrates examples.

Virtualizing database workloads on vSphere significantly reduces the number of physical systems your organization requires, while achieving more effective utilization of datacenter resources. Clients realize tangible savings from this consolidation along with operational cost savings from reduced datacenter floor space, power, and cooling requirements. Figure 1-7 illustrates an example of Oracle database servers on vSphere architecture with application services and infrastructure services.

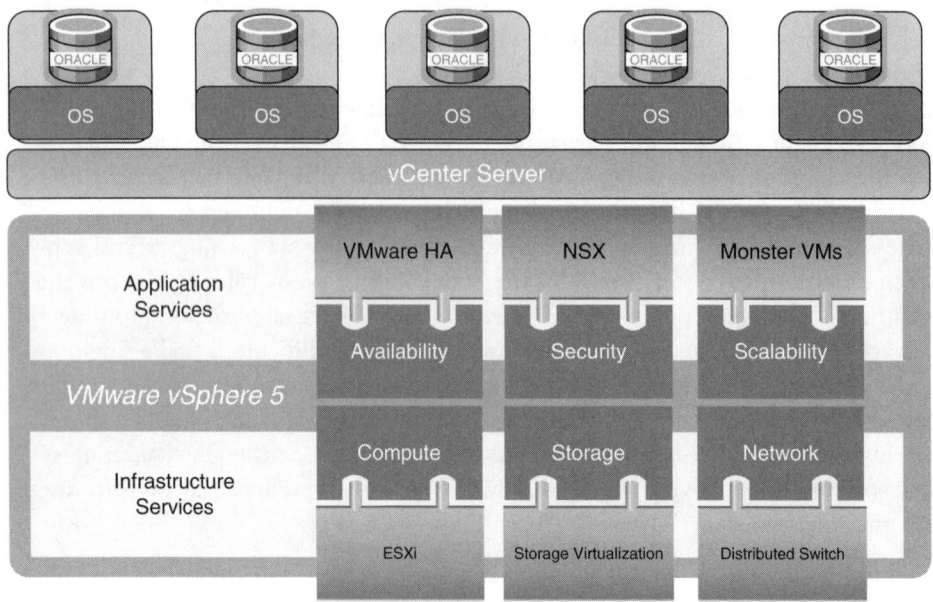

Figure 1-7 Oracle databases on VMware vSphere

Oracle Databases and DBA Fundamentals

DBAs wear many hats and play many roles within an organization. A DBA is the administrator who designs, implements, tests, operates, and maintains databases for an organization. Figure 1-8 illustrates the DBA's general tasks, and the list that follows provides further explanation.

- **Database design, storage, and capacity planning**: DBAs play a major role in designing the database along with determining disk storage requirements and future database growth. Monitoring database growth trends is important so that the DBA can advise management on long-term capacity plans.

- **Install, configure, upgrade, migrate, and provisioning**: Although system administrators are generally responsible for the hardware and OS on a given server, installation of the database software is typically done by the DBA. This role requires knowledge of the hardware prerequisites and requirements so that the database server runs efficiently, and then communicating those requirements to the system administrator. The DBA installs the database software and selects from various options to configure it for the purpose for which it is being deployed. As new releases and patches are made available, it is the DBA's role to determine which are appropriate and to complete the installation. If the server is a replacement server, it is the DBA's role to transfer the data from the old server to the new one. The more seasoned DBA will take a highly cautious approach to any data transfer or migration operation because data loss is a potential consequence of sloppy transitions. DBAs are tasked to provision database servers on demand for development, testing, QA, and reporting.

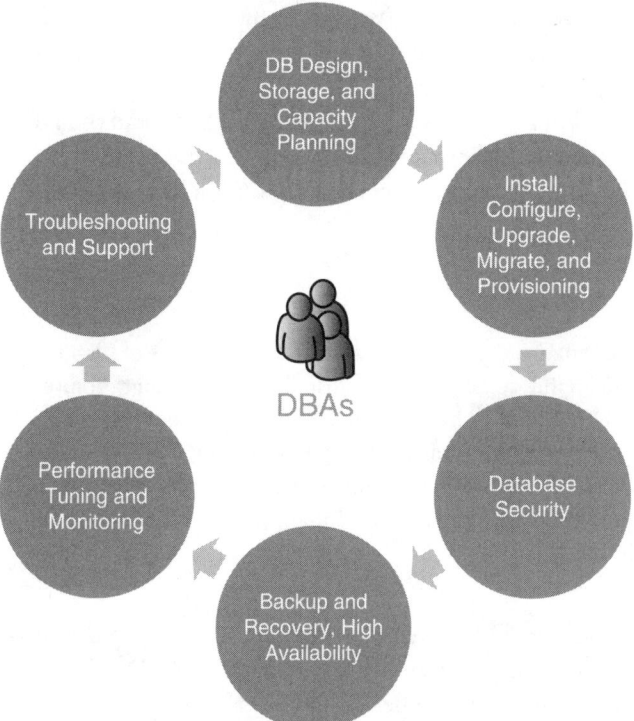

Figure 1-8 General tasks for DBAs

- **Database security**: Databases centralize the storage of data and are attractive targets for hackers. DBAs must understand the particular security model that the database product uses as well as the security requirements of the application and how to effectively control data access. The three basic security tasks are authentication (setting up user accounts to control logins to the database), authorization (setting permissions on various schemas and database objects), and auditing (tracking user movements and actions within the database). The auditing task is particularly important as regulatory laws, such as Sarbanes-Oxley (SOX), the Healthcare Insurance Portability and Accountability Act (HIPAA), and Payment Card Industry (PCI), have security and reporting requirements that require adherence.

- **Backup and recovery, high availability**: DBAs are responsible for developing, implementing, and periodically testing a backup and recovery plan for the databases they manage. Even in large organizations where a separate system administrator performs server backups, the DBA has final responsibility for ensuring that the database backups are done as scheduled and that they include all the files necessary to make database recovery possible after a failure. When failures do occur, the DBA needs to know how to use the backups to restore the database to operational status as quickly as possible, without losing any transactions that were committed. There are several ways a database can fail, and the DBA must have a strategy to recover from each type of failure. From a business standpoint, there is a cost to doing backups, and the DBA makes management aware of the cost/risk trade-offs of various backup methods. DBAs use techniques such as online backups, clustering, replication, and standby databases to provide higher availability.

TIP

"When running on vSphere Oracle remains the same" is one of the main pillars of Oracle on vSphere. This nugget of wisdom applies to all backup philosophies. Upon migration to virtualized infrastructure, DBAs can maintain all backup process and techniques previously used. However, DBAs should consider incorporation of the capabilities of virtualization into their back strategy. The classic approaches to include the use of Recovery Manager (RMAN), storage vendor snapshot database tools, and the manual copying of database files remain the most popular methods.

- **Performance tuning and monitoring**: DBAs are responsible for monitoring the database server on a regular basis to identify bottlenecks and remedy them. Database server tuning is performed at multiple levels. The capacity of the server hardware and the way the OS is configured can become limiting factors, as can the database software configuration. The way the database is physically laid out on the disk drives and the types of indexing chosen also have an effect. The way queries against the database are coded can dramatically change how quickly results are returned. A DBA needs to understand which monitoring tools are available at each of these levels and how to use them to tune the system. Proactive tuning involves designing performance into an application from the start, rather than waiting for problems to occur and fixing them. It requires working closely with developers of applications that run against the database to make sure that best practices are followed so that good performance will result.

- **Troubleshooting and support**: When things go wrong with the database server, the DBA needs to know how to quickly ascertain the problem and to correct the issue without losing data or making the situation worse. DBAs provide 24x7 support, 365 days a year.

Understanding Oracle Database Architectures

The Oracle Server is a relational database management system (RDBMS) that provides an open, comprehensive, and integrated approach to information management. An Oracle server consists of an Oracle database and an Oracle instance. Figure 1-9 describes the relationship between the database and the instance.

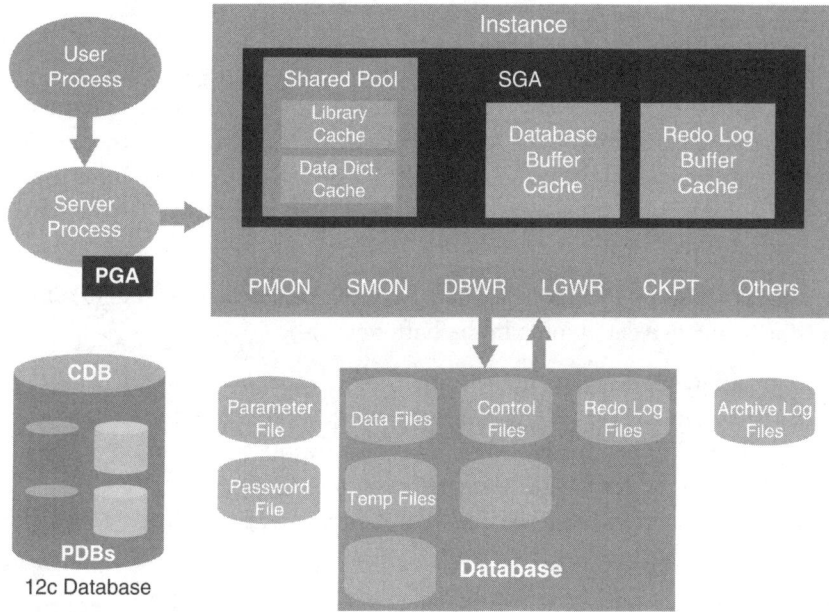

Figure 1-9 Oracle database server architecture

However in Oracle RAC, there may be more than one instance accessing the same database. An instance and a database may have a many-to-one relationship when using RAC, and a one-to-one in case of single-instance non-RAC Oracle deployments.

The following steps describe a basic Oracle configuration where the user and associated server process are on separate machines connected via a network:

- An instance is running on the computer that is executing Oracle, often called the host or database server.

- A computer used to run an application (a local machine or client workstation) runs the client as a user process. The client application attempts to establish a connection to the server using the appropriate SQL*Net/Oracle network driver.

- The server is running the proper SQL*Net/Oracle network driver. By default, the server detects the connection request from the application and creates a (dedicated) server process request on behalf of the user. Other types of database connections are possible, such as "shared server" connections as well as connections coming from application servers by proxy through connection pools.

- The user executes a SQL statement and commits a transaction. For example, the user changes a name in a field or row of a table.

- The server process receives the statement and checks the shared pool for a SQL statement resident in the shared SQL area that contains an identical SQL statement. If a shared SQL statement is found, the server process checks the user's access privileges to the requested data and the previously existing shared SQL statement is used to process the new statement; if not, a new shared SQL area is allocated for the statement so that it can be parsed and processed.

- The server process retrieves any necessary data from the actual data file (tables) after checking for the respective data blocks in the buffer cache.

- The server process may modify data in the buffer cache, which is a primary component of the system global area (SGA). Once the transaction is committed, the log writer (LGWR) process immediately records copies of the transcription of the transaction from the log buffer to the online redo log file. At this point, the database writer (DBWR) process writes modified data blocks permanently to the data files on disk when doing so is efficient.

- If the transaction is successful and disk acknowledgment is received, the server process sends a message across the network to the application. If it is not successful, an appropriate error message is transmitted.

Throughout this entire procedure, the other background processes run, watching for conditions that require intervention. In addition, the database server manages other user transactions and attempts to minimize contention such as locking, deadlock conditions, and bottlenecks on processing resources.

Summary

The most important advancement in twenty-first century computing technology has been the inception and maturity of virtualization, more precisely VMware vSphere. At this point in the evolution of the industry, it is indisputable that 99.9% of all database or data management systems should be considered candidates for virtualization on vSphere. Oracle databases and software are prime candidates to consider migrating to virtualized infrastructure. Subsequent chapters discuss the ever-evolving role of the DBA, which will be delivered with a heartfelt admonition: to consider the direction of technology growth and the projection of your own position in the next decade. Only one conclusion is rational because only one path is sustainable: Embrace virtualization as the next phase of the ever-expanding province of the DBA or face obsolescence.

## Chapter 2

Virtualization and High-Performance Oracle Workloads

Virtualized Oracle Environments on vSphere Key Benefits

Even though this chapter's title refers to high workloads, the discussion extends to all business-critical applications (BCAs), or in a broader sense, important applications. Often, the terms Tier 1 and BCA are used as synonyms, but the overlapping use of the terms is more of a commingling of the ideas. BCA refers to those applications that are critical to the moment-by-moment functioning of the business, whereas Tier 1 usually refers to an application with a regularly high workload, such as a data warehouse (DWH) application. Of course, a Tier 1 application with high resource requirements may also be paramount to the success of the company; so in that case, the application is both Tier 1 as well as a BCA.

This chapter discusses the four V's shown in Figure 2-1. This chapter is important to database administrators (DBAs) who want to understand the viability of running an important and resource-intensive application on vSphere and who want to know the specific features that add value to their environment and to themselves as database professionals. The versatility aspect becomes important as different high-workload-capable architectures are considered, and the intrepid DBA will want to know what future features (even those features that cross into the realm of science fiction) will be applicable to the existing architecture.

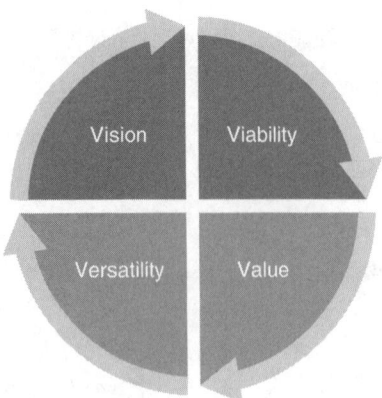

Figure 2-1 Four V's approach

As we move the discourse into the most critical areas of the viability discussion, it is useful to draw attention to a component of information technology (IT) that although highly visible is often overlooked when diagnosing the reasons for success or failure of a given IT department or individual project. The most essential factors influencing the achievements of any IT group are the officers in the upper levels of IT management. The modern chief information officer (CIO) and chief technology officer (CTO) (sometimes more than one) are the individuals who make the decisions that ultimately set the course of the IT organization.

Later in this book, we discuss the extraordinary influence of the Oracle DBA, but at the moment, we want to suggest certain essential attributes of a successful IT decision maker. First, that individual must have an imposing personal presence, similar to a military field commander. Second, the IT leader must have a thorough understanding of the technologies being considered, to include the eventual architectural components chosen as well as the feasible alternatives.

Technical personnel tend to focus on their personal niche in the organization, which can sometimes resemble "herding cats." Later in this chapter, we discuss the makeup of the successful Oracle DBA. All of these disparate personalities and skill sets can make the IT leader's job quite difficult. However, if the leader has the approach of a field commander (proceeding with an inspiring and self-confident presence), all IT personnel will take notice. The decisions will be delivered with effervescent self-assurance, garnering commitment to the precepts behind the implementation. The purpose of the deployment will be understood and accepted, and "buy-in" will be established. Most importantly, a commitment to the philosophy of the implementation will be palpable. No single component of a modern computing architecture facilitates this leadership presence more effectively than the inclusion of VMware as the essential component of any and every implementation.

Chances are, VMware's customers and the successful C-level management personnel of those companies will probably agree. Figure 2-2 shows example of an IT organization hierarchy.

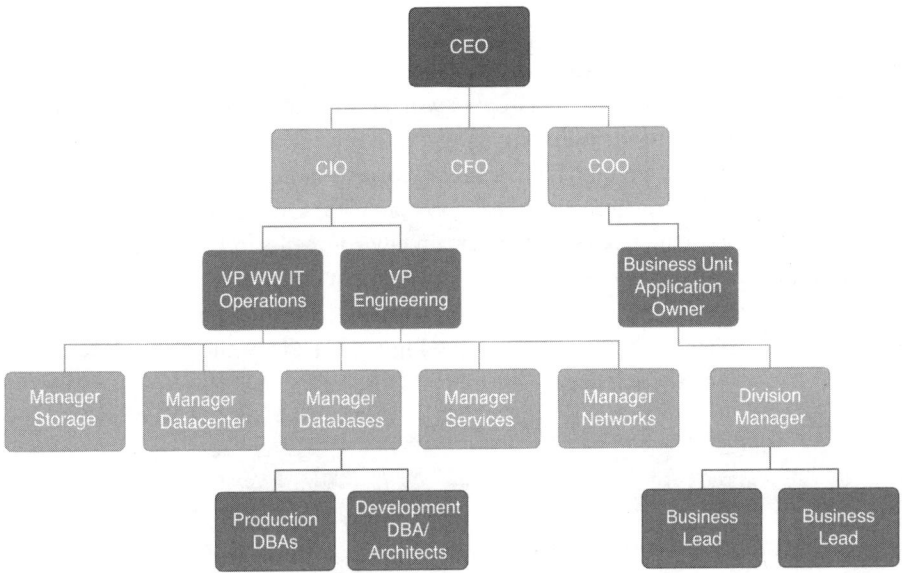

Figure 2-2 IT organization hierarchy

Consolidating Platforms to Reduce Datacenter Costs

Customers can run Oracle databases on vSphere efficiently by consolidating into fewer, scalable, available, and reliable enterprise-class servers, as shown in Figure 2-3. This reduces total datacenter cost without compromising performance and manageability.

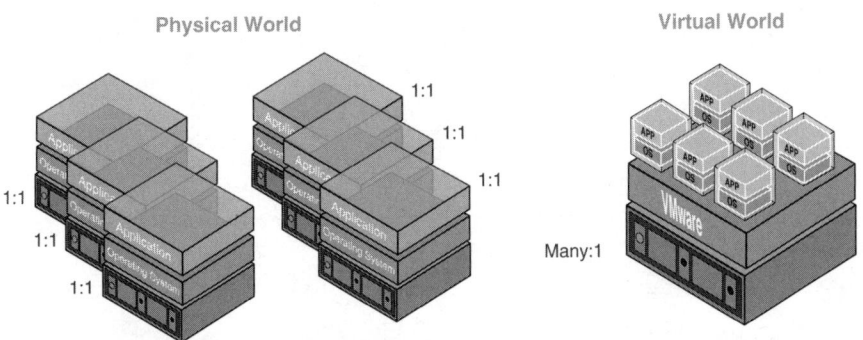

Figure 2-3 Virtualizing Oracle datacenter

Customers can create performance-driven, manageable, and cost-effective Oracle environments with the following unique features:

- **Memory oversubscription**: More efficient use of physical random-access memory (RAM) by reclaiming unused physical memory and consolidating identical memory pages among virtual machines (VMs) on a host. The general principals of best practices for the more "important" workloads, often times referred to as *production*, *Tier 1*, or *business-critical applications* (BCAs), will usually require guaranteed physical memory corresponding to the memory allocated to the VM. To accomplish this, the DBA/VMAdmin will set a memory reservation corresponding to the total amount of shared memory used by the guest operating system (OS) Oracle instances. Oversubscription of memory may make sense in certain environments in which high performance is not a factor, but in environments in which performance delineates the line between success and failure, oversubscription (also called overcommitment) will not be an effective implementation methodology. Figure 2-4 shows the vCenter screen used to set the memory reservation.

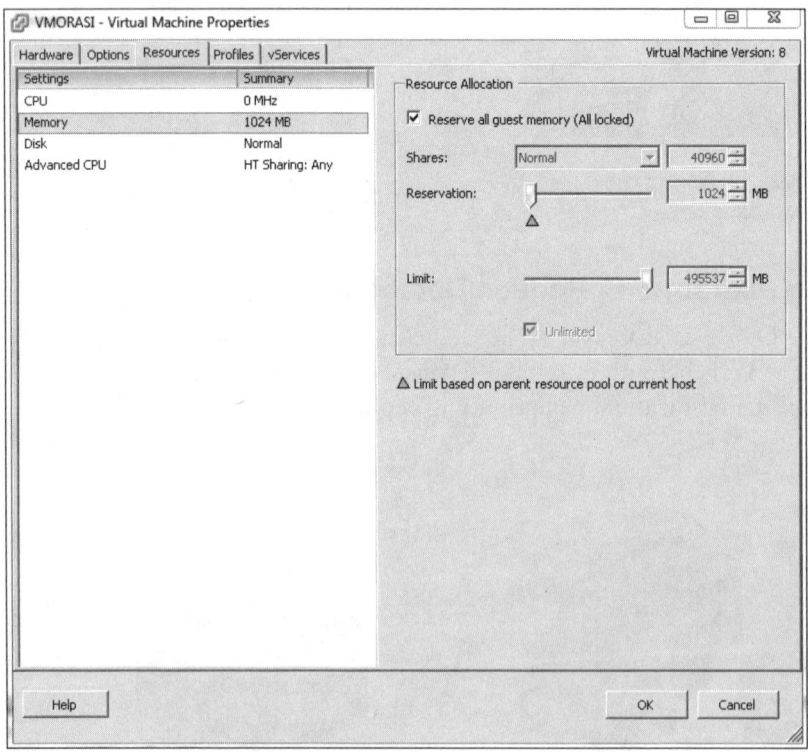

Figure 2-4 Virtual machine memory reservation

- **High-performance scheduler**: Can account for central processing unit (CPU) and input/output (I/O) needs of VMs by dynamically allocating more resources and larger processor time slices to prescribed VMs.

- **VMware vSphere Distributed Resource Scheduler (DRS) with resource pools**: Dynamically load balance VMs across a cluster so that applications get required resources when they need them. This is a "safety net" that allows administrators to run individual servers at higher utilization levels while meeting service level agreements (SLAs) for performance. Figure 2-5 shows the VMware distributed resource scheduling where VM are moved as per DRS rules.

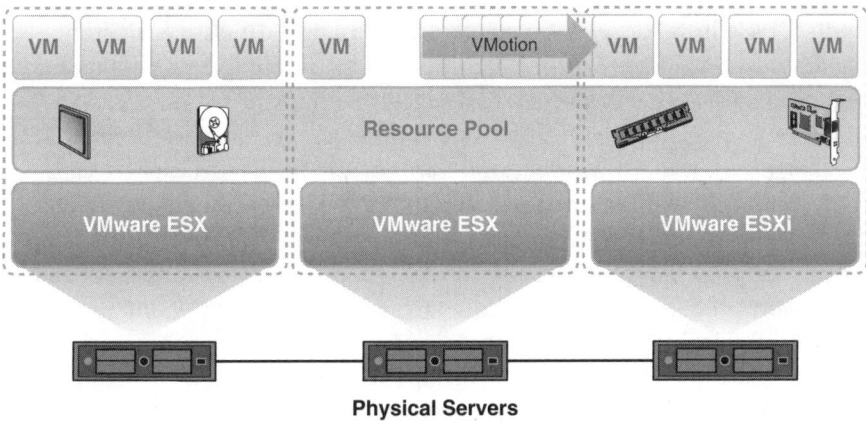

Figure 2-5 VMWare distributed resource scheduling

- **Direct driver model**: VMware ESXi can achieve very high I/O throughput and can handle the I/O requirements for more VMs simultaneously requesting hardware resources.

- **Support for large memory pages (called Huge Pages in Linux) and nested/extended page tables**: Optimized memory access can provide substantial performance benefits for mission-critical, memory-intensive applications and can reduce CPU resource consumption by up to 15%. See Chapter for 4, "Oracle on vSphere Best Practices," for more information on large pages.

Enhancing Database Availability and Cost-Effective Disaster Recovery

Customers can deliver enhanced availability with VMware for Oracle databases. By doing so, it becomes much easier to implement a disaster recovery (DR) platform that enables production Oracle database VM servers to be recovered after failure. The following capabilities are particularly valuable to customers:

- VMware vSphere High Availability (HA) is an innate feature of vSphere that continuously monitors all physical servers in an ESXi cluster and restarts VMs affected by host or server/guest OS failure. Customers isolating their databases based on SLAs and looking for maximum availability have two categories of options: Real Application Cluster (RAC) or Data Guard (DG). Oracle 12c Maximum Availability Architecture documentation lists seven unique approaches to HA. The "fast start failover" feature of DG can be used as an HA tool. Both RAC and DG can be used in conjunction with VMware HA as they are complementary technologies. RAC allows for multiple Oracle instances to concurrently access a single database facilitating extremely fast session failovers. Oracle DG provides log shipping between the source and target databases using either sync or async log streaming or remote archive streaming. Combining either with VMware HA provides increased availability. Generally speaking, the advanced Oracle features are complementary to vSphere capabilities. It is very important to note that VMware HA will allow for failover of the entire guest and all the processes running within that guest. vSphere HA will determine the most appropriate available host on which to restart a particular guest and subsequently any processes that have been set to start automatically within the OS of that guest will start. vSphere HA is a cost-effective available option for most database environments that can protect them from unexpected hardware failures. Figure 2-6 shows Oracle DG in action protecting Oracle databases.

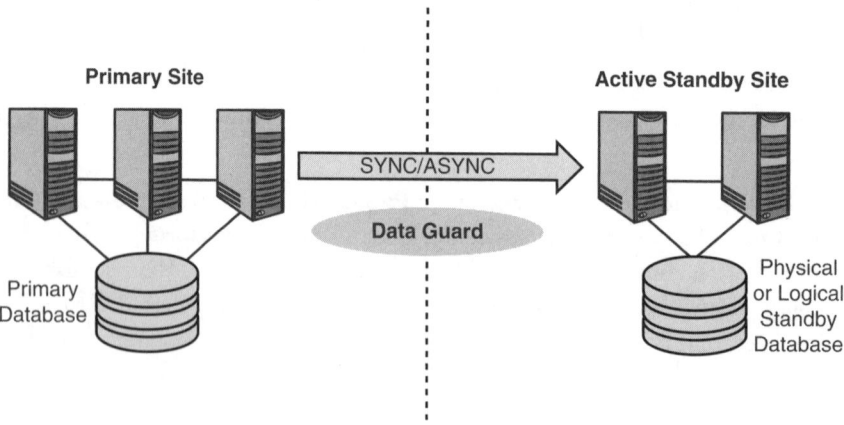

Figure 2-6 Oracle Data Guard

- VMware vCenter Site Recovery Manager (SRM) is a workflow orchestration system that streamlines and automates datacenter transition and can be used for disaster recovery by leveraging vSphere and partner storage replication software via the storage replication adaptors (SRAs) developed by the storage vendors. SRM delivers centralized management of recovery plans, automation of DR testing, and DR Failover, as well as datacenter migration. Figure 2-7 shows logical architecture of VMware SRM.

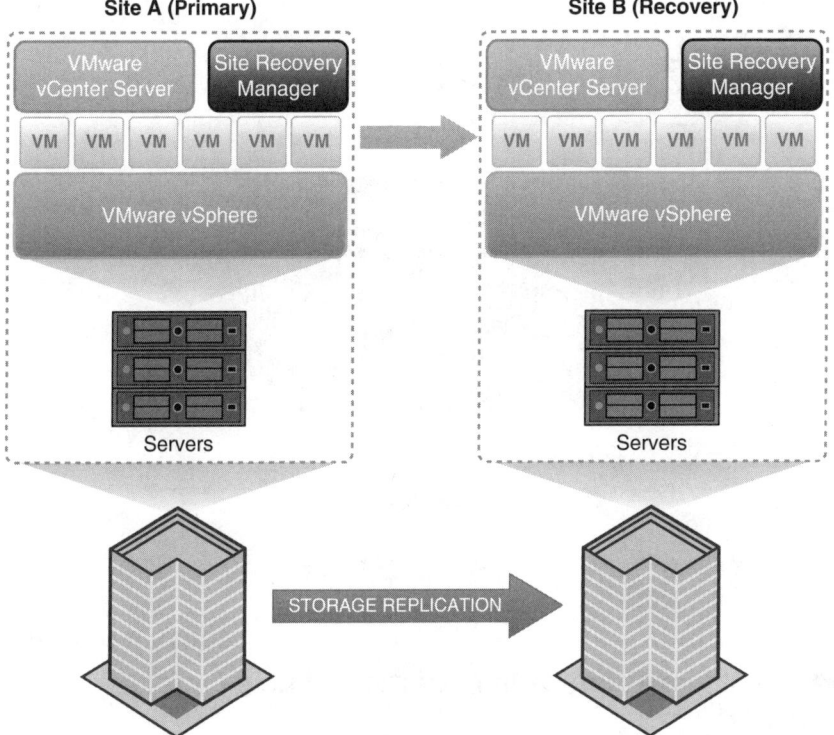

Figure 2-7 VMWare Site Recovery Manager

Provisioning Rapid and New Database Server Environments

Customers can take advantage of VM libraries and VM templates to provision new pre-configured Oracle database environments in minutes on a vSphere platform. The Cloud architecture products, such as vFabric Data Director, which has been migrated into vFabric Application Director and vCloud Automation Center (vCAC), constitute advanced framework systems for provisioning, management, and monitoring of all applications. In 2014, each of these products will be integrated into vCAC. vCAC will contain multiple "out-of-the-box blueprints" for "well-known" deployments, and customers will be able to create any other blueprints to organize their application deployments for all purposes. Database-as-a-service (DBaaS) will become a reality. Figure 2-8 shows creating clones of a production database through golden copy using vCAC DBaaS.

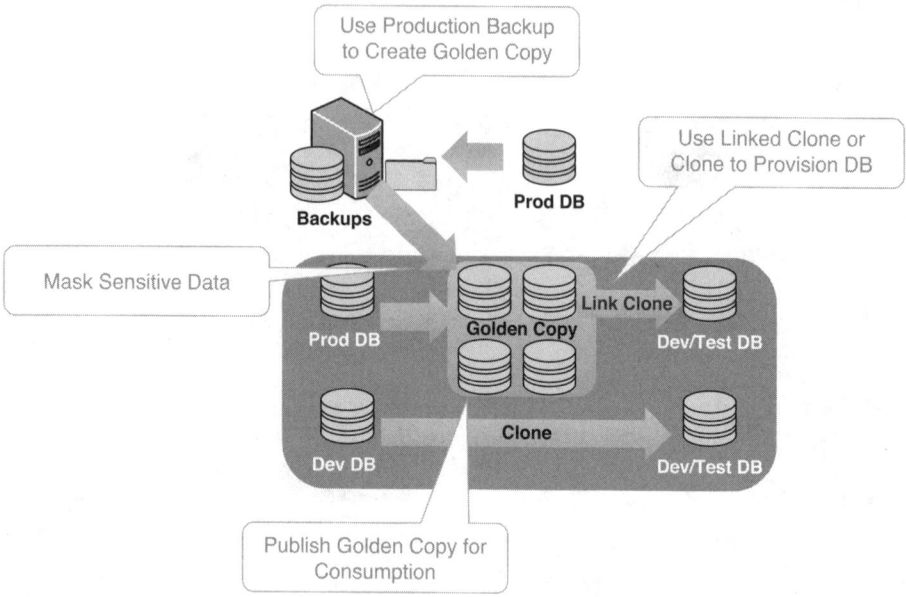

Figure 2-8 VMware vCAC – DBaaS

Reducing Planned Downtime with Migration of Live Oracle Database Servers

Customers can use VMware vSphere vMotion technology to migrate/transition live Oracle database servers in VMs from one physical server to another. With vMotion, DBAs can perform hardware maintenance without system downtime that disrupts business operations. A VMAdmin simply places the host to be fixed into "maintenance" mode, and then the VMs running on that host are transitioned to available hosts within the ESXi cluster, effectively eliminating downtime for hardware maintenance. Figure 2-9 shows VMware vMotion.

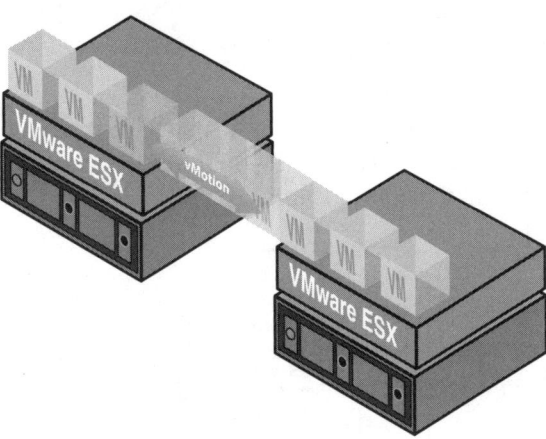

Figure 2-9 VMware vMotion

Guaranteeing Resources in a Shared Environment

In a virtualized environment, comprehensive resource sharing can be achieved through the combined exploitation of resource pools and Distributed Resource Scheduler (DRS). Resource pools allow for the prioritization of resource allocation. DRS dynamically distributes VMs between the physical hosts based on the availability of resources and prioritization. The most important VMs, in this case, are probably the production database servers, with the objective being to isolate them from other less important and potentially disruptive servers. A VMAdmin will create rules and policies to prioritize how resources are allocated to VMs. DRS will load balance VMs across the physical nodes within an ESXi cluster so that database servers receive required resources when they need them. Enforcing prioritization rules to evacuate VMs from a host during peak workloads, using reservations to guarantee memory, and allocating shares to set priorities on the resources allocated to VMs helps to guarantee desired resource distribution in a shared environment.

This approach addresses two classic vSphere consolidation challenges: the "noisy" neighbor and the "nosey" neighbor. The noisy neighbor is a VM/server that demands significant system resources, often has inconsistent utilization of those resources, and is generally disruptive. The nosey neighbor is a VM/server that does not have adequate security considerations or access rights to run on the same physical host as a more important and security sensitive VM. DRS will use load-balancing capabilities to address the Noisy Neighbor and DRS affinity rules can be combined with VMware advanced security capabilities to solve the Nosey Neighbor predicament. Together these tools help empower business units to build and manage VMs in their resource pools while giving central IT control over hardware resources.

Achieving IT Compliance

Customers take advantage of vSphere to drive compliance in Oracle database environments by enforcing the use of standard, compliant operating system and database images across the datacenter with master templates and cloning capabilities. Figure 2-10 shows how VMware helps to clone and archive a previous environment for compliance.

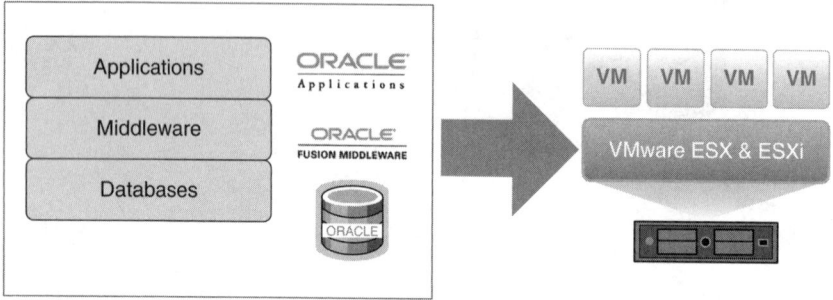

Figure 2-10 VMware cloning for compliance

Zeroing In on Key Trigger Events

After unambiguous viability has been established, the application and database management teams will want know the value of vSphere to both the company and themselves individually. Every few years, the hardware falls out of style, and they need to endure the anxious uncertainty of the new and "better" hardware and the tedious drudgery of the migration itself. Why should they take the risk of yet another migration? The answer is simple. VMware vSphere provides intrinsic value to the company as well as to IT. And the value of the new skill set acquired by technical personnel, especially the DBA, can be a career-advancing decision. DBAs should consider championing virtualization when one of the following events is imminent.

Key trigger events to deploy Oracle on vSphere include the following:

- Refreshing hardware

- Solving compliance and security issues

- Application or database version migration

- Introducing new business units requiring Oracle databases

- Migrating from traditional UNIX/mainframe environments to x86 platforms to reduce costs and provide an open platform

- Creating cost-effective development and testing environments quickly

- Growing a virtualization footprint in an IT business unit

- Introducing new DR requirements without additional fiscal resources having been allocated

- Imposing greater application availability requirements without additional fiscal resources having been allocated

- Onboarding underutilized Oracle database servers that will benefit from consolidation

Solving Oracle Database Deployment and Management Issues Using VMware

VMware technology addresses and provides solutions for most Oracle database deployment and management issues. DBAs use classic tools to manage databases, and they typically use primitive methods to provision databases. Oracle Enterprise Manager, in its many forms, has been the staple of Oracle management tools for two decades. Copying database files and re-creating the control file has been the most common method of provisioning or "cloning" an Oracle database for even longer. Oracle DBAs approach their craft with a very conservative mindset. "If it isn't broke, don't fix, change it, or even touch it, please" is a common sentiment of the well-seasoned Oracle professional. This attitude is totally reasonable when considering the daunting responsibility of protecting the data that is so valuable to the company, and no one understands the magnitude of the potential impact of small mistakes better than the Oracle DBA. However, even the most grizzled Oracle professional should consider many tools and techniques because those tools will make the DBA more effective and make the company's overall IT infrastructure easier to manage. It is possible that the DBA may no longer have to spend quite so much time on the minutiae of the mundane metrics and even minimize the time dedicated to worrying about backups completing. A wise DBA once posed a sports analogy to waiting for backups to finish by taking a classic analogy and raising the level of irony: "Waiting for backups to finish is like going to a domed stadium and watching the artificial grass grow."

Modern database management tools help the DBA, the system admin, the VMAdmin, the storage admin, and the network admin all see the same view of the stack. This holds true especially if all these jobs are held by the same person. Oracle Enterprise Manager and its broader system Grid/Cloud Control (Cloud Control in 12c) are comprehensive systems for metrics collection which encourage thoughtful analysis. VMware tools such as *vCenter*, the main vSphere management system and vCenter Operations Manager Suite (vCops), a modern performance analytics tool, collects metrics and performs trending analysis. More about vCops later, but suffice it to understand that these VMware and Oracle tools are totally complementary. Blue Medora Corporation has developed a VMware plug-in for Oracle Enterprise Manager 12c, and additionally they have an Oracle adapter for vCops. So, the administrators can view metrics from each perspective. Also, there are many third-party tools such as Ignite for Oracle (formally IgniteVM) from Confio, which is now a part of Solar Winds Corporation.

Database deployment can be accomplished through most of the tools mentioned here, and we will spend ample time on the idea of DBaaS later in the book, but VMware has dedi-cated significant resources to developing a well-organized approach to service-oriented architectures (SOAs). In 2012, VMware developed vFabric Data Director to provision many types of databases, including SQL Server, vPostgres, MySQL, and of course, Oracle. Applications Director (AppD) allowed for the construction of "blueprints" for the provi-sioning of "virtual appliances" (vApps). VMware then acquired DymanicOps Corporation, and from that acquisition emerged vCloud Automation Center (vCAC). VMware also has vCloud Orchestrator, which as its name conveys acts as a workflow orchestration genera-tor. In 2014 and beyond, components of these robust tools are being merged into vCAC to provide a single Cloud provisioning system. At this point, the science fiction of com-prehensive DBaaS will become a reality. For more information on VMware management tools, see Chapter 8, "Performance Management and Monitoring."

Implementing Dynamic Oracle Datacenter Resource Management

Running on dedicated physical servers and resizing applications requires reprovisioning on larger physical hosts, which is a time-consuming and highly disruptive undertaking. DBAs must forecast capacity requirements years in advance and translate those estimates into system specifications, including CPU and memory. This is the art of "right-sizing." It is an art that is fueled by arithmetic metrics, but certainty in this exercise is always elusive. When conditions change, the database must be reprovisioned, causing downtime, disrup-tion, and negative business impact.

vSphere provides a number of capabilities that enable IT operations to scale applications dynamically. Capabilities such as "hot-add CPU" allow for the dynamic addition of vCPUs (vSockets), while DRS initiates live migrations of VMs in a DRS cluster by automati-cally moving a resource starved VM from an overutilized host to one with more available capacity.

VMware Site Recovery Manager as well as the aforementioned vCloud Orchestrator can be used to seamlessly migrate entire datacenters across great geographic distances in very short periods of time. General Electric Appliances and Lighting, with the help of House of Brick, do exactly that and have delivered powerful speaking sessions at VMworld (both in San Francisco and Barcelona) in 2013 on the subject.

Most profoundly, the simplicity of augmenting an ESXi cluster by adding a new and possibly disparate physical host and using a "host profile" to configure the new ESXi host exemplifies the notion that "vSphere is a platform of virtualized hardware."

Minimizing Server Sprawl

Oracle database deployments can generate significant server sprawl (although this is typically less of an issue than that caused by other relational database management systems [RDBMS]) due to the need to provision separate systems for development, quality assurance/test, and production environments. As a result, the number of Oracle database implementations can increase exponentially, leading to the ironic situation in which even smaller implementations can have a relatively large IT footprint. In a typical production or nonproduction deployment, every database server environment is hosted on dedicated physical systems that are not fully utilized much of the time. Many businesses also implement a hardware replacement policy that states that all hardware must be refreshed every 3 to 5 years. Replacement cost combined with ongoing hardware maintenance expenditures often constitutes a significant portion of the average corporate IT budget. Oracle database server consolidation with vSphere helps to reduce hardware costs and increase server utilization.

Meeting SLA Demands for Database Performance, Availability, and Disaster Recovery

Oracle database and IT administrators must meet SLAs to provide availability and performance to Oracle users. VMware technologies help the DBAs and IT administrators by allowing them to take advantage of VMware HA, vMotion, and DRS to meet SLAs and provide acceptable levels of HA. Protecting the production datacenters running Oracle databases during disasters is critical to any business. SRM provides protection against an Oracle datacenter site disaster. SRM will be discussed in Chapter 9, "Business Continuity and Disaster Recovery."

Supporting a Dynamic Business Environment

Mergers and acquisitions present significant challenges to an IT organization. IT integration may be incomplete, delayed, and costly, and this can frustrate business owners as their goals become unachievable and consequently undermine the success of a merger. VMware virtualization reduces the cost and complexity of merging disparate IT environments by converting current Oracle database server environments to VMs. These virtualized workloads can run on the latest industry-standard servers and are easily incorporated into a single environment. As data and processes of the acquired company are integrated into the existing database servers, the virtualized architecture provides greater flexibility to effectively address the mixed workload on the systems.

Minimizing License Costs

Consolidation saves resource and therefore money! That is hardly a controversial statement, because it is obvious when a firm uses less physical space, less power, retires physical machines in lieu of faster more efficient machines, and more efficiently assigns personnel, everybody wins. However, there is enough uncertainty concerning this subject that is warrants an entire chapter in this book. For a more in-depth study of support and licensing, see Chapter 7, "Support and Licensing." Regardless, it is somewhat obvious that Oracle databases and IT administrators may take advantage of the consolidation of licenses by deploying Oracle databases in vSphere clusters. VMware does not offer guidance on third-party licensing. Oracle has publicly available pricing and licensing information at Oracle's website.

When you access VMware's website, search for the publication corresponding to Oracle licensing for more information.

Maximizing Oracle Workloads and Sizing

A perception still exists in the DBA community that virtualization introduces a performance constraint on larger applications, which have an overabundant appetite for storage access in all forms especially I/O-intensive applications such as databases. This perception most certainly originated with early versions of the VMware hypervisor, which had scalability limitations and material overhead. It is fair to say that the authors of this book were aware of the real limitations of virtualized infrastructure in the early years after Y2K. However, the latest versions of VMware vSphere 4.x/5.x have advanced significantly over the early product generations. VMware placed a significant focus on maximizing the performance of VMs and vSphere 5.x offers tremendous progress in I/O, CPU, and memory scalability over early product generations.

Today, VMs on vSphere 5.5 can scale to 64 virtual CPUs, 1TB of memory, and over 1,000,000 disk I/O per second (IOPS) per VM, while keeping overhead limited between 2% to 10% for the majority of performance metrics with the majority of applications. Figure 2-11 shows the performance metrics statistics of each vSphere version.

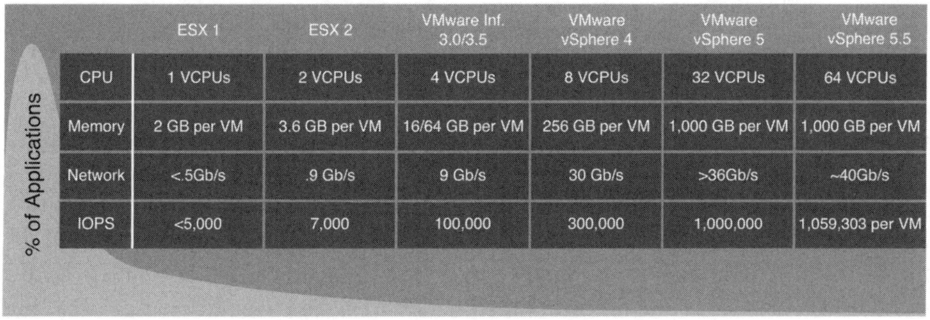

		ESX 1	ESX 2	VMware Inf. 3.0/3.5	VMware vSphere 4	VMware vSphere 5	VMware vSphere 5.5
% of Applications	CPU	1 VCPUs	2 VCPUs	4 VCPUs	8 VCPUs	32 VCPUs	64 VCPUs
	Memory	2 GB per VM	3.6 GB per VM	16/64 GB per VM	256 GB per VM	1,000 GB per VM	1,000 GB per VM
	Network	<.5Gb/s	.9 Gb/s	9 Gb/s	30 Gb/s	>36Gb/s	~40Gb/s
	IOPS	<5,000	7,000	100,000	300,000	1,000,000	1,059,303 per VM

Figure 2-11 Performance metrics and vSphere versions chart

Performance, backup and recovery, and replication in DR scenarios are important topics for database architecture discussions and DBAs' everyday lives. In all these areas, storage is a critical component. Large Oracle database customers will most likely be using either storage-area network (SAN), Information Protocol (IP) storage systems such as network-attached storage (NAS) or Internet Small Computers System Interface (iSCSI) or flash storage arrays from the more common storage vendors in the industry (all of whom are close VMware partners). The DBAs and potentially the storage array vendor should work together on the selection of a storage paradigm for the following reasons:

- Database performance depends heavily on the storage array architecture and design. The storage vendors have their own Oracle database implementation protocols and typically have best practice guidelines for Oracle databases. The guidelines originally developed for Oracle on nonvirtualized infrastructure usually apply equally well on virtualized infrastructure.

- Database consistency is extremely important for DBAs during backup and DR replication scenarios. The storage vendors have their own tools and processes to manage these situations and customers may be utilizing these methods in their existing environment. These methods can also be leveraged in the virtualized environment.

- VMware Site Recovery Manager for DR is based on storage array replication from the storage vendor. Each storage vendor is responsible for developing its own Storage Replication Adapter (SRA) to interface with SRM and allow SRM to coordinate the storage failover with the server/VM failovers.

- The DBA may have developed custom scripts and procedures to manage database backup and recovery. These can be leveraged in the future state virtual environment.

- Customers may have adopted database vendor techniques for DR scenarios such as Oracle Data Guard, Oracle Streams, and Oracle Golden Gate. These procedures can also be used in the future state virtual design.

Oracle database sizing in the virtualized environment should be done with these three options as described in the sections that follow.

Option 1: Sizing the Oracle DB Workload

Oracle DB workload testing is managed and conducted by the application administration team and DBAs, who have their own methods to verify that the application is functioning correctly as well as generating a representative workload. It is imperative to simulate both average and peak workloads. The following methods of workload generation are available:

- **Execute workload tools:** Business or functional users are typically required to generate the business data. This can be an arduous effort. Application data not in the correct state impacts the workload in the application. Data, after being consumed, must be refreshed by operators to rerun a workload, so it might be necessary to take storage-level snapshots or backups before a large test run to allow for a rollback. Workload tools will facilitate the completion of the performance testing phase of each project. This is a preferred methodology for workload sizing.

- **SwingBench online transaction processing (OLTP)/decision support system (DSS) kits:** These kits are common among the Oracle community to test workloads for both OLTP and DSS systems. Each kit's output provides the baseline for how the Oracle database server performs.

- **Oracle Real Application Testing (RAT):** Oracle Real Application Testing option enables helps in capturing production workloads and assessing the impact of system changes before deploying into production. For details, refer to Oracle documentation at the Oracle website.

- **HP Load Runner:** HP Load Runner is another load-testing tool that does performance and test automation. Refer to the HP website for more details.

- **Silly Little Oracle Benchmark (SLOB):** SLOB is another testing tool to performance test Oracle databases. Check Kevin Closson's blog for complete details.

- **HammerDB:** HammerDB is an open source database load testing and benchmarking tool for Oracle, SQL Server, TimesTen, PostgreSQL, Greenplum, Postgres Plus Advanced Server, MySQL, and Redis. Check out the HammerDB website for more details.

- **Benchmark Factory for Databases:** Benchmark Factory for Databases is another database performance testing tool that allows DBAs to conduct database workload replay, industry-standard benchmark testing, and scalability testing. For more details, refer to the Dell/Quest website.

Storage benchmarks tools: The lifetime of a SAN includes firmware upgrades, host driver updates, re-cabling of switches, and other changes. Any of these changes can cause performance problems. VMware recommends building an I/O baseline so that if a change is made to the storage, a benchmarking test can reveal performance problems introduced by the change. After testing the changes, the DBA should record a new baseline. Storage benchmarking is a simple process. The DBA should run two sets of tests: a maximum throughput sequential write test and a maximum throughput sequential read test. Many open source tools available enable you to perform those tests, including these recommended tools:

- Iometer or IOzone

- Linux/UNIX dd

- Oracle ORION

Benchmarking storage is a critical step in the deployment of Tier 1 workloads. It is recommended that customers achieve a defined minimum before considering that the storage is viable for a Tier 1 Oracle workload. Although this is not a high data rate, it serves as a gating factor for preemptive storage performance diagnostics to prevent VMware technology from becoming a predictable, innocent target for performance problems suspicions.

Benchmarking storage provides two benefits. First, any potential storage issues or misconfigurations are flushed out. The second benefit is testing for storage Tier 1 readiness. Often, this entails benchmarking the physical storage performance and comparing the results with the new datastores prepared for the Oracle workload. These types of simple tests can be performed with any type of enterprise ready storage to include SAN, flash, or IP-based storage of any kind. Storage benchmarking must be greater than our established redline to be considered to be a valid Tier 1 test, as depicted in Figure 2-12.

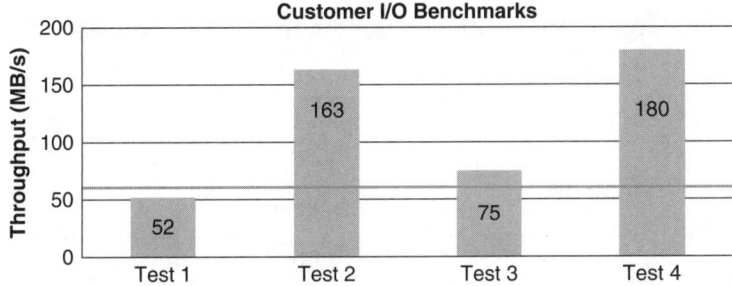

Figure 2-12 Typical customer I/O benchmark redline

Option 2: Sizing the Oracle DB Application Vendor Recommendations

This option can be leveraged based on the application vendor recommendation for sizing. Table 2-1 provides an example for SAP application sizing.

In Table 2-1, we highlight the SAP Application Performance Standards (SAPS) metric, which is derived from the well-known Sales and Distribution (SD) Benchmark test.

Table 2-1 Application Vendor Estimates

Server Specification	Physical SAPS from Hardware Vendor	Virtual SAPS (Assume 10% overhead)	Total # of Cores	SAPS per Core = SAPS per vCPU*
XXXXXXXX	17,777	16,000	16	1,000

*SAPS per vCPU assumes that the total number of vCPUs <= total number of cores.

The SAP business requirements were submitted to the SAP practice of *<Hardware Vendor X>*, which conducted an SAP "Quick Sizer" exercise and returned the following sizing response.

The SAPS rating per vCPU must be provided by the hardware vendor SAP practice. Any SAPS based sizing that has not involved the hardware vendor is *not* supported by VMware. In this example, five SAP products are shown, but there are other products available, each of which would be a separate system.

Table 2-2 shows the SAPS estimates for the target servers based on information from *<Hardware Vendor X>* from which we obtain the SAPS per vCPU.

Table 2-2 Sizing Response from Hardware Vendor

SAP Product	SAPS	DB SAPS	DB vMEM	APP SAPS	App vMEM
ERP	8,100	4,050	30	6,075	60
BW	10,800	5,400	16	8,100	24
SolMan	5,700	1,425	4	4,275	10
Portal	5,400	2,700	10	4,050	30
SCM	2,000	1,000	4	1,500	4

The 10% overhead is a general VMware estimate. Hardware vendors might have a different overhead estimate and might provide only the virtual SAPS per vCPU directly without giving the physical ratings and overhead details as shown in the preceding table. If the physical SAPs ratings is based on hyperthreading, then the hyperthreading benefit of 25% (rule of thumb) should be subtracted. (VMware has seen 20% to 30% increase in SAP OLTP throughput/SAPS due to hyperthreading.) Hyperthreading is the hardware feature that masks the physical core and presents that core as two separate processing threads. For more information on hyperthreading and its effect on the virtualized database environment, see Chapter 8.

Table 2-3 shows estimates for the VM sizes for the database and application tiers (based on 1,000 SAPS/vCPU) and ESX/ESXi hosts with 8 cores per socket.

Table 2-3 DB Tier – Updated Sizing Based on 1,000 SAPS per vCPU (65% CPU)

SAP Product	Hardware Vendor: DB SAPS/mem (GB)	Round SAPS to Nearest 1,000	Estimated DB Virtual Machine	ESX/ESXi Host: 8 Cores per Socket (Standardize on 2-, 4-, 8-way)
ERP	4,050/30	4,000	4 vCPUs, 30GB	
BW	5,400/16	6,000	6 vCPUs, 16GB	Too oversized if increased to 8 vCPUs
Sol Man	1,425/4	2,000	2 vCPUs, 4GB	
Portal	2,700/10	3,000	3 vCPUs, 10GB	Increase to 4 vCPUs
SCM	1,000/4	2,000 decided minimum VM size of 2 vCPU for a DB	2 vCPUs, 4GB	

Figure 2-13 shows an example layout based on 2-socket, 8 cores per socket ESX/ESXi hosts.

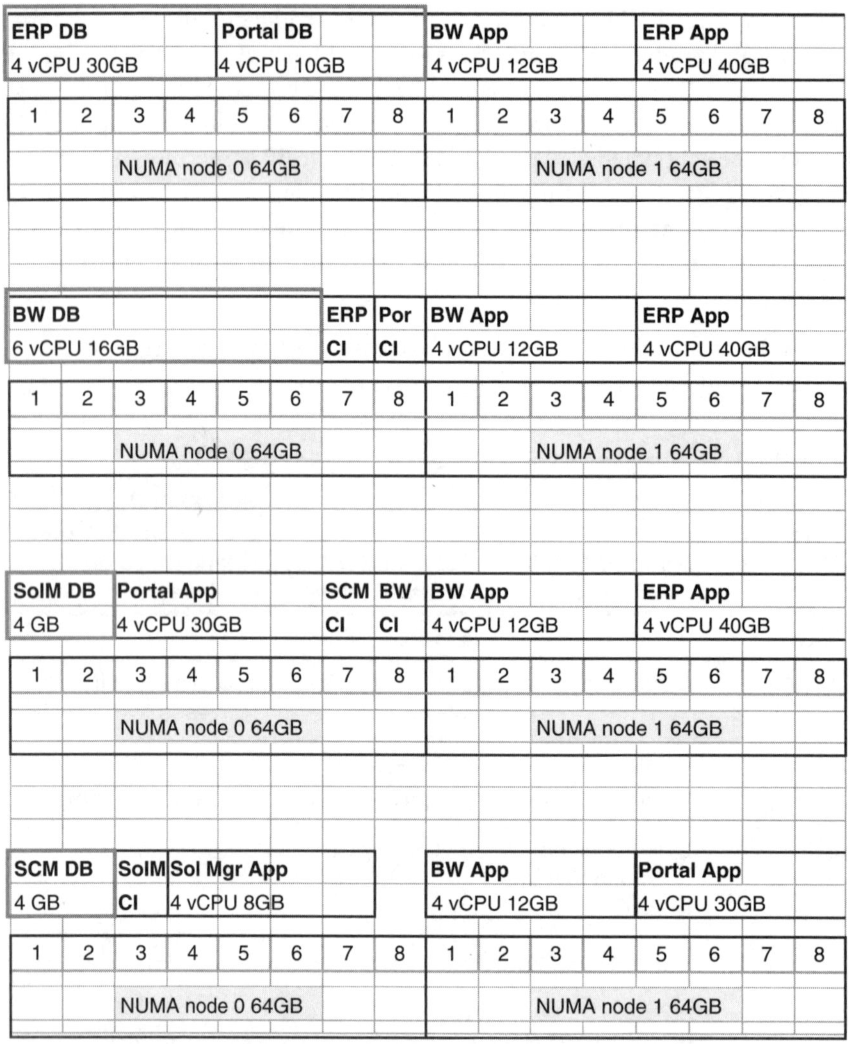

ERP DB		Portal DB		BW App		ERP App	
4 vCPU 30GB		4 vCPU 10GB		4 vCPU 12GB		4 vCPU 40GB	
1	2	3	4	5	6	7	8	1	2	3	4	5	6	7	8
NUMA node 0 64GB								NUMA node 1 64GB							

BW DB				ERP CI	Por CI	BW App		ERP App	
6 vCPU 16GB						4 vCPU 12GB		4 vCPU 40GB	
1	2	3	4	5	6	7	8	1	2	3	4	5	6	7	8
NUMA node 0 64GB								NUMA node 1 64GB							

SolM DB	Portal App		SCM CI	BW CI	BW App		ERP App	
4 GB	4 vCPU 30GB				4 vCPU 12GB		4 vCPU 40GB	
1	2	3	4	5	6	7	8	1	2	3	4	5	6	7	8
NUMA node 0 64GB								NUMA node 1 64GB							

SCM DB	SolM CI	Sol Mgr App		BW App		Portal App	
4 GB		4 vCPU 8GB		4 vCPU 12GB		4 vCPU 30GB	
1	2	3	4	5	6	7	8	1	2	3	4	5	6	7	8
NUMA node 0 64GB								NUMA node 1 64GB							

Figure 2-13 Production VM assignment example

This design assumes the SAP user license covers the database license. That is, there are no licensing restrictions on running the database on vSphere.

Figure 2-13 represents an example logical architecture. The VMs do *not* run exclusively on a particular core; the ESX/ESXi scheduler balances the VMs across the ESX/ESXi cluster based on the workload and if enabled, Distributed Resource Scheduler (DRS) balances and distributes the VMs across the clustered hosts using DRS algorithms. The figure shows total number of vCPUs assigned and demonstrates that for production, the total number of vCPUs <= total number of physical cores. Later chapters discuss non-uniform memory access (NUMA) and NUMA optimization in depth, but to understand the chart, notice that where possible the VM fits within a single NUMA node.

The ESXi host in the following diagram can be configured with or without hyperthreading. When using hyperthreading, and where vCPUs <= total number of cores, the ESXi scheduler by default tries to schedule the vCPU on a NUMA node. For more information on VMware SAP guidelines, see VMware's website and also refer to VMware SAP SME's Virtualizing Business Critical Application blog site.

http://blogs.vmware.com/apps/sap

http://www.vmware.com/business-critical-apps/sap-virtualization/index.htm

Option 3: Sizing Oracle DB Server Vendor Guidelines

Use this option when the VM/server vendor has guidelines for sizing the Oracle database server. Table 2-4 provides an example where Oracle has developed single-click configurations that include all the necessary CPU, memory, and storage resources to meet predetermined levels of user demand. Oracle offers several different single-click configuration options to start.

Table 2-4 Oracle Single-Click Configurations

	Entry Configuration	Standard Configuration	Power Configuration	Enterprise Configuration	Datacenter Configuration
Max Named Users*	Up to 60	Up to 125	Up to 400	Up to 1,000	Up to 2,000
DB Size (TB)	1.2	3	4.2	2.7	2.7
Licensed X86 CPU Cores	6 at 2.53GHz	12 at 2.53GHz	12 at 3.46GHz	20 at 2.4GHz	40 at 2.4GHz
System Memory Size	24GB	72GB	144GB	512GB	1TB
Flash	N/A	N/A	N/A	2 x F20	4 x F20
Basic Server Models	Sun Fire X4170 M2	Sun Fire X4170 M2	Sun Fire X4270 M2	Sun Fire X4470 M2	Sun Fire X4470 M2
Oracle Database Edition	11g R2 Standard Edition One 64-bit	11g R2 Standard Edition 64-bit	11g R2 Standard Edition 64-bit	11g R2 Enterprise Edition 64-bit	11g R2 Enterprise Edition 64-bit

*A named user is a human or a nonhuman operating device that can access Oracle database at any time.

Refer to the Oracle website for Oracle single-click configurations.

Testing the Limits: Performance Studies and Stress Tests

Throughout the last half decade, VMware along with a plethora of VMware partners and third-party companies, all with an interest in testing the limits of technology, has run a broad range of performance and stress tests on vSphere. Throughout this book, we discuss many of those tests and describe the various results. Tests such as the RAC Workload Characterization Study performed by VMware in conjunction with Cisco unambiguously proved the viability of Oracle RAC running on vSphere 4.1. The functional stress tests executed by Principled Technologies showed the complete abstraction between the guest OS and the virtualized hardware. Those same tests showed impressive albeit unique usage of vSphere features, such as vMotion and the vSphere 5.5 feature of the vFlash Read Cache (vFRC). All modern versions of the Oracle RDBMS from 10g to 12c as well as a decent sampling of the applications have been used throughout this veritable library of test procedures. Other high-workload tests have been performed, including the famous one million IOPS workload tests, proving the innate ability of ESX to access storage. We refer to these tests throughout the text and include some of the links here.

vSphere 5.5 advanced features Flash Read Chache and vMotion—

http://principledtechnologies.com/vmware/vFRC_Oracle_12c_0414.pdf

vSphere 5.1 with Oracle RAC vMotion—

http://www.principledtechnologies.com/VMware/vMotion_Oracle_RAC_1013.pdf

Achieving a Million I/O Operations per Second from a Single VMware vSphere® 5.0 Host—

http://www.vmware.com/files/pdf/1M-iops-perf-vsphere5.pdf

Summary

Oracle performance testing can be arduous, mundane, and time-consuming, or it can be exhilarating and enlightening and actually quite fun. If the DBA has a working knowledge of the tools available, the process may not be entertaining, but it will be effective. If the performance testing is a facet of a greater virtualization project, the result will be a triumph of modern computing, and everyone involved will experience the benefits of virtualized infrastructure. DBAs still need to manage, monitor, provision, and back up databases, but the capabilities of VMware and the qualities innate in the four V's of vSphere as a platform of virtualized hardware will make this experience a much more satisfying journey to 100% virtualization.

Oracle Databases and Applications in Virtual Infrastructure: Architectural Concepts

VMware vSphere is the industry's most trusted virtualization platform. In fact, it is correct to say that vSphere is the world's only "platform of virtualized hardware." The main focus of the idea of virtualized infrastructure is to transform datacenters into dramatically simplified cloud infrastructures and to enable the next generation of flexible, reliable information technology (IT) services. VMware vSphere virtualizes and aggregates the underlying physical hardware resources across multiple systems and provides pools of virtual resources to the datacenter.

In this book, we adhere to the framework of the four V's: viability, value, versatility, and vision, as shown in Figure 3-1. This chapter focuses on the viability and versatility of vSphere when running Oracle as well as other industrial-strength relational database management systems (RDBMS).

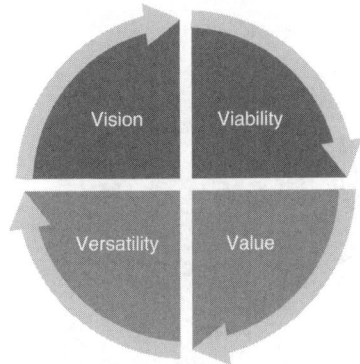

Figure 3-1 Four V's approach

VMware ESXi Hypervisor

The VMware ESXi hypervisor architecture is an architecture designed to provide the most robust virtualized infrastructure available in the IT industry. The main categories of capabilities include the potential for consolidation of hardware, licenses, and other facets of the system as well as the resource management capabilities innate in the platform (and finally, the features that allow the architect to build systems that meet the requirements of the various service level agreements [SLAs]). VMware ESX/ESXi hypervisor architecture provides the following unique capabilities:

- A true thin Type 1, non-paravirtualized hypervisor (144MB).

- No underlying operating system (OS). (Note that when ESX became ESXi, all the embedded OS components were eliminated.)

- Drivers optimized for virtual machines (VMs). Through VMtools, which is a VMware provided package added on top of the guest OS, the user may choose to implement the various paravirtualized drivers such as pvSCSI and VMXNET3. These drivers are beneficial to the running Oracle environment and are discussed in Chapter 8, "Performance Management and Monitoring."

- Transparent Page Sharing (TPS) delivers greater VM density.

- The physical resources of the host are completely owned and managed by the hypervisor, resulting in minimal hypervisor management overhead.

- Optimized scalability through the efficient use of all the available physical resources on the host. vSphere has the capability of managing all resources that are part of the virtualized infrastructure at a highly granular level to include processing, memory, network, and storage access.

Figure 3-2 illustrates the VMware ESXi hypervisor architecture.

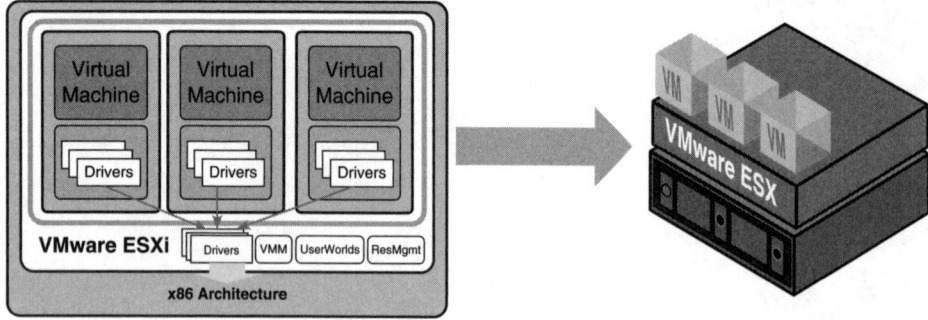

Figure 3-2 ESXi architecture

Oracle databases are excellent candidates to take advantage of these features. They run successfully on vSphere, providing significant scalability, availability, and performance benefits. Virtualizing database workloads on vSphere significantly reduces the number of physical systems your organization requires while achieving more effective and efficient utilization of datacenter resources. Customers realize tangible savings from this consolidation along with operational cost savings from reduced datacenter floor space, power, cooling requirements and more effective use of personnel.

VMware customers who run Oracle databases on vSphere leverage the following benefits:

- Maximize availability of the Oracle environment at a lower cost.

- Deploy Oracle database servers rapidly for staging, training, development, testing, and even production.

- Maximize uptime during planned maintenance. It is fair to say that downtime for hardware maintenance can be effectively eliminated.

- Minimize Oracle datacenter costs for floor space, energy, cooling, hardware, and labor.

- Minimize unplanned as well as effectively eliminate planned downtime.

- Automate testing and failover of Oracle datacenter environments for disaster recovery (DR) and business continuity.

- Aids in achieving IT security compliance.

- Realize immediate return on investment (ROI).

Virtualization is rapidly eliminating the old "one server one application" model and has freed applications from physical constraints. You can virtualize the hardware resources of an x86-based machine to create a fully functional VM that can run its own OS and behaves similarly to a physical computer. By encapsulating an entire machine, including the central processing unit (CPU), memory, operating system, and network devices, the VM is completely compatible with all common x86 operating systems, applications, and device drivers. Virtualization enables the customer to run multiple VMs on a single physical machine as well as pool hardware resources for dynamic delivery to the applications that need those resources. It is the job of the administrators to include the database administrators (DBAs), the VMAdmins, and the system admins to become familiar with the broad array of tools and features that constitute the platform capabilities of vSphere, which allow for effective sharing of resources and therefore true mixed-workload environments. Different VMs can run different operating systems and multiple applications on the same physical host computer.

Organizations are increasingly virtualizing their enterprise applications in production, and databases are no exception. Experienced DBAs recognize that virtualization unlocks capabilities that were hidden in physical environments. Throughout this book, we discuss database performance on vSphere, examine the general tasks assigned to DBAs, and introduce VMware technologies and tools that assist DBAs in designing, implementing, testing, operating, and maintaining databases in a virtual environment.

Today's challenge for DBAs is to provide 24x7 database services to application owners with the flexibility and autonomy they expect while keeping the infrastructure as simple and economical as possible. Traditional databases running on fixed physical hardware are often oversized, underutilized, protected by complex and expensive clustering solutions, and require rigorous processes for version control and continued application compatibility.

VMware virtualization creates a layer of 100% abstraction between the physical resources required by an application and OS and the underlying hardware that provides those resources. By decoupling the OS and applications from the underlying hardware, vSphere allows virtualized servers running databases to dynamically react to changes in underlying system resources such as CPU, memory, storage, and network to deliver near native database performance with minimal overhead. By running multiple VMs on a single physical server, throughput can be scaled to match fluctuating demands. From a single management console, you can use virtual images to easily deploy thousands of database servers to remote and local locations.

Today, VMs on vSphere 5.x can scale to 64 virtual CPUs (vCPUs), 1TB of memory per VM, over 36Gbps of network throughput between ESXi hosts (prior to the introduction of 40G cards), and more than 1,000,000 disk I/O per second (IOPS). All this while keeping overhead limited to between 2% to 10% for any performance metric of any dimension of performance. In some cases, these modern capabilities constitute a 25x performance increase from the early versions of ESX. This clearly demonstrates that VMs running on vSphere can scale to meet the demands of the largest workloads. At this point in time, it is fair to state that for 99.9% of the database implementations in existence, it makes sense to consider running them in virtualized infrastructure. VMware is 100% committed to 99.9% virtualization. In addition, vSphere maximizes the performance achieved from physical hosts by enabling multiple database systems to efficiently share the large capacity of multicore servers.

Modern 64-bit servers feature an ever growing number of CPU cores, higher memory limits, and increased network bandwidth. The majority of database applications can run comfortably with a fraction of the physical server capacity. The traditional deployment model of one application per server is not maintaining pace with the latest enhancements in hardware and virtualization. Virtualizing infrastructure for databases on vSphere simultaneously consolidates the RDBMS and optimizes compute resources, while maintaining application flexibility by providing the option to isolate each database in its own VM. Also, you can migrate databases from physical to virtual environments in their current state without expensive and error-prone application migrations.

The value of virtualization goes far beyond basic consolidation. Virtualizing database applications on vSphere can improve application quality of service (QoS) and accelerate application lifecycles, reducing application costs:

- **Improve application QoS:** Databases are very difficult to size on physical servers. With VMware, databases can scale dynamically (through features such as hot-add) to meet variant throughput and processing requirements. You can leverage vSphere High Availability (HA), vSphere Fault Tolerance (FT), VMware vMotion, Dynamic Resource Scheduling (DRS), and VMware vCenter Site Recovery Manager (SRM) to create robust availability with minimal configuration changes. If needed, these solutions can also be combined with more traditional database clustering and replication options to provide even higher levels of availability. It is feasible to build out a system that can tolerate the most tactically challenging hardware failures while addressing the most strategically ominous disaster scenarios.

- **Accelerate application delivery:** DBAs can provision new databases on demand in a matter of minutes from preconfigured virtual appliances or simple templates. They can test multitier applications quickly and efficiently by easily cloning production databases. They can automate release cycles and deploy standard, preconfigured databases at the click of a button, promoting consistency between production and nonproduction databases and minimizing manual configuration overhead and configuration drift.

- **Reduce application costs:** Databases are among the most overprovisioned applications in the datacenter. Because of this massive overprovisioning, databases have tremendous consolidation potential. With server consolidation, which requires the exercise of "right-sizing," not only are hardware footprints reduced, but the costs of expensive database licenses can also be reduced.

Designing Databases on VMware

By decoupling the application and OS from the physical hardware, the VMware virtualization platform addresses many difficult design problems such as scalability, HA, and resource isolation that traditionally dominate the physical environment. With VMware features and tools, a customer can design database solutions that can be scaled on demand to meet any resource requirement or organizational growth requirement, implement higher availability and DR solutions with less complexity, and leverage available hardware resources while maintaining full application isolation.

Designing for Scalability on Demand

Capacity planning is one of the most challenging tasks in designing a database solution. How much of each resource (CPU, memory, storage, and network) is needed? Are available resources adequate to handle peak server load? What is the expected growth rate? What happens when the company decides to support another geographic region with the application? These are all difficult problems that DBAs face daily in the nonvirtualized environment. Undersizing a system may result in underperformance, which will affect business operations or event availability. Often, DBAs have no choice but to size a physical server many times larger than the workload to address spikes that occur during peak hours that may only happen once a year or to handle an unexpected anomalous resource demand.

With VMware vSphere, resources are managed in pools. CPU, memory, storage, or networking can be increased or decreased dynamically or manually with just a few mouse clicks.

Working with VMware Hosts, Clusters, and Resource Pools

VMware hosts, clusters, and resource pools provide flexible and dynamic techniques that facilitate the organization of aggregated computing and memory resources in the virtual environment and link them back to the underlying physical resources.

A host represents the aggregate computing and memory resources of a physical x86 server. An ESX/ESXi or vSphere cluster acts and can be managed as a single entity. It represents the aggregate computing and memory resources of a group of physical x86 servers sharing the same network and storage arrays. Cluster membership is maintained through a quorum system and sustained by an intranode heartbeat. For example, if the group contains 8 hosts with 4 dual-core CPUs (total 64 cores) each running at 4GHz and 32GB of memory, the cluster has an aggregate 256GHz of computing power and 256GB of memory available for running VMs.

Resource pools are partitions of computing and memory resources presented from a single host or a cluster. Resource pools can be hierarchical as well as nested. You can partition a resource pool into smaller resource pools to further divide and assign resources to different groups or for different purposes.

Working with VMware Hot-Add

The VMware hot-add feature enables dynamic addition of CPU/memory to a running VM. As applications grow over time and require more CPU or memory resources, a DBA can scale up VMs dynamically. The Oracle RDBMS (10g and later) will automatically detect the new capacity, reconfigure itself dynamically (in terms of dynamic latch counts and parallelism), and make use of the additional resources in subsequent operations.

Working with VMware vMotion

VMware vMotion enables live migration of VMs from one physical server to another without service interruption as shown in Figure 3-3. vMotion uses the VMware cluster file system (Virtual Machine File System [VMFS]) to control access to a VM's storage. During a vMotion migration, the active memory and precise execution state of a VM is rapidly transmitted over a high-speed network from one physical server to another and access to the VM's disk storage is instantly switched to the new physical host. Because the network is also virtualized by the VMware host, the VM retains its network identity and connections, resulting in a seamless migration process.

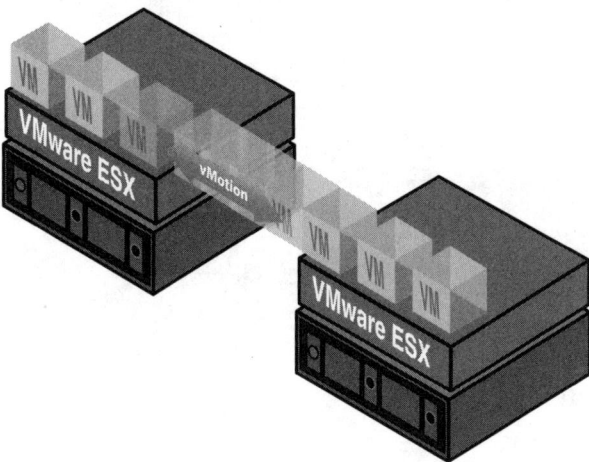

Figure 3-3 VMware vSphere vMotion

The amount of time that a vMotion takes is determined by three factors: the amount of memory allocated to the VM, the amount of activity on the VM during the vMotion operation, and the available network bandwidth during that operation. vSphere is capable of using up to 36Gbps of network bandwidth when streaming multiple vMotions concurrently over up to four 10Gb teamed network cards (as of vSphere 5.x). A number of tests referenced throughout this book have recorded up to 23.9Gbps of network usage for a single vMotion operation. vSphere can perform up to eight simultaneous vMotions from a single ESXi host.

Working with VMware Distributed Resource Scheduler

VMware Distributed Resource Scheduler (DRS) takes the VMware vMotion capability a step further by adding an intelligent scheduler. DRS allows you to set resource assignment policies that reflect business needs. VMware DRS does the calculations and automatically handles the details of physical resource assignments. It dynamically monitors the workload (CPU and memory usage) of the running VMs and the resource utilization of the physical servers within a cluster.

VMware resource pools, hot-add, vMotion, and DRS features enable DBAs to design database solutions to scale on demand, as illustrated in Figure 3-4.

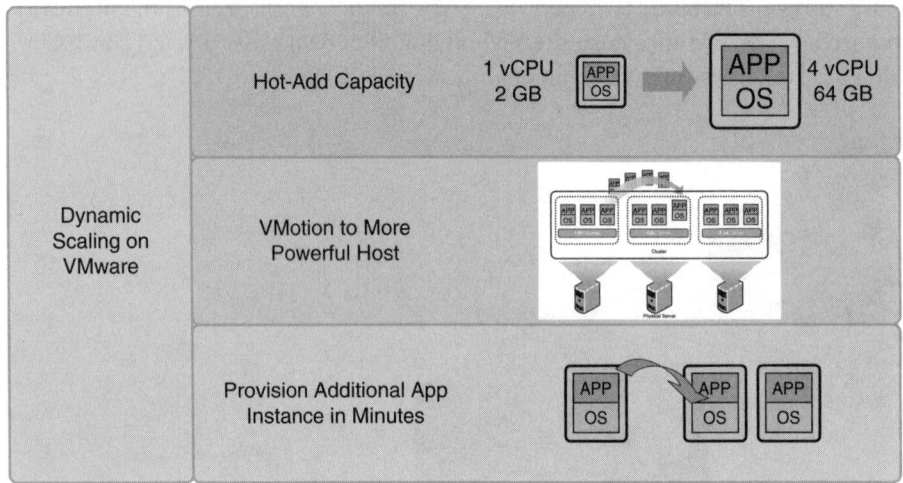

Figure 3-4 Scale applications on demand

In this way, vSphere allows the DBA to effectively "future-proof" the greater system. For example, a retail database may be 10% utilized normally, but during the Christmas shopping season, it may be 95% utilized. The Christmas shopping season only lasts for 30 days. Instead of sizing the database for the Christmas peak capacity initially (wasting resources for the other 11 months), you may size the database VM for normal workloads, live migrate the database to a more powerful host using vMotion, and hot-add CPU to the VM before Christmas shopping season starts to proactively address the increased resource demands during the holiday season.

Designing for High Availability

The Oracle database Server provides a variety of options for high availability and DR (for example, Oracle Real Application Cluster [RAC] and Oracle Data Guard [DG]). Though all of these are effective choices to address a variety of database recovery circumstances, the application-centric nature of these technologies usually result in costly, complex, high operational overhead systems. These advanced Oracle architectures should be selected based on the application's service level agreement (SLA). Implementing extreme HA/DR for every database in a physical environment is often not practical.

The VMware vSphere platform ships with built in HA. By decoupling the OS and application from the underlying physical server hardware, you can restart a VM easily on an appropriate and available node in the ESXi cluster. Think of the VMs being moved around seamlessly and automatically between nodes on the cluster in response to server-level failures.

Maximizing vSphere HA Capabilities

vSphere HA monitors VMs and detects OS and hardware failures. It then restarts VMs on different physical servers without manual intervention. This protects applications from OS failures by automatically restarting VMs when an OS failure is detected. DBAs no longer have to worry about the database becoming unavailable because of OS, host bus adapter (HBA), network card, or other hardware failures (see Figure 3-5).

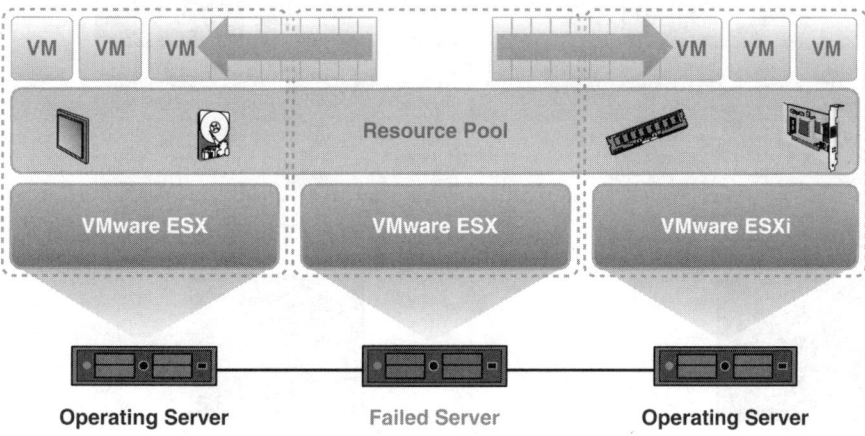

Figure 3-5 VMware HA

HA can be configured with a few clicks from within the vSphere Client interface to provide failover protection for all VMs within an ESX/ESXi cluster without requiring the complex setup and configuration of other types of clustering. DBAs can design uniform, cost-effective failover protections against OS and server failures for all databases regardless of the server hardware or OS used by the database VM. vSphere HA provides a simple and reliable "first line of defense" for all databases against a myriad of failures without the cost and the hassle of traditional database high availability options. The simplicity of this HA solution is underscored by the fact that upon restart of the VM, all the processes (the Oracle DB) within the guest OS that are set to automatically restart will do so. vSphere

HA can also be used in combination with native database HA options, such as Oracle RAC and Oracle DG, to provide complete protection from both hardware and application software failures.

Protecting Datacenters from Disasters Using VMware Site Recovery Manager

Protecting production datacenters and the respective components running Oracle databases during disasters is critical to any business. VMware vCenter SRM complements the application availability capabilities that Oracle provides to an enterprise datacenter by automating the testing and failover of Oracle production datacenters to a DR environment. Figure 3-6 illustrates a basic SRM configuration. SRM, covered in Chapter 9, "Business Continuity and Disaster Recovery," is a workflow orchestration tool (part of the vCloud Suite), which will facilitate coordination between the storage and server components of the virtualized infrastructure during a DR event.

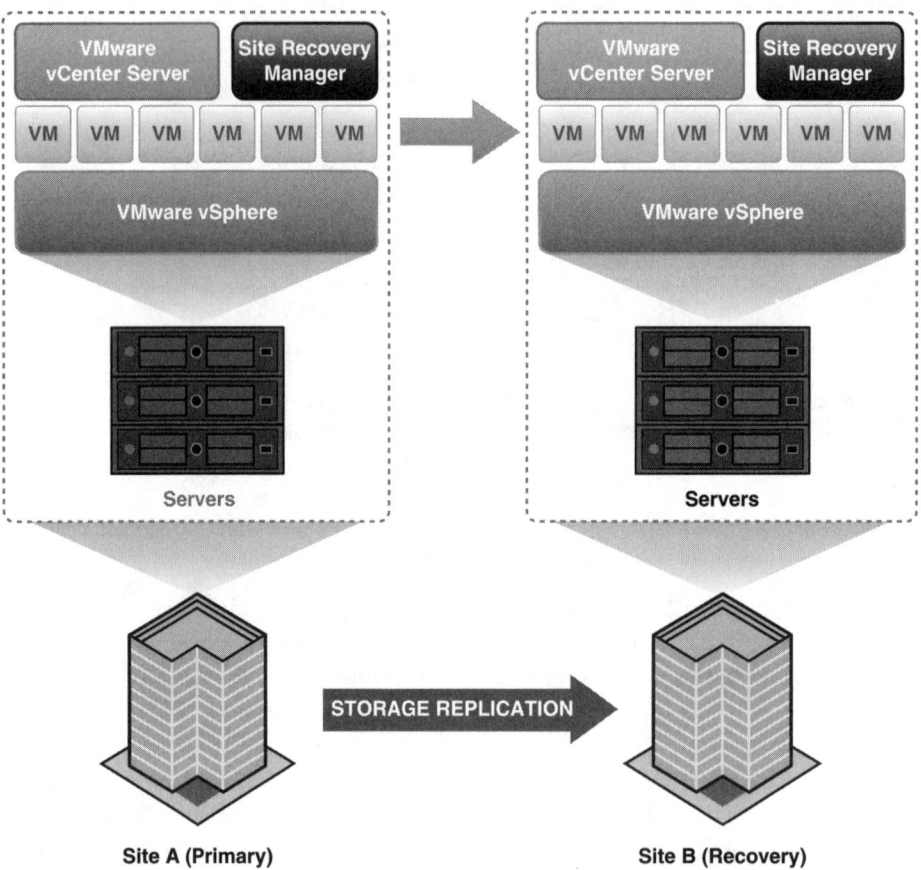

Figure 3-6 VMware vCenter Site Recovery Manager

In case of disaster, SRM fails over all designated components, most importantly the VMs running the Oracle instances onto the DR site (B). SRM then brings up the failover target VMs, which subsequently restart the application environments. SRM integrates and leverages the storage replication software from leading storage vendors by the integration of the respective storage replication adapters (SRAs) to simplify the use of storage replication software with vSphere. The SRAs are built and maintained by the respective storage vendors.

Testing DR scenarios is a complex and time-consuming process to set up and execute. SRM can automate the testing process as part of the VMware vCenter management interface. Some key SRM features include the following:

- Nondisruptive testing
    - Create and manage recovery plans directly from the vCenter management interface.
    - Extend recovery plans with custom scripts to provide for Oracle database instance failover and restart. Store, view, and export results of test and failover execution from vCenter.
    - Connect VMs to an existing isolated network for testing.
    - Automate the execution of recovery plans.
    - Automate the cleanup of testing environments after completing failover tests.
- Failback capabilities were included in SRM 5.x, but the use of this feature would be difficult to coordinate with running Oracle databases.
- Automated failover
    - Monitor the availability of a remote site and alert users of possible site failures.
    - Initiate recovery plan execution from vCenter with a single button click.
    - Execute user-defined scripts and halts during recovery.
    - Reconfigure Oracle VMs to match network configuration at a failover site.
    - Manage and monitor the execution of recovery plans within vCenter.
    - Include callout scripts to be executed as part of the workflow orchestration.

In summary, the key VMware HA and DR benefits include the following:

- Automatic restart of failed Oracle database servers in VMs using VMware HA
- Indigenous capacity planning capability to support Oracle VM failovers

- Migration of Oracle application VMs from failing server hardware using vMotion without disruption to end users

- Automated testing and failover of Oracle datacenter environments for DR and business continuity

Maintaining Compliance

Organizations must understand their IT assets, including both structured and unstructured data residing in corporate databases. They must define what types of business records are vital and how long they must be maintained and stored. Older hardware requires refreshing to stay compliant and current. Compliance with regulatory requirements, such as the Sarbanes-Oxley (SOX) Act, the Health Insurance Portability and Accountability Act of 1996 (HIPAA), and Payment Card Industry standards (PCI), as well as internal IT policies, may require older Oracle environments and data to remain active beyond normal hardware and software upgrade cycles. The need for dedicated hardware to host these legacy environments beyond their maintenance or warranty cycle often leads to additional cost.

vSphere provides enhanced capabilities to manage compliance in Oracle database environments by

- Helping to provide standard, compliant OS and database images that are enforced across the datacenters by leveraging master templates and cloning capabilities

- Helping hardware infrastructures stay updated and compliant by rehosting applications from older hardware onto newer datacenter infrastructures

- Archiving older VMs with their respective databases and configurations for compliance and auditing

- Taking VM snapshots to capture point-in-time data for future reviews and audits

vSphere also contains a plethora of security-focused capabilities that allow the DBA to manage compliance and internal security as an attribute of vSphere.

Consolidating Database Servers

There are three approaches to consolidation within database environments. Database consolidation in general with vSphere is illustrated in Figure 3.7. First, you can consolidate by adding individual "schemas" or databases to a solitary instance. As depicted in Figure 3-8, Oracle 12c makes use of this idea with the paradigm of "container" and "pluggable" databases. Sybase and SQL server have used this methodology from their inception. Second, you can consolidate instances onto an individual server (logical or physical). And finally, third, a modern architect will consolidate the servers onto the vSphere platform. In the third case, the database architect will consider isolating each Oracle instance within a separate VM to maximize the capabilities of vSphere. There may be completely valid reasons to create an architecture that is built with a one-to-many approach, but the one-to-one should be considered because in this way each instance/application can be given the precisely required resources, and security can be applied to meet the exact requirements of that system. It is also important to point out that the architect may choose to utilize a databases-to-instance approach first, such as the Oracle 12c model encourages. In that case, the value proposition of virtualization does not change. There are simply more database schemas being managed by the single instance, which is managing the greater "container database." All other aspects of the value proposition of virtualization remain the same.

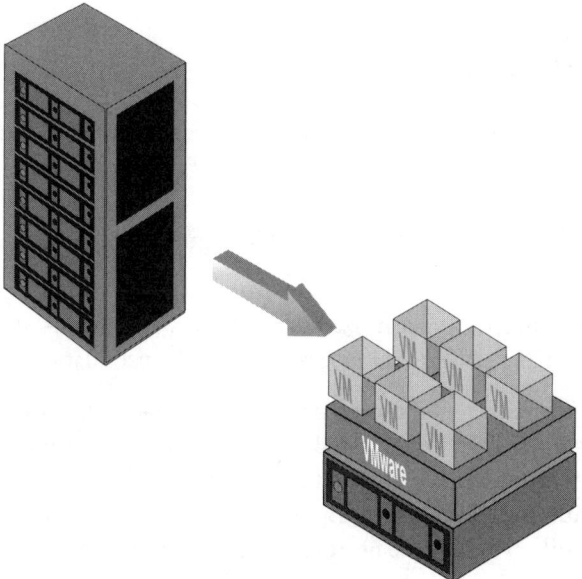

Figure 3-7 Consolidation methods

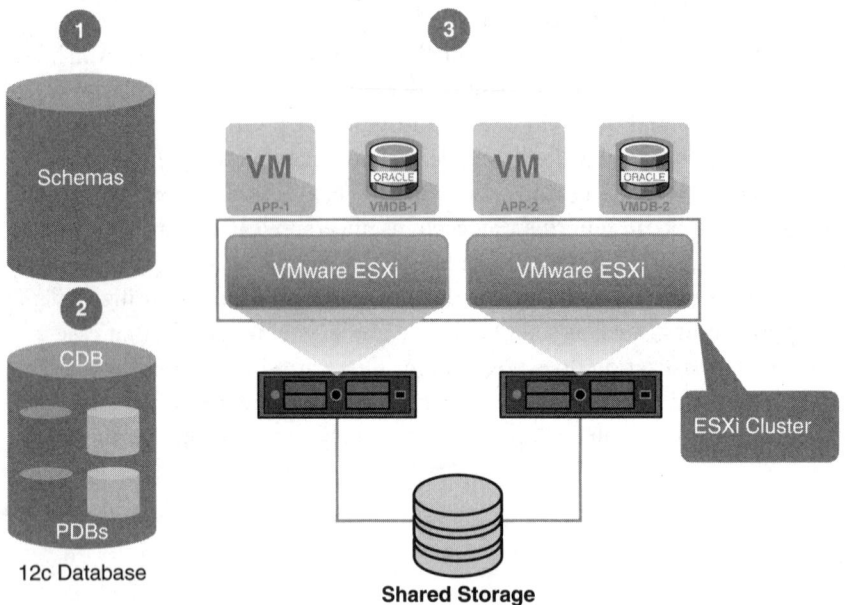

Figure 3-8 Oracle database server consolidation

The third method offers superior architectural benefits as depicted in Figure 3-9 over the first two methods in the following ways:

- **Optimal resource utilization:** Run multiple underutilized database server environments on a single virtualized system and deliver a high level of server consolidation.

- **Legacy application rehosting:** With vSphere, consolidating existing legacy databases is simple and straightforward. Databases can be migrated with a simple physical-to-virtual (P2V) migration or re-provisioned in a VM with their existing OS and database configurations. This eliminates the requirement to retest databases that run on standardized operating systems while avoiding the need to retain old hardware.

- **Isolation:** Databases consolidated on vSphere preserves complete isolation between instances (configuration, failure, security, and resource isolation). Databases can run on their own operating systems and database versions, and a single OS failure impacts only a single database. Security can be customized to the specific application/database pair. This is a unique benefit of virtualization that is impossible with conventional database consolidation approaches.

- **Resource guarantees:** Oracle database servers requiring additional resources can be automatically moved to other virtualized servers (hosts) using vMotion. By performing host-level server-based load balancing, DRS delivers optimal resources to maintain database performance and service levels. This helps with resource guarantees and provides right-sized Oracle database environments that do not require overallocation of datacenter resources.

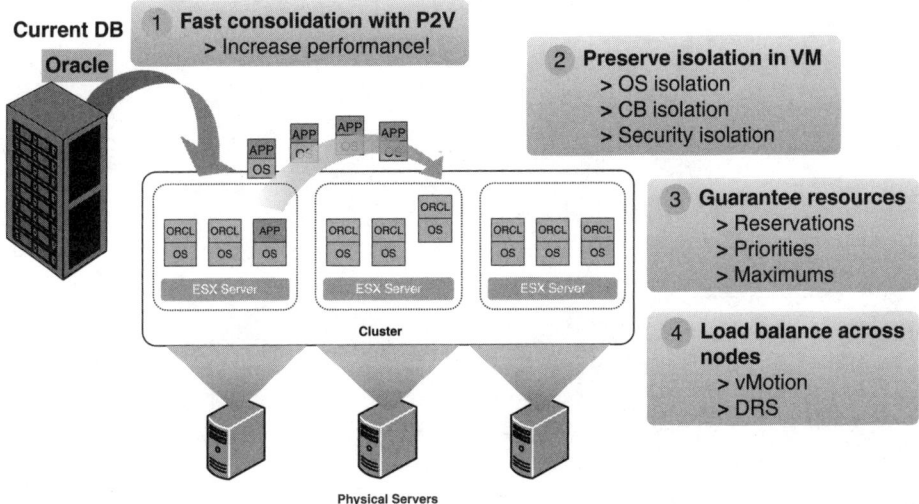

Figure 3-9 Oracle database server consolidation steps

Virtualizing Oracle RAC

Oracle Real Application Clusters (RAC) is a clustered database system that utilizes a shared database cache architecture providing highly available and scalable database solutions for business applications. Multiple Oracle instances usually residing on different logical servers and managed through Global Cache Service (GCS) allow for concurrent access from multiple database instances to database files and data. The RAC node cluster membership is managed through the Grid Infrastructure (formally called Cluster Ready Services [CRS]). The deployment of RAC on vSphere is essentially congruent to nonvirtualized environments, with the exception that each RAC node corresponds to a separate VM, which typically resides on a separate ESX/ESXi host, as shown in Figure 3-10.

The features of a virtualized RAC deployment are as follows:

- **Facilitates consolidation:** While each RAC node VM usually resides on a separate ESX/ESXi host, spare capacity on each ESX/ESXi host allows hosting of other VMs on that same physical host.

- **Provision new RAC nodes using VMware templates:** DBAs can preinstall and patch the operating system, and then store it in a template from which further VM RAC nodes can be created. The inclusion of the newly created RAC node can be automated through the automation of the RAC "add-node" process. Chapter 4, "Oracle on vSphere Best Practices," delves into the details of these advanced vRAC implementations. (VMware Professional Services Organization has such a service.)

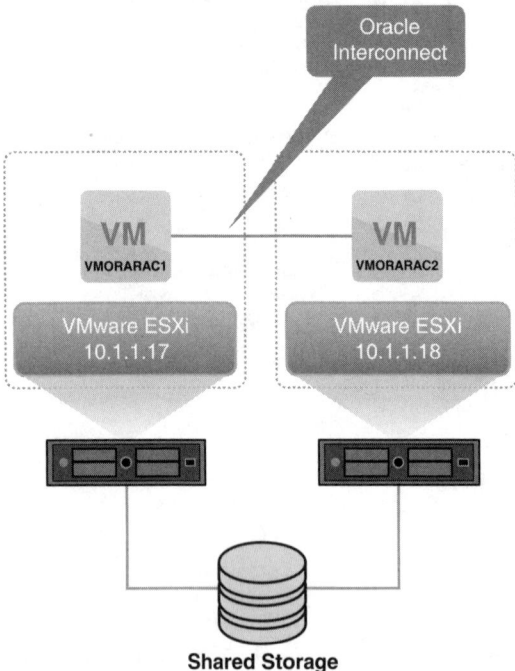

Figure 3-10 Oracle RAC on VMware – two-node RAC

In training environments, DBAs can install RAC in multiple VMs on the same ESX/ESXi host. This minimizes the need for multiple physical machines but still enables RAC functionality to be tested and deployed in a similar functional manner to production environment. For more information about Oracle RAC, including the VMWare supported and recommended implementation methodologies, see Chapter 4.

Identifying Key Stakeholders

This chapter has described compelling features of several possible Oracle architectures. It is useful for every DBA and application architect to know what options are available so that they can identify the best way to address their challenges. However, the point of this entire book may be lost if the key stakeholders of applications and databases do not understand what their organizations stand to gain (as described in this chapter) through the marriage of Oracle and virtualization. Without that understanding, an Oracle virtualization project may have a hard time getting off the ground. Here is a list of key stakeholders in basically every organization and what they are responsible for delivering. This will help DBAs, architects, managers, and business executives alike identify the benefits described in this chapter that will give them the justification and comfort level they need to move ahead with designing virtualized environments for Oracle based applications.

Figure 3-11 provides an organization chart that identifies key stakeholders for virtualizing Oracle database servers.

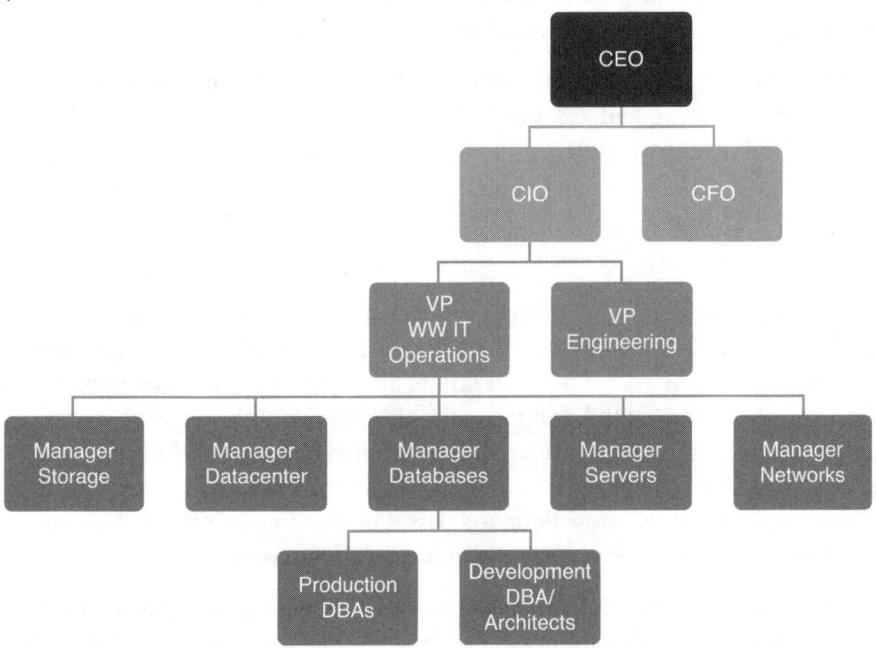

Figure 3-11 Key stakeholders

The key stakeholders for virtualizing Oracle database server opportunities include the following:

- **Vice president, worldwide IT operations:** Responsible for all IT operations and controls and manages datacenter operations, servers, networks, databases, and storage. Goal: Reducing costs through maximum utilization, consolidation, availability, and DR for production systems of high importance.

- **Manager, databases:** Manages all production and development databases with a team of DBAs. Goal: Provide required resources and make the environment available. The same considerations of availability will be of great importance to the mid-level management staff.

- **Production DBAs and database architects:** Concerned with scalability, performance, and overall resource management. Database architects are interested in providing cost-effective architectures that include efficient consolidation, rapid provisioning, and automation capabilities as well as the architectural components of availability that correspond are established by the SLAs associated with an individual architecture. Goal: Leverage current skill sets to perform their roles.

- **Business owners (CIO, CFO, line-of-business VPs, and so on):** Decision makers responsible for controlling budgets. Goal: Lower total cost of ownership (TCO) and higher return on investment (ROI).

Summary

The architectural concepts discussed in this chapter constitute a small sample of the variety of permutations that a VMware customer may use for their virtualized infrastructure. All types of customers from the recent business school graduate to the intrepid entrepreneur to the well-seasoned Oracle DBA will recognize the innate viability of vSphere as the premier platform to adopt when considering their twenty-first century IT architecture options. The versatility of vSphere is on full display when an attendee of a major IT conference roams the alleys of the show floor and passes booth after booth, all of which include some aspect of virtualization in their individual value proposition.

Detailed examination of VMware's colossal customer base will reveal that each and every application, RDBMS and hardware option has been successfully implemented in one form or another. Through the remaining nine chapters of this book, we delve deeper into the various technical, emotional, business, and fiscal components of the use of these variant architectures, and we will unambiguously prove that those who embrace the leading-edge of virtualization technology benefit substantially. The leaders often outlast and outlive the laggards, but in the case of virtualized infrastructure, we may see the laggards fade into obsolescence.

## Chapter 4

Oracle on vSphere Best Practices

The notion of best practices is at the very heart of the question of viability. Without the implementation of the general best practices for Oracle on vSphere, or at least an alternate and well thought-out plan, there are very few successful implementations. A basic pillar of Oracle on vSphere is that the fundamental approach to implementing Oracle does not change and that therefore the skill set of the database administrator (DBA) does not have to be appreciably altered to successfully install, configure, maintain, and run Oracle on vSphere.

The thoughtful DBA will recognize that due to continuous evolutionary forces deeply embedded within the DNA of information technology (IT), change is inevitable. An honest historical analysis will reveal that the DBA's job was naturally extended into the network realm with the introduction of Oracle Cluster and later Oracle Parallel Server and finally Real Application Clusters (RAC). Further scrutiny divulges the fact that within the past decade, the introduction of Automatic Storage Management (ASM) has effectively required the DBA to become a storage administrator, because most professional storage administrators do not enthusiastically embrace management of the ASM instance. Continued analysis will expose the phenomena that the Oracle DBA's professional responsibilities are constantly evolving, and that in the twenty-first century, that evolution has progressed in the direction of virtualization. We will discuss the unofficial titles of the vDBA, the vRACDBA, and the Cloud DBA in later chapters, but suffice it for now to recognize the trend that unambiguously leads the Oracle DBA to become the resident expert in any area that affects data.

Figure 4-1 illustrates the four V's approach. In this chapter, we focus on viability aspect.

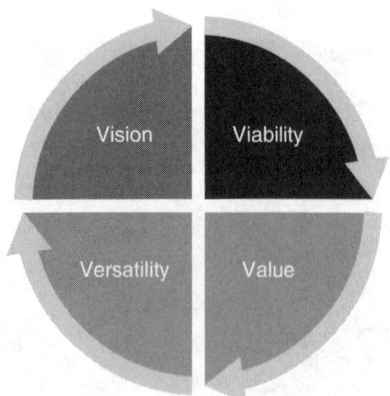

Figure 4-1 Four V's approach

The successful deployment of Oracle on VMware vSphere 5.X is similar to deploying Oracle on nonvirtualized machines. DBAs can fully leverage their current skill sets while delivering the benefits associated with virtualization.

VMware virtualization solutions provide numerous benefits to DBAs. VMware virtualization creates a layer of abstraction between the resources required by an application, its operating system (OS), and the underlying hardware that provides those resources. This abstraction layer provides value for the following:

- **Consolidation:** VMware technology enables multiple application servers to be consolidated onto a single physical server, with little or no decrease in overall performance.

- **Ease of provisioning:** VMware virtualization encapsulates an application into an image that can be duplicated or moved, greatly reducing the cost of application provisioning and deployment.

- **Manageability:** Virtual machines (VMs) may be moved from server to server with zero downtime using VMware vMotion, which simplifies common operations, such as hardware maintenance, and reduces or eliminates planned downtime.

- **Availability:** If an unplanned hardware failure occurs, VMware High Availability (HA) restarts affected VMs on another host in a VMware cluster. With HA, you can reduce unplanned downtime and provide higher service levels to an application. VMware Fault Tolerance (FT) features zero downtime and zero data loss, providing continuous availability in the face of server hardware failures for an application running in a single-vCPU VM.

Now, let's take a look at the common best practices for successful Oracle deployment on vSphere.

Implementing ESX Host Best Practices

The adherence to the basic premises described in this chapter is essential to a successful implementation of Oracle on vSphere. Generally speaking, successful customers follow the principles embedded in these best practices, whereas customers that need assistance after their initial attempts at deployments are most often guilty of not following these guidelines. Although the previous statement is axiomatic, deviation from these best practices is not prohibitive, and although often correlated with, it is not causal of any particular failure. Significant examples of sophisticated and unique implementation methodologies exist, many of which utilize their own specific practices that are sometimes better than the best practices listed in this chapter. EMC-IT for example (see Chapter 12, "Case Studies," for an extended look at the EMC-IT success story) has a number of somewhat unique techniques that are especially effective. Through the half million customer base in the VMware universe, there are a plethora of interesting and innovative approaches. It is important, however, to recognize that these basic best practices are well known, well understood, and well accepted. Deviate at your own risk, and when you are successful, write a white paper.

Table 4-1 provides several host systems' (physical machine) best practices.

Table 4-1 Host Systems' Best Practices

Item	Comments
Recommendation	Create a computing environment optimized for vSphere.
Justification	ESX/ESXi host BIOS settings can be specifically adjusted to maximize compute resources (such as disabling unnecessary processes and peripherals) to Oracle databases. These principals apply to each dimension of performance, compute, memory, networking, and storage.
Recommendation	Create templates or "golden images" of configured and optimized guest operating systems using vSphere cloning and templatization technologies.
Justification	After the operating system has been prepared with the appropriate patches and kernel settings, install Oracle in a VM using the same approach as it is installed on a physical system. This accelerates the provisioning process of each new database server.
Recommendation	Upgrade to the latest version of vSphere.
Justification	VMware and database administrators can realize a substantial performance boost after upgrading to the latest vSphere release from previous versions. This often applies to all dimensions of performance.

Item	Comments
Recommendation	Allow vSphere to choose the best VM monitor (VMM) based on the central processing unit (CPU) and guest OS combination.
Justification	By default, vSphere will choose the best VMM based on the CPU and guest OS combination. The hypervisor will automatically select the VMM appropriate for the CPU/MMU Virtualization option. MMU refers to Memory Management Unit, which is an attribute of either or both the OS and the physical processor. Advances in virtualization technology have included the offload of the memory management tasks from software to hardware, such as when Extended Page Tables (EPT) are enabled in the BIOS.

Maximizing Performance Using BIOS Settings

Often, default installations of any OS on any hardware include superfluous and unnecessary processes and settings. System, VM, and database administrators should endeavor to minimize these processes and customize all settings, both OS and hardware (BIOS), to optimize database performance. You can set X-86 server BIOS settings to disable unnecessary processes and peripherals to maximize performance.

Table 4-2 describes the optimized settings as well as the usual default OS processes that should be considered for elimination from a database server.

Table 4-2 BIOS Settings Maximized for Performance

BIOS Setting	Recommendations	Description
Virtualization Technology	Yes	Necessary to run 64-bit guest operating systems.
Turbo Mode	Yes	Balanced workload over unused cores.
Node Interleaving	No	Disables non-uniform memory access (NUMA) benefits if disabled.
VT-x, AMD-V, EPT, and RVI	Yes	Hardware-based virtualization support.
C1E Halt State	No	Disable if performance is more critical than saving power.
Power-Saving	No	Disable if performance is more important than saving power.
Virus Warning	No	Disables warning messages when writing to the master boot record.

BIOS Setting	Recommendations	Description
Hyperthreading	Yes	For use with some Intel processors. HT is always recommended with Intel's newer Core i7 processors, such as the Xeon 5500 series.
Video BIOS Cacheable	No	Not necessary for database VM.
Wake On LAN	Yes	Required for vSphere Distributed Power Management feature.
Execute Disable	Yes	Required for vMotion and Distributed Resource Scheduler features.
Video BIOS Shadowable	No	Not necessary for database VM.
Video RAM Cacheable	No	Not necessary for database VM.
Onboard Audio	No	Not necessary for database VM.
Onboard Modem	No	Not necessary for database VM.
Onboard Firewire	No	Not necessary for database VM.
Onboard Serial Ports	No	Not necessary for database VM.
Onboard Parallel Ports	No	Not necessary for database VM.
Onboard Game Port	No	Not necessary for database VM.

Operating System Processes

VMware, Oracle, and any experienced Oracle professional will recommend disabling unnecessary foreground and background processes within the guest OS (absent a specific reason to run those processes) because these process provide no discernible added value absent some specific reason.

- Examples of unnecessary Linux processes include `anacron`, `apmd`, `atd`, `autofs`, `cups`, `cupsconfig`, `gpm`, `isdn`, `iptables`, `kudzu`, `netfs`, and `portmap`.

- Examples of unnecessary Microsoft Windows processes include Alerter, Automatic Updates, ClipBook, Error Reporting, Help and Support, Indexing, Messenger, NetMeeting, Remote Desktop, and System Restore services.

- For Linux installs, the DBA should request that the system administrator compile a monolithic kernel that will only load the necessary processes and features.

- Whether you intend to run Windows or Linux as the final optimized OS, these host installs should be cloned by the VMware administrator for reuse.

- After the OS has been prepared, install Oracle the same way you would normally install in a nonvirtualized environment. Use the recommended kernel parameters listed in the Oracle Installation Guide. Also, it is a good practice to check with Oracle Support for the latest settings before beginning the installation process.

- For a Linux guest OS, set IO Scheduler to NOOP. By setting this guest, the OS will do little input/output (I/O) processing before it passes it along to ESX/ESXi.

Upgrading the Version of ESX/ESXi and vSphere

vSphere includes numerous performance and scalability enhancements that provide a substantial performance boost compared to earlier versions of vSphere. Each new version of vSphere includes updates to existing features as well as enhancements. Consult the latest Configuration Maximums Guide, which is published simultaneously to each vSphere release and available through www.vmware.com.

Table 4-3 summarizes the evolution of the capabilities of the hypervisor by including current metrics for each dimension of performance on vSphere.

Table 4-3 Performance and Scalability Improvements by ESX Version

	ESX 2.0	ESX 3.0	ESX 3.5	ESX 4	ESXi 5
Overhead	30% - 60%	20% - 30%	10% - 20%	2% - 10%	2% - 5%
CPU	1 vCPU	2 vCPU	4 vCPU	8 vCPU	64 vCPU
Memory	< 4GB	16GB	64GB	255GB	1TB
Network	380Mbps	800Mbps	9Gbps	30Gbps	> 36Gbps
IOPS (Storage)	< 10,000	20,000	100,000	> 350,000	Up to 1 million/VM

VMware vSphere supports large-capacity VMs, so it can support larger-sized Oracle databases and system global area (SGA) footprints. vSphere host and VM specifications are as follows:

- Each VMware ESXi 5.x host supports up to 4TB RAM.

- Each VMware ESXi 5.x host supports up to 512 vCPUs.

- An individual VM can be configured with up to 1TB.

- An individual VM can be configured with up to 64 vCPUs.

Maximizing Support for a Hardware-Assisted Memory Management Unit

For best performance, VMware recommends using servers with the latest chip generations that support a hardware-assisted Memory Management Unit (MMU). Hardware-assisted MMU refers to hardware support for Memory Management Unit virtualization. Features that provide the support are available from Intel and AMD and are called Extended Page Tables (EPT) and Rapid Virtualization Indexing (RVI). Support consists of an additional level of page tables implemented in hardware. These page tables contain guest physical to machine physical memory address translations.

On processors that support it, vSphere by default uses hardware-assisted MMU virtualization for VMs. You can configure this default behavior in the "VM settings" using the vSphere Client, by setting the **CPU/MMU Virtualization** parameter to **Automatic** (which is default).

Implementing Memory-Related Best Practices

Business-critical applications use significant amounts of memory. The best practices associated with memory allocation to the VM are in reality requirements for the Tier 1 application with any substantive performance requirements.

Table 4-4 outlines the memory-related best practices.

Table 4-4 General Best Practices for Memory

Item	Comments
Recommendation	Set memory reservations equal to or greater than the size to the Oracle SGA. Included here is a formula for the calculation of the memory that should be allocated to the VM when running a single Oracle instance. Use the following formula, and the memory component for the VM running a single Oracle instance will be properly right-sized.
	SGA(SGA_MAX_SIZE) + 2XPGA_Aggregate_Target + 1.5Mb x (each background and foreground process) + (OS + Oracle_Home) executables + 15%

Item	Comments
Justification	To avoid swapping between ESX/ESXi and the host or the guest OS swapping to its page file, set a memory reservation, which guarantees that the memory allocated to the VM has corresponding physical memory. This is essential because operating Oracle databases can be memory intensive.
Recommendation	Use large memory pages.
Justification	Large page support, also called Huge Pages in Linux is enabled by default in ESX versions 3.5 and later, and is supported from Oracle version 9iR2 for Linux operating systems and version 10gR2 for Windows. Enable large pages in the guest OS to improve the performance of Oracle databases on vSphere. In addition, the use of Huge Pages will prohibit swapping (however Huge Pages can be broken down into small pages under extreme memory pressure circumstances). Huge Pages are not supported with the Oracle 11g feature of Automatic Memory Management (AMM). However, most metrics and anecdotes show that the benefit of Huge Pages is substantial and this feature should be used. Only the ASM instance must use AMM, and therefore the use of Huge Pages is prohibited with an ASM instance. Refer to the Oracle Database Administrators Reference Manual.

For further background on VMware memory management concepts, refer to the vSphere Resource Management Guide on the VMware website.

When consolidating Oracle database instances, vSphere presents the opportunity to share memory across VMs that may be running the same operating systems, applications, or other components. In this case, vSphere uses a proprietary Transparent Page Sharing (TPS) feature to reclaim memory, which allows databases to run with less memory than on a physical machine. TPS also allows DBAs to overcommit memory without performance degradation. Refer to vSphere Resource Management - http://pubs.vmware.com/vsphere-51/topic/com.vmware.ICbase/PDF/vsphere-esxi-vcenter-server-51-resource-management-guide.pdf.

In production environments, carefully consider the impact of overcommiting memory and only overcommit after collecting data to determine the amount of overcommitment possible. Before the decision to overcommit memory is made, the DBA must fully understand the existing memory utilization metrics. Although ESX/ESXi has sophisticated memory management capabilities, it is not advisable to allow these capabilities to become active. Although the features embedded in ESX/ESXi, known as TPS and memory compression, work subtly and effectively, the other memory management capabilities are more intrusive. Ballooning, discussed in Chapter 8, "Performance Management and Monitoring," allows the VMs to exchange memory when memory pressure is detected. Swapping can occur within the guest OS as well as within ESX/ESXi itself. It is advisable to avoid each of these performance-draining situations. To determine the effectiveness of memory sharing and the degree of acceptable overcommitment for a given database, run the workload, and use the ESX command-line performance analysis tools rEsxtop or Esxtop to observe the actual savings.

Figure 4-2 shows the screenshot of Esxtop/rEsxtop.

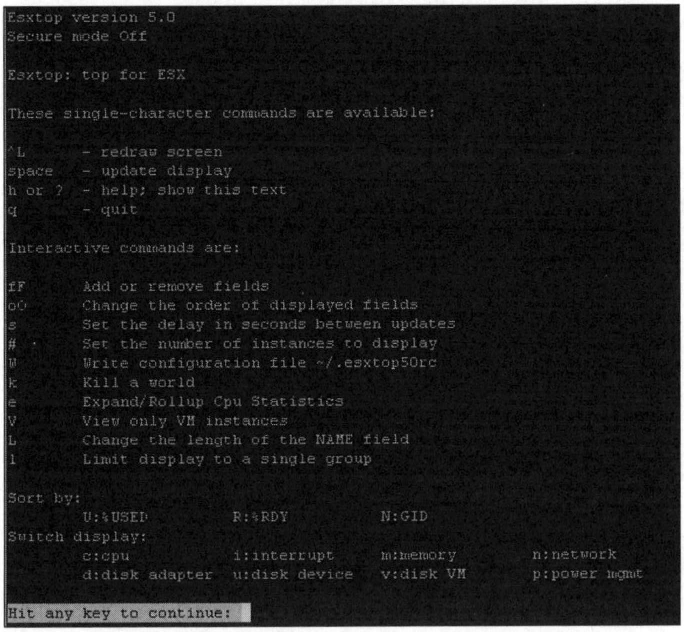

Figure 4-2 Esxtop/rEsxtop

Because Oracle databases can be memory intensive, and to account for situations where performance is a key factor (and avoid kernel swapping between ESX/ESXi or swapping of the guest OS to its swap file in mission-critical production environments), VMware recommends the following:

- Set the memory reservation equal or greater than the size of the Oracle SGA. Use the formula stated earlier.

- Where the Oracle database is part of a third-party commercial enterprise application (enterprise resource planning [ERP]), follow virtualization guidelines from the ERP vendor.

- Note that setting reservations may limit vMotion. A VM can only be live migrated if the target ESX host has free physical memory equal to or greater than the size of the reservation.

- Do *not* disable the balloon driver. Although a well-designed system will not make use of the balloon driver, it is better to have it enabled as a safety mechanism as opposed to the next step, which is swapping.

- The guest OS within the VM still needs its own separate swap/page file. Follow the same swap space guidelines given for nonvirtualized environments.

Though VMware recommends setting memory reservations equal or greater than the size of the Oracle SGA in production environments, it is acceptable to overcommit memory more aggressively in nonproduction environments, such as development, test, or QA. In these environments, a DBA can introduce memory overcommitment to take advantage of VMware memory reclamation features and techniques such as the aforementioned TPS and memory compression. Even in these environments, the type and number of databases that can be deployed using overcommitment largely depend on their actual workload.

Supporting Large Pages

vSphere supports large pages in the guest OS. The use of large pages results in reduced memory management overhead and can increase hypervisor performance. Oracle supports the use of large memory pages in version 9iR2 for Linux operating systems and in version 10gR2 for Windows. The following MyOracleSupport.com (formerly known as Metalink) notes are relevant when setting large pages:

- Note 361323.1—*Huge Pages on Linux: What It Is... and What It Is Not...*

- Note 361468.1—*Huge Pages on 64-Bit Linux*

- Note 401749.1—*Shell Script to Calculate Values Recommended Huge Pages/Huge TLB Configuration*

- Note 46001.1—*Oracle Database and the Windows NT Memory Architecture, Technical Bulletin*

- Note 46053.1—*Windows NT Memory Architecture Overview*

- Note 1557478.1—*Be Cautious When Using Transparent Huge Pages (THP) in the Oracle Enterprise Linux (OEL) and Red Hat Linux 6.x Versions.*

Standard Huge Pages is a manual setup. Basically, the vm.nr_hugepages setting in /etc/sysctl.conf file is set to a static limit, which then sets the size of the standard Huge Page pool limit.

- Huge Pages is set at the time the machine boots. They can be arduous to manually manage and often difficult to implement effectively. Red Hat Enterprise Linux 6.x uses Transparent Huge Pages (THP). THP is an abstraction that automates most aspects of assigning, managing, and utilizing Huge Pages. THP is only used if Huge Pages is not explicitly configured.

- Paraphrasing MyOracleSupport note 1557478.1, THP can cause unexpected node reboots and performance problems with RAC. Therefore, Oracle advises users to disable the use of THP. In addition, THP can cause problems in single-instance environments because performance can be unpredictable. Consequently, Oracle recommends disabling THP on all Oracle database servers.

Implementing Compute (vCPU)-Related Best Practices

Processing power should be allocated to each VM in a judicious manner. A DBA should understand the exact level of processing power necessary for both common and peak demand for a specific application running a specific Oracle instance. The "right-sizing" exercise is especially important here because underallocated VMs will underperform, but overallocated VMs will experience degradation as well because ideal vCPUs are not actually ideal. Only assign the exact processing power necessary to meet the objectives of the performance service level agreement (SLA).

Table 4-5 outlines vCPU-related best practices.

Table 4-5 General Best Practices for vCPUs

Item	Comments
Recommendation	Use as few vCPUs as possible but as many as demand requires.
Justification	If monitoring of the actual workload shows that the Oracle database is not benefitting from the increased vCPUs, the excess vCPUs impose scheduling constraints and can degrade overall performance of the VM.
Recommendation	Enable hyperthreading whenever applicable.
Justification	For example, with the release of Intel Xeon 5500 series processors, enabling HT is recommended. Under certain circumstances, HT can increase overall CPU performance by as much as 30%.

VMware uses the terms *virtual CPU* (vCPU) and *physical CPU* (pCPU) to distinguish between the processors within the VM and the underlying physical x86-based processors. VMs with more than one virtual CPU are also called SMP (symmetric multiprocessing) VMs.

VMware virtual symmetric multiprocessing (virtual SMP) enhances VM performance by enabling a single VM to use multiple physical processors simultaneously. vSphere supports use of up to eight vCPUs per VM. The biggest advantage of an SMP system is the capability to utilize multiple processors to execute multiple tasks simultaneously, thus increasing processing capacity (for example, the number of transactions per second). Only workloads that support parallelization (including multiple processes or multiple threads that can run in parallel) will benefit from SMP. The Oracle architecture is multithreaded and includes multiple processes, which makes it a good candidate to take advantage of virtual SMP.

With the release of ESX 4, the CPU scheduler underwent several improvements to provide better performance and scalability; for details, see *VMware vSphere: The CPU Scheduler in VMware ESX 4.1*. Although this is a document from the archives, the content is still valid and applicable (and therefore warrants reference in this section). Though larger VMs are possible in vSphere 5.x, up to 64 vCPUs, VMware recommends reducing the number of vCPUs if monitoring of the actual workload shows that the Oracle database is not benefitting from the increased number of vCPUs. For more information, see "ESX CPU Considerations" in *Performance Best Practices for VMware vSphere 5*.

Hyperthreading technology enables a single physical processor core to behave like two logical processors, essentially allowing two independent threads to run simultaneously. Unlike having twice as many processor cores—which can roughly double performance— HT can provide anywhere from a slight to a significant increase in system performance by keeping the processor pipeline busier. For example, an ESX host system enabled for HT on an 8-core server sees 16 threads that appear as 16 logical processors. With the release of Intel Xeon 5500 series processors, enabling HT is recommended. Prior to the 5500 series, VMware had no uniform recommendation with respect to HT because the measured performance results were not consistent across applications, run environments, or database workloads.

Hyperthreading (HT) can be a confusing subject. When using HT in a nonvirtualized environment, the OS will perceive the number of threads resulting from HT to be equivalent to the number of hyperthreads. For example, if there are 8 cores on a particular machine and HT is enabled, the OS will perceive 16 processors. Features such as Oracle parallelism, which is dependent on the perceived number of CPUs in the OS, will be configured based on 16 CPUs rather than 8. (Oracle DBAs can issue a `show parameter cpu_count` command within SQL*Plus to display the number of processors.) However, when running vSphere, the guest OS will perceive only the number of vCPUs assigned to the VM even though HT is set on the underlying system. ESX/ESXi will take advantage of HT, but the mechanism differs from the nonvirtualized system.

An analogy that is helpful is that of the classic fast-food drive thru. Think of the station in which one orders their "Number 4, Cheerful Meal" and subsequent station at which one receives said "Cheerful Meal" as equivalent to the processor and the I/O interface. However, it is often the case that the line from which one orders that meal splits off into two stations, both of which accept orders. However, only one station exists to dispense that order, which means that the bottleneck will occur at the station where the customer accepts the meal. This is the same for HT because multiple logical processing threads may speed up the aggregate processing but the I/O will still be the ultimate constraint.

Figure 4-3 illustrates the HT-using the Burger Joint analogy.

Figure 4-3 Burger Joint analogy

VMware recommends the following practices for allocating CPU to Oracle database VMs:

- Start with a thorough understanding of your workload. Database server utilization varies widely by application. If the application is commercial, be sure to follow published guidelines where appropriate. If the application is custom written, work with the application developers to determine resource requirements. VMware Capacity Planner can analyze your current environment and provide resource utilization metrics that can aid in the sizing process.

- If the exact workload is not known, start with fewer vCPUs and increase the number later, if necessary. Only allocate multiple vCPUs to a VM if the anticipated database workload can truly take advantage of all the vCPUs.

TIP

For Linux implementations, if the VMAdmin/DBA configures the VM with at least two vCPUs, the "SMP kernel" is automatically configured, which will allow the simple increase of the number of vCPUs if demand requirements change at a later date; otherwise, the VM must be either rebuilt or a new SMP kernel must be installed.

- When consolidating multiple VMs on single ESX host, proper hardware sizing is critical for optimal performance. Make sure that aggregate physical CPU resources on a host are adequate to meet the needs of the VMs by testing the workload in the planned virtualized environment. CPU overcommitment should be based on actual performance data to avoid adversely affecting VM performance.

Configuring Storage-Related Best Practices

One of the main pillars already mentioned regarding running business critical applications on vSphere is that the application itself, in this case Oracle, does not change in any substantive way. Agnosticism, with regard to the use of specific storage and other hardware, constitutes another make pillar of this proposition. Simply put, VMware supports nearly every possible permutation of hardware. VMware supports an almost unlimited variety of fiber-based storage products as well as Internet Protocol (IP)-based storage products to include Network File System (NFS), Internet Small Computer System Interface (iSCSI), and Fibre Channel over Ethernet (FCoE). Flash-based storage has also become popular in recent years, and VMware has storage partners, many of whom are mentioned in Chapter 8. Also, there are a number of newer VMware storage paradigms to consider, including virtual storage-area networks (vSANs) and virtual volumes (vVOLs) as well as competing products.

Table 4-6 outlines storage-related best practices.

Table 4-6 General Best Practices for Storage

Item	Comments
Recommendation	For IP-based storage such as iSCSI, NFS, or FCoE, enable jumbo frames when 10Gb network cards are being used.
Justification	Jumbo frames should be enabled for ethernet frames to have larger "payload," allowing improved performance.

TIP

Ensure that each hop in the network chain has jumbo frames enabled as well as 10Gb bandwidth; otherwise, the "least common denominator" of the network bandwidth will apply, and the aggregate bandwidth will be based on the slowest network segment.

Item	Comments
Recommendation	Create dedicated datastores to service database workloads.
Justification	The creation of dedicated datastores for I/O-intensive databases is analogous to provisioning dedicated logical unit numbers (LUNs) in the physical world. This is a typical design for a mission-critical enterprise workload. This advice may not be necessary or possible in all modern storage arrays, but it is still a proper, best practices approach to database storage design.
Recommendation	Use vSphere Virtual Machine File System (VMFS) for single-instance Oracle database deployments.
Justification	To balance performance and manageability in a virtual environment, deploy Oracle using VMFS. VMware recommends the use of VMFS in all cases by default because the stated direction of VMware is to use VMFS. Therefore, any new features that will be introduced are guaranteed to be supported with VMFS, and those features may not be supported with raw device mappings (RDMs), although RDMs will be supported. The use of IP storage is a recommended methodology as well. Chapter 8 covers the various IP storage products in more detail. There are, however, a number of side cases that may require RDMs to include the existence of database files over 2TB (until vSphere 5.5, in which support for 62TB virtual machine disks [VMDKs] exists). Storage vendors often purport the use of RDMs as an easier approach to using their storage based snapshot tools.
Recommendation	Make sure that VMFS is properly aligned. Specifically, the VMDKs should be physically aligned with the storage blocks. This is called partition alignment. From the Performance Best Practices Guide, "To manually align your VMFS partitions, check your storage vendor's recommendations for the partition starting block. If your storage vendor makes no specific recommendation, use a starting block that is a multiple of 8KB."
Justification	Like other disk-based file systems, VMFS suffers a penalty when the partition is unaligned. Use VMware vCenter to create VMFS partitions because it automatically aligns the partitions.

Item	Comments
Recommendation	Use Oracle Automatic Storage Management (ASM).
Justification	Oracle ASM provides an integrated disk container system and volume management capabilities for managing Oracle database files. ASM simplifies database file creation while delivering near-raw device file system performance.
Recommendation	Use your storage vendor's best practices documentation when laying out the Oracle database.
Justification	Oracle ASM cannot determine the optimal data placement or LUN selection with respect to the underlying storage infrastructure. For that reason, Oracle ASM is not a substitute for close communication between the storage administrator and the DBA.
Recommendation	Avoid silos when designing the storage architecture.
Justification	At a minimum, designing the optimized architecture should involve the DBA, storage administrator, network administrator, VMware administrator, and application owner.
Recommendation	Use paravirtualized Small Computer System Interface (SCSI) adapters for Oracle data files with demanding workloads.
Justification	The combination of the new paravirtualized SCSI (pvSCSI) driver and additional ESX/ESXi kernel-level storage stack optimizations dramatically improves storage I/O performance.

TIP

When minimizing latency is the main objective, the use of the pvSCSI driver for the controller of the VMDKs containing the Oracle redo log files may not be optimal. The LSI SAS driver might be considered because the pvSCSI driver, despite reducing overall overhead, may introduce minimal amounts of extra latency.

Storage configuration is essential for any successful database deployment, especially in virtual environments where you may consolidate many different Oracle database workloads on a single ESXi host. Your storage subsystem should provide sufficient I/O throughput as well as storage capacity to accommodate the cumulative needs of all VMs running on your ESXi hosts.

Categorizing Storage Virtualization Technologies

VMware storage virtualization can be categorized into three layers of storage technology:

- The physical storage array is the bottom layer, consisting of physical disks presented as logical disks (storage array volumes or LUNs) to the layer above.

- The next layer is the virtual layer defined by vSphere. Storage array LUNs are presented to ESX/ESXi servers as datastores and are formatted as Virtual File Machine System (VMFS) volumes. Other paradigms of storage could be considered specifically IP storage. Network-attached storage (NAS), also referred to as Network File System (NFS), can be used in a variety of ways, as discussed in Chapter 8.

- VMs consist of virtual disks (VMDKs) that are created in the datastores and presented to the guest OS as disks that can be partitioned and used in file systems.

VMware VMFS the File Systems of the Virtualized Infrastructure

VMFS is a cluster file system that provides virtualized storage optimized for VMs. Each VM is encapsulated in a set of files (VMDKs). VMFS is the default storage system for these files on physical SCSI disks and partitions. VMFS allows multiple ESX/ESXi instances to access shared VM storage concurrently. It also enables virtualization-based distributed infrastructure services, such as vMotion, VMware Distributed Resource Scheduler (DRS), and VMware High Availability (HA) to operate across a cluster of ESX hosts (up to 32 physical hosts).

Accessing a Volume on the Physical Storage Subsystem Using Raw Device Mapping

VMware also supports raw device mapping (RDM). RDM allows a VM to directly access a volume on the physical storage subsystem, and can only be used with Fibre Channel or iSCSI. RDM can be thought of as providing a symbolic link from a VMFS volume to a raw volume or some other alternate storage. The mapping makes volumes appear as files in a VMFS volume. The mapping file, not the raw volume, is referenced in the VM configuration.

Understanding Storage Protocol Capabilities

When deploying vSphere, the choice of a networked storage system has little to do with virtualization. As with any nonvirtualized Oracle deployment, the main considerations are still price, performance, and manageability. In addition, the protocols available with vSphere (Fibre Channel, hardware iSCSI, software iSCSI, and NFS) are capable of achieving throughput levels that are limited only by the capabilities of the storage array and its connection to vSphere. During its testing, VMware has found that wire speed is the limiting factor for I/O throughput when comparing the storage protocols. VMware ESX/ESXi can reach the link speeds in single VM environment, and can also maintain the throughput up to 32 concurrent VMs for each storage connection option supported. For details, refer to the *Comparison of Storage Protocol Performance in VMware vSphere 5.x* white paper. Fibre Channel may provide maximum I/O throughput, but iSCSI and NFS may offer a better price-performance ratio.

When selecting networked storage systems and protocols, it is critical to understand which vSphere features are supported, because failure to do so may result in the selection of a protocol that does not have support for necessary vSphere features. Table 4-7 describes the capabilities of each of the protocols available in vSphere.

Table 4-7 Storage Protocol Capabilities

Type	Boot VM	Boot vSphere	VMotion HA/DRS	VMFS	RDM	SRM
Fibre Channel	Yes	Yes	Yes	Yes	Yes	Yes
iSCSI	Yes	Yes	Yes	Yes	Yes	Yes
NAS	Yes	No	Yes	No	No	No
Local storage	Yes	Yes	No	Yes	No	No

Jumbo frames are recommended for the IP-based storage protocols iSCSI and NFS. Jumbo frames must be enabled individually for each vSwitch through the vSphere command-line interface (CLI). Also, if you use an ESX/ESXi host, you must create a VMkernel network interface enabled with jumbo frames. It is also necessary to enable jumbo frames on the hardware as well, including the network switches and storage arrays. As mentioned earlier, it is imperative to enable jumbo frames at all levels and network hops from point to point. Figure 4-4 describes the point-to-point configuration. For more information on jumbo frames, search www.vmware.com.

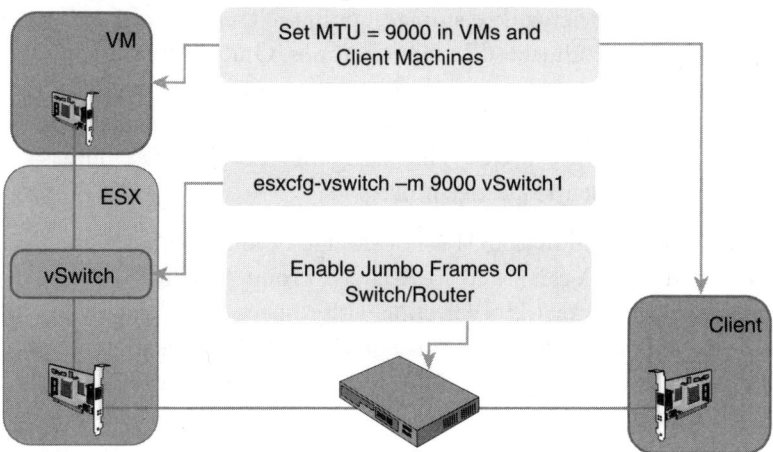

Figure 4-4 Configuring jumbo frames

Understanding Database Layout Considerations

The Oracle Optimal Flexible Architecture (OFA) is a set of naming standards and best practices used when installing and configuring Oracle software. It is a generally accepted best practice to follow the OFA standards for Oracle installations on virtualized infrastructure as well. Beginning in 10g, Oracle introduced Automated Storage Management (ASM), which also conforms to the OFA naming conventions.

Managing Files Using Oracle Automatic Storage Management

Oracle ASM is a disk container system that provides an integrated clustered file system and volume management capabilities for managing Oracle database files. In addition, ASM simplifies database file creation while delivering near-raw device file system performance.

A vSphere datastore is an abstraction of the storage layer. LUNs can be thought of as abstractions of the disks themselves. For this reason, care must be taken before configuring ASM disk groups. When creating ASM disk groups

- Create ASM disk groups with equal disk types and geometries. An ASM disk group is essentially a grid of disks, and the group performance is limited by the capabilities of the slowest disk within the group. This is a restriction based on the idea of the least common denominator.

- Create multiple ASM disk groups based on I/O characteristics. At a minimum, create two ASM disk groups: one for log files, which are sequential in nature; and one for data files, which are random in nature.

When running on vSphere and using networked storage, configure the ASM disk groups with external redundancy. Do *not* use Oracle ASM failure groups. Oracle failure groups consume additional CPU cycles and can operate unpredictably after suffering a disk failure. When using external redundancy, disk failures are transparent to the database and consume no additional database CPU cycles. The management of the disk failure is offloaded to the storage arrays and their respective processors.

It is extremely important to understand that ASM is not storage-aware. In other words, whatever disks are provisioned, a DBA can use to create a disk group. Oracle ASM cannot determine the optimal data placement or LUN selection with respect to the underlying storage infrastructure. For that reason, Oracle ASM is not a substitute for close communication between the storage administrator and the DBA. Refer to your Oracle Installation Guide to create ASM disk groups.

Working with Oracle Clustered File System: OCFS/OCFS2

The Oracle Clustered File System is a POSIX-compliant shared disk cluster file system for Linux that can be used with Oracle Real Application Clusters. OCFS was the predecessor to Oracle ASM that was introduced in Oracle 10g. ASM is the recommended clustering technology for all RAC implementations. Also, Oracle now recommends the use of ASM for non-RAC implementations.

Working with Consolidated or Dedicated Datastores

It is a generally accepted best practice to create a dedicated datastore if the application has a demanding I/O profile. Databases fall into this category. The creation of dedicated datastores allows DBAs to define individual service level guarantees for different applications and is analogous to provisioning dedicated LUNs in the physical world.

It is critical to understand that a datastore is an abstraction of the storage tier and that it is, therefore, a logical representation of the storage tier, not a physical representation of the storage tier. So, creating a dedicated datastore to isolate a particular I/O workload (whether log or database files) without isolating the physical storage layer as well does not have the desired effect on performance.

Implementing an Oracle Database Storage Layout on VMware vSphere

For mission-critical databases, it is common practice in physical environments to spread the database over multiple LUNs to maximize I/O performance (for example, placing log and data files in separate LUNs). Similar guidelines should be followed as virtualized infrastructure best practices. Figure 4-5 shows a layout example.

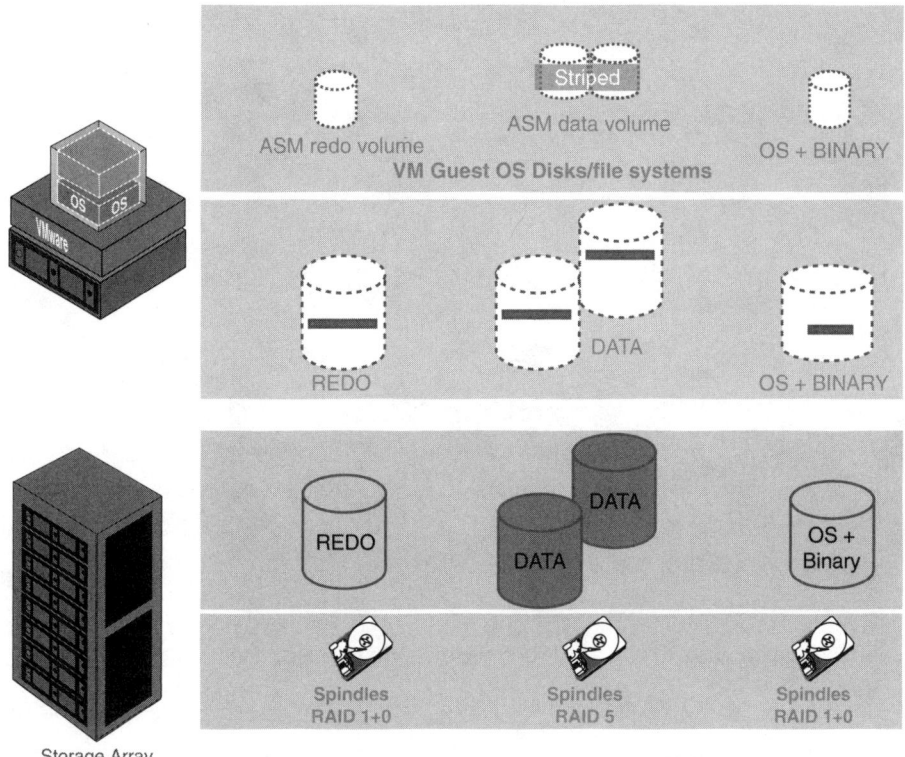

Figure 4-5 Storage presentation on VMware

Figure 4-6 follows the generic diagram above by adding a usage methodology to the generalized architecture. The following example depicts a storage layout of an Oracle online transaction processing (OLTP) database on VMware vSphere.

Figure 4-6 shows an example of storage design for a virtualized Oracle OLTP database. The design is based on the following principles:

- At a minimum, an optimized architecture requires collaboration between the database, VMware, and storage administrators.

- Follow storage vendor best practices for database layout on their arrays (as is done in the physical world).

Note that Figure 4-6 is only an example and that actual configurations for customer deployments may differ.

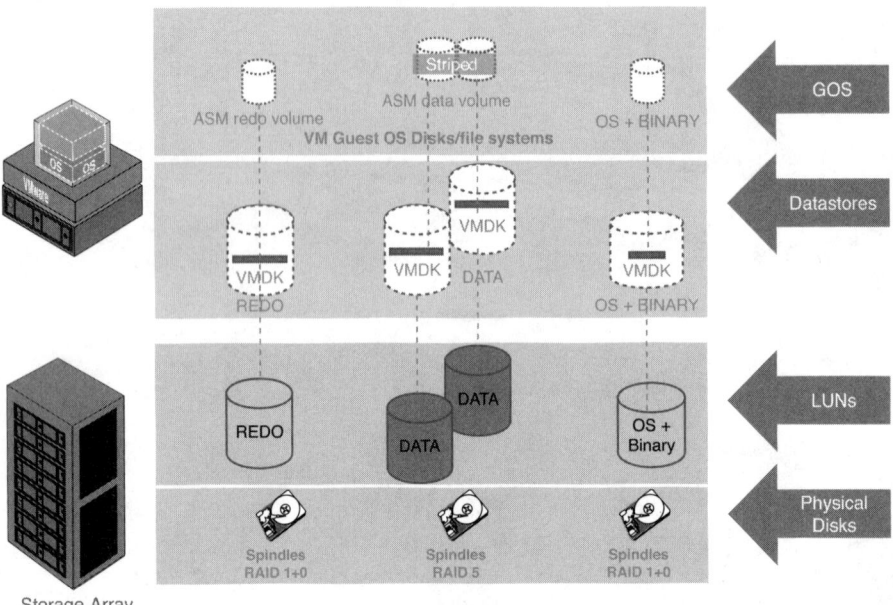

Figure 4-6 Storage layout of an Oracle OLTP database on VMware example

Working with Virtual SCSI Controllers

Use multiple virtual SCSI controllers (up to a limit of 4 until vSphere 5.5, in which a new SATA controller was introduced that has a limit of 8) for the database VMs or VMs with a typical production database high workload profile . Each virtual SCSI (vSCSI) controller processes an isolated I/O stream which results in parallelization of the aggregate I/O workload. The classic Oracle database storage layout best practices still apply as well. Always separate the redo/log I/O throughout from the data file I/O and the tempfile I/O throughput by using discreet virtual SCSI controllers. As a best practice, the DBA should use a single controller for OS and swap, one controller for redo log files, and one or more controllers for DB data files (depending on the amount and size of DB data files). Refer to the VMware Administration Guide for how to add additional virtual SCSI controllers.

Comparing VMFS to RDM: Performance and Functionality

VMware is often asked which offers better performance, VMFS or RDM? Both VMFS and RDM volumes can provide similar transaction throughput. For more details, refer to the *Performance Characterization of VMFS and RDM Using a SAN*.

VMware generally recommends VMFS, but in some situations, RDMs may be required. Table 4-8 summarizes some of the options and trade-offs between VMFS and RDM. For a more complete discussion, see the *VMware SAN System Design and Deployment Guide*.

Table 4-8 VMFS and Raw Disk Mapping Trade-Offs

VMFS	RDM
Volume can host many VMs (or can be dedicated to one VM).	Maps a single LUN to one VM, so only one VM is possible per LUN.
Increases storage utilization, provides better flexibility, easier administration, and management.	More LUNs are required, so it is easier to reach the LUN limit of 256 that can be presented to an ESX host.
Can potentially support clustering software that does not issue SCSI reservations, such as Oracle Clusterware. To configure, follow VMware KB: 1034165.	RDM may be required to leverage third-party storage array-level backup and replication tools.
Oracle RAC node Live Migration.	RDM volumes can help facilitate migrating physical oracle databases to VMs. Alternatively, enables quick migration to physical in rare Oracle support cases.
	Required for Microsoft Cluster Services (MSCS) quorum disks.
2TB size limit prior to vSphere 5.5. 62TB size limit in vSphere 5.5.	64TB size limit.

Aligning File Partitions

Aligning file system partitions is a well-known storage best practice for database workloads. Partition alignment on both physical machines and VMware VMFS partitions prevents performance I/O degradation caused by I/O crossing track boundaries. VMware test results show that aligning VMFS partitions to 64KB track boundaries results in reduced latency and increased throughput. VMFS partitions created using vCenter are aligned on 64KB boundaries as recommended by storage and operating system vendors.

It is considered a best practice to

- Create VMFS partitions from within vCenter. They are aligned by default.

- Align the data disk for heavy I/O workloads using `diskpart`.

- Consult with the storage vendor for alignment recommendations on their hardware.

- Consult with storage vendors regarding partition alignment considerations when performing snapshots.

For more information about this topic, see the white paper titled *Performance Best Practices for VMware vSphere 5.x.*

Improving Performance Using Paravirtualized SCSI Adapters

A variety of architectural improvements have been made to the storage subsystem of VMware vSphere 4 and later. The combination of the new paravirtualized SCSI driver (pvSCSI) and additional ESX kernel-level storage stack optimizations dramatically improves storage I/O performance.

VMware recommends that you create a primary adapter for use with a disk that will host the system software (boot disk) and separate pvSCSI adapters for the disks that will store the Oracle database files.

Results of tests conclude that pvSCSI is not recommended for VMs performing fewer than 2,000 (input/output operations per second [IOPS]) and issuing greater than four outstanding I/Os. This issue is fixed in vSphere 4.1, so that the pvSCSI virtual adapter can be used with good performance, even under this condition.

Follow guidelines from these VMware KB articles:

- 1010398—*Configuring Disks to Use VMware Paravirtual SCSI (pvSCSI) Adapters*

- 1017652—*Do I Choose the pvSCSI or LSI Logic Virtual Adapter on ESX 4.0 for Non-IO Intensive Workloads?*

Networking Guidelines

The virtualized architecture is incomplete without recognition to the networking dependencies and therefore the best practices. This section and Table 4-9 outline the networking-related best practices.

Table 4-9 Networking-Related Best Practices

Item	Comments
Recommendation	Use the VMXNET family of paravirtualized network adapters.
Justification	The paravirtualized network adapters in the VMXNET family implements an optimized network interface that passes network traffic between the VMs and the physical network interface cards with minimal overhead. When choosing a network adapter for your VM, refer to the VMware KB article 1001805.

Item	Comments
Recommendation	Separate infrastructure traffic from VM traffic for security and isolation.
Justification	VMs should not see infrastructure traffic (security violation) and should not be impacted by infrastructure traffic bursts (for example, vMotion).
Recommendation	Use network interface card (NIC) teaming for availability and load balancing.
Justification	NIC teams can share the load of traffic among some or all of its members, or provide passive failover in the event of a hardware failure or a network outage.
Recommendation	Take advantage of Network I/O Control (NIOC) to converge network and storage traffic onto 10GE.
Justification	This can reduce cabling requirements, simplify management, and reduce cost.
Recommendation	Use jumbo frames whenever employing 10Gb network cards.
Justification	Jumbo frames will take advantage of the capacity of the 10Gb cards. For an Oracle RAC, interconnect use jumbo frames. Consult the KB article on enabling jumbo frames on virtual distributed switches (10388278).

The standard VMware networking best practices apply to running Oracle databases on vSphere. For more information, follow the networking design guidelines in VMworld 2010 session TA859—*Virtual Networking Concepts and Best Practices*. This includes designs to efficiently manage multiple networks and redundancy of network adaptors on ESX/ESXi hosts.

Monitoring Performance on vSphere

Monitoring performance validates the viability of the proposed architecture during testing and after implementation. This section outlines performance monitoring-related best practices.

Table 4-10 shows performance monitoring-related best practices.

Table 4-10 Performance Monitoring-Related Best Practices

Item	Comments
Recommendation	Use VMware vCenter and/or the Esxtop/rEsxtop utility for performance monitoring in the virtual environment.
Justification	Guest OS counters can be used to get a rough idea of performance within the VM, but, for example, CPU and memory usage reported within the guest OS can differ from what ESX reports. Oracle DBAs should pay close attention to the counters listed in Table 4-11.

Table 4-11 lists a few key counters that should be added to the list of inspection points for Oracle DBAs.

It is useful to focus on certain performance metrics and counters. Table 4-11 lists a number of useful values to follow.

Table 4-11 ESX/ESXi Performance Counters

Subsystem	Esxtop Counters	vCenter Counter
CPU	%RDY	Ready (milliseconds in a 20,000ms window)
	%USED	Usage
Memory	%ACTV	Active
	SWW/s	Swapout Rate
	SWR/s	Swapin Rate
Storage	ACTV	Commands
	DAVG/cmd	deviceWriteLatency & deviceReadLatency
	KAVG/cmd	kernelWriteLatency & kernelReadLatency
Network	MbRX/s	packetsRx
	MbTX/s	packetsTx

Chapter 8 provides additional information on the counters listed here. But, in the meantime, it is useful to highlight a few points for the DBA to always focus on:

- The total used time indicates system load.
- Ready time indicates overloaded CPU resources.

- A significant swap rate in the memory counters clearly indicates a shortage of ESX memory, and high device latencies in the storage section point to an overloaded or misconfigured array.

- Network traffic is not often the cause of most database performance problems except when large amounts of iSCSI storage traffic are using a single network line. Check total throughput on the NICs to see whether the network is saturated.

- To determine if there is any swapping within the guest OS, use the in-guest counters in the same manner as in physical environments.

Timekeeping in Virtual Machines

A lack of coordination of timing between the OS and ESX/ESXi can result is subtle but profound inconsistencies throughout the system. VMware recommends the use of the Network Transfer Protocol (NTP) timekeeping as opposed to the Oracle process Cluster Time Synchronization Service (CTSS).

Table 4-12 outlines timekeeping best practice for VMs.

Table 4-12 VM Timekeeping-Related Best Practices

Item	Comments
Recommendation	To minimize time drift in VMs, follow guidelines in KB articles 1006427(Linux) and 1318 (Windows).
Justification	The impact of high timer-interrupts in some operating systems can lead to time synchronization errors.

Most operating systems track the passage of time by configuring the underlying hardware to provide periodic interrupts. The rate at which those interrupts are configured to arrive varies for different operating systems. High timer-interrupt rates can incur overhead that affects a VM's performance. The amount of overhead increases with the number of vCPUs assigned to a VM. The impact of these high timer interrupts can lead to time synchronization errors.

To address timekeeping issues when running Oracle databases, follow the guidelines in these VMware KB articles:

- KB 1006427—*Timekeeping Best Practices for Linux Guests*

- KB 1318—*Timekeeping Best Practices for Windows*

Summary

Following best practices is always a good idea as much in everyday life as it is when implementing Oracle on vSphere. The viability of vSphere as a platform of virtualized hardware for Oracle depends on a close coordination of the administrators of the virtualization, the OS, the storage, and the database layers. Otherwise, the interfaces between those layers constitute impenetrable boundaries, and the resulting silos of activity neither resonate nor complement. However, when all these seemingly disconnected professions are properly coordinated, the resulting harmony is both high technologically and professionally dazzling. This result resembles a veritable symphony of technology as the generated technological harmonics are both esthetically beautiful and practically useful. As the tag line of the author of this book states, "Serious databases require serious virtualization."

## Chapter 5

Oracle Database High Availability: Planned and Unplanned Downtime

High availability (HA) refers to the design attribute that determines the percentage of time an application, database, or server is accessible to its users. Availability is an intrinsic aspect of the implementation of a specific service that pertains to the percentage of time that particular service is capable of providing functionality to its users. It is often the most important aspect of a service level agreement (SLA). Database architects factor this into the system design to protect business critical operations from both unplanned downtime (an outage due to infrastructure failure) and possibly planned downtime (an outage required for system maintenance).

Let us once again consult the theme of this book: the four V's (see Figure 5-1). The requirement for varying levels of HA falls within the realms of value and versatility (value because the need for HA is often not recognized until a system fails). Moreover, when the HA requirement is explicitly expressed, it is often difficult to set up and manage. HA on vSphere is so simple that a child could accomplish the setup. We often refer to vSphere HA as "Fisher Price HA" because a child could easily accomplish the few mouse clicks that it takes to set up vSphere HA for the entire ESXi cluster. Versatility is also a major facet of the HA proposition as this capability extends to a plethora of different architectural permutations. We discuss the different innovative possibilities throughout this chapter.

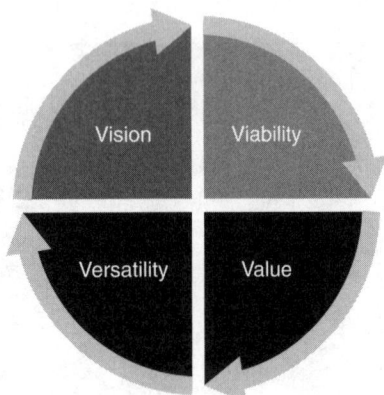

Figure 5-1 Four V's approach

Protecting the Virtualized Environment with vSphere High Availability

The vSphere feature, simply known as High Availability, continuously monitors all VMware ESX/ESXi nodes (hosts/servers) in an ESXi cluster and detects a variety of failures. An ESXi cluster is a group of loosely connected nodes, each running an ESXi hypervisor. VMware vCenter Server manages the nodes' resources jointly such that the cluster owns all the central processing unit (CPU) and memory resources of all nodes. The VMware HA agent placed on each host maintains a heartbeat link with the other nodes in the cluster. Each server sends heartbeat signals to the other servers in the cluster at regular intervals. If any server loses the heartbeat signal, VMware HA reacts by restarting all virtual machines (VMs) affected on available nodes. VMware HA will protect against server failure regardless of the cause. From many operating system (OS) crashes to network outages and physical host failures, vSphere HA will allow for each of the logical servers (VMs) to be restarted somewhere else in the cluster within minutes.

After a failure event, vSphere HA fails over and restarts a VM. At that point, startup scripts/services are required to autostart the Oracle instance or any other process in the guest OS. This is similar to a restart on a physical system. In the case of the VM, the new host is in actuality different hardware, but no manual intervention is needed. The concept of "intelligent fanout failover" facilitates the restart of each affected VM on a physical host with available physical resources. ESXi samples resource utilization real time when performing a vSphere failover. The level of sophistication of the approach is quite impressive. For instance, if the amount of memory being used on a host that has been selected as a failover target changes during the startup of that VM, the system may choose to halt the restart. Subsequently, the system may choose a different host to restart that VM upon.

Distributed Resource Scheduling (DRS) makes the decision as to which host the VM is ultimately started on. Classic HA systems require administrators, at implementation time, to define a failover target hierarchy.

Figure 5-2 shows three ESXi hosts, two of which are running an Oracle database. This illustrates a typical scenario with multiple VMs that host a single-instance Oracle database. When vSphere HA is applied, which is a configuration often found in real-world installations, each of the VMs on nodes 1 and 3 can be failed over to the failover node 2. Table 5-1 summarizes the configuration's features.

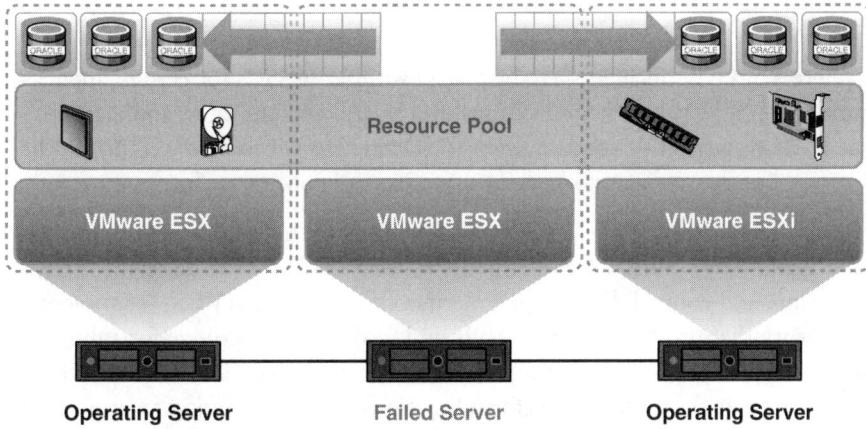

Figure 5-2 VMware HA for Oracle single-instance database

Table 5-1 vSphere HA Capabilities and Limitations

Pros	Cons
Protection against ESX/ESXi server failure.	No monitoring of Oracle instance inside VM. Application awareness is available starting in VS5.5 and from Symantec with a plug-in known as AppHA starting in VS4.1
Auto restart of VMs.	Some downtime for recovery after failure. Time required for VM to restart, OS to boot, and Oracle instance to start and complete instance recovery.

Pros	Cons
VMware HA is easy to configure (VMware "out-of-the-box").	Guest OS and Oracle patching requires downtime.
A cost-effective solution to provide hardware protection to many databases, including nonproduction systems, regardless of the OS inside the VM.	

Protecting Applications with vSphere and Symantec AppHA

Starting in vSphere 5.5, Hyperic agents can be placed within the VMs for certain applications that augment vSphere HA with application-level awareness (and thus, application restart without a VM restart). The specific agent for Oracle has yet to be developed at the time of this writing, but that project is on the near-term roadmap.

The Symantec product AppHA, introduced around the time of the release of vSphere 4.1, is an application availability solution that augments VMware HA to provide application visibility, monitoring, and control. Based upon Veritas Cluster Server (VCS) technology, it utilizes a framework that provides an extendable and flexible methodology for supporting a wide range of applications. Agents interface with this framework known as the *agent framework*. Agents provide the ability to perform functions, such as bringing an application online or offline or monitoring it for proper operation. The installation of AppHA adds a tab to vCenter to allow for management of the product, which acts like a vSphere plug-in.

Symantec provides many out-of-the-box agents for the different supported applications. These include agents that monitor critical resources, such as file system mount points and Virtual Internet Protocol (VIP) addresses as well as various applications. An agent is available to monitor a single-instance Oracle database. The agent communicates with a central process that is installed within the guest OS, relaying information about the state of the Oracle resource. This central process coordinates the activities of the agent so that the resource is brought online and offline as needed while making sure dependencies are met. For example, an Oracle instance is not brought online before the storage it requires is online first.

The database administrator (DBA) can configure AppHA to automatically restart the Oracle application and dependent resources if a failure is detected. If this restart fails to solve the application issue, it can then communicate with vSphere HA to trigger a restart of the VM. This is accomplished using an application programming interface (API) that was jointly developed by VMware and Symantec. The failover is accomplished as AppHA communicates to vSphere through the API and vSphere HA rehosts the VM.

Implementation of the AppHA solution is simplified because Symantec provides a method to automatically discover the target application and dependent resources it requires at configuration. Symantec further simplifies matters by providing a plug-in into vSphere that enables an administrator to view the status of an application and perform start/stop operations.

Figure 5-3 shows the Oracle application failing in the absence of either the VM or the host failing. Under those circumstances, vSphere HA takes no action. However, AppHA augments vSphere HA with application-level awareness and the Oracle application failure ultimately results in a rehosting of the VM.

Table 5-2 following the figure summarizes the features of this configuration.

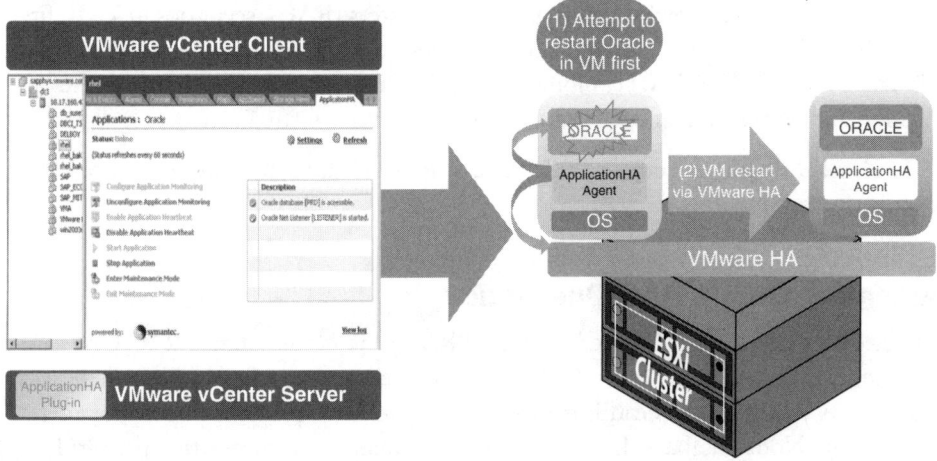

Figure 5-3 Logical architecture of Symantec AppHA for a virtualized single-instance Oracle database

Table 5-2 Symantec AppHA Capabilities and Limitations

Pros	Cons
Builds upon VMware HA to allow for application-level availability.	In case of Oracle failure, there is minimal downtime so that the agent can restart the Oracle instance.

Pros	Cons
Does not impede the functionality of VMware features, such as DRS, vMotion, Distributed Power Management (DPM), and so on.	If VMware HA is invoked, downtime is incurred for the VM to restart, OS to boot, and Oracle instance to start and complete instance recovery.
Ability to manage from a single pane of glass (vSphere).	Guest OS and Oracle patching requires downtime.
Oracle agent starts and stops the Oracle and dependent resources in the required order.	Only able to monitor a single application per VM.
Simple to set up and configure.	

Understanding Oracle RAC in Virtual Machines

This section discusses two Oracle Real Application Clusters (RAC) scenarios in VMs: first "RAC One Node," and second, the traditional multinode RAC deployments. The implementation of Oracle RAC in VMs combines the uptime features of clustering with the consolidation and workload management benefits of VMware virtualization.

As per My Oracle Support document ID 249212.1, RAC 11.2.0.2 and later is supported by Oracle on VMware.

Implementing Oracle RAC One Node

With Oracle Database 11gR2, Oracle introduced RAC One Node. Oracle RAC One Node is a single instance of an Oracle RAC-enabled database running on one node in a RAC cluster. A RAC cluster (Grid Infrastructure) is the prerequisite for installing an Oracle RAC One Node database. In a VMware environment, this means that the Grid Infrastructure is installed and running on multiple VMs. You can install Oracle RAC One Node in a VM in the same manner as on a physical server. The pillar, mentioned in this book multiple times, which states that "Oracle does not change in any substantive way when run on virtualized infrastructure" applies. This is especially true as RAC One Node functionality does not differ on a virtualized server from a nonvirtualized server. If an ESX/ESXi host failure or a failure of the database instance occurs, the failed database instance fails over to another Oracle server on a different VM. Subsequently, the VM itself may be failed over as well and so the logical RAC One Node Cluster will return to its full server capacity.

Oracle RAC One Node uses the Oracle Omotion utility, which allows the individual RAC instance to seamlessly transition from one node in the RAC cluster to another to manage the instance-level failover. This proves particularly useful when performing software maintenance on a node and minimizes the downtime of the database instance. For more information about Omotion, see the Oracle documentation at www.oracle.com.

Figure 5-4 shows a logical architecture of a RAC One Node deployment in VMs in which the single Oracle RAC instance is transitioned from one node to the second node. Notice that this architecture is the same regardless of the presence of virtualized infrastructure. This again verifies the first pillar of Oracle on vSphere, which is that Oracle functionality does not change on vSphere.

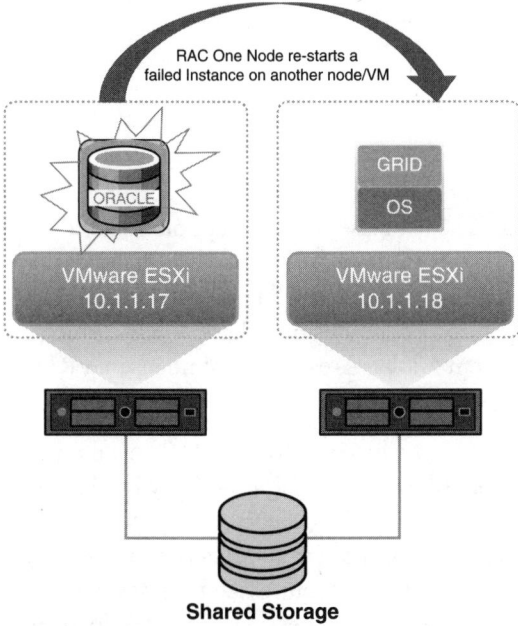

Figure 5-4 Logical architecture of Oracle RAC One Node in VMs

Table 5-3 summarizes the pros and cons of deploying Oracle RAC One Node on vSphere.

Table 5-3 Using Oracle RAC One Node in the Virtualized Environment

Pros	Cons
Failure detection in case of instance or ESX/ESXi host failure; Oracle service relocated to second VM.	RAC skills required: Generally more complex solution, but unlike multimode RAC, an interconnect is not required.
Oracle instance can be migrated to another node (via Oracle Omotion) for guest OS and Oracle patching.	In case of failure, some downtime is incurred for the Oracle instance to start and complete instance recovery on the second node.

Pros	Cons
Overall a similar setup to a traditional clustering solution.	During Omotion, existing transactions are allowed to complete on the original instance, but Oracle experiences some downtime as instance is stopped and then restarted on the failover target node.
Follow VMware KB article 1034165, *Disabling Simultaneous Write Protection Provided by VMFS Using The Multi-Writer Flag*, to deploy RAC on VMFS.	

Implementing Multinode RAC

A multinode RAC in the physical environment consists of several nodes (or servers) connected to each other by a private interconnect. The database files are kept on a shared storage subsystem, where they are accessible to all RAC nodes. The same implementation can be deployed in the VMware virtual environment whereby each node corresponds to a separate VM. The private interconnect is used for Cache Fusion (Phase 1 or 2), which enables the shipping of blocks between the System Global Area (SGA) of nodes in a RAC cluster.

Oracle RAC features rolling upgrades that enable some instances of the RAC installation to be available during the scheduled outage required for patch upgrades. Only the RAC instance that is being patched needs to be brought down. The other instances can continue to remain available, thus minimizing downtime for application users. Patches that involve alterations to the Oracle Data Dictionary (SYS schema) will require database downtime unless the DBA uses the 11g Data Guard capability known as the Transient Standby Database. For more information on Transient Standby Database, refer to www.oracle.com

Figure 5-5 shows a logical architecture of a RAC deployment in a VM. The logical RAC nodes are VMs, which run within the ESXi cluster. All the capabilities of vSphere resonate with the capabilities of RAC.

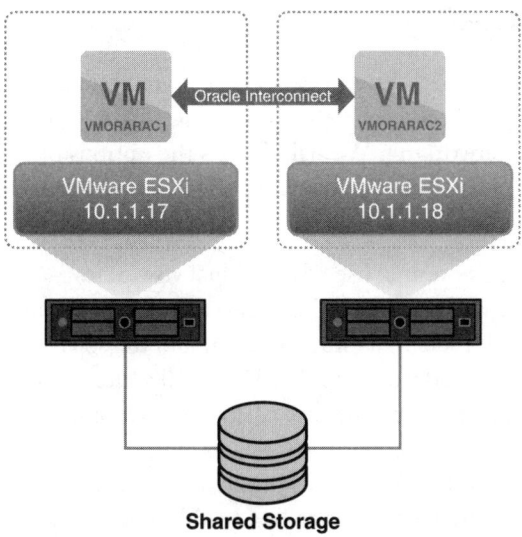

Figure 5-5 Logical architecture of Oracle RAC in VMs

Table 5-4 summarizes the pros and cons of running Oracle RAC on vSphere.

Table 5-4 Running Oracle RAC on vSphere

Pros	Cons
Protection against ESX/ESXi host failure.	RAC skills required: Generally a more complex and costly solution with respect to time and resources to implement and maintain.
In case of a node failure, Oracle instance is still available on the remaining nodes.	In case of a node failure, Oracle instance is still available on remaining nodes, but transactions on failed node produces errors except for "select" statements.
Guest OS and Oracle patching requires no downtime.	
Follow similar deployment techniques as for RAC on physical. For more information, review the VMware KB article 1034165, *Disabling Simultaneous Write Protection Provided by VMFS Using the Multi-Writer Flag* to deploy RAC on VMFS.	

Deploying Oracle RAC on vSphere

When deploying Oracle RAC on vSphere, a number of significant choices are available to the database administrator (DBA), whom we should refer to as the vRAC-DBA. Many of those choices revolve around storage and networking. We will discuss the options in both of these categories in greater detail in Chapter 8, "Performance Management and Monitoring."

The considerations for the network include the potential use of individual vSwitches as compared to the use of a Virtual Distributed Switch (VDS). This approach will allow the DBA to guarantee network bandwidth for the Oracle RAC interconnect, and the separation of the network traffic for public access. In addition, a vRAC-DBA will route any potential vMotion traffic through a segregated network path and, of course, that omnipresent RAC interconnect must be guaranteed a minimum of 1Gig bandwidth all the time (i.e., not in the aggregate). These are all important areas of focus of the database architect. The potential use of Network I/O Control (NIOC) to prioritize bandwidth to the more important networks is often considered specifically for the interconnect network traffic. In Chapter 4, "Oracle on vSphere Best Practices," we discussed the use of 10Gig networks when available along with the application of jumbo frames and the use of the paravirtualized network driver VMXNET3.

Traditionally, raw device mappings (RDMs) were the primary storage option when running RAC on vSphere. Since December 2010, however, the default and recommended implementation methodology is to use Virtual Machine File System (VMFS). The Oracle RAC Deployment Guide, referenced in the link provided, provides each and every supported storage option. As discussed in Chapter 8, there is very little difference in the throughput realized when using an RDM as compared to VMFS; however, rumors and misinformation continue to pervasively roam the Internet to suggest the contrary. A variety of tests run over the past 6 years show conclusively that the difference in throughput is negligible. Although there is some added simplicity to the use of storage-based snapshots when using RDMs, there is very little tangible reason to continue to use RDMs.

http://www.vmware.com/files/pdf/solutions/oracle/
Oracle_Databases_VMware_RAC_Deployment_Guide.pdf

The recommendation of VMware is to use VMFS for all implementations whenever possible, including Oracle and Oracle RAC implementations. However, when implementing Oracle RAC, the DBA must share storage to each server running an Oracle RAC node. The DBA will use Automatic Storage Management (ASM) to store the database files. The VM admin will present disks to vSphere running VMFS as "datastores." Each datastore is available to each VM. The VM admin creates a VM disk (VMDK) for each VM on the datastore, which appears to the OS as a unique disk (vDisk). The disk can be translated to a disk partition using Fdisk or some other disk-partitioning tool. That partition can be presented to ASM as an ASM disk and become part of an ASM disk group. At this point, Oracle database files can be created through one of the mechanisms available to the DBA to create databases or add database files to an existing database. Those database files are then judiciously placed in the ASM disk group to be managed by ASM.

The use of the SCSI multi-writer Flag (SMWF) is well-known technology borrowed from the technology of VMware Fault Tolerance (FT). FT allows a running server to be mirrored as the memory and processing between two separate servers are kept in sync to the microsecond level via a process known as *lockstep*. For this capability to work, it is necessary to have shared storage (active-active) between the two hosts running the mirrored VMs. The SMWF removes the responsibility of concurrency control from ESXi, allowing the application above to accept responsibility for the concurrent access from distinct VMs. Obviously, the potential negatives of allowing simultaneous writes from multiple locations are significant. One might say that the feature is riddled with dangerous consequences. Obviously, it was perfect for Oracle RAC. So when Oracle extended the Oracle on vSphere support statement to RAC (11.2.0.2 and beyond), the SMWF proved to be the ideal solution. At that point, VMware made the SMWF a visible feature for Oracle RAC as well as all Oracle Cluster File Systems (OCFS) on vSphere. (Other CFSs can take advantage of the CFS as well to include Global File System [GFS], General Parallel File System [GPFS], OCFS2, and others.) For complete guidelines, refer to the Oracle RAC deployment guide on vSphere at www.vmware.com.

The following figures show the architectures that you can deploy for RAC on vSphere.

Figure 5-6 shows the RAC on vSphere architecture when using vSwitches.

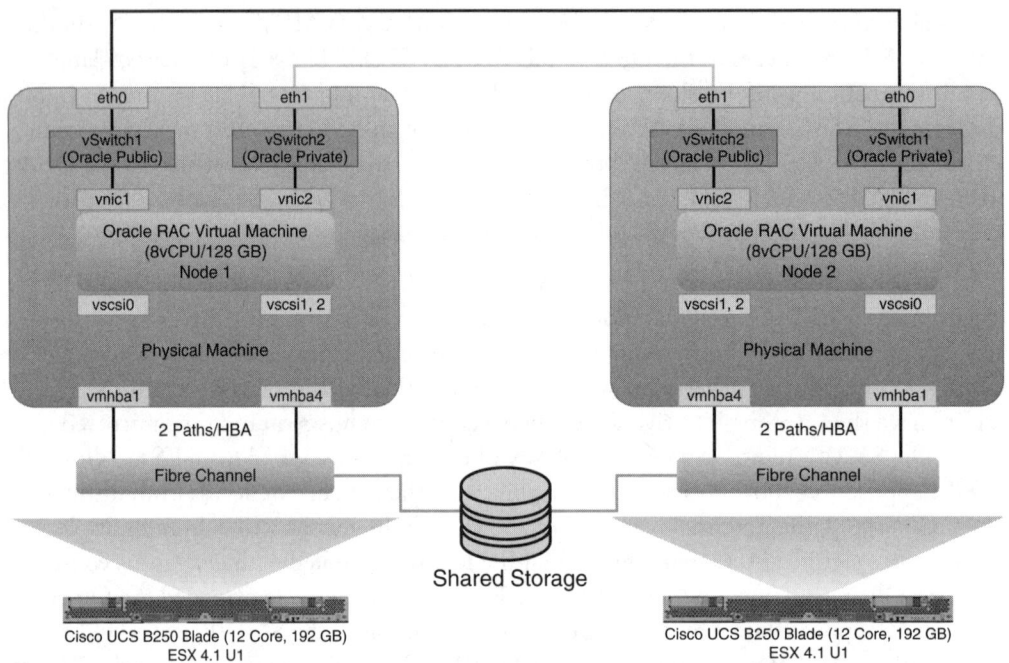

Figure 5-6 Oracle RAC on vSphere logical architecture with vSwitch

Figure 5-7 shows Oracle RAC on vSphere logical architecture using vSphere distributed switch (vDS).

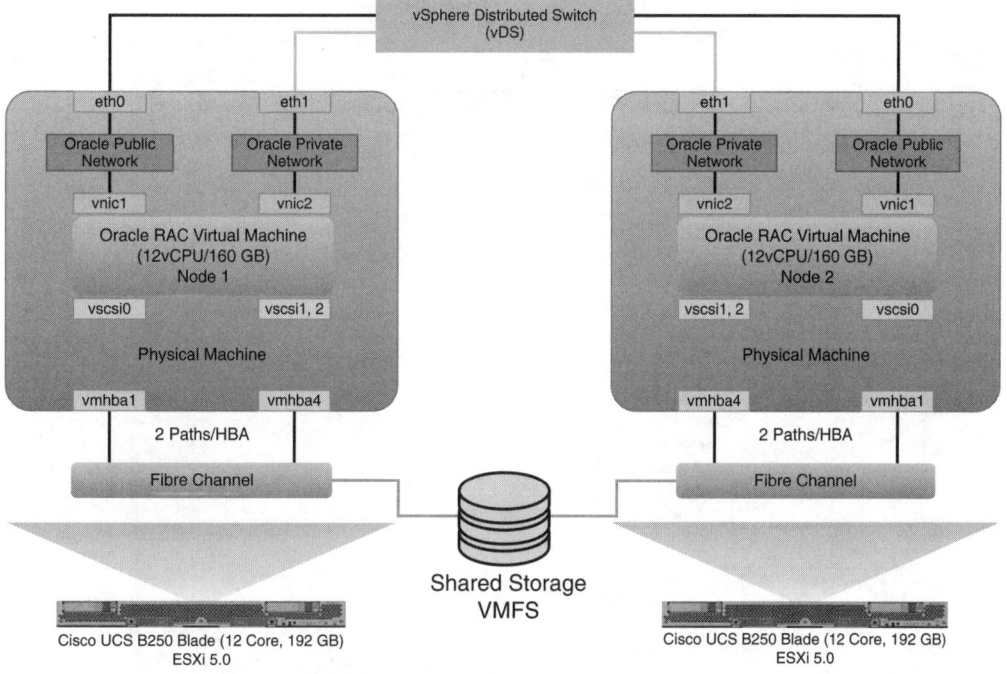

Figure 5-7 Oracle RAC on vSphere logical architecture with vSphere distributed switch (vDS)

Figure 5-8 shows the configuration of the VMS file (the main VM configuration and parameterization file) for use with the SMWF.

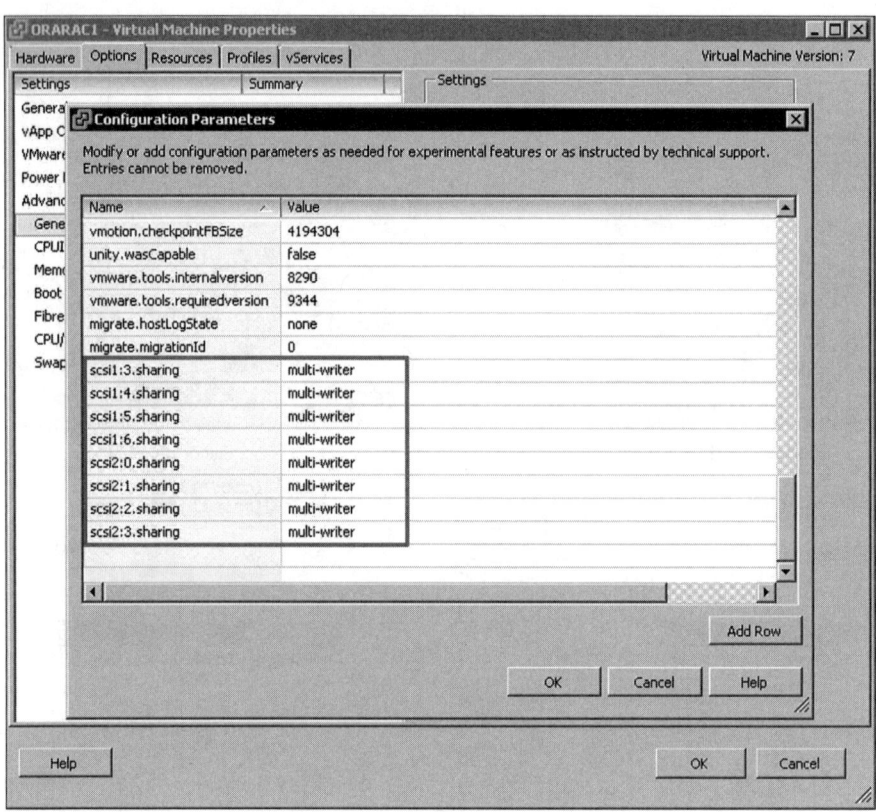

Figure 5-8 Adding SCSI multi-writer flag to VM VMX file

Figure 5-9 shows a specific reference to the configuration of the SCSI-bus-sharing parameter when using the SMWF. This particular screen is highlighted because it is somewhat counterintuitive in that it would appear that the intention is to share disks. This is true on a level well above the SCSI-bus-sharing, which therefore must be disabled (set to None) for the SMWF to behave as desired.

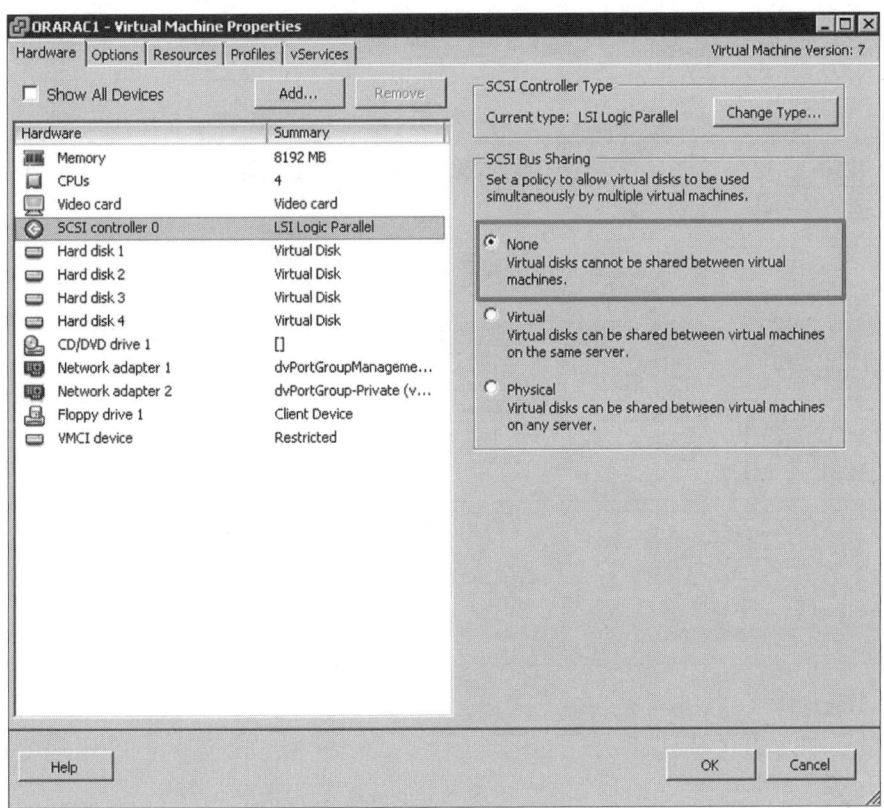

Figure 5-9 SCSI-bus-sharing set to None

Figure 5-10 shows the steps that need to be applied to automate the deployment of RAC on vSphere. The boxes highlighted in green depict the steps that the average production DBA can take to create RAC templates that will act as the base template for the addition of new RAC nodes to the ESX cluster. The vRAC-DBA will save the configuration in a template and use that template when running the RAC adding a RAC node to the RAC cluster through the RAC "addnode" process. VMware Professional Services Organization (PSO) offers a specific service to deploy a methodology for creating templates for the entire RAC deployments process to include the steps in all four "swimlanes" depicted in the figure.

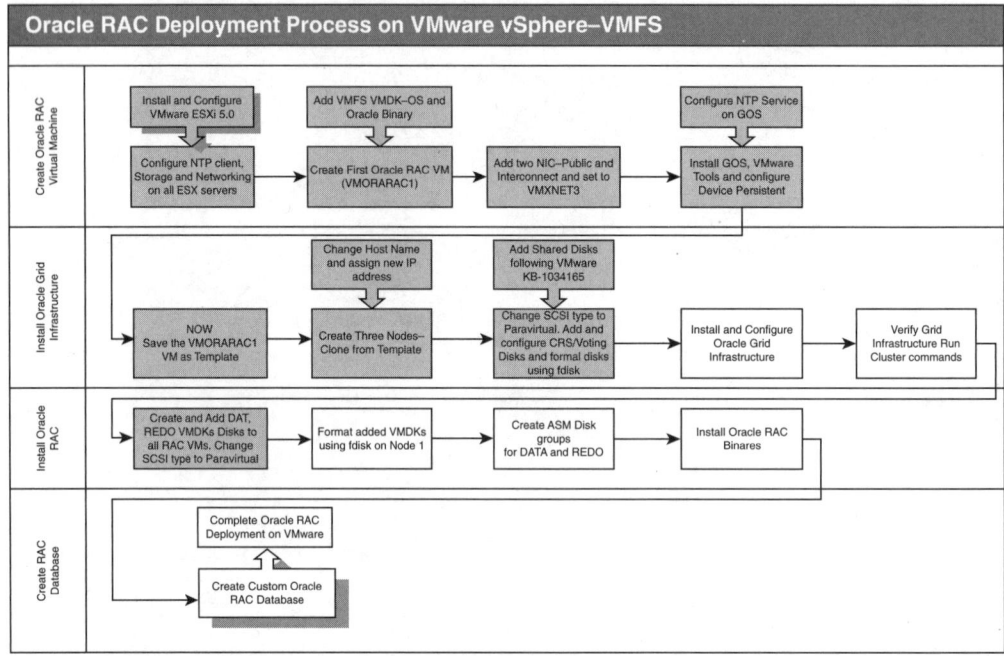

Figure 5-10 Oracle RAC on vSphere deployment steps: VMFS

Protecting Oracle Databases Against Downtime

Each of the previous scenarios provides varying degrees of protection for an Oracle database against downtime. Table 5-5 summarizes and compares the high availability scenarios described in the previous sections.

Table 5-5 Summary of High Availability Scenarios

Oracle DB in VM Scenario	ESX Host Protection	Oracle DB Protection	Minimizes Downtime for Guest OS and Oracle Patching	Oracle Available During Failover	Session/ Select Persistence Through Failover Oracle TAF	Cost/ Complexity
VMware HA	Yes	No	No	No	Medium	Low
VMware HA + Symantec ApplicationHA	Yes	Yes	No	No	Medium	Medium

Oracle DB in VM Scenario	ESX Host Protection	Oracle DB Protection	Minimizes Downtime for Guest OS and Oracle Patching	Oracle Available During Failover	Session/ Select Persistence Through Failover Oracle TAF	Cost/ Complexity
Oracle RAC One Node in Cluster	Yes	Yes	Yes	No	Medium	High
Oracle RAC Multiple Nodes	Yes	Yes	Yes	Yes	Very High	Very High

The DBA should factor in the following points when deciding on an HA solution for Oracle databases on VMware:

- It takes multiple scenarios, rather than just one, to maintain high levels of uptime, because overall system availability also depends on redundancy designed into the other parts of the infrastructure, such as network, power, and storage.

- Symantec AppHA provides an effective solution that bridges the gap between VMware HA and RAC by providing application awareness of the Oracle database instance inside a VM.

- RAC solutions provide the higher degrees of protection and are preferred options for businesses that require near zero downtime in availability for the Oracle database. For organizations that can tolerate moderate downtime of around 5 minutes, VMware HA and Symantec AppHA scenarios can offer a cost-effective solution to address the required service levels.

- What is the business's SLA with respect to uptime/downtime, or how much downtime is the business willing to tolerate?

- What is the business cost/uptime trade-off? RAC deployments are generally more expensive, and VMware is the most cost-efficient solution. Therefore, willingness to incur additional costs for increased availability is a key consideration.

- Most production databases will be configured to run with multiple CPUs. However under the rare circumstances that a database is run with a single vcpu and at the same time requires extremely high levels of HA, the feature of vSphere named Fault Tolerance (FT) would be a suitable alternative. FT allows for instant failover of the VM to a pre-designated failover node by using memory and process mirroring, which is a technology known as Lockstep. The version of vSphere at the time of the writing of this book is vSphere 5.5 and with this version, FT is limited to a single vCPU; therefore, it is not normally a legitimate option to use for extreme HA. However it is possible that in future versions of vSphere, FT will allow for multiple vCPUs and become a viable option for extreme HA requirements. We do not spend significant time in this book on FT precisely because it is not presently a real option for business critical Oracle implementations.

Figure 5-11 charts the degree of availability in a deployment against the associated cost to deliver each solution. We see here a pattern of diminishing returns where at some point the organization receives less and less extra levels of availability for additional investment into the solution.

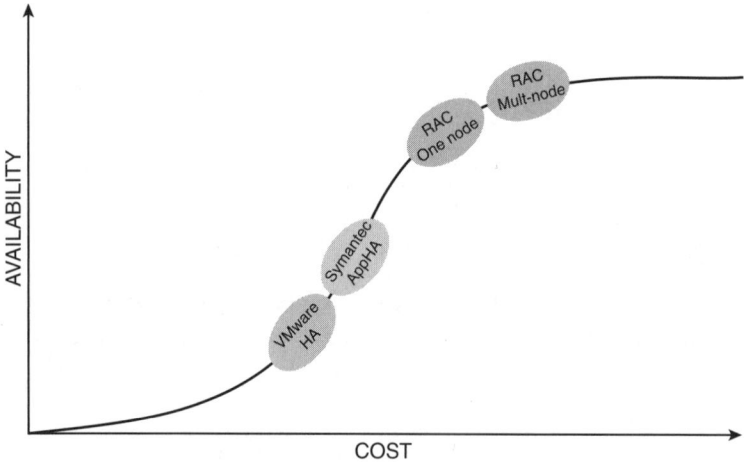

Figure 5-11 Availability versus cost trade-off

The final design choice depends on how much downtime a business can tolerate versus the cost they are willing to incur in the extra resources and skills to install, configure, and operate advanced Oracle RAC and the respective software necessary to maintain a stable environment.

Transitioning RAC Nodes Between Hosts Using VMware vMotion

VMware's feature vSphere vMotion is a highly mature capability, which allows a logical server (VM) to be transitioned from one physical host within the vSphere cluster to another. This live migration capability has been a staple of VMware technology for the past decade. The key point being that the server itself remains largely unaffected during the transition. The factors that influence the efficiency of a vMotion operation include the available bandwidth between the physical hosts, the degree of activity on the server being transitioned at the time of the vMotion, and the size of the memory allocated to the VM. Although the degree of activity is a significant factor in the time that it takes to complete a vMotion, the specific application, which happens to be running on the VM at the time, is irrelevant.

VMware vMotion has many benefits. These benefits include the increase of availability for systems that would otherwise be affected by hardware maintenance. All an administrator needs to do is to place the ESX/ESXi host that requires hardware maintenance in "maintenance mode" and each VM running on that node will be automatically transitioned to available nodes within the ESX/ESXi cluster via DRS. When the maintenance is complete and the node is removed from maintenance status, VMs are eventually transitioned back to that node effectively eliminating downtime for hardware maintenance. vMotion can also be used for load balancing of the servers in the cluster through DRS, although it is important to consider the implications of continuous movement of the VMs between physical hosts especially for large, high workload profile, or otherwise business critical systems.

Figure 5-12 shows Host 2 is in Maintenance, RAC node 2 vMotioned to Host 4.

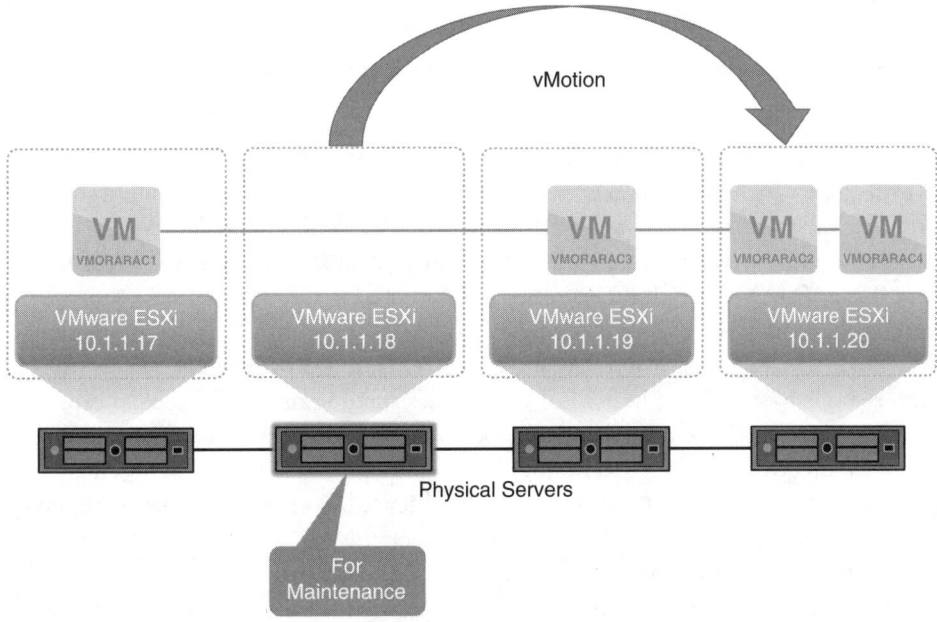

Figure 5-12 Oracle RAC vMotion: Server maintenance

Figure 5-13 shows Host 2 completed its maintenance, RAC node 2 vMotioned back to Host 2.

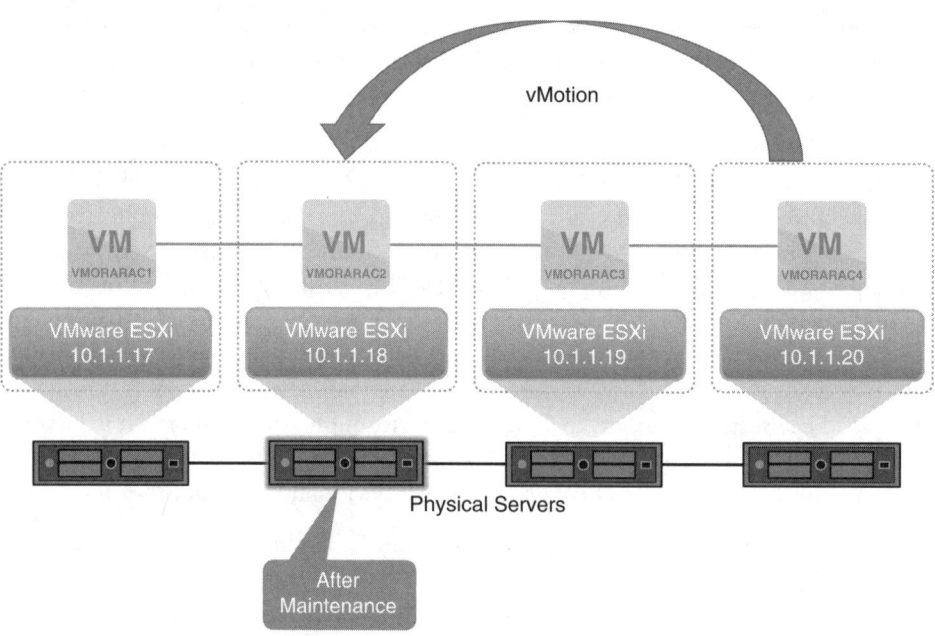

Figure 5-13 Transitioning RAC Nodes Between Hosts Using VMware vMotion After Maintenance

In 2013, VMware in collaboration with EMC and Cisco sponsored an Oracle Functional Stress Test Study, which focused on extreme usage of vMotion imposed on highly stressed RAC nodes. This stress test, executed by Principled Technologies, included the use of the Benchmark Factory tool to simulate a TPC-C-like workload, vSphere 5.1, Oracle RAC 11.2.0.3, a VMAX-CE (Cloud Edition), and Cisco UCS B200 M3 blades. A single VM running a logical RAC-node was configured on each of the three Cisco UCS hosts. Initially a single live, highly stressed RAC node was transitioned between two hosts. At this point, a single host had two individual RAC nodes running on it. The second experiment consisted of two RAC-nodes being swapped between two hosts. The third and most impressive test involved all three RAC-nodes being simultaneously moved between all three physical hosts. As expected, some performance degradation resulted, but no disruption of service occurred. No false evictions or fencing operations were recorded for the iterations of these tests. The impressiveness of these repeatable results cannot be overstated. It is an axiom of science that to truly understand what something consists of, one must heat it up! In this case, Principled Technologies, at the behest of the collaboration group, effectively created a RAC & vMotion "Super-collider." All hyperbole aside, even under these extreme circumstances, Oracle RAC was not affected by the transition of multiple RAC-nodes between physical hosts occurring simultaneously. Oracle RAC has built-in designed hypersensitivity. One might say that the prime directive of all Oracle software and RAC in particular is to protect data from all rogue access. Euphemistically, it has been stated that "RAC is built to fail," that is if the failure which manifests as an eviction or a fencing operation is necessary to protect the data. Yet even with this functional understanding under these conditions of extremely high stress, this set of tests did not produce any deleterious results. These conclusions underscore one of the main pillars of running Oracle on vSphere, which is the idea that ESX/ESXi creates a true layer of abstraction between the OS and the physical hardware so that these types of extreme conditions are managed via the virtualization layer and the effect on the OS or the application running in that OS is negligible. Refer to www.principledtechnologies.com for Oracle RAC vMotion testing.

To RAC or Not to RAC

Oracle RAC and vMotion are completely complementary technologies. When deciding to use Oracle RAC for an individual application, Oracle professionals must perform a comprehensive and diligent analysis on that application and the respective SLA attached to that application. Often, the decision to use RAC is solely based on the need for significant HA. However, the extreme level of HA that can be accomplished with RAC is often unnecessary to meet the requirements of the actual SLA (assuming all stakeholders are genuinely consulted and all costs are considered). For many years, the industry has worked on the assumption that common applications need extreme levels of HA. Often referred to as four or five nines, this "mythology of the five nines," has permeated the industry for the better part of the past two decades. If a customer has an application that was developed with Oracle Call Interface (OCI) and instrumented to use Oracle Transparent Application Failover (TAF), and that customer enables Fast Connection Failover through the Oracle Notification Services (ONS), it is possible to achieve the result of extremely minimal downtime. If that same customer sets up the failover using the *preconnect* option in the connect string, which initiates a prestarted server process on the failover target instance, it is certainly possible to achieve active session status upon RAC node failure failover within a range of 60 seconds. Of course, only the session and select statements as opposed to actual transactions remain persistent through the failover.

TIP

Oracle 12c has capability to maintain persistence of transactions spanning session failovers.

It is also important to remember that other factors are involved in the assessment of effectiveness of that session failover. Many applications have not been instrumented to use TAF. Also the classic problem, known as the brownout—or the time required to complete the reconfiguration of the Oracle Parallel Server (OPS) (pre-cursor to RAC) Lock

Database—is no longer a factor, and reconfiguration of Distributed Lock Manager (DLM) locks through the cache fusion mechanisms of the Global Cache Service (GCS) occurs almost immediately. The sessions will be distributed among the surviving nodes via the services model as well. However, there is still the issue of the failed instance being recovered by a surviving instance. Whichever System Monitor (SMON) process discovers the failed instance first will be responsible for recovering the failed instance. Also the buffer cache(s) and the Shared Pool objects must be repopulated (for those old school DBAs who still remember and use those terms) which is still a factor. These operations usually take minimal time but certainly constitute factors that the DBA should remain aware of.

The preceding discussion, notwithstanding Oracle RAC, is the most sophisticated and powerful relational database management system (RDBMS) technology in history with no other candidates in the comparison equation. When the right circumstances are present, that is, extreme HA is a stated requirement, the use of Oracle RAC is easily justified. Oracle RAC should be used when a customer has comprehensively determined that extreme levels of HA are truly required to meet the specifications of the application SLA. However, for applications that can withstand about 5 minutes downtime, vSphere HA is more than adequate to the task. vSphere HA takes a few minutes and a few mouse clicks to set up for the entire ESXi cluster. To set up the cluster, start the VM, then the OS software, and finally the applications that are set to start automatically on that server. Remember one of the main pillars, that upon failover, the exact same logical server is restarted on a different physical machine.

Summary

VMware vSphere HA, vMotion, and Oracle RAC are completely complementary technologies. If a customer has completed due diligence and concluded that the use of Oracle RAC for extreme session-level HA is necessary for a particular application, then by logical extension, that customer should run RAC on virtualized infrastructure. In a nonvirtual environment, a physical machine failure will result in the degradation of service capability due to the temporary but open-ended loss of the physical RAC-node. However, in the virtual environment, vSphere HA will restart the VM running a RAC node just like any other VM restarting. Therefore, vSphere HA allows the DBA to address the problem with the respective physical node when deemed convenient rather than in the reactionary manner required by the nonvirtualized system. When these capabilities are combined with the fact that vMotion eliminates downtime for hardware maintenance, the conclusion to use vSphere for a production-level RAC implementation is without antithesis. Although the "methodology of the five-nines" may still be unachievable in reality, the combination of these two magnificent technologies moves one closer to this HA nirvana.

## Chapter 6

Performance Workload and Functional Stress Test Studies

As we progress through the various subject areas related to running Oracle on vSphere, it is important that we continue to reiterate how those subject areas correspond to our initial principals of the four V's: viability, value, vision and versatility (see Figure 6-1). This chapter and the studies described within highlight the comprehensive viability and extensive value innate within the proposition of running Oracle on vSphere.

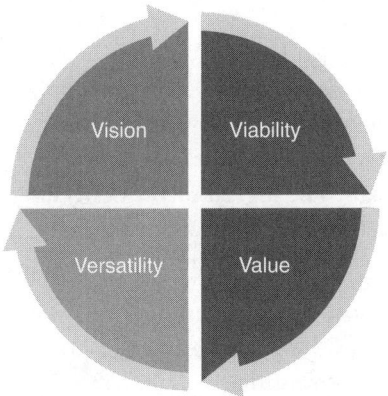

Figure 6-1 Four V's approach

We will describe the Oracle single instance and Oracle Real Application Clusters (RAC) workload characterization studies, which are well-known studies that have been circulated widely over the years. The more recent studies with *Principled Technologies*, which were collaborative efforts between VMware, EMC, and Cisco, provide impressive scenarios that

100% prove the true abstraction between the operating system (OS) and the hardware when using vSphere while highlighting the more sophisticated capabilities of vSphere that complement Oracle as well as the capacity of the overall stack.

Oracle Single-Instance Workload Study

The original workload characterization study of virtualized Oracle databases (11gR2) on VMware ESXi 4.1 produced results that show that virtualized Oracle databases on vSphere effectively service intensive online transaction processing (OLTP) loads in single and multi-virtual machine (VM) scenarios. The findings show the following:

- A single Oracle database VM linearly scaled from two to eight vCPUs; the transactions per minute (TPM) increased in a nearly linear fashion as more vCPUs were added.

- A single ESXi server can manage the workload of multiple Oracle databases in separate VMs. Consolidation is achieved both in terms of the central processing unit (CPU) and storage. Total vCPU count can exceed the number of physical cores, and multiple databases can share the same Virtual Machine File System (VMFS) datastores.

The results were *not* achieved by oversubscribing memory resources. The total memory of the VMs was less than or equal to the physical memory available on the ESXi host machine.

A live migration of a VM running an Oracle database OLTP load, using VMware vMotion, experienced zero transaction errors and no loss of data integrity, though a temporary dip in throughput was observed during the migration. This conclusion is particularly important because vMotion causes the logical server to be *transitioned* between physical hosts as the memory pages are copied page by page. The logical server (VM) does not experience an outage, but there is usually minimal performance impact during the operation. However, there will be no disruption of service or destruction of data.

Hot-add of vCPU helps in dynamically scaling the processing resources, improving overall performance and throughput of a saturated VM running an Oracle database server processing an OLTP load. This can be accomplished with zero downtime.

Test Methodology

You can use many different load tools to execute the various types of workload tests. We chose to use Swingbench to perform these tests. In this specific case, the Large-Scale Order Entry Benchmark Kit with Swingbench was used. The Swingbench kit consists of scripts and load drivers that generate business transactions, which simulate large-scale order entry OLTP loads that are input/output (I/O) intensive. It is a Transaction Processing Performance Council – Level C (TPC-C)-like workload generator that includes a data generator tool, which is used to create larger schemas to generate much higher levels of I/O (more index lookups). Data is loaded to grow the database size to 1TB, and the workload has a read/write ratio of 60/40.

You can find more information about the Swingbench benchmark kit at Dominic Giles's website.

http://dominicgiles.com/swingbench.html

Test Setup/Infrastructure

Initially, we describe the physical and logical infrastructure used to build out this workload study.

Table 6-1 summarizes the hardware and software used in the tests.

Table 6-1 Hardware and Software Used for Workload Characterization Tests

	1 x Cisco UCS B-250 blade server: 2 socket, 6 cores each, Intel Xeon X5670 @ 2.93GHz 192GB RAM (running ESXi 4.1)
	1 x Cisco UCS B-250 blade server: 2 socket, 6 cores each, Intel Xeon X5670 @ 2.93GHz 192GB RAM (running ESXi 4.1)
	1 ESXi host used to run database server VMs, the other used in the vMotion scenario and to run Swingbench clients in VMs (1 Swingbench client for each database server)
	1 x B200 blade server running Windows 2008 and Virtual Center
	Network: 10GB Ethernet
Hardware	Shared storage: EMC Clariion CX4-240 (Flare 30) with 75 Fibre channel 15K RPM spindles
VMware software	VMware Hypervisor ESXi 4.1
	vCenter Server 4.1
	vCenter Client 4.1
	vMA (Virtual Management Appliance)
Guest OS and Oracle database software in VM	Oracle Enterprise Linux 5.4 x86_64
	Oracle 11gR2 Enterprise Edition Single Instance x86_64
Oracle OLTP workload	Oracle Swingbench Load Generator – Large-Scale Order Entry Benchmark

Figure 6-2 shows the physical architecture used for the workload tests. As in many of the tests, the physical hardware included both EMC and Cisco components.

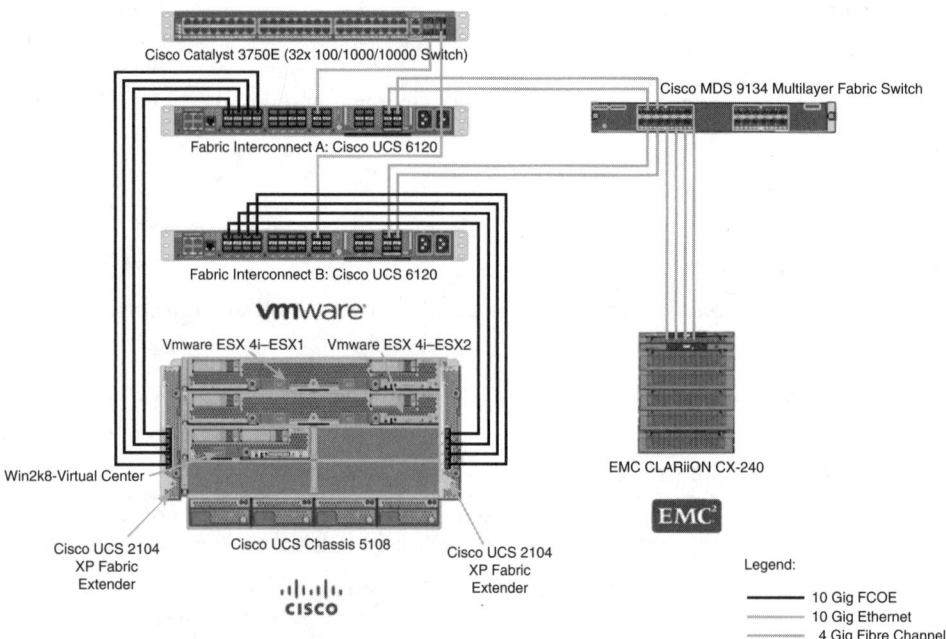

Figure 6-2 Physical architecture

Test Scenarios Summary

Table 6-2 summarizes the test scenarios.

Table 6-2 Summary of Test Scenarios

Scenario	Virtual Machine (vCPU, RAM)	Test Description
Scaling up single Oracle database VM (HT OFF)	2 vCPUs/8GB	Run Swingbench Large-Scale Oracle Entry Benchmark user load against each VM configuration
	4 vCPUs/16GB	
	6 vCPUs/24GB	4 separate test runs
	8 vCPUs/32GB	300 concurrent users
		Min and max think time = 5 and 10ms (milliseconds)

Scenario	Virtual Machine (vCPU, RAM)	Test Description
Scaling out and consolidating multiple VMs running an Oracle database (HT ON)	4 vCPUs/16GB (1 to 5 VMs)	Run Swingbench Large-Scale Oracle Entry Benchmark user load against each VM configuration
		5 separate test runs
		200 concurrent users per VM
		Min and max think time = 50 and 100ms
Live migration of Oracle database in a VM (vMotion)	4 vCPUs/16GB	Run Swingbench Large-Scale Oracle Entry Benchmark user load
		300 concurrent users
		Min and max think time = 5 and 10ms
VMware hot-add CPU of Oracle database in a VM	2 vCPUs/8GB (hot-add 2 vCPUs)	Run Swingbench Large-Scale Oracle Entry Benchmark user load
		100 concurrent users
		Min and max think time = 5 and 10ms

Test Result Details

These sections describe in detail the setup and results for all the test scenarios. Performance results were obtained from the following:

- Performance data was captured by the VMware Esxtop utility.

> **NOTE**
>
> When this test was performed, Esxtop was used. In more recent versions of vSphere, because the service console was removed from ESXi, rEsxtop will be used rather than Esxtop.

- Output data comes from the Oracle Swingbench generator. In this case, performance is measured by transaction throughput, which is transactions per minute (TPM).

Single Virtual Machine: Scale-Up Test

In the scale-up test, we ran four separate test iterations against a single VM configured with two, four, six, and eight vCPUs. The goal was to demonstrate increasing transaction throughput by enhancing the VM with additional processing capability. Table 6-3 shows the test configurations, and Figure 6-3 shows the scale-up test details.

Table 6-3 Single VM: Test Configurations

No. of vCPUs	Database Size (TB)	Concurrent Users (Min, Max Think Time, ms)	VM Memory	Oracle Server SGA Size
2	1.1	300 (5,10)	8GB	6GB
4	1.1	300 (5,10)	16GB	10GB
6	1.1	300 (5,10)	24GB	16GB
8	1.1	300 (5,10)	32GB	20GB

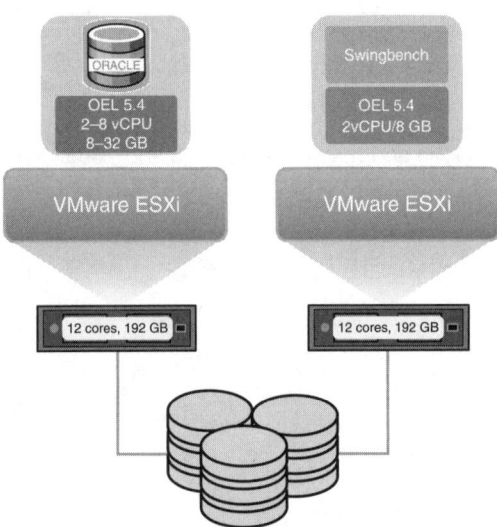

Figure 6-3 Single VM: Scale-up test

Next we look at the storage layout of the single Oracle database VM.

Storage Layout for a Single Virtual Machine

Figure 6-4 represents the storage layout of the Oracle database. Following the pillar that "Oracle does not change when run on vSphere," the standard and well-known approaches to storage allocation for Oracle will still apply. The common and Oracle-endorsed methodology for storage configuration known as Optimal Flexible Architecture (OFA) applies in the virtual world in the same way it applies in the nonvirtual world. The following is the storage configuration for the single Oracle database VM:

- LUN 1–8 (1TB each – RAID 5) -> Data: datastore 1–8 VMFS -> 8 x VMDKs (900GB each) (managed by Oracle ASM)

- LUN 9–10 (1.5TB each – RAID 10) ->Redo: datastore 9–10 VMFS -> 2 x VMDKs (1TB each) (managed by Oracle ASM)

- LUN 11 (1.5TB – RAID 10) - > VMORA: datastore 11 VMFS -> 2 x VMDKs (30GB for OS, 50GB for binary)

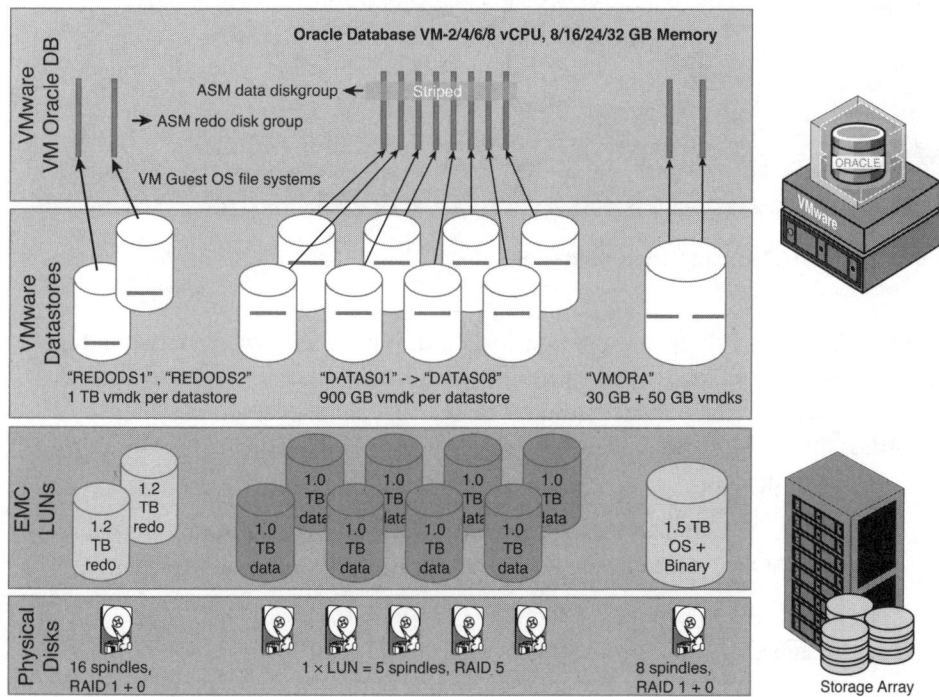

Figure 6-4 Single VM: Storage layout

Next we will consider the implications on dynamic scalability.

Single Virtual Machine Scale-Up Results

Figure 6-5 shows the results of the test runs. The chart shows the transaction throughput, measured in TPM, against the size of the VM. In all iterations, CPU utilization within the VM was near 100%.

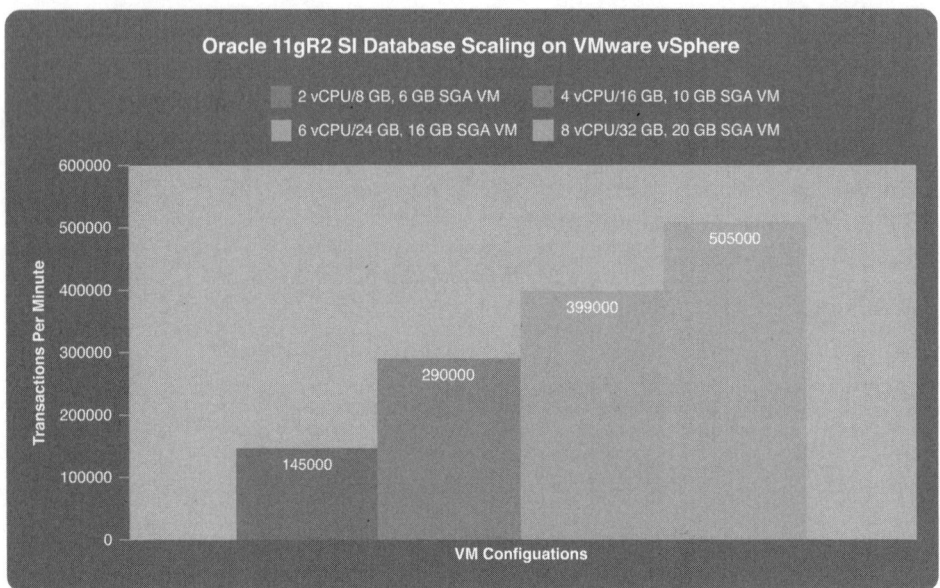

Figure 6-5 Single VM: Scale-up chart

The results in Figure 6-5 show that the Oracle database scaled linearly from two to four vCPUs. It did not scale as well to eight vCPUs, but still exhibited sizable performance gains. It was observed in the case of eight vCPUs the VM memory spans non-uniform memory access (NUMA) nodes. Chapter 8, "Performance Management and Monitoring," discusses NUMA in detail.

Figure 6-6 shows the CPU and I/O statistics for the eight-way configuration iteration. Although we did see a drop off in linearity, the results are nonetheless impressive.

This is a highly utilized VM producing 505,000 TPM with CPU near 800% (as per standard Esxtop reporting, which corresponds to near 100% CPU utilization of the aggregate individual vCPUs). The disk statistics of one of the data logical unit numbers (LUNs) reported 1120 input/outputs per second (IOPS) (commands/sec) with latency of 9.5ms/cmd.

These findings show that a single database deployed in a VM can be scaled to handle larger transaction throughput. At the time of this test with vSphere version 4.1, VMs could be sized up to a maximum of 8 vCPUs, whereas the maximum with vSphere 5.5 is 64 vCPUs.

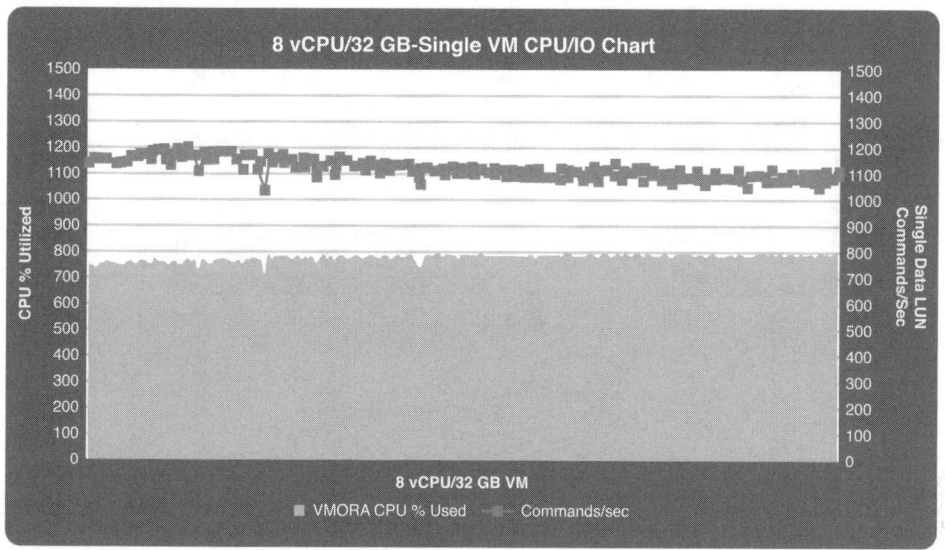

Figure 6-6 Single VM CPU/IO chart: 8 vCPUs/32GB

Multiple Virtual Machines: Scale-Out Test

In the scale-out test, we ran five separate iterations from one to five VMs, with each VM configured with the same number of vCPUs and allocated memory. Each VM ran the same database. The goal was to demonstrate increasing total transaction throughput when adding multiple VMs. Table 6-4 and Figure 6-7 describe the tests. All five VMs shared the same LUNs/datastores.

Table 6-4 Multiple VMs: Test Configuration

No. of vCPUs per VM	Database Size (TB)	Concurrent Users (Min, Max Think Time, ms)	VM Memory	Oracle Server SGA Size
4 (1 to 5 VMs)	1.1TB	200 (50,100)	16GB	10GB

Figure 6-7 shows the logical layout of the scale-out test architecture.

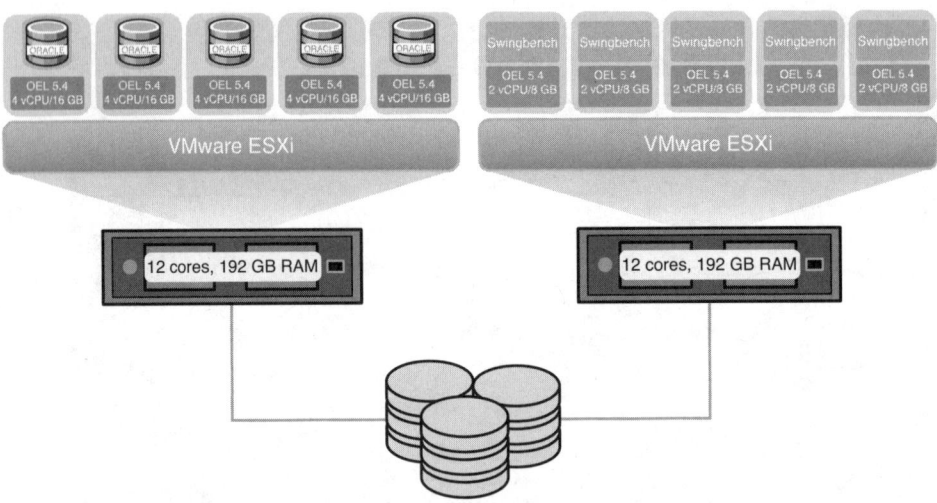

Figure 6-7 Multiple VMs: Scale-out test

Storage Layout for Multiple Virtual Machines

Figure 6-8 represents the storage layout for the Oracle databases used in the scale-out test. The multiple Oracle database running on individual VMs share the same Automatic Storage Management (ASM) disk groups (DGs). ASM, a database disk container system, allows database administrators (DBAs) to manage "disks" (ASM disks) that are presented to a specialized Oracle instances known as the ASM instance. The DBA can then build out the ASM DG and place each database file within that ASM DG, thus allowing the Oracle process to manage the logical storage. You can find a detailed description of ASM at the Oracle Technology Network (OTN) website.

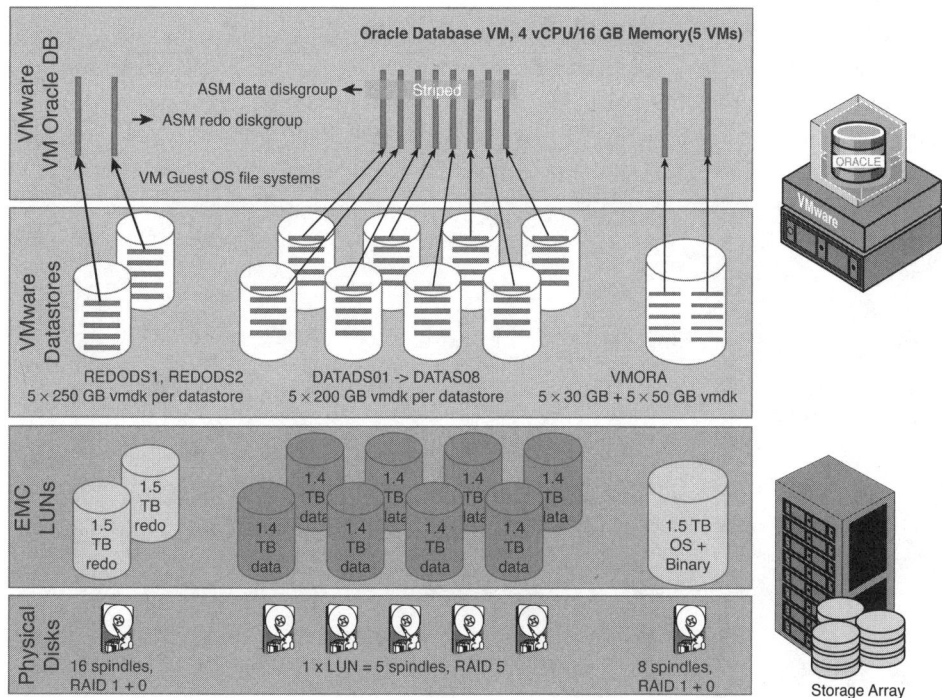

Figure 6-8 Multiple VMs: Storage layout

Here we show the results of the test in terms of transaction throughput.

Now we will look at the LUN layout used for the ASM disks and to build out the ASM DG. External redundancy, which allows for the redundancy (RAID level) to be established on the storage as opposed to the ASM layer, was used in this test:

- **LUN 1–8 (1TB each – RAID 5) -> Data:** datastore 1–8 VMFS -> 8 x VMDKs (200GB each) for each Oracle database (managed by Oracle ASM); each VM has one VMDK from each datastore

- **LUN 9–10 (1.5TB each – RAID 10) -> Redo:** datastore 9–10 VMFS -> 2 x VMDKs (250GB each) for each Oracle database (managed by Oracle ASM); each VM has one VMDK from each datastore

- **LUN 11 (1.5TB – RAID 10) -> VMORA:** datastore 11 VMFS -> 2 VMDK (30GB for OS, 50GB for Binary) for each Oracle database; each VM has two VMDKs from the same datastore

Multiple Virtual Machines Scale-Out Results

Figure 6-9 shows the results of the five test runs in the scale-out test. The chart shows transaction throughput, measured in TPM, against the number of simultaneous VMs. Each bar is broken down to show the TPM value of the individual VM.

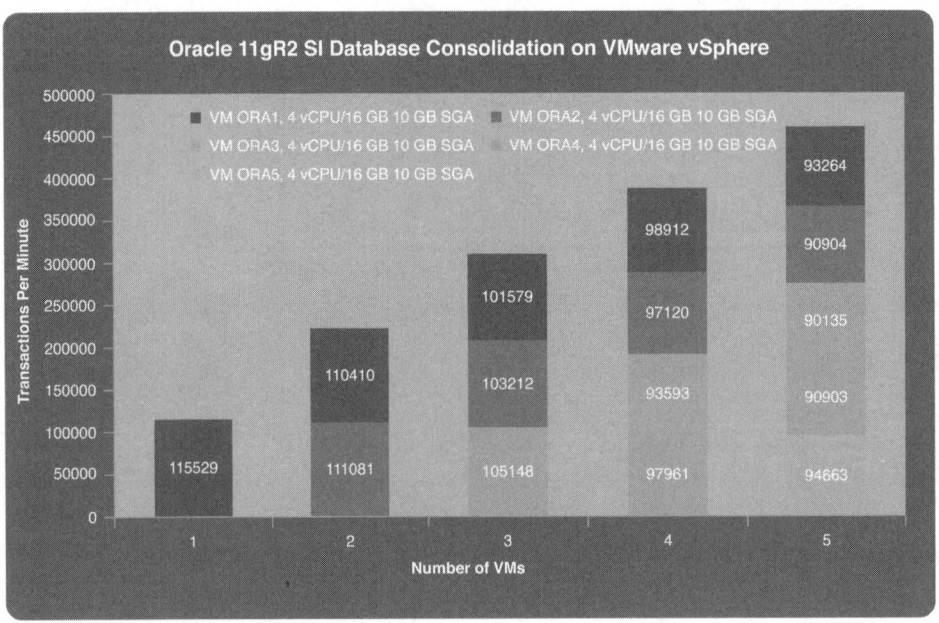

Figure 6-9 Multiple VMs: Scale-out chart

> **NOTE**
>
> Because storage was limited, we could not scale out beyond five VMs. With five VMs running, CPU utilization within each VM averaged 45%.

Figure 6-9 demonstrates that the total throughput increases fairly linearly with additional VMs. The ESX host was able to handle the workloads of the multiple VMs:

- With five VMs, the total number of vCPUs was more than the physical number of server cores.

- Databases across all the VMs were able to share the same VMFS LUNs.

- The memory assigned to all the VMs was within the memory capacity of the ESX host so that the ESX balloon driver was not invoked during the scenarios.

The results show that ESX/ESXi is able to fairly distribute CPU resources across the VMs. CPU utilization of each VM, when all five VMs were running, was similar. When multiple identical VMs are running, identical performance is expected from each. This is demonstrated by the similar TPM values processed by each VM and is attributed to the fairness properties of the vSphere scheduler.

The scale-out capabilities of vSphere enables the consolidation of database VMs and allows customers to get more out of their resources and lower their total cost of ownership (TCO).

Live Migration of Virtual Machine (vMotion)

In the vMotion test, the VM running an Oracle database under a heavy OLTP load was live migrated to demonstrate minimal impact to the workload. The test was executed as follows:

- VM VMORA1 running Oracle database server on ESXi Host 1

- Execute 300-user Swingbench Large-Scale Order Entry Benchmark for approximately 1 hour with minimum and maximum think time of 5 and 10ms respectively

- Live migrate the VM to target server ESXi Host 2

Figure 6-10 shows the throughput variance during the vMotion. The chart shows transaction throughput against time. The first line marks the start of live migration, and the second line marks the end of live migration.

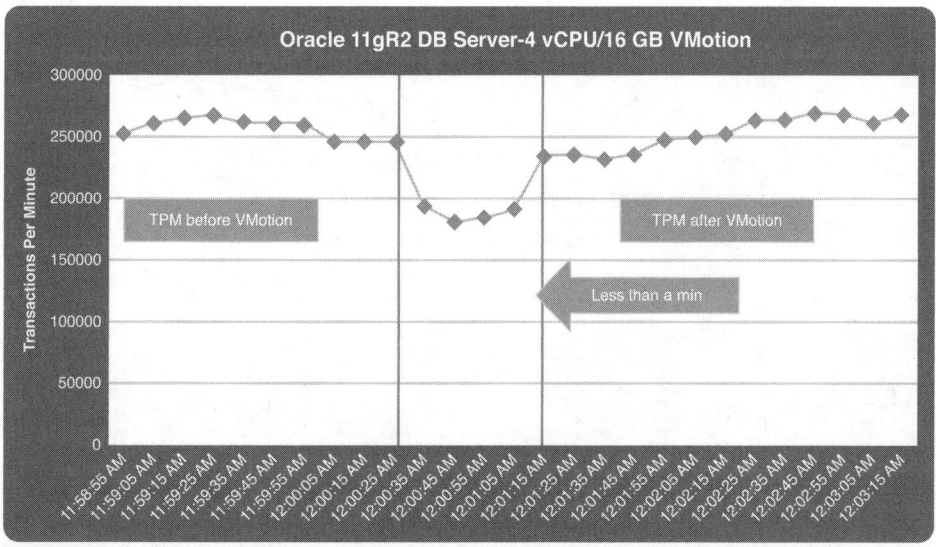

Figure 6-10 Oracle database transactions per minute during migration with vMotion

Figure 6-10 shows a decrease in throughput during migration, but the pre-vMotion transaction rate is restored immediately upon complete migration. The time taken to complete the migration is less than a minute.

Figure 6-11 and Figure 6-12 show the Esxtop CPU panel during the migration. vMotion creates a process on the source (vmotion-src) and target (vmotion-dest) servers that consume CPU in addition to the business workload.

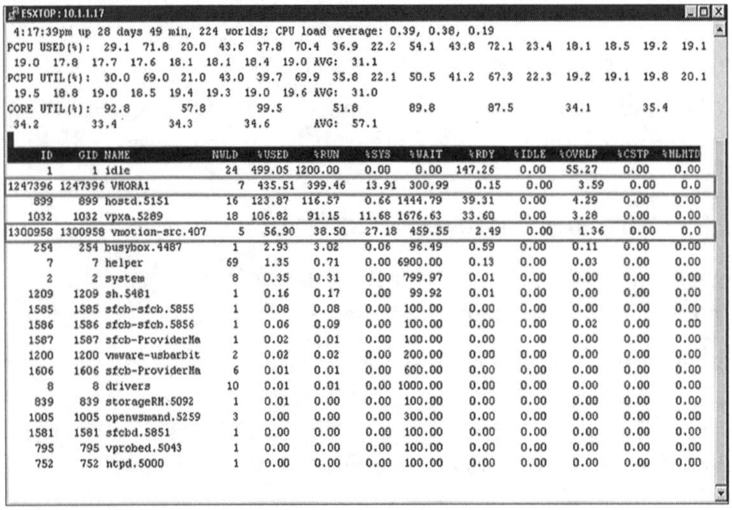

Figure 6-11 ESXi Host 1: Source

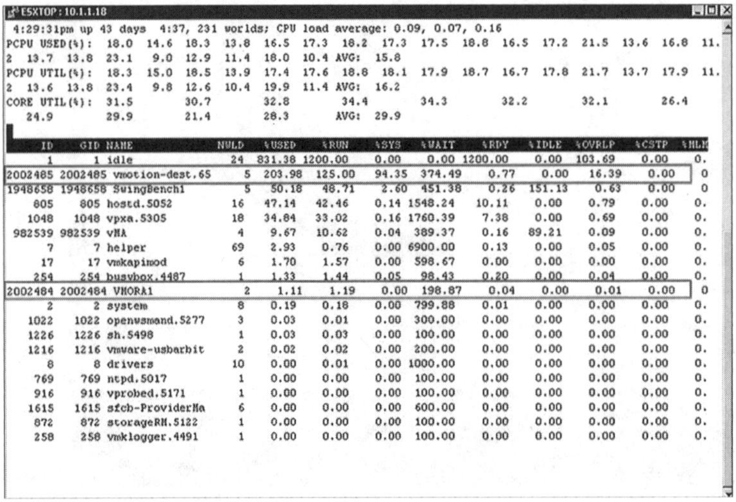

Figure 6-12 ESXi Host 2: Target

VMware vMotion presented minimal impact to the Oracle OLTP workload and no impact on the user or on database consistency. System administrators gain substantial flexibility in being able to balance VMs freely across ESX/ESXi hosts, thus improving performance. In addition, impact on end users can be eliminated when performing host maintenance.

VMware vCPU Hot-Add

In the hot-add scenario, we tested the vSphere hot-plug feature for virtual devices, which supports addition of vCPUs to a VM without powering off the VM. The test was executed as follows:

- VM VMSUSE (Oracle database 11gR2 with SUSE Enterprise Linux 11 x_64 – VMware hot-add vCPU supported guest OS) running on ESXi Host 1 with CPU saturated near 100%.

- Execute 100 users Swingbench Large-Scale Order Entry Benchmark load against 2 vCPUs/8GB VM for approximately 1 hour with minimum and maximum think time of 5 and 10ms, respectively. Hot-add vCPU to VMSUSE (2 vCPUs to 4 vCPUs).

Figure 6-13 shows transaction throughput, measured in TPM against time. It shows the TPM values of the VM before and after the hot-add vCPU operation. The line marks the point in time that the hot-add operation was initiated in the vSphere Client.

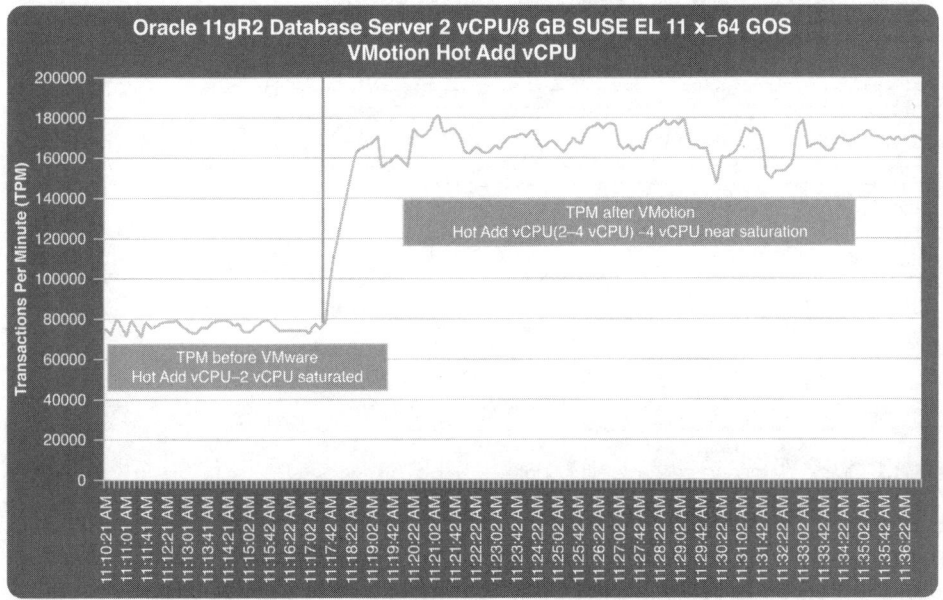

Figure 6-13 Oracle database transactions per minute with VMware hot-add vCPU

The chart shows the VM initially delivered performance at just below 80,000 TPM. After a hot-add of two vCPUs, transaction throughput approximately doubles.

The Oracle database is aware of the extra vCPUs. Figure 6-14 shows detection of the change of CPU count in the Oracle alert log, and Figure 6-15 shows that the Oracle database parameter CPU_COUNT changed from 2 to 4.

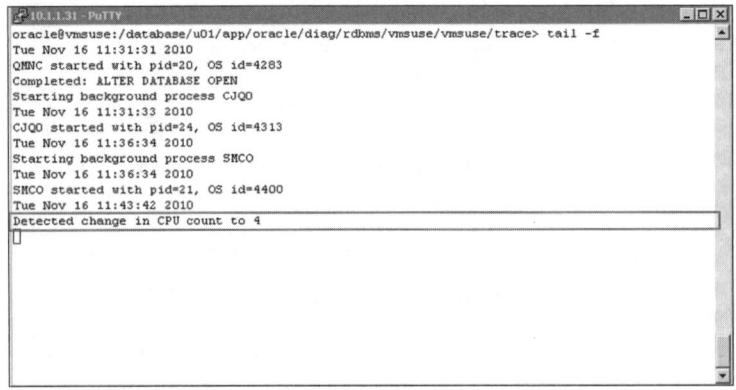

Figure 6-14 Detecting the change of CPU count in the Oracle alert log

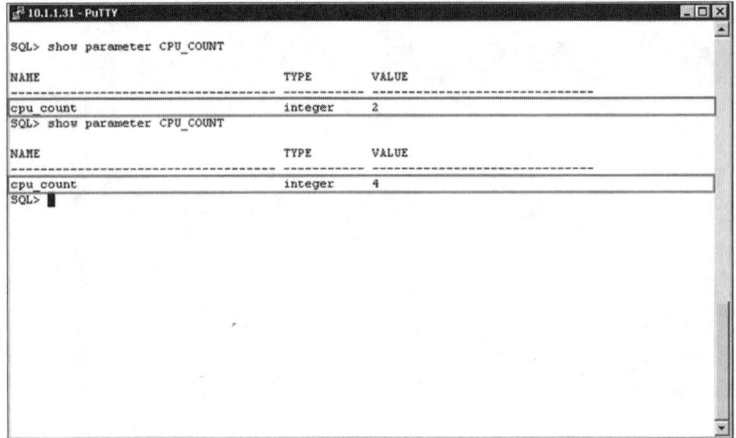

Figure 6-15 Oracle database server CPU count

This test shows that Oracle DBAs can take advantage of the VMware hot-add CPU feature to add vCPUs on-the-fly without restarting the database or the VM. Databases can be sized in a smaller VM, but as workload increases beyond initial estimates, no downtime is required to add more processing capability.

For example, a retail store that is expecting a precipitous increase in sales the day after the Thanksgiving (known as Black Friday) may want to allocate more resources from a pool of available resources to address the expected increase in demand. With the hot-add vCPU feature, the customer can add a vCPU (or vSocket in later releases of vSphere).

> **TIP**
>
> With the introduction of virtual NUMA (vNUMA) in vSphere 5.x, the enabling of hot-add vCPU disables vNUMA.

Oracle RAC Workload Characterization Study

The deployment of Oracle RAC on VMware is similar to physical environments except that each node corresponds to a separate VM that typically resides on a separate ESX host. The features of a virtualized Oracle RAC deployment include the following:

- **Facilitates consolidation:** While each Oracle RAC node VM resides on a separate ESX host, spare capacity on each ESX host allows hosting of other VMs.

- **VMware templates can quickly provision new Oracle RAC nodes:** The OS can be preinstalled and patched in a template from which further VM Oracle RAC nodes can be created.

- **In training environments, Oracle RAC can be installed in multiple VMs on the same ESX host:** This minimizes the need for multiple servers, but still enables Oracle RAC functionality to be tested and deployed in a similar manner to production environments.

vMotion and VMware HA

vMotion can move a live, running Oracle database VM from one ESX host to another with no downtime. Because VMs running on vSphere are abstracted from the underlying hardware, vMotion can even move VMs across hardware from different vendors and between physical machines or servers having different hardware configurations (as long as the CPUs meet compatibility requirements).

VMware vSphere vMotion is an invaluable tool for Oracle DBAs because of its capabilities, such as the following:

- **Avoiding planned downtime:** You can move Oracle RAC node VMs off an ESX host that requires downtime (hardware replacement/upgrade, firmware upgrade, and the like) with no loss of service.

- **Simplifying server refresh cycles:** Server refresh cycles can be challenging as the application and OS typically need to be reinstalled. With vMotion, moving an Oracle RAC node onto new hardware can be done in minutes, with no downtime.

- **Troubleshooting suspected issues:** Moving Oracle RAC node VMs onto a different ESX host can be an effective tool for troubleshooting suspected issues with underlying hardware.

An Oracle RAC node failure in a virtual deployment results in user failover that is the same as physical RAC environments; that is, user sessions fail over to the remaining nodes (assuming configuration of Oracle session failover functionality, Transparent Application Failover [TAF]). A multinode Oracle RAC deployment by design is highly available, so the use of VMware HA in this environment is not critical for protection against hardware failure. However, VMware HA can coexist with and complement a virtualized Oracle RAC installation in the following ways:

- While Oracle RAC maintains database availability, VMware HA can automatically restart the failed RAC VM node on another ESX host where no other Oracle RAC node exists in order to return to full capacity as soon as possible. As of vSphere 4.1, affinity rules are possible to enforce placement of Oracle RAC VMs such that they reside on separate ESX hosts. Note that the restart of the Oracle RAC node VM on a new ESX host after a VMware HA event requires that the target ESX host be licensed. For more information, see "VMware High Availability (HA): Deployment Best Practices" at the VMware website. Refer to VMware vSphere High Availability 5.0 Deployment Best Practices.

  http://www.vmware.com/files/pdf/techpaper/vmw-vsphere-high-availability.pdf

- Disabling automatic restart of Oracle RAC VM nodes if there is an ESX host failure. In this case, impacted user sessions fail over and continue to be processed on the remaining nodes in a "degraded" state (because there are fewer nodes). This is only temporary until the failed server is repaired and brought back into the cluster, at which point the failed VM node can be manually restarted.

Large-Scale Order Entry Benchmark Kit (Swingbench)

The Swingbench kit consists of scripts and load drivers that generate business transactions that simulate I/O-intensive, large-scale order entry OLTP loads. It is similar to a TPC-C workload generator that includes a data generator tool, which was used to create larger schemas that generate much higher levels of I/O (larger index lookups). This workload has a read/write ratio of 60/40.

You can find more information about the benchmark kit at Dominic Giles's website.

Architecture

This section describes the physical and logical architecture, hardware and software used, network configuration, storage layout, and workload test conducted with four-node Oracle RAC VMs on VMware vSphere.

Table 6-5 summarizes the hardware and software used in the RAC workload characterization tests.

Table 6-5 Hardware and Software Used

Item	Description
Hardware	4 x Cisco UCS B-250 blade server: 2 socket, 6 cores each, Intel Xeon X5670 @ 2.93GHz 192GB RAM (running ESXi 5.0)
	1 x B200 blade server for Swingbench load generator VM
	1 x B200 blade server running Windows Server 2008 and vCenter
	Network: 10GB Ethernet
	Shared storage: EMC VNX5500 unified storage, running the following:
	VNX OE for block: level 05.31.000.5.008
	VNX OE for file: level 7.0.13
VMware software	ESXi 5.0
	vCenter Server 5.0
	vCenter Client 5.0
Guest OS and Oracle database software in VM and multipathing software	Oracle Enterprise Linux 5.5 x86_64
	Oracle Database 11gR2 (with Oracle RAC and Oracle Grid Infrastructure) Enterprise Edition
	EMC PowerPath/VE 5.7
Oracle OLTP workload	Oracle Swingbench 2.4 Load Generator – Large-Scale Order Entry Benchmark

Figure 6-16 shows the physical architecture used for the RAC workload characterization tests. Although the version of vSphere used in this study was version 5.1, the results are applicable to all versions of vSphere 5.1 and later.

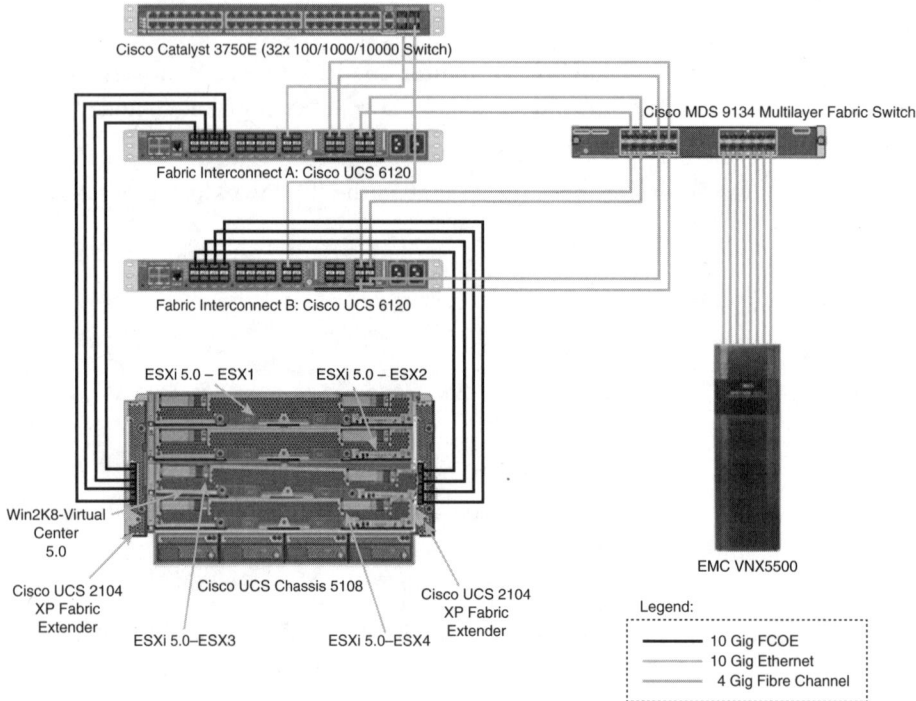

Cisco Catalyst 3750E (32x 100/1000/10000 Switch)

Cisco MDS 9134 Multilayer Fabric Switch

Fabric Interconnect A: Cisco UCS 6120

Fabric Interconnect B: Cisco UCS 6120

ESXi 5.0 – ESX1   ESXi 5.0 – ESX2

Win2K8-Virtual
Center
5.0

Cisco UCS 2104
XP Fabric
Extender

Cisco UCS Chassis 5108

ESXi 5.0–ESX3   ESXi 5.0–ESX4

Cisco UCS 2104
XP Fabric
Extender

EMC VNX5500

Legend:
——— 10 Gig FCOE
——— 10 Gig Ethernet
——— 4 Gig Fibre Channel

Figure 6-16 Physical architecture

The server and network hardware is based on the Cisco Unified Computing System (UCS), which provides centrally controlled and managed compute, network, virtualization, and storage resources. These resources are stateless and are provisioned dynamically by the Cisco UCS Manager, which handles every aspect of system configuration, from a server's firmware and identity settings, to the network connections that connect storage traffic to the destination storage system.

Figure 6-17 shows two of the four Oracle RAC nodes.

Each VM Oracle RAC node was configured with eight vCPUs and 128GB of memory. Each ESX host had 12 cores and hyperthreading (HT) was enabled so that there were a total of 24 threads/logical CPUs.

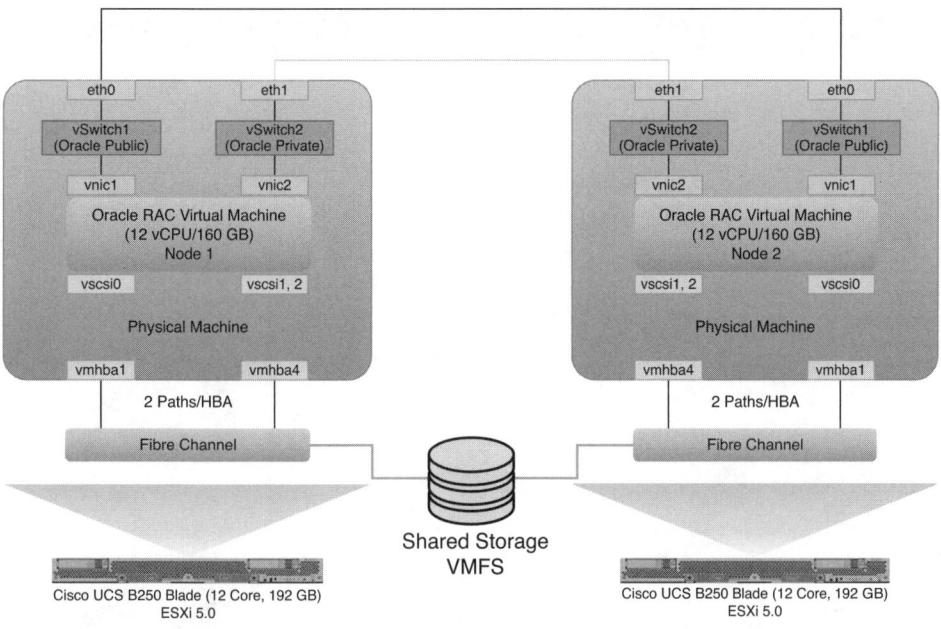

Figure 6-17 Logical architecture: Oracle RAC nodes (only two shown)

Network Configuration

In this example, four separate vSwitches (corresponding to four separate physical subnets) were created in each ESX host for the VMware system console, vMotion, public networks, and private networks.

Figure 6-18 shows the vSwitch configuration as viewed from vCenter.

The ESX host/UCS blade network adapters are based on the Cisco UCS Fabric Interconnect, which consists of a 10Gbps unified fabric that combines storage and network I/O. The network interface card (NIC) redundancy was not factored into this lab design, but it is a best practice recommendation for production deployments. Follow the VMware networking best practice guidelines described in the "VMworld 2010 Breakout Session: TA8595 – vNetwork Concepts and Best Practices at VMworld.com Using VMworld 2010 Access Privileges."

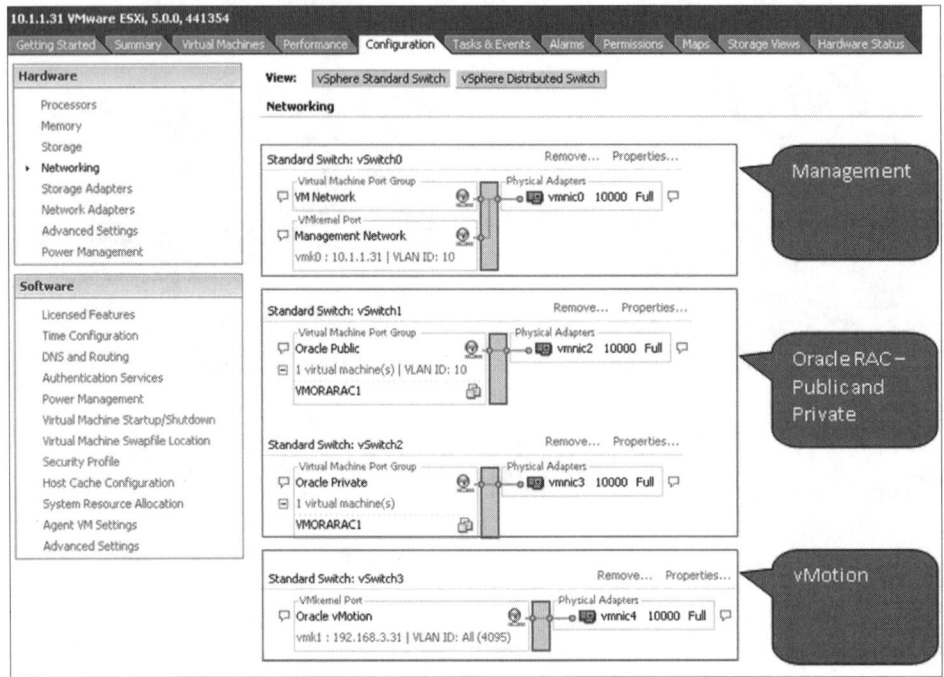

Figure 6-18 vSwitch configuration

Storage Layout

The VNX 5500 was initially configured to use 58 x 600GB SAS drives. Because the Oracle RAC data service scales to higher node counts, the combined I/O demand from the different instances starts to queue up within the storage, creating increasingly higher transaction response time. So EMC Fully Automated Storage Tiering (FAST) and FAST Cache technologies were engaged. 14 x 100GB flash drives were allocated for FAST cache to improve transaction response times.

EMC FAST technology is storage-array-based software that provides a policy-based auto-tiering solution for enterprise applications transparently. The goal of FAST technology is to leverage storage tiers to lower customers' TCO and to increase performance by keeping hotter slices of data of the different LUNs provisioned on higher-performance tiers and colder slices on lower tiers. High locality of data is important to realize the benefits of the FAST technology. FAST operates at sub-LUN level, with the storage automatically sensing the usage frequency of different pieces of data and relocating more active data to faster drives, such as flash drives, for performance and less active data to slower rotational drives (the Fibre Channel drives in this case), thereby *optimizing* storage usage to reduce costs.

FAST data is transparent to the host environment. For more information on how to use EMC FAST Cache for Oracle OLTP databases, refer to the EMC document "Leveraging EMC FAST Cache with Oracle OLTP Database Applications" at the EMC website ../../../../Users/uclevch/Users/sullivand/AppData/Local/Temp/Temp1_ch06_to_AR.zip/www.emc.com/collateral/software/white-papers/h8018-fast-cache-oracle-wp.pdf.

Ten flash drives were placed in an EMC FAST tier (4+1 RAID 5) and four flash drives were used to implement EMC FAST Cache (mirrored RAID) in this test configuration. Space was also allocated for hot spare drives. Figure 6-19 depicts the back-end storage connectivity after this reconfiguration.

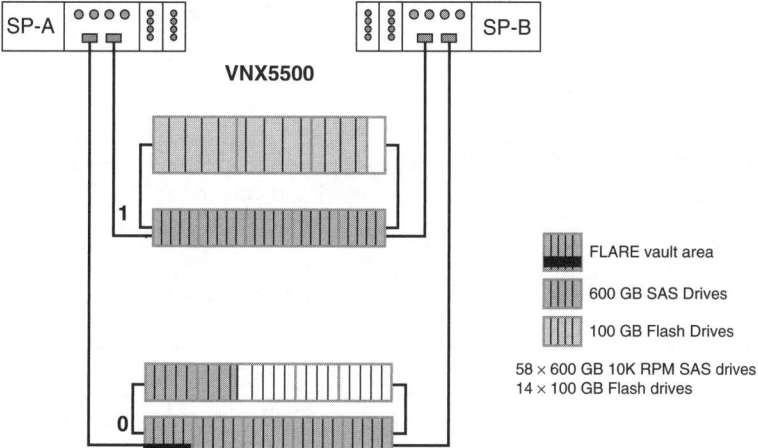

Figure 6-19 Back-end storage connectivity

Generally, faster storage access results in better aggregate database performance. Although this point is axiomatic, the subtleties are often elusive. Flash storage (provided by a number of companies to include Pure, EMC, Tintri and Violin), although presently more expensive than magnetic disk, provides millisecond storage access times. This allows the circumvention of the most prevalent cause of bad performance in the great majority of Oracle database environments: inadequate storage access.

Rerunning the stress tests using the configuration leveraging flash drives and EMC's FAST technologies resulted in the expected performance outcome with latency no longer a constraint.

The other option would have been to add a much larger number of Fibre Channel drives to achieve the same performance results.

The LUNs were configured as shown in Table 6-6.

Table 6-6 Storage Layout Configuration

RAID Group and Type	LUN	Virtual Device	Size	VMFS Datastore	Purpose	Storage Processor Owner
RAID Group 0, RAID 5 4+1	LUN 1	N/A	20GB	N/A	ESXi 5 boot LUN	SP-B
RAID Group 0, RAID 5 4+1	LUN 2	N/A	20GB	N/A	ESXi 5 boot LUN	SP-A
RAID Group 0, RAID 5 4+1	LUN 3	N/A	20GB	N/A	ESXi 5 boot LUN	SP-B
RAID Group 0, RAID 5 4+1	LUN 4	N/A	20GB	N/A	ESXi 5 boot LUN	SP-A
RAID Group 0, RAID 5 4+1	LUN 5	N/A	20GB	N/A	ESXi 5 boot LUN	SP-B
RAID Group 1, RAID 1+0	LUN 6	SCSI 0:0	1TB	VMDATASTORE	Virtual machines and Oracle binary	SP-A
Pool 0, RAID 5	LUN 7	SCSI 1:0	20GB	CRS1	OCR and voting – Oracle ASM	SP-A
Pool 0, RAID 5	LUN 8	SCSI 1:1	20GB	CRS2	OCR and voting – Oracle ASM	SP-B
Pool 0, RAID 5	LUN 9	SCSI 1:2	20GB	CRS3	OCR and voting – Oracle ASM	SP-A
Pool 0, RAID 5	LUN 10	SCSI 1:3	300GB	DATA1	Data disks – Oracle ASM	SP-A
Pool 0, RAID 5	LUN 11	SCSI 1:4	300GB	DATA2	Data disks – Oracle ASM	SP-B
Pool 0, RAID 5	LUN 12	SCSI 1:5	300GB	DATA3	Data disks – Oracle ASM	SP-A
Pool 0, RAID 5	LUN 13	SCSI 1:6	300GB	DATA4	Data disks – Oracle ASM	SP-B
Pool 0, RAID 5	LUN 14	SCSI 1:8	300GB	DATA5	Data disks – Oracle ASM	SP-A
Pool 0, RAID 5	LUN 15	SCSI 1:9	300GB	DATA6	Data disks – Oracle ASM	SP-B
Pool 0, RAID 5	LUN 16	SCSI 1:10	300GB	DATA7	Data disks – Oracle ASM	SP-A

RAID Group and Type	LUN	Virtual Device	Size	VMFS Datastore	Purpose	Storage Processor Owner
Pool 0, RAID 5	LUN 17	SCSI 1:11	300GB	DATA8	Data disks – Oracle ASM	SP-B
Pool 0, RAID 5	LUN 18	SCSI 1:12	300GB	DATA9	Data disks – Oracle ASM	SP-A
Pool 0, RAID 5	LUN 19	SCSI 1:13	300GB	DATA10	Data disks – Oracle ASM	SP-B
RAID Group 1, RAID 1+0	LUN 20	SCSI 2:0	64GB	REDO1	Redo disks – Oracle ASM	SP-A
RAID Group 1, RAID 1+0	LUN 21	SCSI 2:1	64GB	REDO2	Redo disks – Oracle ASM	SP-B
RAID Group 1, RAID 1+0	LUN 22	SCSI 2:2	64GB	REDO3	Redo disks – Oracle ASM	SP-A
RAID Group 1, RAID 1+0	LUN 23	SCSI 2:3	64GB	REDO4	Redo disks – Oracle ASM	SP-B

In this lab example, RAID 1+0 was used for the Oracle redo disks and RAID 5 for the Oracle data disks. Customer deployments may differ in their RAID choices, and they should follow the database best practices recommended by their specific storage array vendor.

For each LUN, a storage processor was chosen as the default owner so that the storage array service processors were evenly balanced.

Workload Test

The load was based on the Swingbench Large-Scale Order Entry Benchmark, which was implemented as follows:

- A single Swingbench load generator was used that was load balanced to evenly spread user load across Oracle RAC nodes.

- Minimum and maximum think time = 5 and 10ms.

- Performance data was collected using VMware rEsxtop and Oracle AWR (Automatic Workload Repository) reports.

- One thousand users were loaded and run continuously over a 24-hour period.

Now we describe the steps to install and create partial templates for the virtualized RAC environment. This is the point at which the DBA becomes a vRAC-DBA.

Oracle RAC Installation Overview

Figure 6-20 shows a flow diagram of the high-level steps required to install Oracle RAC on the virtualized platform. The diagram consists of 4 "swim lanes," which constitute separate categories of steps. The steps highlighted in other shades of gray can easily be included in a template. The OS and some basic storage elements should be included in the building of the template, which can then be used to add a VM to an existing virtualized RAC cluster (for the purpose of adding a new RAC node). The template can also be used to build out entirely new virtualized RAC clusters.

A final point is that although the process is quite sophisticated, VMware Professional Services offers a specific service to create templates to include each step in the greater process displayed here. Other elite VMware Oracle implementation partners have successfully taken different approaches to creating comprehensive templates for entire RAC systems.

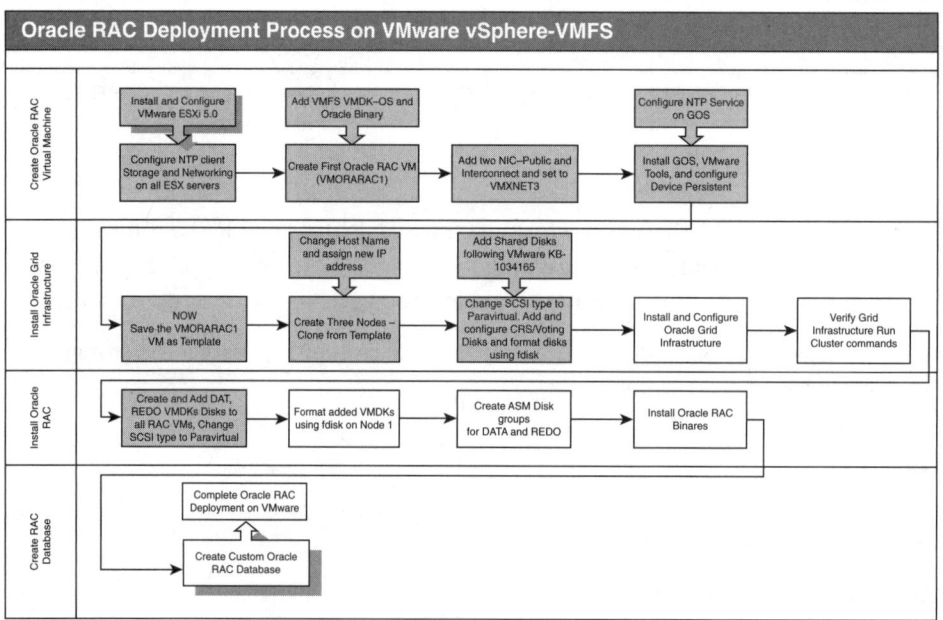

Figure 6-20 Oracle RAC installation on VMware VMFS

Finally, we extended the RAC workload characterization test to run for an entire 24 hours.

24-Hour Workload Test

This section describes the results of the 24-hour workload test. Performance results were obtained from the following:

- Performance data captured by the VMware rEsxtop utility viewed in Windows Performance Monitor

- Output data from the Oracle SwingBench generator

- Oracle Automatic Workload Repository (AWR) report based on snapshots taken at the beginning and end of the run

Table 6-7 summarizes some of the key findings.

Table 6-7 24-Hour Workload Test Results

Result	Value
Total runtime	24 hours
Swingbench average transactions per second	12,787
Swingbench maximum transactions rate	804,191
Swingbench average response time	35ms
CPU utilization of each Oracle RAC node (during last 12 hours)	90% to 93% approximately (Source: vCenter performance charts)
ESX host core utilization (during last 12 hours)	88% to 92% (approximately)
Total IOPS (all four Oracle RAC nodes)	32,000 to 36,000 (approximately)

The results show the following:

- Workload stabilized in the last 12–15 hours of the run such that all the performance counters leveled out.

- The workload was evenly distributed across the four Oracle RAC nodes. Each node showed similar CPU utilization (90%+) and generated a similar number of IOPS (8,000–9,000 approximately).

- The redo LUN latency was less than 10ms after the workload leveled out. Values below the 10ms threshold indicate good I/O performance (see *Using Esxtop to Identify Storage Performance Issues* at VMware KB:1008205). The 10ms threshold is a guideline, and it is possible for applications to experience satisfactory response times with higher disk latencies.

- The approximate interconnect traffic measured by the Oracle AWR report was 146MBps. rEsxtop network counters reflected similar numbers.

- The AWR top five wait events for the 24-hour period demonstrates that latency due to the Oracle RAC interconnect was less than 5%.

- Overall throughput of Swingbench transactions did not degrade, and there were zero transaction errors.

Oracle RAC Node vMotion Test

This section describes the results of an Oracle RAC node vMotion test. It demonstrates the elimination of application downtime from planned server maintenance. The use case assumes live migration is initiated at a time when workload is not at peak so that one ESX host can temporarily host two Oracle RAC nodes. (vCPU overcommitment occurs when the total number of vCPUs exceeds the number of cores on a host.) This consolidation is possible without impact to transaction performance as long as the CPU utilization of two Oracle RAC nodes can be sustained on one ESX host.

All the results were obtained from the following:

- Performance data captured by the VMware rEsxtop utility

- Output data from the Oracle Swingbench generator

- Oracle cluster logs and database alert logs

Table 6-8 shows the configuration of four virtualized Oracle RAC nodes and the respective ESXi hosts.

Table 6-8 Oracle RAC Node vMotion Test Configuration

ESX Host	RAC Node VM	# of vCPUs	Memory (GB)	Oracle SGA (GB)
ESX1 – 12-Core, 192GB RAM	VMORARAC1	8	64	40
ESX2 – 12-Core, 192GB RAM	VMORARAC2	8	64	40
ESX3 – 12-Core, 192GB RAM	VMORARAC3	8	64	40
ESX4 – 12-Core, 192GB RAM	VMORARAC4	8	64	40

The intent of the configuration is to establish a definition for the server constituting the RAC node. The following is the procedure for testing Oracle RAC node vMotion migration:

1. All four nodes are running with their respective ESXi hosts (see Figure 6-21). The Swingbench Large-Scale Order Entry Benchmark was run against all four nodes with 400 users. ESXi2 must be taken down for hardware maintenance (such as a firmware upgrade).

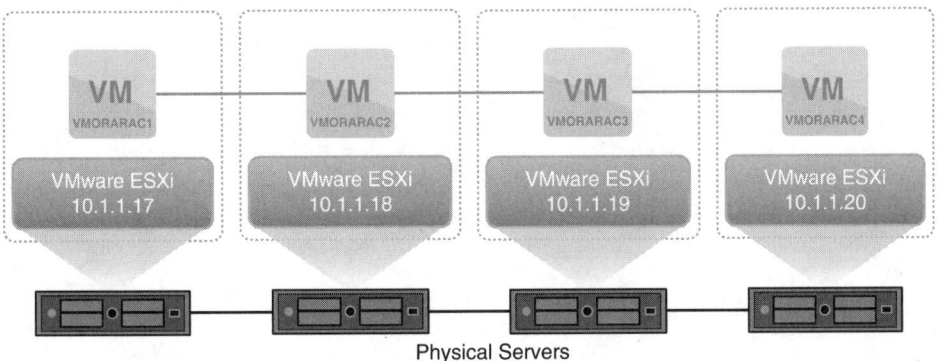

Figure 6-21 Four-node Oracle RAC with four ESXi hosts

Migrate the Oracle RAC node VMORARAC2 from ESXi2 (10.1.1.18) to ESXi4 (10.1.1.20) so that ESXi2 can be taken down for a firmware upgrade (see Figure 6-22).

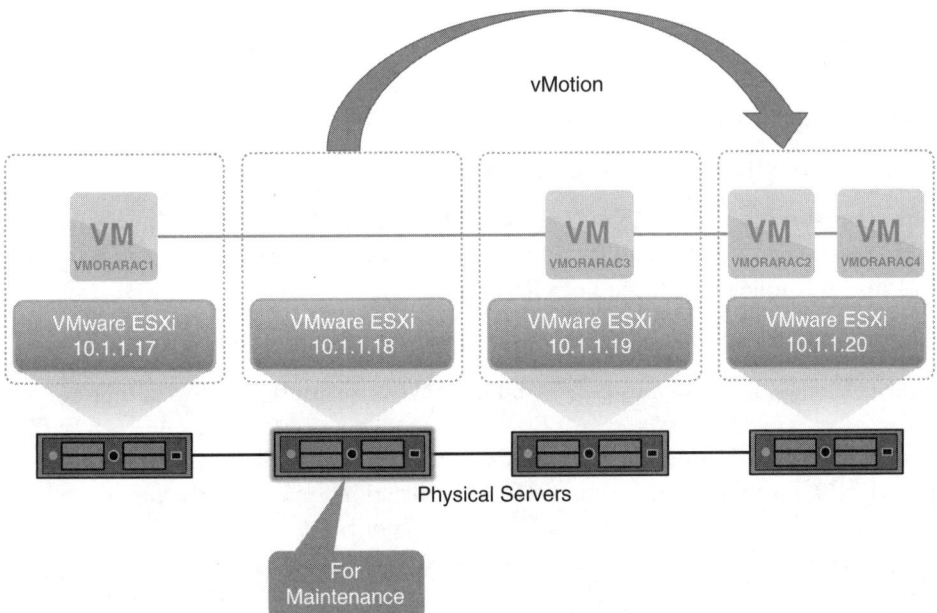

Figure 6-22 Oracle RAC node 2 migration to ESXi Host 4

2. After the hardware maintenance is completed on ESX2, move VMORARAC2 from ESXi4 (10.1.1.20) back to ESXi2 (10.1.1.18), as shown in Figure 6-23.

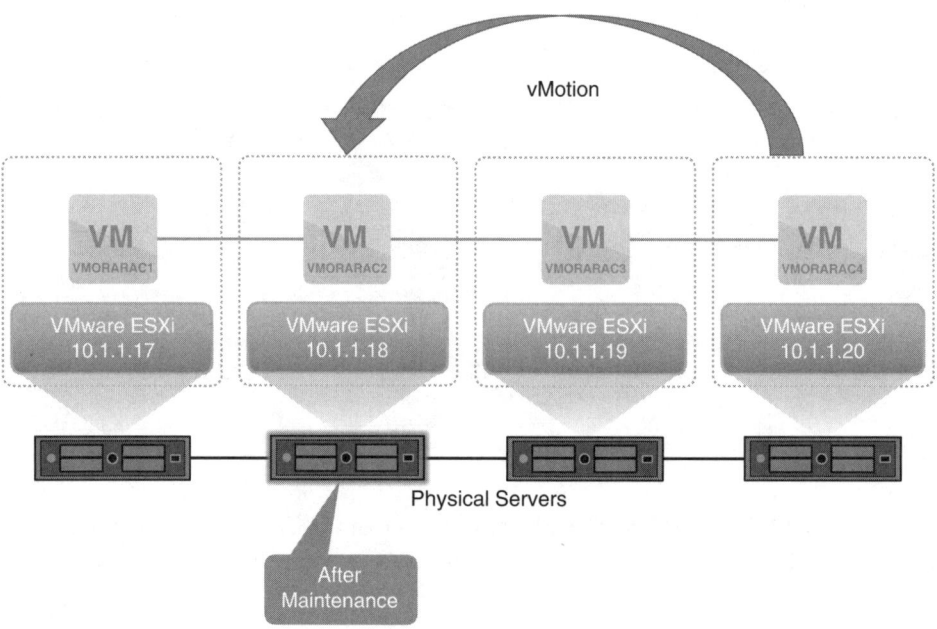

Figure 6-23 RAC node 2 migration to ESXi Host 2

Results show the following:

- CPU usage on all four ESXi hosts was approximately 40% to 41%.

- After migration of VMORARAC2 (RAC node 2) from ESXi2 to ESXi4, ESX4i had a CPU usage of 80% to 81%. CPU of this host was not saturated, which shows that it was able to handle the loads of both RAC nodes.

- Transactions per minute (TPM) are similar before and after vMotion migration.

- Oracle database logs and cluster logs did not have errors during vMotion migration.

The chart in Figure 6-24 shows the CPU utilization of both the ESXi2 (10.1.1.18) and ESXi4 (10.1.1.20) host during vMotion test. CPU utilization for ESXi4 is approximately 80% to 81%, which is the sum of the two Oracle RAC nodes (VMORARAC2, approximately 40%; and VMORARAC4, approximately 41%).

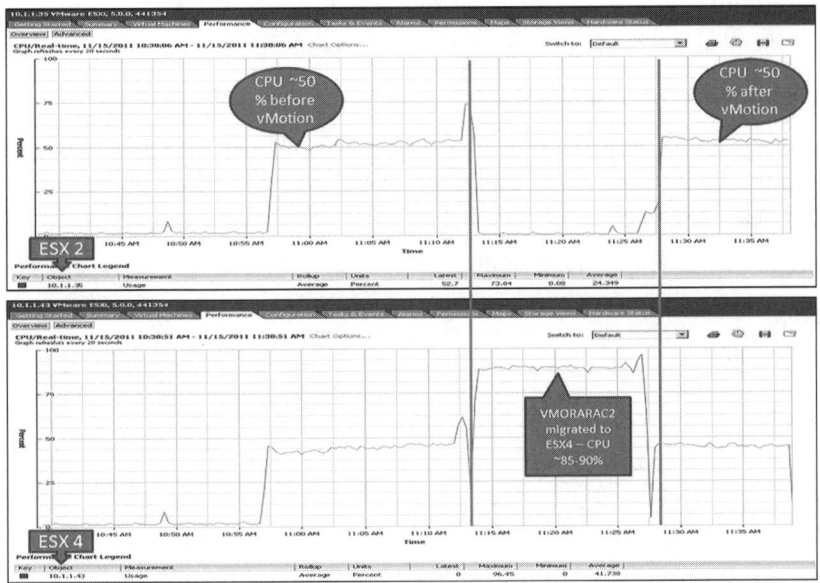

Figure 6-24 Host CPU utilization during vMotion test: vCenter chart

Mega vMotion-RAC Functional Stress Test

Throughout 2013, a collaborative effort (first described in Chapter 5, "Oracle Database High Availability: Planned and Unplanned Downtime") between EMC, VMW, and Cisco, along with Principled Technologies, built a robust stack for the purpose of conducting a functional stress test focused on Oracle RAC working in conjunction with vMotion under very high stress. One of the main purposes of this test was to prove the 100% abstraction between the OS and the hardware. This point could be made intuitively obvious by subjecting the RAC nodes to extremely high stress and utilizing vMotion (as described earlier in the RAC workload characterization study). In this case, however, the study group increased the proverbial stakes significantly. All (three) RAC nodes were transitioned to different physical hosts in the ESXi cluster via vMotion simultaneously. The amazing implications of this test were self-evident. It simply does not matter whether Oracle is running on virtualized hardware or nonvirtualized hardware with the non-paravirtualized hypervisor ESXi. Since that landmark moment, a number of tests have replicated this initial effort. Those tests serve as validations of the original effort. The original stack, which included some of the most capable storage that EMC or the industry in general has to offer, and the Cisco blades and networking, which are equally as impressive, show the impressive overall capability that exists in a well thought-out system tied together by vSphere. Some details of the stack and the test are described here, and the complete report is available at the Principled Technologies website and referred below.

http://www.principledtechnologies.com/VMware/vMotion_Oracle_RAC_1013.pdf

The statement that Oracle RAC and vMotion are completely complementary technologies has been repeated in this book. It should be repeated because it is very important because even RAC nodes often need server-side availability.

The hardware was chosen and configured as follows:

- **Chassis/fabric:**

    - Cisco UCS 5108 chassis

    - 2x Cisco Fabric Interconnects 6248UP

    - 2x Nexus 5548UP switches

- **Compute:**

    - 3x Cisco B200 M3 blades

    - 384GB RAM

- **Storage:**

    - EMC VMAX Cloud Edition (VMAX 10K 1 engine)

    - 48GB usable cache, 96GB raw

    - Drives: 16 – 2TB SATA, 106 – 300GB FC 15K, 24 – 100GB SSD

    - Service levels: Silver2, Gold4, Diamond1

The software was chosen and configured as follows:

- **Hypervisor and management:**

    - VMware vSphere 5.1

    - VMware vCenter Server 5.1

- **Guest OS:** Oracle Enterprise Linux 6.4 x86_64 Red Hat Kernel
- **Database:**

    - Oracle database 11gR2 for Linux 64-bit (11.2.0.3)

    - Oracle Grid 11gR2 for Linux 64-bit (11.2.0.3)

- **Test Harness:**
    - Benchmark Factory for Databases 6.9.1
    - Oracle Client for Windows

The OS and the Oracle instance configuration:

- **Guest:**
    - Six vCPUs
    - 156GB RAM, 145GB Oracle SGA
    - Three NICs
    - Tuned profile: Enterprise storage

- **Database configuration:**
    - Redo logs: Gold service level
    - Data files: Diamond service level
    - VM OS files: Gold service level

The tests:

- One large VM per blade, for a total of three VMs
- Approximately 1-hour TPC-C like test load
- Initiated three vMotion events
    - **Single vMotion:** VM from HostA to HostB
    - **Double vMotion:** VM from HostA to HostB, and VM from HostB to HostA
    - **Triple vMotion (merry go round):** VM from HostA to HostB, VM from HostB to HostC, and VM from HostC to HostA

Figure 6-25 shows the multiple vMotion operations. All three logical RAC node VMs are simultaneously migrated between the existing hosts.

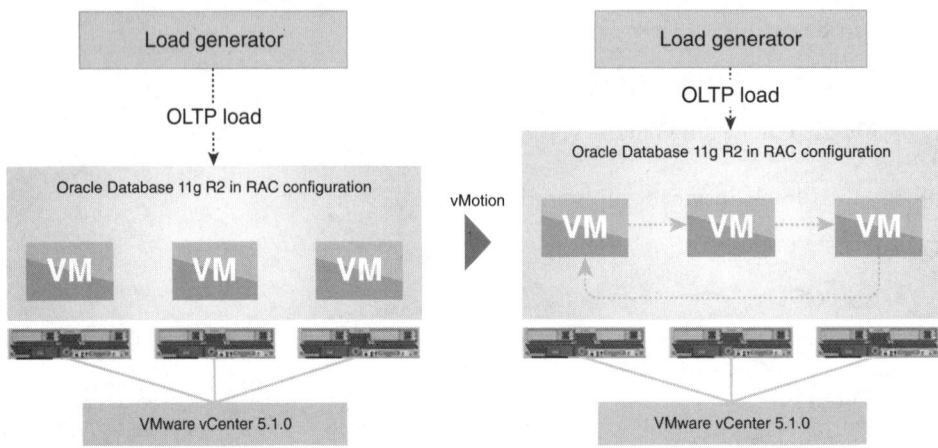

Figure 6-25 Multiple concurrent Oracle RAC vMotion operation

Figure 6-26 shows the hardware used in the concurrent vMotion study. The Cisco UCS servers acted as the ESXi hosts, and the VMAX Cloud Edition was used for the storage array. This impressive stack was used to display the equally impressive capabilities of vSphere. The load was generated with the intention of simulating the most intensive workload environment that a customer may encounter so that the subsequent vMotion operations would surpass anyone's most lofty expectations.

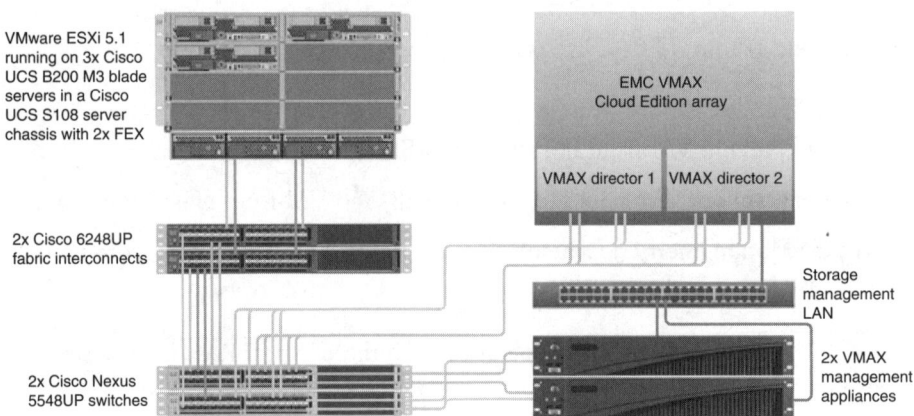

Figure 6-26 Physical architecture for concurrent vMotion

Summary

The business value of the complementary nature of Oracle Real Applications Clusters (RAC) and vSphere is self-evident. The workload and functional tests described in this chapter highlight the undeniable fact that Oracle is enhanced when run on virtualized infrastructure. Oracle RAC is the most sophisticated and powerful database management technology in history, but it is difficult to implement and expensive to maintain because those high-priced vRAC DBAs do not work cheap.

Although it can be easily argued that the great majority of RAC implementations are the product of excessive caution in the approach to system availability and ubiquitous access to sophisticated technology, many RAC implementations are totally appropriate. It is often the case that the application SLA truly does require extreme levels of HA. Of course, there are other valid reasons to use RAC, including the multi-instance scalability, partial rolling-patch ability, and the DBA's desire to increase his professional standing. However, as time marches on in IT, the most prevalent reason to use RAC is the extreme levels of HA that can be provided with a well-conceived RAC design. This is why RAC running on vSphere makes sense. In the absence of increased node evictions and significant performance degradation, the features and capabilities of vSphere, including vMotion, provide a compelling argument to run RAC on vSphere.

The Principled Technologies test has gained significant notoriety and garnered tremendous visibility for the simple fact that when running these high stress tests, nothing happened: no RAC node ejections, false or otherwise; no fencing operations either. In fact, nothing noteworthy happened at all. But what emerges from within this seemingly boring result set is the breathtakingly profound notion that virtualized hardware works just as effectively as nonvirtualized hardware. The remainder of this book is dedicated to communicating the broad value of vSphere (there appears the second *V*), and one should ask this simple question: *If virtualized hardware is as effective as nonvirtualized hardware and if the overhead of virtualization is near negligible, why wouldn't I embrace the idea?*

## Chapter 7

Support and Licensing

Contemplating Oracle Software Support and Licensing

The increasing virtualization of infrastructure for Oracle software raises important questions regarding the impact of virtualization on Oracle support and licensing. Unfortunately, in this space, confusion often rules the day. The purpose of this section is to provide customers with information about certification, support, and licensing of Oracle software when running on virtualized hardware with VMware vSphere. This information is based on the experience and knowledge that has been accumulated from years of working with many customers who are successfully running Oracle on vSphere.

In the context of the four V's (viability, value, versatility, and vision; see Figure 7-1), which are thematic to this book, nothing is more important to the acceptance of the viability of running Oracle on vSphere than the details pertaining to how the software is supported and how it is licensed. Support and licensing constitute the true essence of the viability discussion. Misinformation runs rampant here, whether spread through negligence or worse, and the result is considerable confusion in the industry. Directly stated, Oracle software running on vSphere has been supported by Oracle since the introduction of MetaLink Note 249212.1 in 2007. And licensing Oracle software on virtualized infrastructure, if planned with care, should not add additional expense to the joint customers of Oracle and VMware. There are side cases, some of which will be addressed in the pages of this chapter, but ultimately the specific details of the licensing arrangements are the sole province of the relationship between Oracle and the Oracle customer and the details of the resulting contracts. However, remember that all red herrings are most effective when they are both distracting and deceptive, and often what is commonly misconstrued about Oracle on vSphere support and licensing aptly parallels this description.

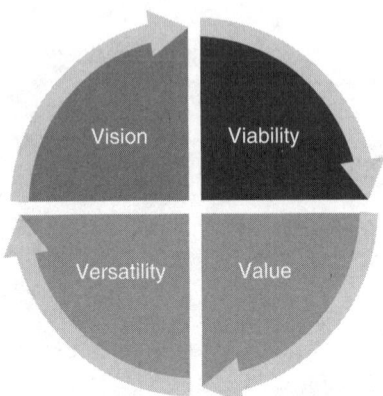

Figure 7-1 Four V's approach

There is a shared understanding throughout the community of Oracle professionals with regard to the lofty status of the experienced Oracle database administrator (DBA). This perception is even higher for those information technology (IT) professionals who embrace virtualization technologies, especially VMware. This widespread consensus about the Oracle DBA extends from the singular importance of that role under the most consequential circumstances that inevitably confront each and every company: the prospect of catastrophic data loss. In this regard, there is a particular, albeit unofficial, status that is often attained by the veteran Oracle DBA. This almost mythical status is independent of official rank, compensation, or title. This standing is as irrespective to personal income as it is transparent to any of the more worldly attributes of modern commerce.

In matters involving data, the opinions and positions of the experienced Oracle DBA, especially management-level Oracle DBAs, are often adhered to without question. At very least, the advice tendered by the veteran DBA is often considered a vital component in any decision-making process that involves data. This is understandable because Oracle software is often the most important and expensive software in an enterprise and because it often stores and protects companies' most important and valuable asset, their data. Oracle products can be extremely complicated and unwieldy to manage, and at the time of a crisis, an Oracle DBA who can successfully recover invaluable data that would otherwise be lost to the ether becomes quite simply the most valuable person in that company.

It is the combination of years of professional interest in this most sophisticated relational database management system (RDBMS) and the composure of a Major League Baseball relief pitcher that renders this mythical status to the Oracle DBA. In this sense, the Oracle DBA is similar to the Praetorian Guard of ancient Rome. The Praetorian Guard was initially instituted by Augustus Caesar (wisely realizing that given Julius Caesar's demise, a change of approach to security was necessary) through the selection of the most loyal and elite fighters from the Roman legions. This elite group (and early form of the "secret service") was charged with protecting the most important assets of the emperor (which, of course, was the emperor himself and his family), and they were paid accordingly. However, an unintended consequence was that they had influence well beyond their apparent official status and pay grade. Emperors of later years (most notably Caligula and Nero, who were assassinated by this same group) would learn to neither ignore the Praetorian Guard nor inspire their enmity. So today, as it is with the Oracle DBA, where the Praetorian Guard of data protects perhaps the most important asset of the modern institutions of our age. This analogy has been posed to help those who are interested in the virtualization of their infrastructure for their Oracle software to understand that without the support of the Oracle DBAs, the likelihood of strategic success in this effort is low. The Oracle DBA must understand the viability of this proposition, and often that discussion must start with the realities of Oracle support.

This chapter does not provide official policies or legal advice concerning a customer's license or support agreement with Oracle or any third party. Customers should always discuss these issues directly with Oracle. The detail of a customer's contract is more important than an expert opinion or otherwise (any blog entry, any conference session, any conversation with any sales team, or any section in any book). In other words, there is no shortage of opinions on how all this works. Note that in many cases the resolution of these issues depends on the specific commercial relationship between the customer and Oracle. So, this chapter is intended to help customers understand the issues and better prepare for discussions with Oracle as well as with third-party vendors.

Understanding Oracle Certification and Support for VMware Environments

Oracle has an official support policy for virtualization on VMware vSphere, articulated in My Oracle Support (formerly known as MetaLink) document ID 249212.1, which customers can access with a valid My Oracle Support login. In November 2010, Oracle extended this support policy to include Oracle Real Application Clusters (RAC 11.2.0.2 or later) on vSphere. VMware sees this as a tacit acknowledgment by Oracle both that customers are increasingly running even their most mission-critical systems on vSphere and that vSphere is a technically sound platform for running these applications. The support extension was not accompanied by any particular recommendation, restriction, or limitation (other than the version number of RAC). That extension inspired a number of enthusiastic and dedicated individuals from VMware to immediately produce the RAC Deployment Guide, in which a number of different methods for deploying RAC on vSphere are discussed along with the recommended methodology of using Virtual Machine File System (VMFS) with the SCSI multi-writer flag (SMWF).

Certification of Oracle on VMware vSphere

The first line of the support statement 249212.1 states that Oracle has not certified any of its products on VMware vSphere. This makes sense because Oracle, in the case of software, certifies to the operating system (OS) layer and third-party infrastructure elements below the OS are generally not considered. However, the "certification" of complete or partial stacks does occur often, resulting in reference architectures that are widely promoted as those architectures that have been carefully constructed and, therefore, have well-known and documented performance profiles. It is also true that even in the nonvirtualized world (some would still use the term *physical*), the idea of certifying the plethora of permutations of hardware is simply impractical. Of course, it is often the case that individual hardware companies, such as HP, Dell, or IBM, have the option of executing the certification kits from Oracle that are readily downloadable. You can find links to the certification kits on Oracle's public website. For quick reference, go to www.oracle.com/webfolder/technetwork/hcl/overview.html for an example of the hardware certification process.

Hardware companies often complete the certification process for very specific hardware components. Regardless of a certification process, though, customers normally do not allow this to limit their choice of deployment platforms. The Oracle hardware division (formerly Sun Microsystems) has a public website specifically for the Sun Fire x86 server series, which lists a variety of different Sun Fire products. This list includes hardware and software components of the stacks, some of which contain vSphere. Customers exercise their options by deploying on noncertified hardware because certification has no relation to support. You can find links to the information pertaining to the Sun Fire systems on Oracle's public website.

https://wikis.oracle.com/display/SystemsComm/Sun+Server+X2-4

https://wikis.oracle.com/display/SystemsComm/Sun+Server+X2-8

http://sun.systemnews.com/articles/141/1/Performance/22439

Although Oracle officially certifies only its own virtualization product, customers should not allow this to limit their options. As in the physical world, customers should choose the virtualization platform that best meets their needs. As long as customers run a certified OS on VMware, and that OS is certified to Oracle software, customers should feel confident that rigorous testing has occurred across the different layers of the stack. The next section covers some attributes of the Oracle support process. It is also interesting to note that Oracle has certified its Linux variant, Oracle Enterprise Linux, with the specialized kernel known as the Unbreakable Enterprise Kernel (UEK) to vSphere. You can find these links to information about the UEK on Oracle's public website.

http://linux.oracle.com/hardware-certifications

In addition, for quick reference, go to http://virtualization.info/en/news/2013/10/oracle-linux-fully-supported-to-run-on-vmware-esxi-and-hyper-v.html for more information.

Obtaining Oracle Support

Oracle has an official support statement for VMware, which is My Oracle Support document 249212.1, as mentioned earlier. The Oracle support policy states that "Oracle will only provide support for issues that either are known to occur on the native OS, or can be demonstrated not to be as a result of running on VMware." This statement can create a perception that customers are somehow at risk, but customers running Oracle on VMware vSphere (an exponentially growing number) have chosen to do so after carefully weighing the benefits against this implied but obscure risk. We believe that three considerations are especially relevant to the assessment:

You can evaluate the risk (or lack thereof) by considering the following facts:

- VMware ESX/ESXi is a Type 1, non-paravirtualized hypervisor and therefore does not modify the native (guest) OS, so the solution Oracle provides for the native OS is fully expected to work for that same OS running on VMware vSphere. Summarizing this most important point and reiterating one of the main pillars of the Oracle on vSphere proposition: Oracle does not change when running on virtualized hardware (where as all software may be affected when running on a paravirtualized hypervisor). The well-honed skills of the Oracle DBA do not change when Oracle is running on vSphere.

- At the time of this writing, VMware has received no reports of incidents in which ESX/ESXi/vSphere was determined to have caused or been the root cause of a technical issue in an Oracle application or database.

- In a worst-case scenario, Oracle might ask a customer to reproduce the issue on different hardware, particularly if Oracle's proposed solution fails. This request is seldom made, and often dismissed when properly handled, especially when the customer involves VMware's Global Support Services (GSS) Oracle Support team. Even in the nonvirtual world, Oracle or any software vendor reserves the right to request reproduction on different physical hardware in a similar situation. In fact, this disclaimer constitutes the exact same support proposition for any software running on any hardware, virtualized or nonvirtualized. It is intuitively obvious that if the party responsible for one part of a stack believes that the cause of a presented problem occurs in an area of the stack that they do not own, that party will request that the customer either involve the vendor in question or simply ask the customer to prove that the responsibility for the problem is theirs to begin with. Unfortunately, this type of "passing of the buck" happens far too often in the IT industry.

Obtaining Oracle Support from VMware

VMware GSS has an elite Oracle Support team. At the time of this writing, the GSS Oracle Support team accepts all Oracle-related technical service calls. This gives the customer two separate channels of obtaining expert assistance when running Oracle on vSphere. Obviously, the VMware Oracle support team does not write patches for Oracle software, and they do not configure applications (as that is the province of the VMware Professional Services Organization as well as the VMware Oracle implementation partners). However, they do accept any and all tickets related to Oracle, maintain active status on that ticket until its resolution, and open tickets on behalf of the customer with Oracle Support under the rare circumstances that they cannot solve a particular issue. Through TSANet (www.tsanet.org/), tickets can be opened between vendors to facilitate thorough and seamless support for customers, especially when multiple vendors participate in the construction of a particular customer's stack. TSANet works as a "Geneva Convention" of sorts for technology vendors, giving the customer access to collaborative support for the more challenging technical issues that may be presented. Oracle and VMware both actively participate in TSANet collaborations for the benefit of their mutual customers on a regular basis.

Figure 7-2 describes the VMware GSS Oracle Support process flow.

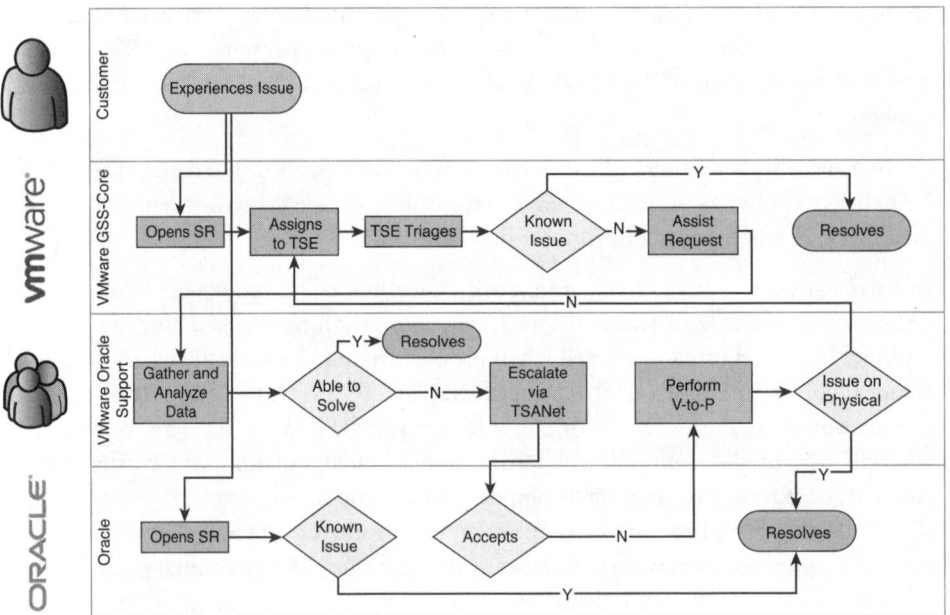

Figure 7-2 VMware GSS process flow diagram

Negotiating with Oracle

A customer can seek to negotiate the terms in their support agreement with Oracle and insist that Oracle provide the support commitment that meets that individual customer's needs. This, of course, may include support for Oracle products running on vSphere. It is important to work through the details of an individual contract to attain clarity with regards to Oracle support for Oracle products running on any platform, virtualized or nonvirtualized.

VMware has its own policy to support customers running Oracle applications on VMware. The VMware support policy link is easily accessible from the VMware website. For quick reference, go to www.vmware.com/support/policies/oracle-support.html for more information. VMware accepts all Oracle software-related requests for support from VMware customers who are current on their production-level support contracts. An Oracle-related service request (SR) will be addressed in its entirely as a best effort attempt to provide a solution to the comprehensive problem. If ambiguity as to the root cause of a particular presented problem persists, GSS may open a ticket with Oracle Support through TSANet.

The document titled "Understanding Certification, Support and Licensing Guide" describes the VMware positions and policies in exacting detail. You can find the link on VMware's public website along with the link to the VMware support policy regarding Oracle.

http://www.vmware.com/files/pdf/techpaper/
vmw-understanding-oracle-certification-supportlicensing-environments.pdf

https://www.vmware.com/support/policies/oracle-support

As shown earlier, VMware will take ownership of the SR and pursue rapid resolution, in collaboration with the Oracle Support organization through TSANet, as necessary. Because VMware customers virtualize all types of Tier 1 and business-critical applications, the VMware GSS Oracle Support team has significant interest in making this a seamless support experience. This team has tremendous experience in solving Oracle-related technical issues and a success rate to back up these claims.

The GSS-Oracle Support Team was represented by Matt Scott on a panel moderated by manager Mike Matthies at VMworld 2014 San Francisco. Matt elaborated on the process to engage this elite team as well as their success rate.

Licensing Oracle

It is axiomatic that as effective consolidation of IT resources is accomplished, the overall cost of IT is reduced. Storage, networking, and server consolidation results in lower hardware costs. Software consolidation results in lower licensing expenditures. The respective reduction in support costs should also be acknowledged. Consolidation, in general, will result in material floor space reduction within the physical datacenter, which results in lower power consumption. In addition, general consolidation will result in more effective use of vital and expensive personnel.

Note, as well, that in the absence of a reduction in resource consumption, those resources can be used much more effectively when deployed in virtualized infrastructure. Virtualization facilitates cost savings at every step in the stack and every aspect of the overall IT footprint. In that sense, VMware epitomizes a "green" company through the lessened power consumption from efficient datacenter consolidation using virtualized infrastructure. Some companies produce television commercials bragging about how they have reduced power consumption by x% and are therefore leaders in environmental awareness. VMware has helped countless numbers of companies accomplish the same thing. The theoretical example in Figure 7-3 depicts how a customer might achieve significant savings when consolidating with vSphere.

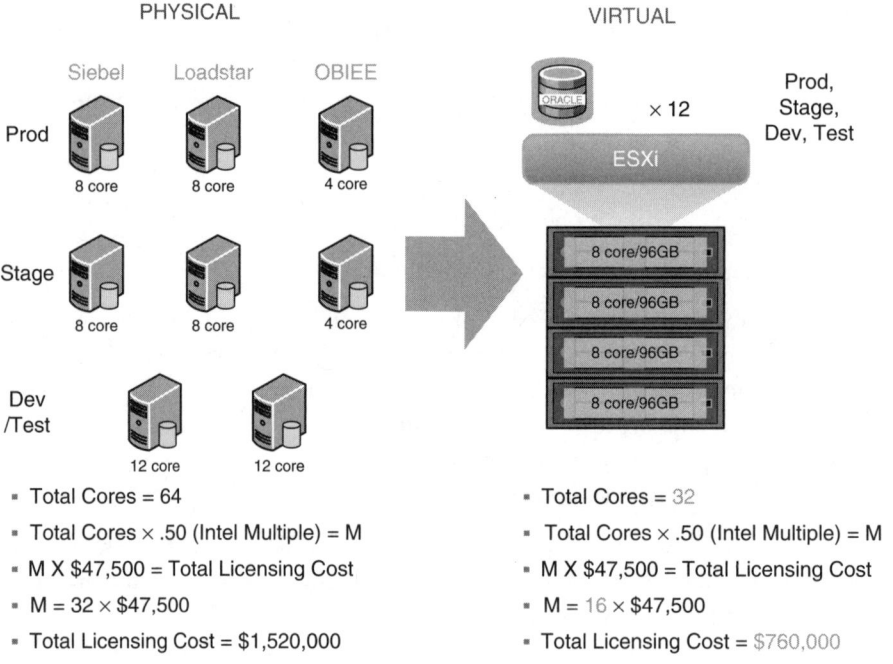

Enterprise Edition Pricing per *Oracle Technology Global Price List*, July 3, 2014

Figure 7-3 VMware Oracle licensing example

Any reduction in the usage of a particular part of an IT system will reduce the respective expense of that entity. So it is true that when a customer uses fewer Oracle licenses or runs their Oracle software on fewer physical servers, the overall expense of that software and the respective support is reduced.

Advising VMware Customers

Over the years, VMware has dedicated significant resources to helping their customers understand the implications of individual third-party application licensing when running that software on virtualized infrastructure. Each vendor has its own policies and methodologies for maximizing its application revenue. Some vendors have explicit models for licensing their application when running on virtualized infrastructure, and some ignore the presence of virtualization. VMware has developed a guide that specifically addresses the concepts behind Oracle licensing on vSphere: "Understanding Oracle Certification, Support and Licensing Guide for VMware Environments." (This 2011 document covers important aspects of how VMware customers successfully and logically architect Oracle on vSphere to most effectively utilize their IT budget.) VMware fully acknowledges the fact that ultimately any agreements, whether they are standard arrangements or customized arrangements, regarding Oracle licensing on vSphere (or any other platform) are solely the province of Oracle Corporation and the individual customer. In other words, regardless of any information in publicly available documents (that are usually accompanied with disclaimers indicating that they are for educational purposes only), blogs, and opinion pieces or conference sessions, the determinative information is found in the individual contracts.

VMware also emphatically advises that customers properly license each and every server that Oracle software runs on. Oracle has many available public documents that discuss the various aspects of Oracle licensing to include the differences between Enterprise and Standard licensing as well as the ideas of "Named User Plus" licensing. This chapter does not attempt to cover all the nuances of Oracle licensing as much as describe the approaches that the joint customers of Oracle and VMware have utilized when successfully licensing.

In 2012, VMware solidified this position by dedicating prized session slots at both VMworld San Francisco and VMworld Europe in Barcelona to the narrow subject of Oracle licensing. The Barcelona session was recorded and provides useful insight into effectively approaching the general idea of Oracle licensing. For more information on this session, simply search VMware's public website: http://www.vmworld.com/docs/DOC-6144. A simple web search will reveal a plethora of blogs, interviews, and documents that describe the various approaches to licensing Oracle on vSphere.

The partners who participated in the 2012 sessions focused on Oracle licensing in the virtualized environment greatly enhanced the global understanding of this subject. Daniel Hesselink, from License Consulting, presented on both continents, as did representatives of iQuate on their license discovery product iQSonar. A special guest speaker was Judica Krikke, from Stibbe, who spoke to the legal implications of the licensing question. There were other interesting sessions and interviews from that VMworld season, including a very interesting interview about the validity of using host affinity for restriction and management of Oracle servers.

https://www.youtube.com/watch?v=FuXBMS2UwyE&feature=youtu.be

http://www.licenseconsulting.eu/2012/08/29/
vmworld-richard-garsthagen-oracle-on-licensing-vmware-virtualized-environments/

Licensing Oracle Using Three Approaches

In the absence of a virtualization model for licensing from Oracle, VMware and Oracle customers need to consider three approaches to license Oracle software efficiently. To present these approaches clearly, it is important to be precise. For example, the word *cluster* is used many times throughout Oracle documentation. In this book, we use the term cluster to refer to an ESX/ESXi/vSphere cluster. Clustering generally refers to the notion of a set of computers loosely connected through a network managed by a set of membership algorithms and some type of quorum paradigm. The word *partitioning* is almost always confused with regard to not only the differences between *hard* and *soft* partitioning but also the term is often applied to areas of vSphere technology that have nothing to do with "partitioning" of any kind. Hard partitioning refers to the direct connection of physical resources to autonomous servers sharing certain resources all connected through an electrical backplane within a large single frame. Soft partitioning is discussed in the following sections. The word *affinity* is often misused as well. We will carefully use these terms in their proper context.

Implementing the Isolated ESXi Cluster Approach

The most common approach to licensing Oracle on vSphere is the simple idea of creating a dedicated vSphere cluster. The customer will properly "right-size" each virtual machine (VM) so that every hertz of processing power on every core on every socket on every node is dedicated to Oracle to include available headroom for potential failovers. The great majority of VMware/Oracle customers take this approach when licensing Oracle enterprise software, which creates an unambiguous separation of the nodes within that dedicated ESXi cluster from the remainder of the virtualized environment.

Figure 7-4 shows the isolated ESXi cluster approach.

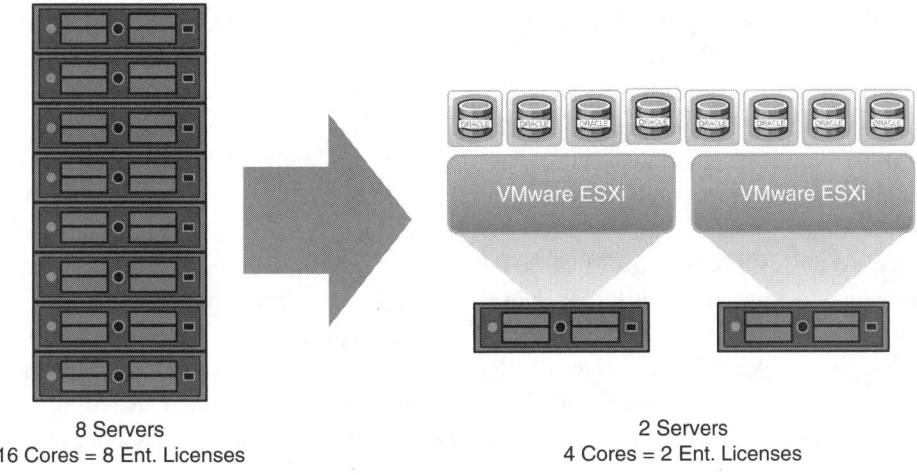

8 Servers
16 Cores = 8 Ent. Licenses

2 Servers
4 Cores = 2 Ent. Licenses

Figure 7-4 Isolated Oracle ESXi cluster

Implementing the Subcluster Approach

Many customers take the approach of licensing using the idea of the logical subcluster. Most of these customers use a feature that was introduced in vSphere 4.1, named DRS/ host affinity, to set the logical boundaries of the subcluster. Host affinity is a feature of Distributed Resource Scheduling (DRS) that sets restrictions on the VMs within an ESXi cluster as to which ESXi hosts a specified VM may be transitioned to automatically. For example, a failure of a VM resulting in a VM failover (a high availability [HA] event) will result in that VM being restarted on a host that is within the lists of hosts allowable based on the rules set up through host affinity. Basically, the system is only allowed to restart that specified VM on the hosts that are designated through the host affinity restrictions.

Also, as DRS attempts to load balance the VMs over the ESXi hosts in the cluster via automatic vMotion, DRS will not move a specified VM outside the boundaries established by the host affinity configuration. Simply put, no automatic movement of a VM will cause the VM in question to be moved to an ESXi host that the VM is prohibited from running on. Logs generated by the main management tool, vCenter, will record all movements of the VMs and be available for audit purposes.

This capability is often confused with "soft partitioning." It is sometimes stated that "VMware is soft partitioning" by individuals who do not understand the technological concepts involved. This assertion is similar to referring to the Empire State Building as a lighthouse. Although this great building, which was once the world's tallest, does produce significant light from its crowning tower, it is obviously far more than a lighthouse. In the same manner, although VMware does possess the capability of soft partitioning, as do all modern virtualization technologies, vSphere does considerably more than soft partitioning. The confusion stems from the use of the word *affinity*. DRS affinity is a mechanism by which vSphere can restrict the automatic movement of an individual VM to a subset of the physical hosts in the greater ESXi cluster. Therefore, no implicit or automatic action, such as an automatic vMotion or even a vSphere HA failover, will result in a VM running on an unintended host. Of course, a VM could be manually moved to a host that has yet to be licensed, which in reality is no different than the fact that at any time that same software could be manually installed on a completely isolated physical machine. The bottom line is that when using DRS affinity to logically define a subcluster, the VMs running Oracle software cannot be run on a node outside the subcluster absent explicit manual action. Figure 7-5 shows an example of an effective architecture, which includes the application of DRS host affinity.

TIP

To prevent manual movement of a VM running Oracle software to an ESXi host that is not licensed to run that software, a VM admin may simply remove access to the virtual machine disk (VMDK) (or raw device mapping [RDM]) that contains the Oracle binaries (Oracle Home) from the hosts that will remain unlicensed.

Figure 7-5 shows an example of a four-host ESXi cluster in which Oracle software is being run on Hosts 1 and 2. Hosts 3 and 4 *cannot* run the displayed Oracle software because the DRS host affinity will not allow any automatic movement to move the VMs running the Oracle software to either of those hosts.

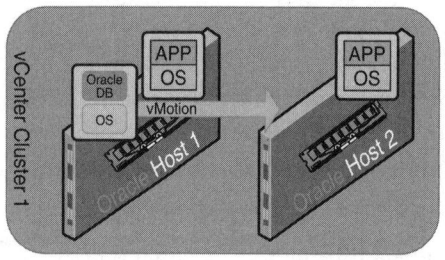

Figure 7-5 Oracle ESXi subcluster

Implementing the Subcapacity Licensing Approach

Often customers would like to license fewer cores than exist on a specific physical host. This is the notion of *subcapacity* licensing. This is the proper use and context of the concept of soft partitioning. A number of terms are often used to describe this form of implementation, including CPU pinning, CPU locking, and *CPU affinity* (there goes that word affinity again). The idea is to lock a particular VM to a specific socket(s). The clear unambiguous theme of Oracle Enterprise licensing, which states that each core on each server that Oracle software is run or installed on must be licensed, results in the following simple conclusion. At the time of this writing, all cores must be licensed on a physical server that is running Oracle software; so therefore, there is no provision for "subcapacity" licensing.

Generally, this is not a roadblock for VMware customers desiring to run Oracle on vSphere. Locking a VM to an individual socket(s) severely limits the capabilities of vSphere for that particular VM because many of the features of vSphere, including vMotion and HA, become either limited or incapacitated. Given these restrictions, it is not advisable for customers to pursue the subcapacity licensing route, and in the absence of a compelling concern, it is not prudent. However, if the customer has a large physical system (for example, an HP DL-980 with 80 cores) and they have a small Oracle instance that they would like to include in their virtual infrastructure, the limitations around subcapacity licensing may prevent the customers from employing this approach entirely. Also, in the case of public Cloud implementations, where by definition the customer does not know how many servers or the physical capacity of those servers that their particular load runs on, the lack of a subcapacity model (licensing by the VM) may be a significant roadblock to the virtualization effort.

It is important to state two points about the idea of subcapacity licensing. First, very few VMware customers are interested in locking VMs to specific sockets because the use of this restrictive feature suppresses and negates some of the most valuable features of vSphere. Under rare circumstances, it makes sense to lock a VM to a socket when using less-capable hypervisor technologies, but when using a true platform of virtualized hardware, the great majority of customers intend on employing the powerful capabilities of vSphere. Second, the great majority of deployments are on systems that have been properly right-sized, so there is no reason to consider the subcapacity approach. Only in the case of public Cloud implementations does the idea of subcapacity licensing become a significant factor.

Summary

The viability of running Oracle on vSphere becomes a legitimate question only after the business factors are considered and settled. Unless the application owners and the upper levels of management are convinced that they will not be required to incur exorbitant and extraneous licensing costs, they will not consider the use of virtualized infrastructure for any of their business-critical applications, including Oracle. In addition, no one would ever consider a profound platform change without the explicit consent of the software vendor. However, a careful examination of the facts and thoughtful discussions with experts should reveal that Oracle software, when run on vSphere, is supported by both Oracle and VMware and, when architected properly, can be achieved in a cost-effective way.

## Chapter 8

Performance Management and Monitoring

This chapter covers the ideas of performance, in addition to the management and monitoring of that performance, of the Oracle database server running on vSphere. All four V's (viability, value, versatility, and vision; see Figure 8-1) are discussed in this subject area. Database administrators (DBAs) need insight into the metrics, which reveal the performance of the database and the levels of the stack that directly and sometimes indirectly affect the running database. The viability of the overall proposition of Oracle running on vSphere is dependent on the performance, and that can be proved only through comprehensive metrics collection and analysis. DBAs are familiar with metric sampling and accumulation through Oracle Enterprise Manager and Automatic Workload Repository (AWR) reports. DBAs are also familiar with the fact that those metrics, which are intimate to the inner workings of the instance, have a long history. From the early days of the awkward use of utlebstat and utlestat, these metrics have not really changed. Of course, the presentation, display, mining methods, and aggregation have changed significantly.

Performance tuning is an art more than a science, and like all artistic endeavors, the proper tools are necessary to ensure that the end product is satisfactory. It is also true that many varied approaches lead to successful results. This chapter focuses on the fundamental concepts of performance tuning and the most effective performance tuning tools, techniques, and approaches. The chapter covers many well-known approaches used by VMware Professional Services (PSO) and Global Technology Solutions (GTS), in addition to approaches used by trusted VMware partners such as House of Brick (HOB). Sections of this chapter parallel material used and developed by VMware and as part of a collaborative effort (sometimes) with partners such as HOB. Note that many ideas in this chapter are often familiar to the career DBA because those concepts have been developed over many years. Those ideas and techniques have survived the test of time. Even the newest and most advanced technological features are often governed by classic well-understood principles. As you progress through this chapter, note the creative approaches to the tuning of Oracle on virtualized infrastructure. It is only when that creativity is rationally and effectively commingled with fundamental principles that effective tuning is accomplished. The vDBAs who can combine the consistency of familiar approaches with techniques that address the specific circumstances of an individual situation will become experts in tuning Oracle on vSphere.

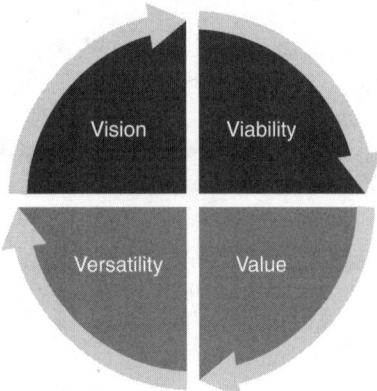

Figure 8-1 Four V's approach

vCenter Operations Manager (vCOPS) is a tool for metrics collection and performance analytics, but many other adapters enable the various administrators who have interest in the virtualized infrastructure to view their application specific data in a context and language that they understand. This point underscores the versatility of the broad product base of VMware. Many logical and physical architectures make sense within the vast set of permutations that vSphere can embrace within the platform of virtualized hardware, and vCOPS will provide value to all of those variations.

The vision of VMware, also known as the software-defined datacenter (SDDC), encompasses the idea of virtualized infrastructure for the entire stack and for all the applications running within each datacenter of every company. DBAs use these performance management and monitoring tools to manage the smallest and largest environments.

To manage and monitor Oracle products on vSphere, the industry offers a number of effective tools. Other industry management and monitoring tools are noted but not discussed in detail in this chapter. For example, Confio's IgniteVM, now called Performance Analyzer and produced by Solar Winds, which provides tremendous optimized visibility into each level of the stack while elegantly tying those elements of the stack to the virtualization layer, is a subject for a different conversation. Another tool, produced by Blue

Medora and known simply as the Oracle Enterprise Manager plug-in for VMware, supports 10g, 11g, and 12c, and is a well-conceived and effective management and monitoring tool. Although these tools, external to VMware, are quite effective and popular, this chapter covers the tools produced by VMware and used by VMware customers. Refer to the individual third-party tools vendor's websites for details. For example refer to Confio's website listed here.

www.confio.com/performance/oracle/vmware/

Performance Management Terminology

The IT industry has a history of overusing certain terms, thus creating a fog of ambiguity around those terms. So, at this point, it will be useful to define certain terms.

The following terms are not only key points that are used when discussing Oracle system performance, but they are also terms that are often used loosely:

- **Cluster:** The most overused term in the industry. Usually the term refers to a set of separate physical hosts loosely connected through a network managed by a set of management algorithms, a heartbeat maintained through an interconnect, and some type of quorum. However, there are many other uses for the term *cluster*.

- **Overhead:** CPU resources needed for the hypervisor on a given physical node. Lower overhead does not necessarily equate to superior performance, because overhead has no impact on performance if adequate CPU resources are available.

- **Response time:** The elapsed time a human operator waits for a screen to refresh, as when activating a drop-down menu or submitting entries in one or more fields for processing. Such operations are also known as online transaction processing (OLTP).

- **Throughput:** The amount of work that can be performed in a given period of time. Throughput can also refer to the elapsed runtime of a batch process or report. Throughput is usually measured in time units and often used in different contexts.

- **Scalability:** System stack capacity to execute multiple jobs or work streams on a server (physical or virtual) in parallel such that the response time of any given screen session and throughput of a batch job or report is not impacted by other jobs or work streams.

- **Latency:** The granular time a processing request spends in a given system stack layer. Processing request response time is the sum of the latencies of each layer in the system stack. For example, a processing request might have a latency of 10ms in the disk subsystem and 2ms in the network, but the total latency in this example, albeit oversimplified, would be 12ms.

- **Isolation:** The degree to which a processing request on a server maintains logical independence and is unaffected by peripheral processing. An isolated operation will retain the same response time or throughput whether running in a dedicated fashion or sharing the server with other sessions or batch jobs.

- **Affinity:** The degree of connection that one entity has to another. For example, often a processor has "affinity" to certain memory segments or a process has "affinity" to a processor. A different use of the term is the feature of host affinity, which is the capability of restricting a VM from automatically moving to any host outside a defined subcluster. Host affinity is described in detail in Chapter 7, "Support and Licensing." However a completely distinct use of the term *affinity* occurs when used in the context of CPU affinity. This ubiquitous capability, which is found in some form in all virtualization technologies, allows a virtual machine (VM) to be pinned (or locked) to a particular processor or set of processors. Host affinity and CPU affinity constitute two completely different uses of the word *affinity*. Note, as well, that we do not recommend using CPU affinity or pinning to manage VMs running Oracle or any business-critical application (BCA).

The Role of the DBA in Performance Management

Virtualization expands the role of an IT administrator to include the DBA. This can be an advantage for the administrators, for IT, and for the overall business. However, this constitutes an important paradigm shift in IT and also requires a significant increase in the attention of those same administrators in the area of performance analysis. To measure performance, the following steps are suggested:

1. Select key performance attributes from these hardware resource groups: I/O, memory, CPU, and network.

2. Adopt average and high water mark metrics for each attribute.

3. When selecting the performance tools, evaluate tools bundled with VMware vSphere, with native Linux, and from the open source community.

4. Author and promote summary conceptual overviews of the performance attributes, the needs they fulfill, and associated service level agreements (SLAs).

5. Regularly publish performance metrics to the organization, including to the C-level and business users.

Figure 8-2 depicts the various levels of the stack, all of which require specific and customized performance analysis.

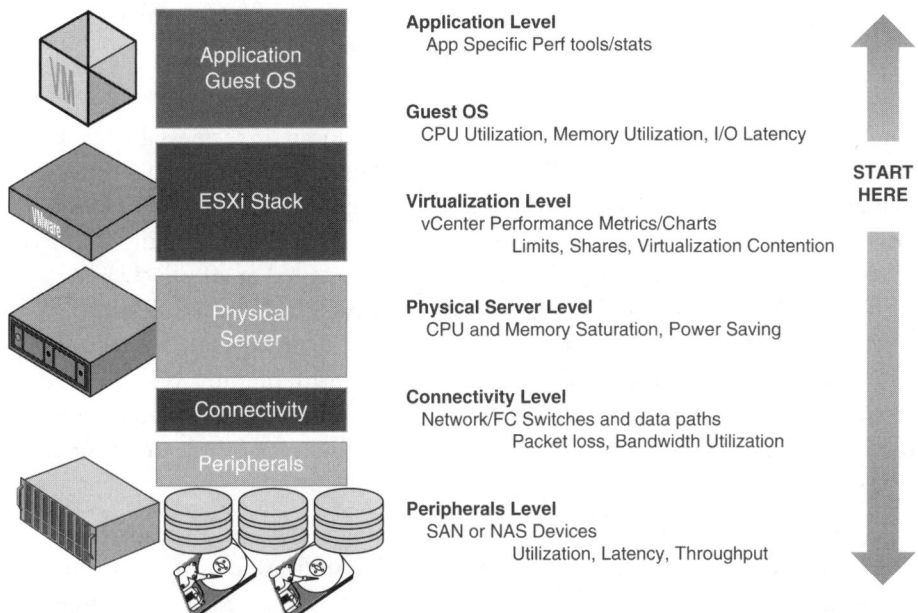

Figure 8-2 Various levels of monitoring

There is significant benefit to IT proactively educating executives and peers on the aspects of performance that directly affect them. For instance, discussing associated SLAs and making the respective performance information easily available when appropriate can enhance communication and project a more positive focus on IT.

To that effort, we separate the dimensions of performance and highlight the more important areas of each dimension. Performance attributes and measurement methods are covered in the "Processing Power, Memory, Networking and Storage Configuration" sections, later in this chapter.

Processing Power: CPU or vCPU

Processing power is generated by the central processing unit (CPU). CPUs exist as microprocessors and fit onto a motherboard on a particular socket. Each socket will have multiple cores, which constitute the individual CPU. In the world of virtualized infrastructure, a virtual CPU (vCPU) will be allocated to a VM. That vCPU is an abstraction from the physical core, so there may be more vCPUs than corresponding cores. This is called overcommitting or oversubscribing of CPU. It should be pointed out that although the use of hyperthreading, as discussed in Chapter 4, "Oracle on vSphere Best Practices," can allow for efficient overcommitment, it is a best practice, when sizing for all high workloads, to not overcommit CPU resources at least until the true CPU usage profile is very well understood.

Determining the proper number of vCPUs that should be allocated is achieved by monitoring the usage through the vSphere CPU performance chart. Overcommitment of CPU resources can cause scheduling problems, as discussed in the section "CPU Ready Time (%RDY)." Properly sizing the Oracle workload is the balance of allocating vCPUs without allocating more than necessary. Because Oracle is designed to effectively use multiple processors (symmetric multiprocessing [SMP] kernel), and because a different operating system kernel is typically installed when only a single processor is available, it is preferred to create VMs and templates to be used for Oracle with multiple vCPUs. You can add additional vCPUs later if needed without having to reinstall the OS, update the kernel, or relink the Oracle binaries. A Tier 1 VM template built for Oracle often contains many vCPUs.

In general, configure workloads so that they use no more than 80% of CPU capacity. VMware recommends a target of 75% for effective resource utilization while providing significant capacity for peak loads and for scalability. To display workload CPU utilization, select the VM, and then click the **Performance** tab. Select **Advanced**, and in the Switch To drop-down menu, select **CPU**.

TIP

Many experts in the field, such as the highly successful DBA team at the EMC IT organization, strictly adhere to a philosophy of not allowing any particular Oracle server to exceed 50% utilization on average. This often allows for a greater amount of CPU overcommitment, as opposed to the IT shops that attempt to fully utilize their server capacity.

The following represents the Oracle virtualized workload's CPU utilization during the batch replay of a test HR payroll calculation. The CPU usage was minimal. During most of this run, CPU consumption averaged around 10% utilization. It is not necessary to configure more than two vCPUs for this workload.

Figure 8-3 depicts VMs configured with four and two vCPUs on a host with four cores. There is no overcommitment on the VMs depicted in this diagram.

Figure 8-4 shows Oracle server VMs with different vCPU configurations.

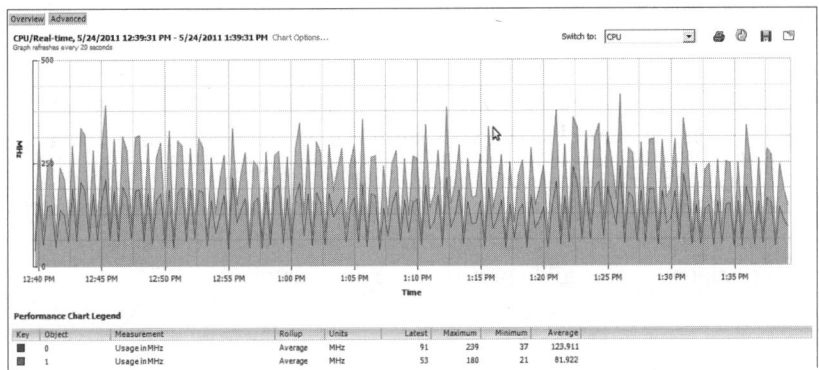

Figure 8-3 Oracle workload vCPU usage timeline

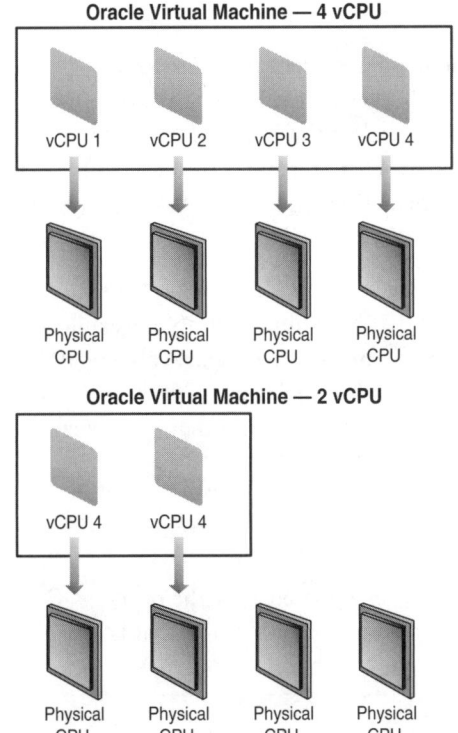

Figure 8-4 Virtual machines with different number of vCPUs

CPU Ready Time (%RDY)

The ESX/ESXi hypervisor schedules CPU resources on behalf of the guest operating system (GOS). When a GOS has an operation to run, it passes an interrupt to the hypervisor. CPU Ready Time aggregates the time that the VM is waiting in a ready-to-run state. The instruction will be scheduled to run on any number of physical processors by the hypervisor. Excessive CPU Ready Time is usually caused by overcommitment of CPU resources in concert with high VM utilization rates. Any value over 5% warrants increased scrutiny because it indicates potential non-negligible performance degradation.

TIP

The values for CPU Ready Time displayed in rEsxtop (%RDY) differ in presentation to those displayed in vCenter. rEsxtop shows a percentage of time the VM is waiting; in contrast, vCenter displays accumulated total ready time.

The DBA will monitor CPU utilization through the vSphere Client or the `esxtop/ resxtop` command. The vSphere Client is preferable because it measures CPU Ready Time in milliseconds. As displayed in Figure 8-5, select the VM and click the **Performance** tab. Select **Advanced > Chart Options > CPU > Real Time > Ready**. Figure 8-6 shows the pertinent CPU Ready Time information, and Figure 8-7 displays the chart used to continuously monitor the variations in CPU Ready Time.

It is normal for a guest to average between 0 and 50ms or more of CPU Ready Time, which is called the guest heartbeat. It is often believed that any value over 300ms can lead to performance problems. However, this number is quite low. On average, a value of 10% per vCPU will not negatively affect performance with a high water mark of 4000ms for a two-way vCPU VM, but anything higher should be considerd a warning that performance is being adversely affected.

TIP

In earlier versions of vSphere, it was advisable to set aside an entire core for the overhead generated by ESX/ESXi; however, in the modern versions of ESX/ESXi, that is unnecessary.

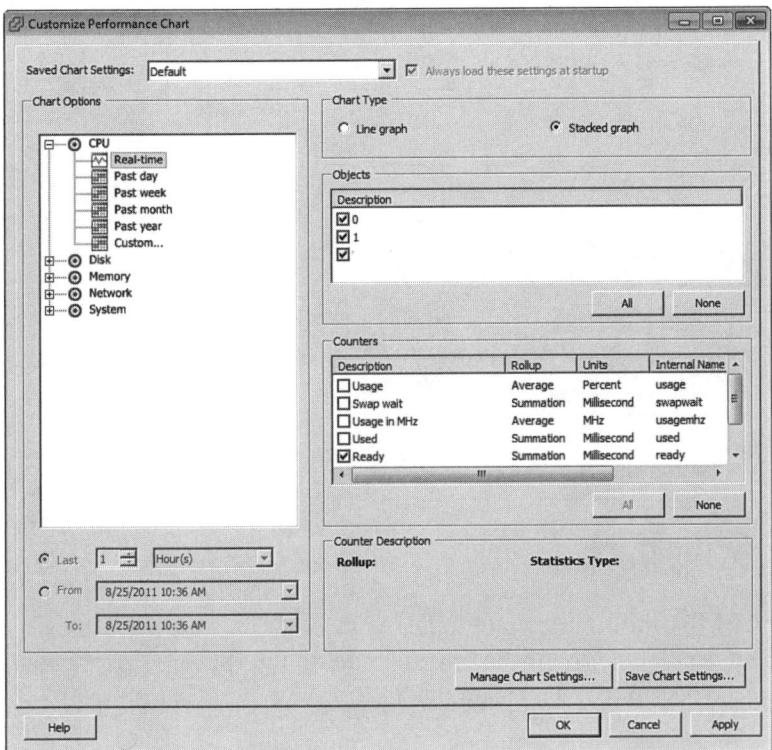

Figure 8-5 Selecting CPU Ready Time

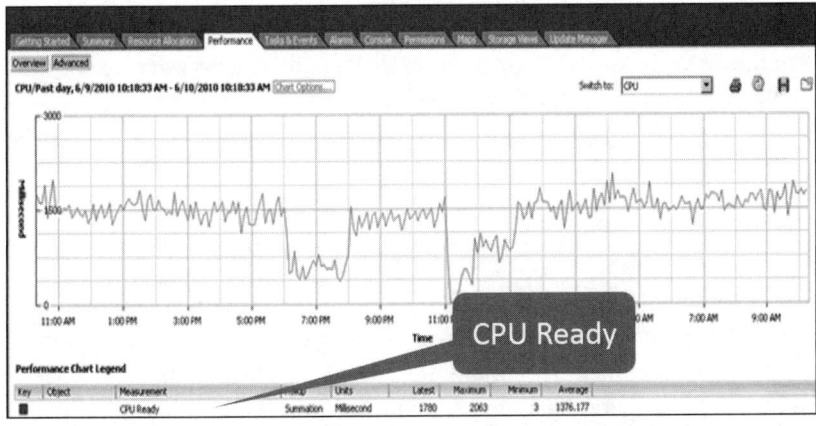

Figure 8-6 CPU Ready Time

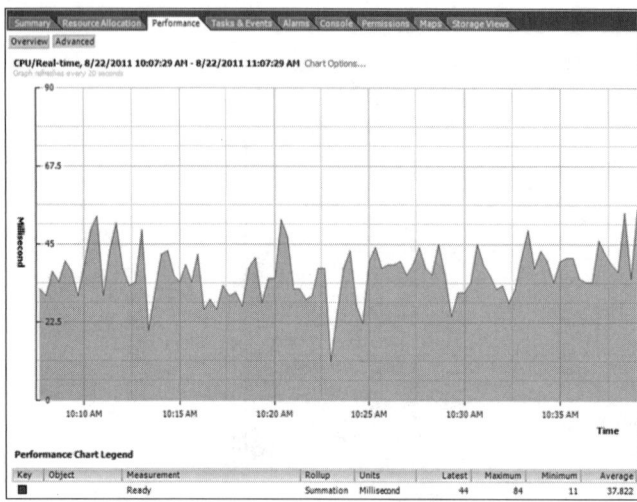

Figure 8-7 Monitoring CPU Ready Time

Although many other CPU performance counters and metrics exist, it is not feasible to discuss them in sufficient detail in this book. So, instead, refer to the vSphere Performance Monitoring Guide, which you can access through the Performance section at the main VMware website.

http://pubs.vmware.com/vsphere-51/topic/com.vmware.ICbase/PDF/
vsphere-esxi-vcenter-server-51-monitoring-performance-guide.pdf

---

TIP

Consider converting the ms value for RDY to a percentage of runtime. This will give you greater clarity into the actual amount of time the vCPUs are waiting for a service.

Memory

This section starts with an unambiguous admonition: Do not oversubscribe/overcommit memory shared by Tier 1 Oracle workloads. VMware vCenter should report no ballooning. The total amount of allocated memory should not exceed the physical memory on the host. Also, with Linux guest operating systems, minimize virtual memory configuration because Oracle data file I/O should be configured for direct I/O, which bypasses any OS-level caching. Accordingly, avoid unnecessary RAM allocation to the guest and improve I/O latency by disabling operating system-level caching. You can do this by persistently setting the Linux kernel parameter swappiness to 0 in /etc/sysctl.conf.

Memory right-sizing is critical to success in virtualizing Oracle Tier 1 workloads. If the ESX/ESXi hypervisor is starved for memory, everything running on the host suffers. In addition, latencies are incurred when overallocating memory resources beyond a VM's actual needs. For that reason, VMware recommends right-sizing VMs based on measured requirements.

Oracle aggressively uses all of the resources available. When an Oracle instance starts up, it allocates memory for the Oracle system global area (SGA). This allows Oracle to use a contiguous space of memory for caching of data and SQL statements. For as long as the instance runs, it does not return the memory even if pages remain unused. Oracle memory is less dynamic than CPU. It tends to level out after the Oracle SGA has been allocated. There might be brief periods of spikes when the process global area (PGA) is used for extended operations such as an Recovery Manager (RMAN) backup, but other than slight anomalies, it tends to be static. As with CPU, measure memory during peak workloads.

VMware recommends memory sizing for Oracle servers using the following tools:

- Oracle SGA Advisor
- Oracle PGA Advisor
- Operating system metric collection (for example, nmon)

Start with the Oracle advisors to determine whether the SGA and PGA are accurately sized. The SGA is critical to VM sizing. If the Oracle SGA is undersized, for example, this affects buffer cache and shared pool hit ratios, negatively impacting performance. It also skews the operating system metric collection. After the SGA and PGA are sized accurately, use the operating system collected metrics to determine the appropriate memory size of the VM.

Make the reservation, at minimum, equal to the Oracle SGA. The Oracle SGA is memory that is allocated during instance startup. The SGA contains many Oracle memory components, including a buffer cache for caching user data and the shared pool for caching PL/SQL and SQL statements for soft parsing. Because the SGA is allocated during startup, set a memory reservation for each guest for at least the size of the Oracle SGA. Figure 8-8 shows the process of setting a memory reservation for an Oracle server running as a VM.

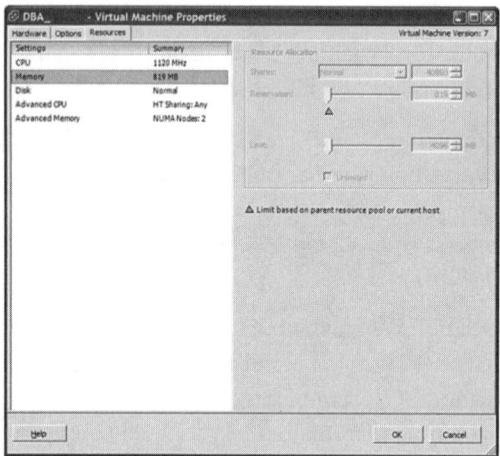

Figure 8-8 Oracle memory reservations

The following graph represents active memory pages. This workload is properly sized in a VM with 8GB RAM. This leaves a modest amount of free memory, giving some additional headroom and growth for the Oracle memory components if needed. Active memory is the memory actively used by the VMs. This does not always equate to the entire SGA but to SGA pages that have been recently accessed.

Figure 8-9 depicts the active memory usage in the vSphere Client. Select the VM and click the **Performance** tab. Then click the **Advanced** tab and choose **Chart Options > Memory > Real Time > Active**.

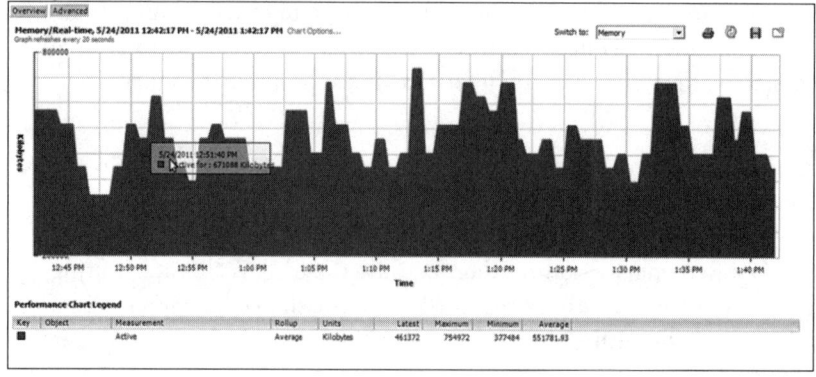

Figure 8-9 Memory usage

The Oracle workload memory reservation is set to the full 8GB allocated to the VMs. VMware recommends, at a minimum, reservation of at least the SGA. To guarantee that the memory allocated to the VM has corresponding physical memory, you should set a memory reservation, which accomplishes the following:

- Reserved memory for the Oracle workload.

- If a vSphere HA event occurs, the VM does not start unless one of the remaining ESX/ESXi hosts has memory available to satisfy the reservation.

- The Distributed Resource Scheduler (DRS) observes the reservation for optimal placement.

TIP

The total size of the memory allocated to the VM should be set to the cumulative size of the SGA, the PGAs, and the background and foreground processes' stack space.

System Huge Pages

This section discusses the use of Huge Pages (or large pages as the feature is referred to in Windows operating systems). Using *huge memory pages* is a technique that allows the operating system to allocate and manage memory using a larger-than-standard page size. This term is synonymous with *large memory pages*. The default page size for most systems is 4KB (4096 bytes). Huge Pages are typically 2MB or 4MB (can be made larger). Managing memory using a larger page size reduces the required number system calls by up to a factor of 1,000.

Due to dramatic improvements in hardware and memory performance, the smaller page size has not traditionally presented a significant problem. However, because memory capacity has the potential to exceed 1TB, and databases can effectively manage hundreds of gigabytes of memory, it becomes significant. Huge Pages were introduced to address this issue. The performance impact associated with the system calls relating to memory management is particularly noticeable when considering very large memory allocations under a hypervisor, because memory operations must be protected. Protected system calls require a degree of serialization, and can experience a measurable performance penalty under a hypervisor. Therefore, reducing the number of system calls has a high return.

So, although natively installed, operating systems benefit from Huge Pages. The effect is much more pronounced for virtual installations of the same operating system. A 14% performance improvement has been shown under load for an Oracle database with a 24GB

SGA when using Huge Pages as compared with standard pages. A 40% improvement was measured for a system with a 96GB SGA with no other changes.

Linux handles Huge Pages gracefully by reserving a pool of memory at system boot time. You can dynamically increase or decrease this amount of memory by using `sysctl`; but for the operation to be successful without a reboot, increases require that the memory is available.

Also, in Linux, using Huge Pages implies memory locking, so user limits must accommodate locking of the entire memory segment for it to be successful.

Figure 8-10 shows the OS parameters for Huge Pages. Refer to Oracle documentation for details.

```
#!/bin/bash
#
# hugepages_settings.sh
#
# Linux bash script to compute values for the
# recommended HugePages/HugeTLB configuration
#
# Note: This script does calculation for all shared memory
# segments available when the script is run, no matter it
# is an Oracle RDBMS shared memory segment or not.
# Check for the kernel version
KERN=`uname -r | awk -F. '{ printf("%d.%d\n",$1,$2); }'`
# Find out the HugePage size
HPG_SZ=`grep Hugepagesize /proc/meminfo | awk {'print $2'}`
# Start from 1 pages to be on the safe side and guarantee 1 free HugePage
NUM_PG=1
# Cumulative number of pages required to handle the running shared memory segments
for SEG_BYTES in `ipcs -m | awk {'print $5'} | grep "[0-9][0-9]*"`
do
    MIN_PG=`echo "$SEG_BYTES/($HPG_SZ*1024)" | bc -q`
    if [ $MIN_PG -gt 0 ]; then
        NUM_PG=`echo "$NUM_PG+$MIN_PG+1" | bc -q`
    fi
done
# Finish with results
case $KERN in
    '2.4') HUGETLB_POOL=`echo "$NUM_PG*$HPG_SZ/1024" | bc -q`;
        echo "Recommended setting: vm.hugetlb_pool = $HUGETLB_POOL" ;;
    '2.6'|'3.8') echo "Recommended setting: vm.nr_hugepages = $NUM_PG" ;;
    *) echo "Unrecognized kernel version $KERN. Exiting." ;;
esac
# End
```

Figure 8-10 Huge Pages setting in Linux

Enabling expanded Automatic Memory Management (AMM) , a feature of Oracle 11g, prohibits use of Linux Huge Pages. This is true of all Database versions 11g R1 and R2 releases and patches, including the Database 11.2.0.2. Database 11g R1 expanded AMM to include PGA. AMM is not active by default in Database 11g and is enabled via the parameters MEMORY_TARGET and MEMORY_MAX_TARGET. However, the Database 10g SGA_TARGET and SGA_MAX_SIZE parameters continue to work as they did previously.

Of the two features, it is strongly recommended that Huge Pages take priority, regardless of the workload characteristics and database instance memory size. In general, using Huge Pages is a performance feature, whereas AMM is a configuration feature.

Database 11.2.0.2 introduced the initialization parameter USE_LARGE_PAGES to provide more Huge Pages-related instance control. Its values are TRUE, FALSE, or ONLY. The default is TRUE and causes Oracle to behave as it always has. Set the parameter to ONLY to enforce the use of Huge Pages and prevent instance startup if sufficient Huge Pages are not available. Finally, although all versions of Oracle since version 7 have supported Huge Pages, Database 11.2.0.2 is the first release that provides any meaningful output in the alert log relating to Oracle's use of Huge Pages.

AMM does not use standard System V-style interprocess communication (IPC) shared memory. Instead, AMM uses memory mapped files in /dev/shm. The problem is that memory mapped files do not support Huge Pages. This is a fundamental problem with AMM if Huge Pages are desired.

Memory ballooning is a common problem in Tier 1 workloads and can cause severe performance problems. Conceptually, the balloon driver is a good idea because it can successfully provide fallback management of memory oversubscription in some situations. However, this can pose a problem with memory-intensive Tier 1 workloads.

For example, Oracle is very aggressive at using all the resources available to it. After an Oracle instance starts up, it uses malloc to allocate memory for the Oracle SGA. This allows Oracle to use a contiguous space of memory for caching of data and parsed SQL. Figure 8-11 depicts memory ballooning within a VM designed to run as an Oracle server.

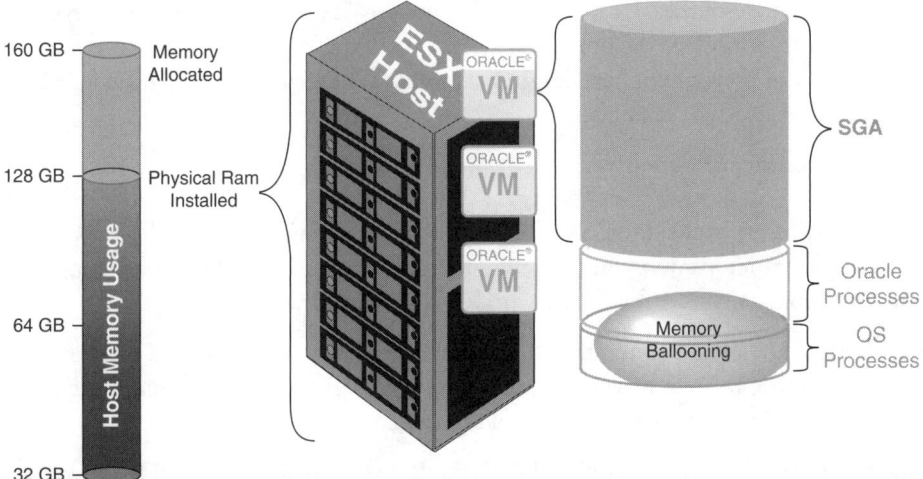

Figure 8-11 Memory ballooning and the Oracle database server

Figure 8-12 shows the VM admin or the DBA how to display memory resources in the vSphere Client. Select the VM, click the **Performance** tab, and then click the **Advanced** tab. In the drop-down menu, switch to **Memory**.

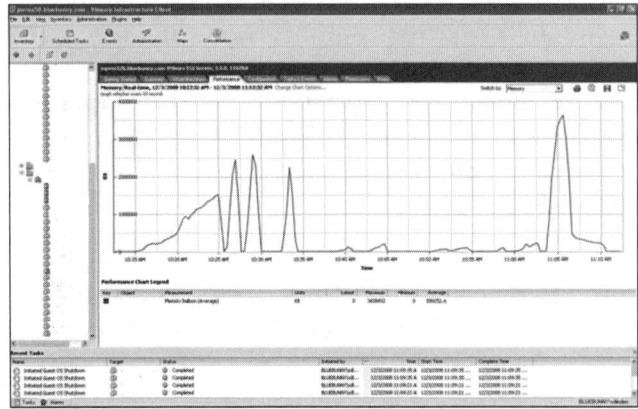

Figure 8-12 Guest memory ballooning and the Oracle database server

Disabling the balloon driver is not a best practice, and VMware recommends leaving it activated. You can combat ballooning in three ways:

- Do *not* oversubscribe memory, especially with Tier 1 workloads.

- Create VMware guest reservations for 100% of the memory for Oracle workloads to prevent ballooning. The reservation also directs DRS to avoid relocation to a host with insufficient resources. Oracle needs the memory it allocates and should never be asked to release it back to the operating system or to the hypervisor. Also, memory reservations can prevent vSphere High Availability (HA) from restarting the VM if the host has insufficient resources.

- Do *not* disable the balloon driver.

With 100% RAM reservations, the ESX/ESXi hypervisor can become starved for memory, at which point everything running on the host suffers. Therefore, a best practice is to consider building a separate cluster for Tier 1 workloads such as Oracle.

Although a VM admin should configure physical memory, guest memory, and memory reservations so that the balloon driver never activates, the balloon driver should not be disabled. It should remain active as a second-level safety net.

The balloon driver is commonly associated with the Linux Out-of-Memory (OOM) killer. If the Linux kernel becomes starved of memory, it uses the OOM killer to kill processes. It starts with the biggest memory consumer, so Oracle is often the victim. Therefore, avoid oversubscription of resources (such as CPU and memory), especially with Oracle database instances and Oracle middle tiers, until after sustained production metrics are evaluated. Even if it appears that actual performance metrics indicate that there is some latitude to oversubscribe resources, a best practice is to not assume to oversubscribe Tier 1 workload memory until sufficient evidence shows that the practice is safe and that same evidence reveals the proper multiple of oversubscription.

Figure 8-13 shows ballooning in action on a guest. Around 1:15 a.m. it asked for 100MB from the Linux guest. The Linux kernel was able to accommodate this without killing any critical processes. Most likely, it sacrificed file system cache. At 4:00 a.m., the balloon drives aggressively asked for 400MB of memory. This caused the OOM killer to kick in and kill Oracle. The OOM killer activity was monitored in /var/log/messages. The vSphere Client is preferred for tracking memory utilization because it measures in kilobytes (KB), whereas Esxtop measures in percent. Ideally, the balloon driver does not activate, and this value is always zero.

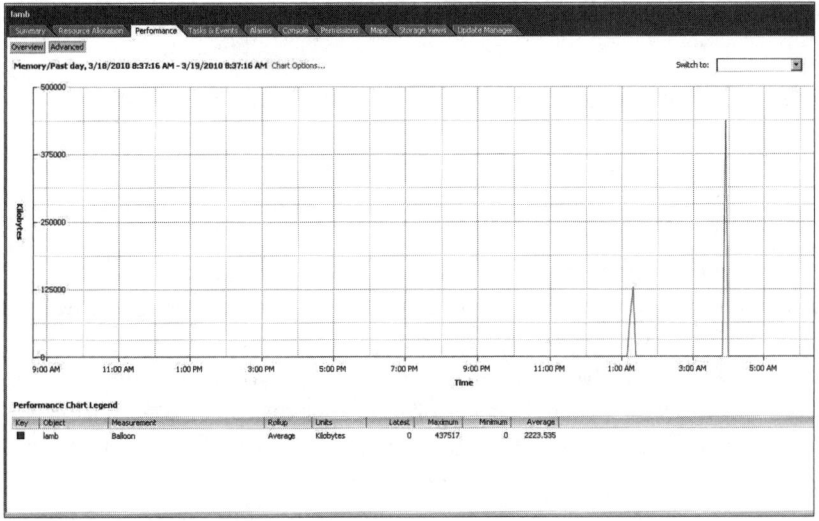

Figure 8-13 Memory ballooning with the Oracle database server

The OOM killer seeks out the highest memory users and starts killing them off until the memory pressure is relieved. Unfortunately, the highest memory users are usually the most important processes on the system. This behavior might result in system instability, which can be difficult to diagnose. The OOM killer timing is often directly related to ballooning activity.

To identify ballooning from vCenter, consult Figure 8-14 and highlight the VM and go to the **Performance** tab. Change the chart options to **Memory** and **Real Time**, and select **Balloon**. This is an example of a VM experiencing severe ballooning.

Figure 8-14 Guest memory ballooning and the Oracle database server

Notice that when the balloon graph spiked, the OOM killer started killing off Java processes, which caused the application to become unstable.

Transparent Page Sharing

It is important to discuss Transparent Page Sharing (TPS), even though the advice will simply be to leave it alone. TPS allows ESXi to effectively dedupe memory pages. The system checks for duplicate memory pages and reduces the amount of total memory used by pointing to the duplicate as opposed to maintaining multiple copies of the same memory page. The degree of overhead when using TPS has proved to be near negligible; so, even in the case of a host that contains many completely disparate VMs (very few opportunities of duplicated pages), it is recommended to leave the TPS driver enabled.

Non-Uniform Memory Access

Non-uniform memory access (NUMA) is an architectural concept that allows a specific processor, also known as a core, to access all memory on the system board regardles of whether that processor is directly attached to the memory being used. Access to memory segments through the capability of NUMA can add very small amounts of latency to memory access time, but it allows for processes to access extremely large amounts of memory across the system board.

In vSphere 5.x, NUMA is mapped between the physical and virtual topologies, which exposes NUMA to the GOS. This allows vSphere and the applications running on vSphere to more effectively utilize the innate value of NUMA. This capability is referred to as virtual NUMA or vNUMA. Although results always vary, the recommendation is to consider the effects of the NUMA node, which is a single physical socket, when architecting the VM.

A physical socket often referred to as a CPU socket is a physical unit of processing that is plugged into a system board that contains one or more processing cores. If the physical server is constructed with sockets , containing four, six, or eight processor cores, it is optimal to build a VM that has no more than a corresponding number of vCPUs allocated to it. In this context, the socket is referred to as a NUMA node. If the number of vCPUs allocated to the VM is smaller than the size of the NUMA node, it is optimal to design the VM with the number of vCPUs equal to an intregal divisor of that socket size. For example, if the socket size is eight cores, the VM should have one, two, four, or eight vCPUs allocated to it. Keep in mind that this advice is not absolute and alternative approaches, although not usually optimal, are not prohibited.

If the VM has more vCPUs allocated to it than the NUMA node and the number of allocated vCPUs is greater than eight, a feature introduced in vSphere 4.1 that recognizes wide VMs, often referred to as wide NUMA, takes effect. A VM that fits into a single NUMA node will be optimal in terms of memory access because that VM has affinity to the memory attached to the NUMA node that it is running on. Alternatively, if the VM size is greater than the NUMA node, memory will be accessed through NUMA. This process is referred to as node interleaving and can result in minor performance degradation. However, the wide NUMA capabilities limit the number of NUMA nodes that will be used to run that process. For example, if the NUMA node size is four and the VM has eight vCPUs, the VM will be limited to run on only two NUMA nodes even if the physical server has many more sockets.

Figure 8-15, which is borrowed from the book *Virtualizing SQL Server with VMware: Doing It Right*, depicts a basic NUMA architecture.

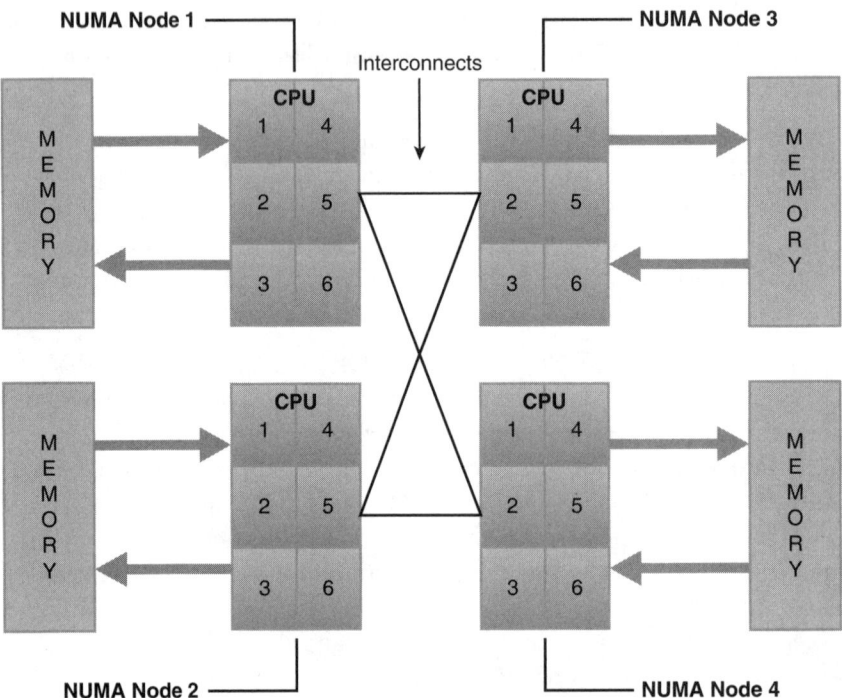

Figure 8-15 NUMA architecture of a physical host with four sockets (or NUMA nodes)

Restrictions and recommendations apply to the use of vNUMA:

- To optimize the VM and take advantage of vNUMA, do not memory-overcommit or CPU-overcommit the host.

- Build the VMs on a host with the number of vCPUs equal to an integral multiple or divisor of the NUMA node. For example, if the physical host has many 4-core sockets and the VM will need a large number of vCPUs, the VM admin or the DBA who intends on leveraging the capability of wide NUMA will build the VM with 8, 12, or 16 vCPUs.

- If the feature hot-add is enabled on the VM, vNUMA is disabled on that VM.

- Refer to the Oracle on vSphere Best Practices Guide along with the vSphere CPU scheduler performance paper on VMware's website for more in-depth information about vNUMA.

- NUMA parameters can be set on the physical host, the virtualization layer, the operating system, and the application level. Starting with Oracle 11g, Oracle does not recommend enabling NUMA on the instance level.

- Oracle NUMA support is disabled by default for 11g and later (see Oracle MySupport Doc ID: 864633.1). In some circumstances, enabling Oracle NUMA may improve performance, but often Oracle NUMA will use an unacceptably high percentage of CPU. The capability should be thoroughly tested before electing to implement the parameter in a production system. VMware recommends enabling NUMA on the physical host BIOS and at the GOS level. These should be the default with most modern servers and guest operating systems.

- The Oracle `init.ora` paramaters regarding NUMA are listed here with their defaults, which disable Oracle NUMA. Any parameter with an underscore (_) is considered to be a hidden parameter and should not be altered in the absence of specific direction from Oracle Support:

```
db_block_numa=1
_enable_numa_optimization=FALSE
```

The Oracle database best practices guide, as well as a white paper describing the inner workings of the ESXi scheduler, are included here to provide the reader deeper insight into the subject of processor focused performance tuning.

www.vmware.com/files/pdf/techpaper/VMware-vSphere-CPU-Sched-Perf.pdf

www.vmware.com/files/pdf/partners/oracle/
Oracle_Databases_on_VMware_-_Best_Practices_Guide.pdf

Networking

The configuration of the network is often addressed without the same degree of importance as other dimensions of performance. However, the network infrastructure can easily be as critical as any aspect of the infrastructure. In the case of a properly designed Oracle Real Application Clusters (RAC) system, the network provided for the RAC interconnect can either allow for success or define failure with extreme prejudice.

Enterprises considering tools for Tier 1 virtual workloads are strongly encouraged to design networks with adequate capacity, including 10GbE for most implementations. The customer has often already made a substantial investment in the storage infrastructure.

The following are the basic network requirements for Oracle and Tier 1 hosts:

- Use a virtual distributed switch (vDS) when available.

- Always use VMXNET3, which is available when loading VMTools on the OS.

- 10GbE (two or more) interfaces.

- 1Gb (5 ports), or preferably 10GbE.

- Always use bonded pairs for redundancy and throughput (also known as teaming).

- It is acceptable to use blade chassis segregation of 10GbE adapters into smaller virtual adapters.

- The RAC interconnect should be on an isolated VLAN. Also consider InfiniBand.

- Set aside a segregated VLAN for all vMotion operations.

- Set up jumbo frames for 10Gb networks when all hops through the network are set up for 10Gb and jumbo frames.

Network Load Testing

Use the network load test to force the maximum throughput through the network fabric and interfaces. Similar to a memory stress test, it flushes out potential issues with drivers, hardware, or network topology.

Iperf is a network testing tool that can create a TCP or UPD data stream between two nodes (or VMs). Iperf is open source software available for both Linux and Windows. The website address is listed here.

http://sourceforge.net/projects/iperf/

To test the maximum throughput of the network interfaces for 500 seconds, perform the following steps and consult Figure 8-16 for the sample benchmark output:

1. On the server node, execute the following command:

   ```
   $ iperf -s -i 5
   ```

2. On the client node, execute the following command:

   ```
   $ iperf -c <server-name> -t 500 -i 5 -m
   ```

```
------------------------------------------------------------
Client connecting to 192.168.11.134, TCP port 5001
TCP window size: 16.0 KByte (default)
------------------------------------------------------------
[  3] local 192.168.11.1 port 59387 connected with 192.168.11.134 port 5001
[ ID] Interval       Transfer     Bandwidth
[  3]  0.0- 5.0 sec   950 MBytes  1.59 Gbits/sec
[  3]  5.0-10.0 sec   919 MBytes  1.54 Gbits/sec
[  3] 10.0-15.0 sec   910 MBytes  1.53 Gbits/sec
[  3] 15.0-20.0 sec   918 MBytes  1.54 Gbits/sec
[  3] 20.0-25.0 sec   913 MBytes  1.53 Gbits/sec
[  3] 25.0-30.0 sec   932 MBytes  1.56 Gbits/sec
[  3] 30.0-35.0 sec   925 MBytes  1.55 Gbits/sec
[  3] 35.0-40.0 sec   930 MBytes  1.56 Gbits/sec
[  3] 40.0-45.0 sec   917 MBytes  1.54 Gbits/sec
[  3] 45.0-50.0 sec   905 MBytes  1.52 Gbits/sec
[  3] 50.0-55.0 sec   865 MBytes  1.45 Gbits/sec
[  3] 55.0-60.0 sec   814 MBytes  1.37 Gbits/sec
[  3]  0.0-60.0 sec  10.6 GBytes  1.52 Gbits/sec
[  3] MSS size 1448 bytes (MTU 1500 bytes, ethernet)
```

Figure 8-16 Iperf sample benchmark

Dropped Packets

Because dropped packets typically indicate congestion in the network or failing hardware, they should not occur on a LAN. Just 1% dropped packets in either direction can throttle throughput by as much as 15%.

You can monitor dropped packets in vSphere by selecting the ESX/ESXi host and clicking the **Performance** tab. Select **Advanced > Network > Real Time**, and select **None** in Counters. Select **Receive packets dropped** and **Transmit packets dropped**.

vMotion and Network Bandwidth

During a vMotion operation, the contents of the VM's memory is transferred from one host to another. With a dedicated 1Gb network, actual throughput of around 60MBps can be expected, or half the theoretical maximum of 120MBps. Basic math produces the following tables (Tables 8-1 and 8-2) of vMotion timings.

Table 8-1 Network Bandwidth at Various speeds

Bandwidth (Units)	100Mb	1Gb	10Gb Jumbo Frame Enabled
Bits/s	104,857,600	1,048,576,000	10,485,760,000
Bytes/s	13,107,200	131,072,000	1,310,720,000
MB/s (max)	13	125	1,250
MB/s (practical)	6	63	625

Table 8-2 vMotion Timings Compared with Network Bandwidth

Memory in GB (75% used)	Time in Seconds for vMotion Operation		
	100Mb	1Gb	10Gb Jumbo Frame Enabled
8	960	96	10
16	1,920	192	19
32	3,840	384	38
64	7,680	768	77
128	15,360	1,536	154
256	30,720	3,072	307

According to these tables, when using a dedicated 1Gb network, expect approximately 96 seconds to complete the vMotion operation for an 8GB guest. During that time, there might be modest performance impact to the VM due to memory synchronization, although the VM continues to operate normally. At the completion of the vMotion operation, a momentary pause of up to the time of one ping can occur, during which the transfer to the new host is completed. If that time exceeds 1 second, the vMotion event can be canceled. If the network is properly sized and configured, it is highly unlikely that the vMotion event will be disrupted.

If the network is shared with other traffic, timings can be slower. Therefore, isolating vMotion traffic increases the likelihood of successful vMotion operations.

TIP

For example, some customers elect to share the vMotion network with the backup network. This carries the risk that backup activity outside the backup window might impact daytime performance. It can also artificially increase recovery times due to competing vMotion traffic.

Storage Network

In addition, the preceding tables, Tables 8-1 and 8-2, translate to anticipated storage performance, assuming the physical storage medium can match the throughput capacity of the network. As with vMotion performance, total throughput is determined by the total amount of traffic on the network segment. Because it is desirable to have consistency in storage throughput, VMware recommends a dedicated network segment here as well.

Virtual Machine Network

It can be desirable to have a VM network dedicated to network traffic between VMs, to provide security controls and adequate bandwidth between VMs. Compare this with a computer room network or server network for physical servers.

Dedicated RAC Interconnect Network

If running clustered databases as guests with a network segment dedicated to VM traffic, an additional network restricted to cluster traffic is recommended.

Teaming and Multipathing

By bonding, or teaming, multiple adapters into an aggregated pair, redundancy is gained for the physical network components, including network interface cards (NICs), host ports, switch ports, and cables. If a member of a network bond goes offline, network traffic continues to flow over the remaining members.

In addition, if the network supports an active/active configuration, it also provides a multiple of the base network bandwidth.

In vSphere, you can also create redundant network paths for storage. This allows for multiple independent NICs (or bonds) and provides the same capability as with Fibre Channel using multiple host bus adapters (HBAs). The following provides the same options as with Fibre Channel:

- **Fixed:** Uses only a single path for all connections

- **Round-robin:** Randomly distributes I/O over available paths as determined on connection or failover

Jumbo Frames

A single default Ethernet frame is 1500 bytes. A jumbo frame maximum transmission unit (MTU) can be increased from the default 1500 bytes to 9000 bytes. The larger payload provides for increased efficiency and higher throughput. For general information, look up "jumbo frames" on common academic websites.

Storage networks with 10GbE topology can benefit from jumbo frames by making the storage network much more efficient by sending larger payloads. The cost of jumbo frames occurs if a packet must be retransmitted because it was dropped or malformed upon receiving it. However, LANs, and in particular storage networks, do not usually experience significant numbers of dropped packets. By enabling jumbo frames on a 10GbE network, an 85% performance improvement has been recorded.

Oracle, by default, uses an 8KB block size to store data in the database. Increasing the TCP/IP payload to 9000+ bytes allows an entire Oracle block to be transmitted as one jumbo frame instead of dividing it up into six separate TCP/IP packets.

Only enhanced VMXNET3 adapters can be used with jumbo frames. Consult VMware KB article 1015556, *Virtual network adapters that support jumbo frames*, for further information.

Implementing jumbo frames requires that jumbo frames be enabled throughout the entire network topology. This can include within the guest VM, virtual switch, physical switch or port, and storage NICs if applicable. Refer to VMware KB article 1007654, *iSCSI and Jumbo Frames configuration*, and to Figure 8-17.

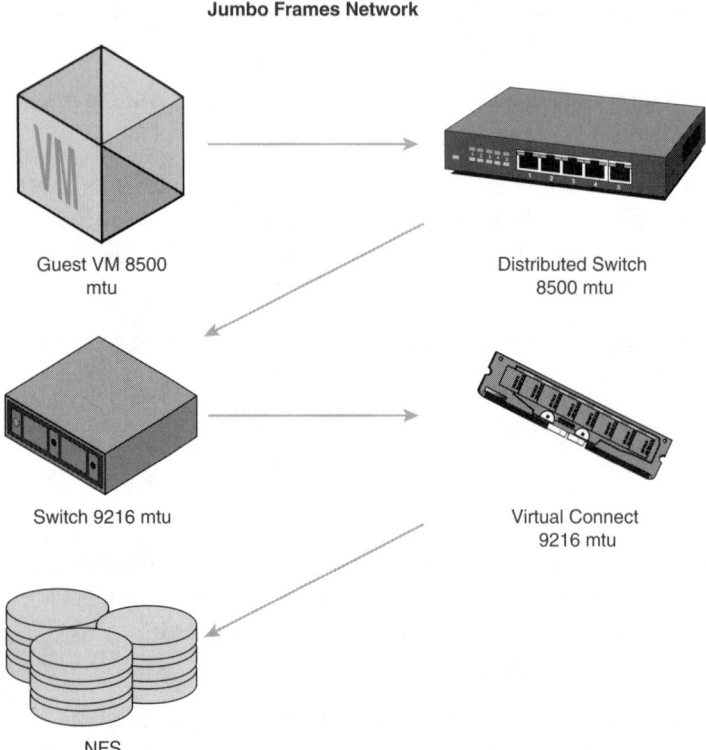

Jumbo Frames Network

Guest VM 8500
mtu

Distributed Switch
8500 mtu

Switch 9216 mtu

Virtual Connect
9216 mtu

NFS

Figure 8-17 Jumbo frame network

To create a jumbo frames-enabled vSwitch, follow these steps:

1. Log in directly to the ESX/ESXi host console.

2. Set the MTU size for the vSwitch with the following command:

   ```
   esxcfg-vswitch -m <MTU> <vSwitch>
   ```

3. Check the new configuration with the following command:

   ```
   esxcfg-vswitch -l
   ```

To enable jumbo frames on a VMkernel interface, follow these steps:

1. Log in directly to the ESX/ESXi host console.

2. Create a VMkernel connection with jumbo frames support using the following command:

   ```
   esxcfg-vswitch -A <vmkernel port group name> <vSwitch#>
   ```

3. Create a VMkernel connection with jumbo frames support with the following command:

```
esxcfg-vmknic -a -i <ip address> -n <netmask> -m <MTU> <portgroup
name>
```

4. Check the new configuration with the following command:

```
esxcfg-vmknic -l
```

Storage Configuration and Utilization

The great majority of performance-related issues according to VMware Global Support Services (GSS) manifest somewhere in the storage stack. Those problems are not necessarily related to the physical storage as much as to the storage configuration. The virtualization layer is usually not the culprit, because the degradation due to vSphere, although not negligible, is not usually significant.

Storage access performance can be perceived from three different perspectives. The application owners are most interested in the latency to their applications, whereas the DBAs and system administrators usually focus on throughput in the form of M/KBps. The storage administrator is interested in I/O operations per second (IOPS). Regardless of the perspective, vSphere should not cause more than 5% degradation, and if the customer is experiencing excessive degradation, they should contact VMware GSS.

By using storage performance monitoring methodologies and tools, the administrator can quickly determine whether the storage performance is adequate. This will save significant time as compared to validating each individual storage configuration parameter.

Of the four dimensions of performance, storage is the most critical component when virtualizing Tier 1 Oracle workloads. Oracle databases, in general, can be I/O intensive. The majority of customers achieve adequate performance upon initial implementation. Successfully implementing Oracle includes the review of the storage capacity, including the following factors:

- Strategic storage concerns
- A thorough understanding of the existing physical and vSphere environments
- An understanding of the capacity of current storage
- Assessment of the storage configuration

SCSI Queues

A complete stack contains many queues, and DBAs, system administrators, and VMAdmins have influence over three different levels of SCSI queues:

- The HBA as it is controlled by ESXi

- The controller queues (vSCSI)

- The queues in the operating system, which should be turned off by setting the parameter `elevator=noop`

Because it is axiomatic that the majority of the issues that arise in virtualized Oracle environments are rooted in the storage stack, the corollary to the axiom is that SCSI queue depth saturation is often the cause of storage performance problems.

The SCSI queue is used to buffer SCSI commands for incoming I/O requests. The SCSI queue configured depth equates to the maximum number of active commands per logical unit number (LUN). Even the most rudimentary commands can trigger many I/O requests. For example, a directory listing can result in a dozen SCSI commands. Often, a VMware vSphere cluster has multiple VMs, and multiple ESXi hosts will access the same datastore concurrently, whereas a typical physical server generally has exclusive access to a specific LUN.

The SCSI queue concept applies to the storage-area network (SAN), ESX/ESXi hypervisor, and VM levels of the stack. If storage switches are involved, some storage switches may have their own SCSI queues; however, this is not usually a concern of the DBA, system administrators, or VMAdmin.

TIP

In addition to adjusting the queue depth, consider dedicating datastores to individual high-profile Oracle workloads.

Each storage layer has only one global SCSI queue maximum depth configuration, although multiple SCSI queues may be associated with each layer. More modern storage systems sometimes present a SCSI queue depth of 32, but some extend to 128. Each storage layer should be set to the optimal SCSI queue depth as recommended by the storage vendor, which you can find within the storage documentation.

A large SCSI queue depth can manifest on a datastore servicing multiple simultaneous I/O requests. If it becomes so large that it spills over to the ESX/ESXi hypervisor memory, it can result in slower I/O performance and unacceptably high disk latency. Refer to VMware KB 1008113, *Controlling LUN queue depth throttling in VMware ESX/ESXi*. Always consult the SAN documentation for optimal and maximum SCSI depth settings and match those same settings to the Oracle database and applications vendor's recommendations.

TIP

Network File System (NFS) is not limited by SCSI queues.

To set the SCSI queue depth on a vSphere ESX/ESXi host through vCenter, complete the following steps and see Figure 8-18:

1. In the VMware vSphere Client, select the host in the Inventory panel.

2. Click the **Configuration** tab and click **Advanced Settings** under Software.

3. Click **Disk** in the left panel, and scroll down to **Disk.SchedNumReqOutstanding**.

4. Change the parameter value and click **OK**.

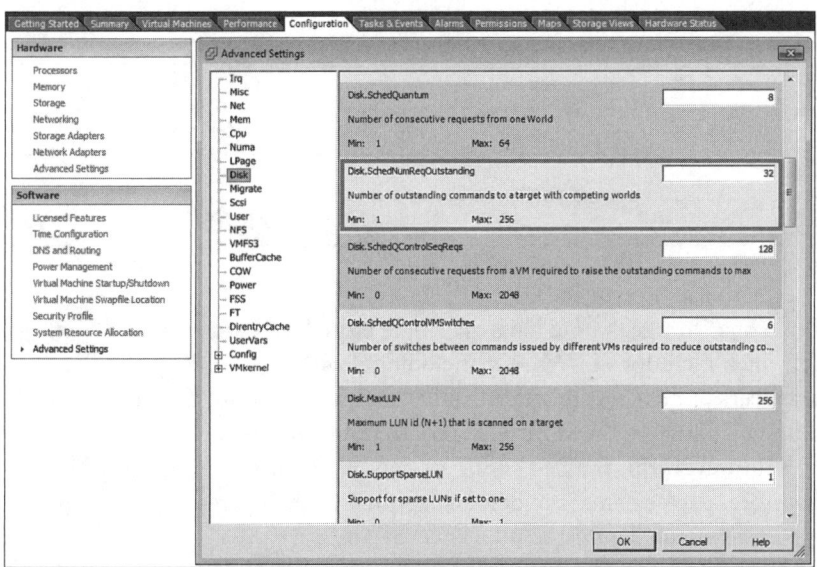

Figure 8-18 Reconfiguration of the queue depth on an individual datastore

For more information, refer to VMware KB 1268, *Setting the Maximum Outstanding Disk Requests per Virtual Machine*.

> **TIP**
>
> Despite setting a higher queue depth on the vSphere host, you might need to increase the queue depth on the HBA driver as well, because the driver setting will take precedence.

A solution to managing SCSI queue depth is to configure datastores exclusively for each Oracle workload. A single datastore is dedicated to each VM. For example, a typical Oracle workload has a separate disk for the operating system to include the Oracle Home and Oracle Inventory on a separate paravirtualized SCSI controller (pvSCSI). The Automatic Storage Management (ASM) virtual machine disks (VMDKs) are housed on the same datastore. The ASM disks remain marked "independent," excluding them during snapshot operations. Generally, you should add about 20% free space for the operating system disk snapshots.

Table 8-3 is an example of the calculations of the total size required for an individual Oracle datastore. A healthy allowance of approximately 15GB free space for snapshots is not included.

Table 8-3 Oracle VMDK Build Example

VMDK	Size
Operating system	30GB
ASM disk 1	100GB
ASM disk 2	100GB
Total datastore size	**240GB**

Consider the example of a storage system having a single large LUN supporting a single VMware datastore, which includes all VMDKs, including database VMDKs. Initially, this configuration appears to be a best practice from a storage viewpoint, thus achieving the best performance and allowing the storage system to optimize data access. From a VMware perspective, however, this is a bad configuration. As the number of active VMs is increased per datastore, performance can degrade because of the decrease in aggregate queues and the respective queue depths.

The impact of adding and removing large VMDKs, as well as manipulating snapshots, has the potential to reduce performance for the entire datastore while these operations are performed. The impact increases as the aggregate number of VMs on the datastore increases.

The foundation concept of good vSphere high-profile workload performance is that the higher the number of storage and access paths available to storage, the greater the total throughput of the cluster. Initially, only one storage access path per LUN exists, but further configuration is permitted. This requires additional HBA or NIC adapters and is not scalable. With more LUNs, redundant paths are available, and therefore the aggregate bandwidth will be optimized.

NFS Storage

NFS does not use SCSI commands to access the disk. Instead, NFS uses file calls to perform disk access. Fibre Channel and iSCSI LUNs are block-level devices. Unlike NFS, they do use SCSI commands for disk access. Block-level devices are not generally comparable to NFS implementations. In fact, TCP-based NFS storage solutions can be very efficient when compared to the Fibre Channel protocol. With 10 and 40GbE NICs, the gap between iSCSI and NFS becomes less important. The soon-to-be-released 120GbE NICs could allow for NFS and IP storage in general to exceed the maximum throughput capabilities of Fibre Channel.

Common Storage Mistakes

When a DBA, inexperienced with virtualization, reports that Oracle on vSphere was attempted but the performance was unacceptable, it is likely that misconfigured I/O was the cause of the performance problem. Figure 8-19 shows an example of a common Oracle storage on vSphere misconception. The example shows a nonvirtualized system versus a virtualized system. The example is an exaggeration of the common problem of oversubscribing storage.

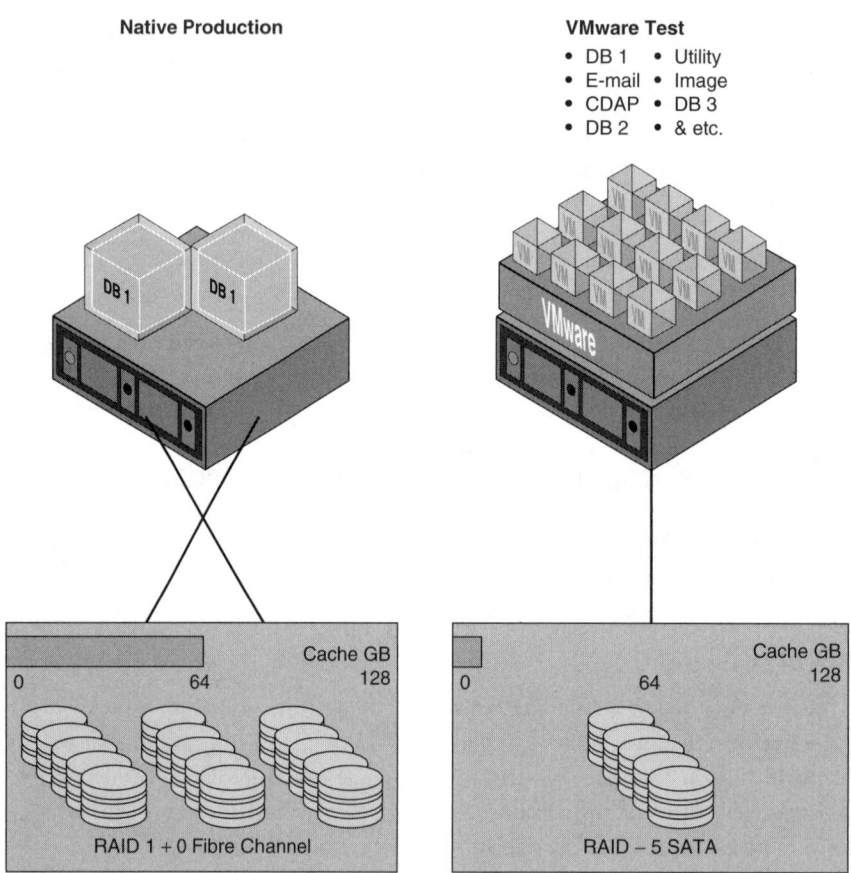

Figure 8-19 Common storage mistake

Storage Performance Monitoring

During each presentation on the viability of vSphere for high-profile Oracle workloads, the conversation will give rise to certain contradictions of the laws of physics. For some reason, normally rational DBAs and other IT professionals fail to consider the consequences of overloading already undersized storage. The result is an unsatisfactory view of the overall initiative. Hopefully, the customer, who has previously suspended disbelief, will then reach out to VMware professionals. The options for help are many, as the customer can contact GSS, VMware Professional Services, or elite implementation partners such as HOB to help them go through the right-sizing exercise and restore their storage-allocation processes to the constraints defined by reality. Ultimately, the conversation ends with the questioner understanding that even though vSphere sometimes seems to work magically, storage allocation is still a matter of arduous arithmetic.

The temptation to apply the server consolidation experience of the nonproduction tiers to the BCA stack, including the storage fabric, is a common fallacy. When you are architecting and troubleshooting hardware stacks, limits for storage I/O have changed little when compared to the past. Whether native or virtual, do not equate storage performance for multiple top-tier workloads to less-important workloads. Consolidating workloads onto a small set of LUNs or datastores using a smaller number of less-capable disks configured in lesser RAID configurations with a fraction of the cache and fewer storage paths will not lead to success when implementing business-critical Oracle workloads.

Storage Access Latency

For day-to-day monitoring of disk throughput, latency is the ideal high-level performance metric. The redline for disk latency should be 20ms or lower. Peaks of greater than 20ms are acceptable for no more than a few moments. For additional information on acceptable latency spikes, refer to the article *Performance Troubleshooting for vSphere* at the VMware website.

www.vmware.com/resources/techresources/10179

The Esxtop and rEsxtop tools monitor disk latency at three distinct layers: the device or HBA, the kernel or ESX/ESXi hypervisor, and the guest or VM. For more information on storage latency, refer to the article *Interpreting Esxtop Statistics* at the VMware website.

http://communities.vmware.com/docs/DOC-9279

To run Esxtop to display device, kernel, guest, and queue latency, follow these steps and see Figure 8-20:

1. Run Esxtop with the following command:

   ```
   $ esxtop v > f > h > i > j >
   ```

2. In the resulting display, view latency in the GAVG, KAVG, and DAVG columns:

   - The GAVG or guest latency is a combination of the device latency + hypervisor (GAVG = KAVG + DAVG).

   - The KAVG is the kernel latency or hypervisor latency. High latency reported at the kernel can be due to high SCSI queues or device drivers.

   - DAVG is the device latency or HBA latency. The term *HBA* is used generically, including an actual Fibre Channel HBA or iSCSI NIC. Device latency usually indicates a bottleneck at the storage or SAN layer. DAVG is the actual storage command round-trip time to array acknowledge and back.

■ QAVG measures the latency of the ESX/ESXi hypervisor. If the hypervisor is inducing any latency, this metric captures it. For example, if the ESX/ESXi hypervisor's SCSI queue is saturated, QAVG latency will be high.

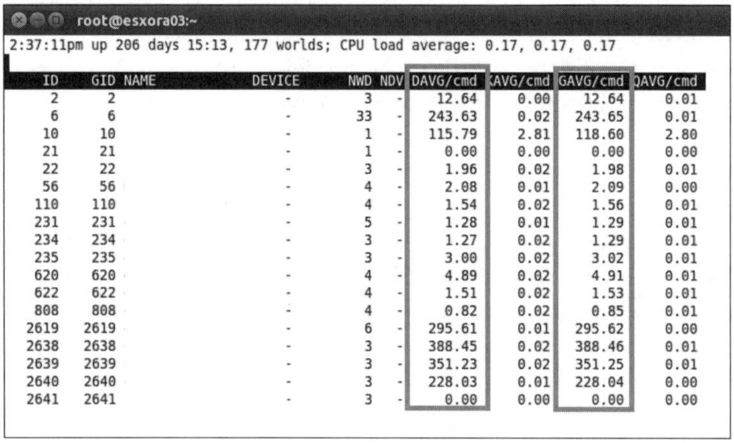

```
⊗ ⊜ ⊕   root@esxora03:~
2:37:11pm up 206 days 15:13, 177 worlds; CPU load average: 0.17, 0.17, 0.17

   ID   GID NAME            DEVICE       NWD NDV DAVG/cmd  KAVG/cmd GAVG/cmd QAVG/cmd
    2     2                    -          3   -    12.64    0.00    12.64    0.01
    6     6                    -         33   -   243.63    0.02   243.65    0.01
   10    10                    -          1   -   115.79    2.81   118.60    2.80
   21    21                    -          1   -     0.00    0.00     0.00    0.00
   22    22                    -          3   -     1.96    0.02     1.98    0.01
   56    56                    -          4   -     2.08    0.01     2.09    0.00
  110   110                    -          4   -     1.54    0.02     1.56    0.01
  231   231                    -          5   -     1.28    0.01     1.29    0.01
  234   234                    -          3   -     1.27    0.02     1.29    0.01
  235   235                    -          3   -     3.00    0.02     3.02    0.01
  620   620                    -          4   -     4.89    0.02     4.91    0.01
  622   622                    -          4   -     1.51    0.02     1.53    0.01
  808   808                    -          4   -     0.82    0.02     0.85    0.01
 2619  2619                    -          6   -   295.61    0.01   295.62    0.00
 2638  2638                    -          3   -   388.45    0.02   388.46    0.01
 2639  2639                    -          3   -   351.23    0.02   351.25    0.01
 2640  2640                    -          3   -   228.03    0.01   228.04    0.00
 2641  2641                    -          3   -     0.00    0.00     0.00    0.00
```

Figure 8-20 rEsxtop display

Monitoring the four distinct layers in this display reveals that the HBA has trouble with the SAN configuration. If the GAVG column is excessively high, absent a corresponding high value of DAVG, focus the evaluation effort on the hypervisor. However, this display indicates severe device latency (DAVG) that requires investigation. This could indicate a SAN issue that must be brought to the attention of the storage administrator and possibly the storage vendor.

In measuring average read time, the following assumptions are made about I/O patterns on systems that are read intensive:

■ Uncached random reads

■ Industry average I/O blend for operational systems of 90% read, 10% write, with writes colliding

The average read time performance attribute is important because there are schema and application designs that can pierce the cache regardless of cache size. Average read time can also be determined using Oracle Statspack and AWR reports at the tablespace and data file level.

You can use the vSphere Client to monitor the disk latency of the Oracle server or to monitor datastore latency.

To display disk latency using the vSphere Client, follow these steps and see Figure 8-21:

1. Select the Oracle prototype VM.

2. Click the **Performance** tab.

3. Select the **Advanced** subtab.

4. Select **Chart Options**.

5. Select **Disk**.

6. Select **Real Time**.

7. Select **Highest Latency**.

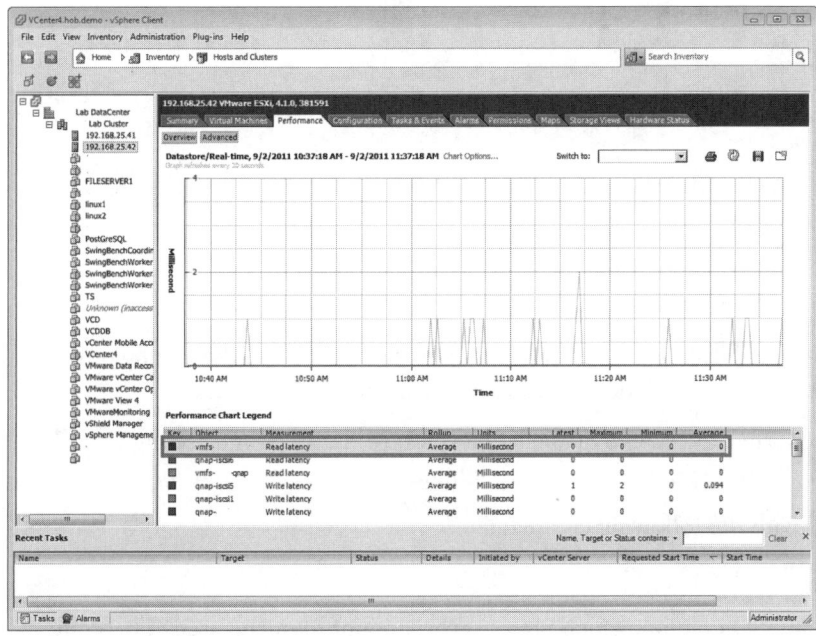

Figure 8-21 Monitoring disk latency

To monitor datastore latency at the datastore level using the vSphere Client, follow these steps and see Figure 8-22:

1. Select **Inventory > Datastores**.

2. Select the datastore in the left column.

3. Select the **Performance** tab.

4. Select **Performance > Average Device Latency per Host** from the drop-down menu.

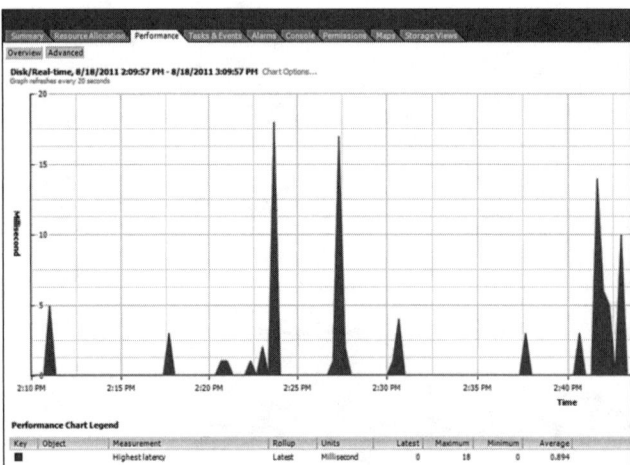

Figure 8-22 Monitoring datastore latency

Spindle Busy Average

The goal for the average disk spindle busy time is less than 50%. Use the Exstop or rEsxtop tool to display device, kernel, or guest, and queue latency.

To display device, kernel, guest, and queue latency, follow the steps and see Figure 8-23. (This Esxtop display also includes storage throughput.)

1. Start Esxtop with the following command:

```
$ esxtop > u > f > i > g > f
```

2. Inspect the %USD column, which presents the amount of queue used. This column is not related to spindle performance but can often be misinterpreted as a component of disk latency. However, this metric proves useful when troubleshooting the entire storage stack.

```
4:42:03pm up 59 days 14:22, 384 worlds; CPU load average: 0.10, 0.10, 0.10

DEVICE              PATH/WORLD/PARTITION DQLEN WQLEN ACTV QUED %USD  LOAD   CMDS/s  READS/s WRITES/s MBREAD/s MBWRTN/s DAVG/cmd KAVG/cmd GAVG/cmd QAVG/cmd
mpx.vmhba0:C0:T       -                    1    -    0    0    0  0.00   0.00    0.00    0.00    0.00    0.00    0.00    0.00    0.00    0.00
mpx.vmhba1:C0:T       -                   32    -    0    0    0  0.00   0.00    0.00    0.00    0.00    0.00    0.00    0.00    0.00    0.00
mpx.vmhba1:C0:T       -                   32    -    0    0    0  0.00   0.00    0.00    0.00    0.00    0.00    0.00    0.00    0.00    0.00
naa.6000eb3d000      -                  128    -    0    0    0  0.00   0.04   0.00    0.00    0.04    0.00    0.00    2.69    0.01    2.70    0.00
naa.6000eb3d000      -                   32    -    0    0    0  0.00   0.00    0.00    0.00    0.00    0.00    0.00    0.00    0.00    0.00
naa.6000eb3d000      -                  128    -    0    0    0  0.00   0.00    0.00    0.00    0.00    0.00    0.00    0.00    0.00    0.00
naa.6000eb3d000      -                  128    -    0    0    0  0.00   0.00    0.00    0.00    0.00    0.00    0.00    0.00    0.00    0.00
naa.6000eb3d000      -                   32    -    0    0    0  0.00   0.00    0.00    0.00    0.00    0.00    0.00    0.00    0.00    0.00
naa.6000eb3d000      -                  128    -    0    0    0  0.00   0.00    0.00    0.00    0.00    0.00    0.00    0.00    0.00    0.00
naa.6000eb3d000      -                  128    -    0    0    0  0.00   0.00    0.00    0.00    0.00    0.00    0.00    0.00    0.00    0.00
naa.6000eb3d000      -                  128    -    0    0    0  0.00   0.00    0.00    0.00    0.00    0.00    0.00    0.00    0.00    0.00
naa.6000eb3d000      -                   32    -    0    0    0  0.00   0.00    0.00    0.00    0.00    0.00    0.00    0.00    0.00    0.00
naa.6000eb3d000      -                  128    -    0    0    0  0.00   0.00    0.00    0.00    0.00    0.00    0.00    0.00    0.00    0.00
naa.6000eb3d000      -                  128    -    0    0    0  0.00   0.00    0.00    0.00    0.00    0.00    0.00    0.00    0.00    0.00
naa.6000eb3d000      -                   32    -    0    0    0  0.00   0.00    0.00    0.00    0.00    0.00    0.00    0.00    0.00    0.00
naa.6000eb3d000      -                   32    -    0    0    0  0.00   0.00    0.00    0.00    0.00    0.00    0.00    0.00    0.00    0.00
naa.6000eb3d000      -                   32    -    0    0    0  0.00   0.00    0.00    0.00    0.00    0.00    0.00    0.00    0.00    0.00
```

Figure 8-23 Storage throughput

Understanding SCSI Queue Depth on an ESX/ESXi Host and Virtual Machine

The SCSI queue depth metric, which reveals the number of SCSI commands that are waiting to be processed, at any layer of the stack should be less than 20. SCSI queues at the ESX/ESXi hypervisor and VM layers can be displayed using VMware utilities. If storage latency is problematic and explained neither by SCSI queues at the ESX/ESXi hypervisor or VM layers, nor by the other storage performance metrics in this section, you should investigate SCSI queues at the SAN and storage switch layer using vendor-proprietary utilities.

To inspect SCSI queue depth at the ESX/ESXi hypervisor layer, follow these steps and see Figure 8-24:

1. Start Esxtop with the following command:

   ```
   $ esxtop > d > f
   ```

2. Verify that QSTATS is selected with an asterisk to the left.

3. The SCSI queue depth of each LUN/datastore is displayed by Esxtop. The ACTV column refers to current/none buffered commands in the queue. This metric should be less than 20 or less than the queue depth that has been manually set. Furthermore, the QUED column refers to commands that are buffered in the ESX/ESXi server memory. Anything greater than 0 is unhealthy and means that the storage is overloaded. Refer to the VMware community docs DOC-9279. See Figure 8-25 for more detail.

   https://communities.vmware.com/docs/DOC-9279

```
Current Field order: ABcdeFGhIjklmnop

* A:  DEVICE = Device Name
* B:  ID = Path/World/Partition Id
  C:  NUM = Num of Objects
  D:  SHARES = Shares
  E:  BLKSZ = Block Size (bytes)
* F:  QSTATS = Queue Stats
* G:  IOSTATS = I/O Stats
  H:  RESVSTATS = Reserve Stats
* I:  LATSTATS/cmd = Overall Latency Stats (ms)
  J:  LATSTATS/rd = Read Latency Stats (ms)
  K:  LATSTATS/wr = Write Latency Stats (ms)
  L:  ERRSTATS/s = Error Stats
  M:  PAESTATS/s = PAE Stats
  N:  SPLTSTATS/s = SPLIT Stats
  O:  VAAISTATS= VAAI Stats
  P:  VAAILATSTATS/cmd = VAAI Latency Stats (ms)

Toggle fields with a-p, any other key to return: ▌
```

Figure 8-24 QSTATS metric

```
9:16:32pm up 3 days  7:39, 237 worlds; CPU load average: 0.09, 0.09, 0.09

DEVICE            PATH/WORLD/PARTITION DQLEN WQLEN ACTV QUED %USD  LOAD
npx.vmhba1:C0:T            -              1    -     0    0    0   0.00
haa.60014052afb           -             32    -     4    0   12   0.12
haa.60014053b84           -             32    -     0    0    0   0.00
haa.600140546a0           -            128    -     1    0    0   0.01
haa.60014057aa            -             32    -     0    0    0   0.00
haa.6001405764b           -             32    -     0    0    0   0.00
haa.6001405a92e           -             32    -     0    0    0   0.00
haa.6001405bdfd           -             32    -     1    0    3   0.03
haa.6001405c63a           -            128    -    33    0   25   0.26
haa.6001405ddfc           -             32    -     1    0    3   0.03
haa.6001405f5da           -             32    -     0    0    0   0.00
:10.ATA     TS1           -              1    -     0    0    0   0.00
:10.ATA     WDC           -              1    -     0    0    0   0.00
```

Figure 8-25 Active queue

Storage Path Throughput

Given a 4Gb Fibre Channel fabric, the goal is to achieve greater than 100MBps/storage path sustained throughput. If less is measured, consider splitting out storage paths.

You can use Esxtop or rEsxtop to display storage throughput. See Figure 8-26 for details. Here is an example of an esxtop command and output.

```
esxtop > u > f > i > g > f
```

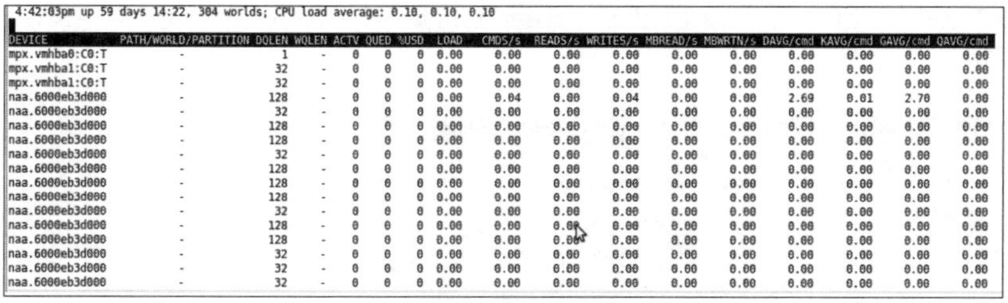

4:42:03pm up 59 days 14:22, 304 worlds; CPU load average: 0.10, 0.10, 0.10

DEVICE	PATH/WORLD/PARTITION	DQLEN	WQLEN	ACTV	QUED	%USD	LOAD	CMDS/s	READS/s	WRITES/s	MBREAD/s	MBWRTN/s	DAVG/cmd	KAVG/cmd	GAVG/cmd	QAVG/cmd
mpx.vmhba0:C0:T	-	1	-	0	0	0	0.00	0.00	0.00	0.00	0.00	0.00	0.00	0.00	0.00	0.00
mpx.vmhba1:C0:T	-	32	-	0	0	0	0.00	0.00	0.00	0.00	0.00	0.00	0.00	0.00	0.00	0.00
mpx.vmhba1:C0:T	-	32	-	0	0	0	0.00	0.00	0.00	0.00	0.00	0.00	0.00	0.00	0.00	0.00
naa.6000eb3d000	-	128	-	0	0	0	0.00	0.04	0.00	0.04	0.00	0.00	2.69	0.01	2.70	0.00
naa.6000eb3d000	-	32	-	0	0	0	0.00	0.00	0.00	0.00	0.00	0.00	0.00	0.00	0.00	0.00
naa.6000eb3d000	-	128	-	0	0	0	0.00	0.00	0.00	0.00	0.00	0.00	0.00	0.00	0.00	0.00
naa.6000eb3d000	-	128	-	0	0	0	0.00	0.00	0.00	0.00	0.00	0.00	0.00	0.00	0.00	0.00
naa.6000eb3d000	-	32	-	0	0	0	0.00	0.00	0.00	0.00	0.00	0.00	0.00	0.00	0.00	0.00
naa.6000eb3d000	-	128	-	0	0	0	0.00	0.00	0.00	0.00	0.00	0.00	0.00	0.00	0.00	0.00
naa.6000eb3d000	-	128	-	0	0	0	0.00	0.00	0.00	0.00	0.00	0.00	0.00	0.00	0.00	0.00
naa.6000eb3d000	-	128	-	0	0	0	0.00	0.00	0.00	0.00	0.00	0.00	0.00	0.00	0.00	0.00
naa.6000eb3d000	-	32	-	0	0	0	0.00	0.00	0.00	0.00	0.00	0.00	0.00	0.00	0.00	0.00
naa.6000eb3d000	-	128	-	0	0	0	0.00	0.00	0.00	0.00	0.00	0.00	0.00	0.00	0.00	0.00
naa.6000eb3d000	-	128	-	0	0	0	0.00	0.00	0.00	0.00	0.00	0.00	0.00	0.00	0.00	0.00
naa.6000eb3d000	-	32	-	0	0	0	0.00	0.00	0.00	0.00	0.00	0.00	0.00	0.00	0.00	0.00
naa.6000eb3d000	-	32	-	0	0	0	0.00	0.00	0.00	0.00	0.00	0.00	0.00	0.00	0.00	0.00
naa.6000eb3d000	-	32	-	0	0	0	0.00	0.00	0.00	0.00	0.00	0.00	0.00	0.00	0.00	0.00

Figure 8-26 Throughput is found in the MBREAD/s and MBWRTN/s columns.

Figure 8-27 shows a sample customer benchmark. Four storage types are selected, ranging in RAID type (RAID 6 and RAID 10) to storage presentation (FC and NFS). The benchmark helps to determine whether the storage is Tier 1 ready. Analysis determines that Test 1 is not qualified for Tier 1 I/O. Test 3 is slightly above the 60-MBps redline, and is minimally qualified. Test 2 and Test 4 show good results. The difference between Test 2 and Test 4 is the RAID type. Because Test 2 with RAID 6 performed nearly as well as Test 4 with RAID 10, the best choice is the Test 2 storage configuration for the Oracle server and future Tier 1 deployments.

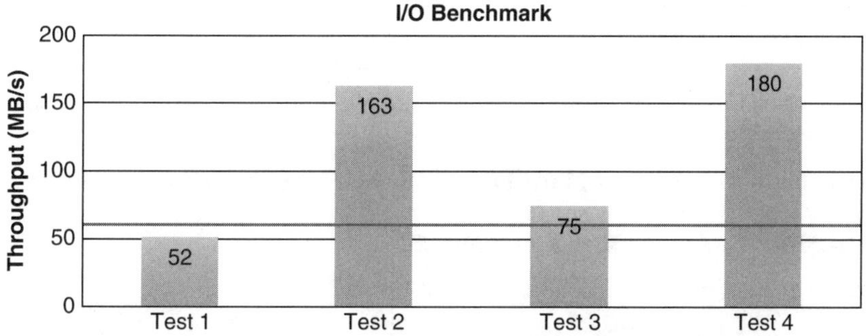

Figure 8-27 I/O benchmark measures in throughput on a series of disparate tests

Storage Benchmarking VMDK

For a substantive benchmarking test, it is recommended to create a new VMDK on a separate controller and to use multiple vSCSI adapters. Choose pvSCSI as the controller type.

This test requires three Oracle Automatic Storage Management (ASM) disks. To create each of the required three disks, follow these steps:

1. Select VM properties by selecting **Edit Settings**. Click **Add** to add the Oracle ASM drives (see Figure 8-28).

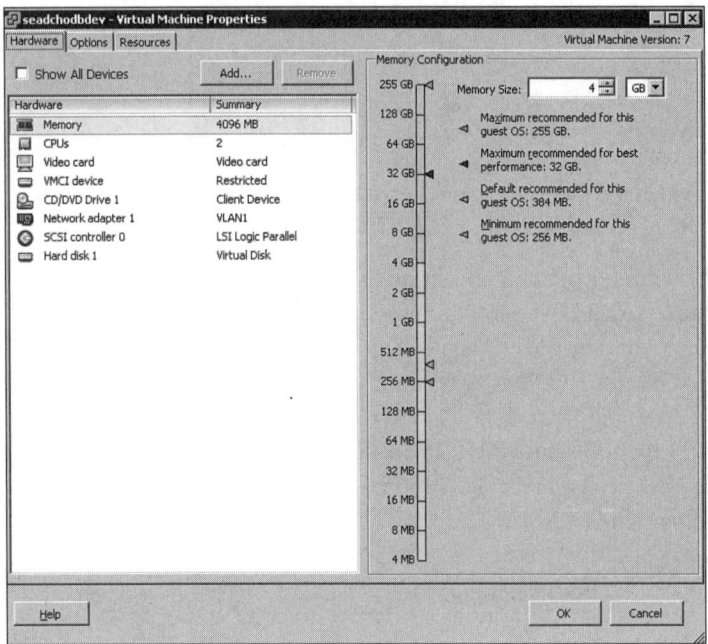

Figure 8-28 Virtual Machine Properties

2. On the Device Type screen, select **Hard Disk**, and click **Next** (see Figure 8-29).

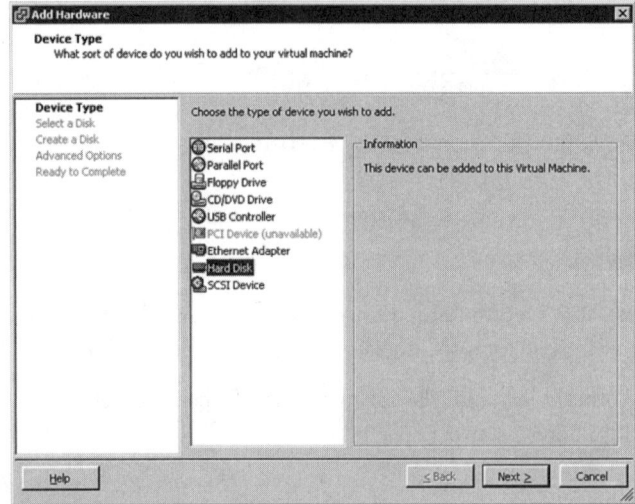

Figure 8-29 Adding ASM drives

3. Check the **Support clustering features such as Fault Tolerance** check box to create an eager-zeroed thick disk so that the disk is completely formatted. Click **Next** (see Figure 8-30).

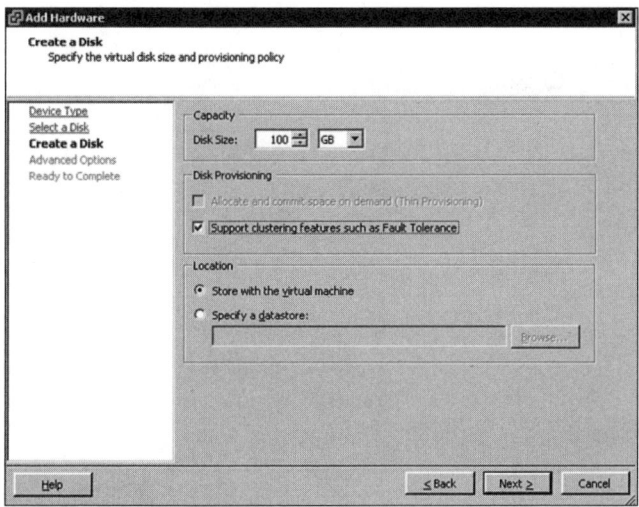

Figure 8-30 Creating a virtual disk

4. In the Advanced Options dialog box that appears, choose **SCSI (1:0)** from the Virtual Device Node drop-down menu. This forces the creation of a new SCSI controller. Click **Next** (see Figure 8-31).

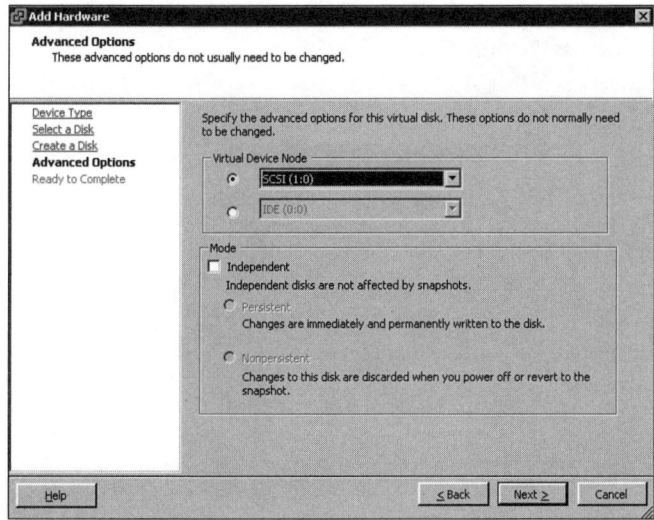

Figure 8-31 Adding a new virtual SCSI controller

5. The **Ready to Complete** screen then appears. Review the summary page and click **Finish** (see Figure 8-32).

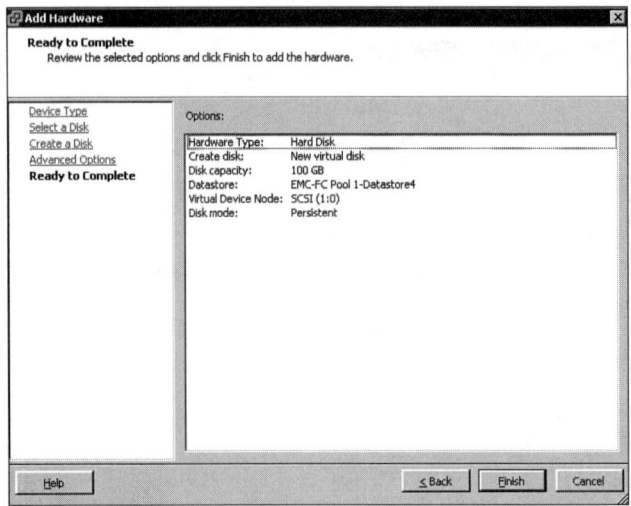

Figure 8-32 Adding disk completed

6. On the Virtual Machine Properties page, select the second controller, labeled **New SCSI Controller**, and then select **Change Type**. In the resulting dialog box, click **VMware Paravirtual**. Click **OK**, and click **OK** again. Because an eager-zeroed thick disk was created, and the entire disk will be formatted, the VMDK creation process takes some time (see Figure 8-33).

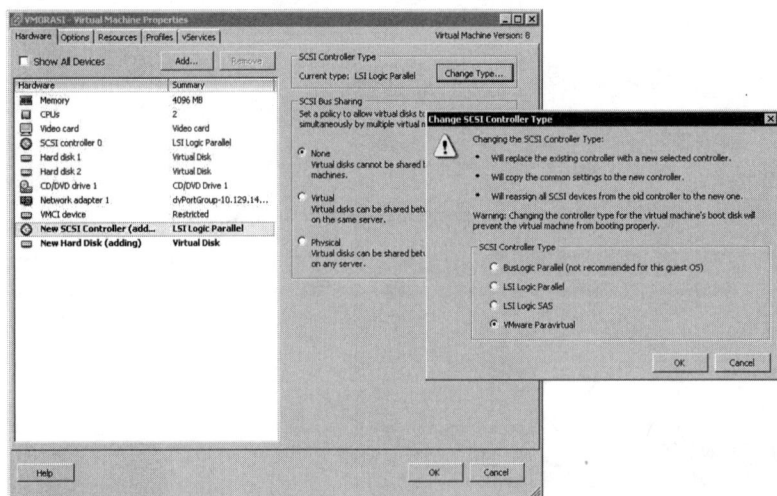

Figure 8-33 Specifying the controller type

Benchmarking and Ongoing Maintenance

The lifecycle of a SAN includes firmware upgrades, host driver updates, recabling of switches, physical movements of the machines, and other changes. Any of these changes can result in performance anomalies, inconsistencies, and problems. You should complete an I/O baseline so that when a change is made to the storage, testing based on the previously collected benchmarks can reveal any performance problems introduced by the alteration. After testing the changes, you should record a new baseline.

The following approaches to performance benchmarking apply to a number of tools, including the most common tools, known as Iometer and dd:

- Consider running the read and write test pairs during different shifts, on weekdays and weekends, and more than once for each time period. This can help to isolate production workload variances that impact the storage subsystem and can reduce the possibility that an I/O spike skews the throughput data.

- Write a test file larger than the storage cache. It is best to make the test file at least 2GB, or whatever size up to 32GB that pierces the SAN write cache.

> **NOTE**
>
> Storage cache greater than 32GB can be difficult to pierce. Do not write a dd output file larger than 32GB. Larger cache sizes can make write sizes larger than 32GB fairly useless, although the test still has value.

- For storage to be viable for a Tier 1 Oracle workload, at least 60MBps for sequential writes is required. If throughput is less than this, you must fix a fundamental storage problem before layering vSphere on top.

- Block size affects test results. A larger block size results in higher throughput as compared with a smaller block size. For the dd example, use 8192 bytes as the default block size for an Oracle database. In the unusual case of a nondefault block size for any of the tablespaces, test with the block size that is used for the majority of the most I/O-intensive tablespaces. Use the same block size for all tests.

- Run a write test to a SAN LUN, preferably through the multipath driver if multipath is in use. A common redline will be 80 to 100MBps on most systems. Determine the minimum performance metric for a sequential write, which is usually around 50 to 60MBps. It is not recommended to continue with the deployment until the storage is able to deliver more than the predetermined minimum. If the throughput is less than the accepted redline, consider repeating the test on different paths (possibly using a root volume group [internal storage] and a non-multipath storage path to the SAN). Testing storage paths incrementally in the direction of greater complexity can highlight a bottleneck.

Iometer

One of the best tools to use to benchmark I/O on an x86 server is Iometer. Iometer was originally developed by Intel and is now released as open source software.

To install Iometer, double-click the executable and follow the prompts. After the installation finishes, click the **Iometer** icon to start the graphical user interface (GUI) and complete the basic configuration.

To run Iometer on Windows Server 2008, follow these steps:

1. Right-click **Iometer** and select **Run as administrator** to run Iometer with administrative privileges (see Figure 8-34).

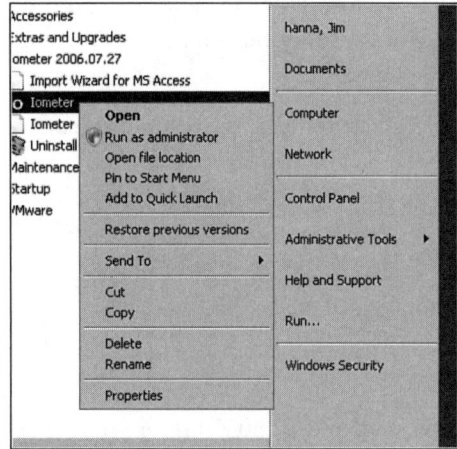

Figure 8-34 Iometer setup first step

2. In the User Account Control window, select **Allow** (see Figure 8-35).

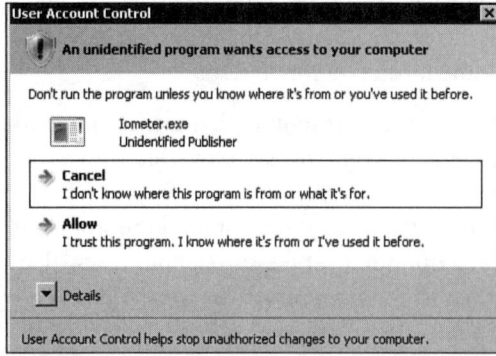

Figure 8-35 User account control

3. After Iometer starts, a window called C:\Program Files (x86)\I... opened with Iometer appears. This thread drives the I/O and file creation. Do not close it (see Figure 8-36).

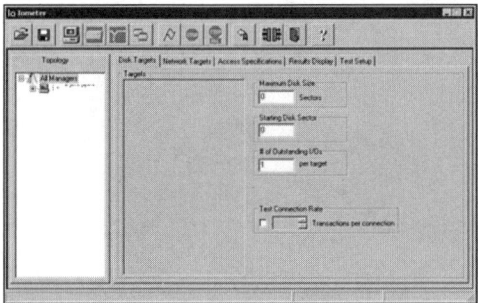

Figure 8-36 Setting the output file location

4. Select **Open** and go to the OpenPerformanceTest.icf configuration file location (see Figure 8-37). The default configuration file is a standard agreed upon by a group of users who test VMware I/O performance. You can modify the file, but the default configuration file is often a good starting point for testing. The file and user forum are available at VMware community thread number 73734.

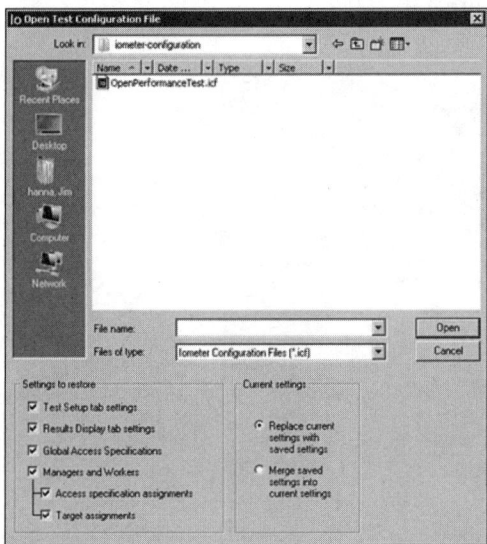

Figure 8-37 Configuring the performance test

5. Select **Worker 1**, and then select the drive. This creates the test output file if it does not already exist. Iometer creates a 4GB test output file by default (see Figure 8-38).

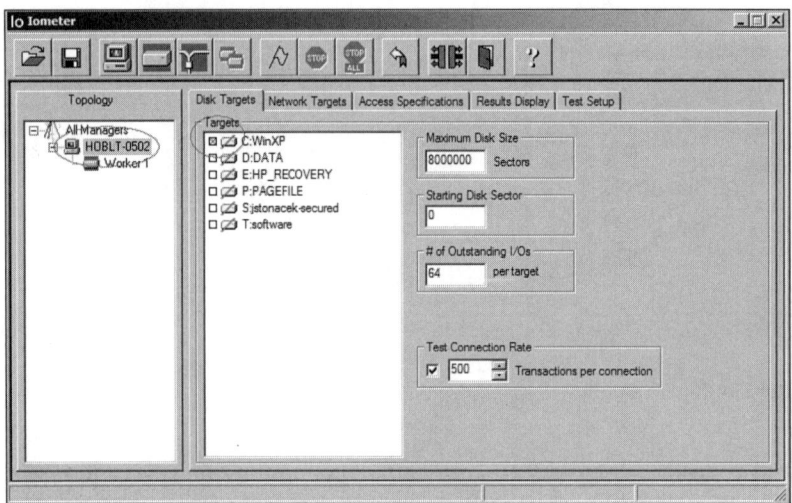

Figure 8-38 Specifying the output file details

6. Under the Access Specifications tab, select a test and click **Add**. This example selects **Max Throughput - 100% Read** (see Figure 8-39).

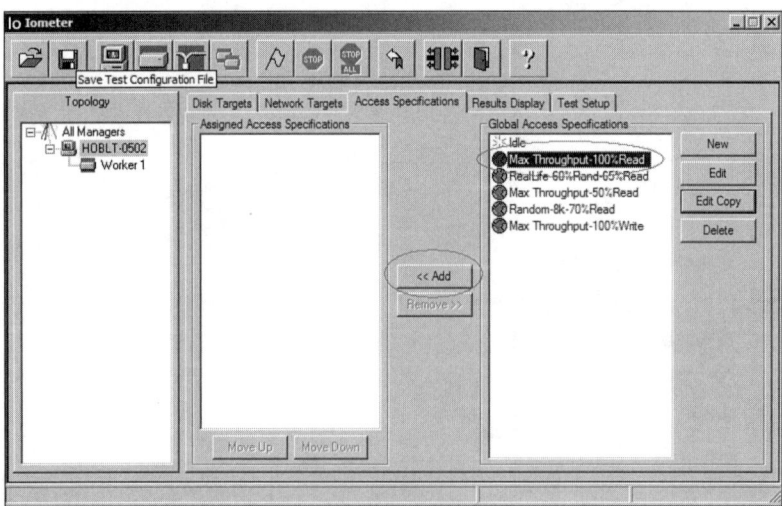

Figure 8-39 Selecting the specific test type

7. Under the Test Setup tab, confirm that the settings are correct. The default values might be okay. You can modify the length of the test in the Run Time section (see Figure 8-40).

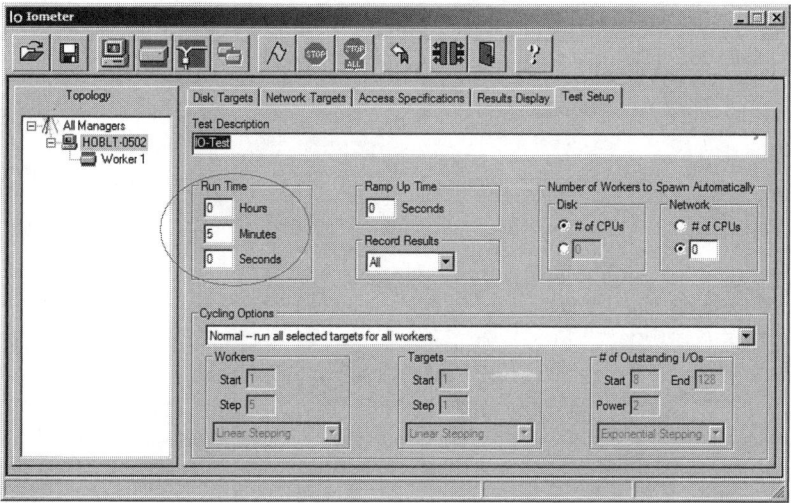

Figure 8-40 Testing the configuration

8. For a write test, select the **Max Throughput - 100% Read** test, select **Edit Copy**, and then change the **Percent Read/Write Distribution** slider to **100% Write** (see Figure 8-41).

For a read test, select **Max Throughput - 100% Read**. This test usually exposes any problems with the storage configuration, ESX/ESXi host, HBAs, or drivers.

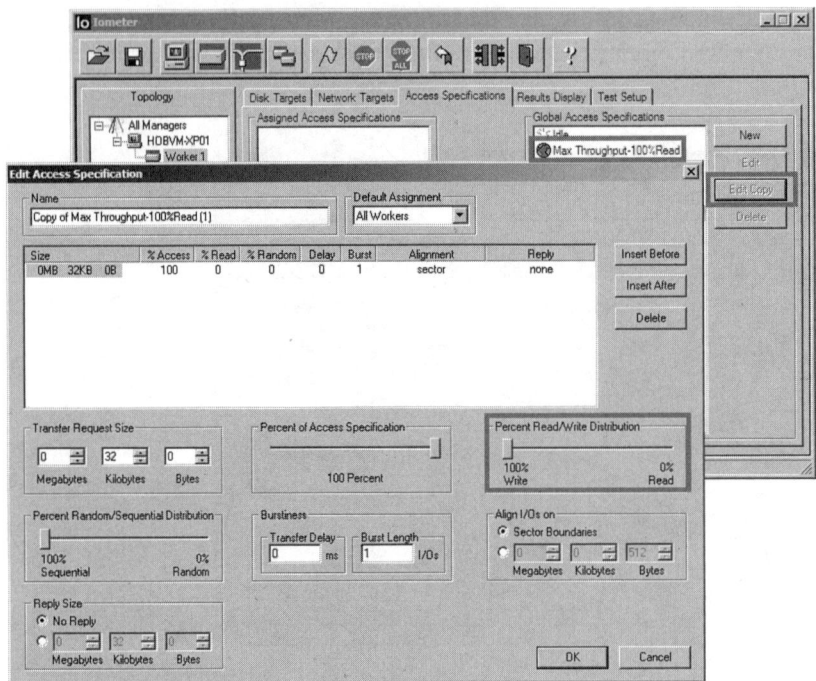

Figure 8-41 Running Iometer

9. Under the Results Display tab, change the **Update Frequency** to **4** and select **Last Update**. Click **Run Test** (the green flag icon; see Figure 8-42).

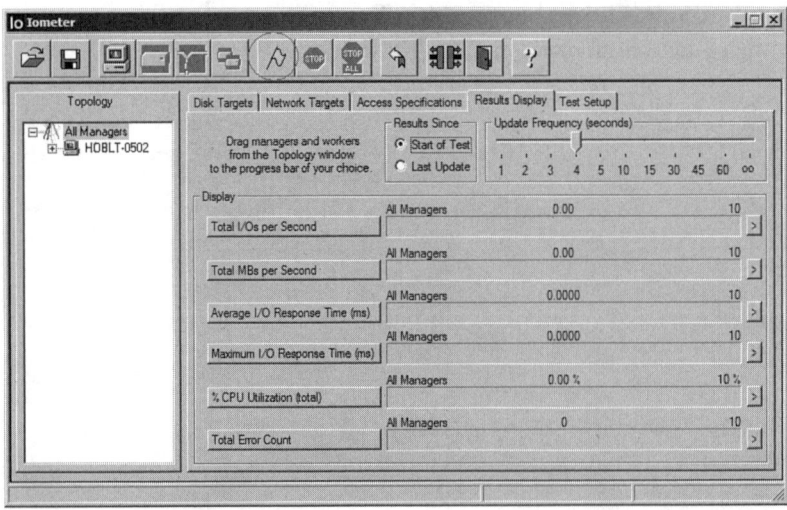

Figure 8-42 Iometer results display

Iometer asks for a filename to save the results. The results are written to a CSV file with the data from the test. After the results file is specified, the test begins.

Iometer first prepares a file for use by the test. If the defaults are used from the ICF configuration file, the file is 4GB and is named iobw.tst. The first time Iometer runs, it generates this file, so the actual test is delayed until the file is ready. Subsequent tests on the same drive use the existing file, so a new file is not generated.

10. Click the **Stop** icon to stop the test if desired. At the end of the test, the average results appear. Examine the **Error! Reference source not found.** to conclude whether the minimum performance redlines determined earlier as the criteria for the test for writes and reads have been achieved. You must manually clean up the iobw.tst file after testing completes.

Oracle ORION

Oracle I/O Numbers (ORION) is an Oracle tool available to benchmark anticipated I/O performance for an Oracle database. It is a simple front-end driver with a current version of Oracle I/O libraries. You can use the tool to simulate an Oracle database I/O workload without an actual database or Oracle installed. The main objective of ORION is to test the readiness of the I/O stack for the inclusion of an Oracle database. It comes with several basic tests to verify correct operation and performs a quick test of the I/O subsystem.

The default options and basic tests included with ORION are read-only tests. Therefore, you can perform read testing on production volumes without risk of destroying data on them. When the default settings are altered, it will clean data on the volumes that ORION uses for the test.

Download the ORION tool and User's Guide from Oracle ORION downloads.

http://docs.oracle.com/cd/E11882_01/server.112/e16638/iodesign.htm

Using ORION

To properly use the ORION tool, follow these steps:

1. Specify the disk devices (or files) for ORION to work on by creating a file with one device or filename per line. For example, you can create a file called test1.lun as follows, which directs ORION to use the ASM disks specified:

```
/dev/oracleasm/disks/DATA01
/dev/oracleasm/disks/DATA02
/dev/oracleasm/disks/DATA03
/dev/oracleasm/disks/DATA04
```

```
/dev/oracleasm/disks/DATA05
/dev/oracleasm/disks/DATA06
/dev/oracleasm/disks/DATA07
/dev/oracleasm/disks/DATA08
/dev/oracleasm/disks/DATA09
/dev/oracleasm/disks/DATA10
```

2. Invoke a simple test called test1 to perform a basic read-only test with the following command:

```
./orion -run simple -testname test1
```

A more complete test can be run by replacing the argument `simple` with `normal`.

3. Upon conclusion of the tests, ORION generates several output files, including comma-separated values (CSV) with data points that can be graphed in a spreadsheet.

4. In addition to the simple and normal tests, a user can specify individual parameters to perform more granular tests. For example, the following command line is an example of the normal test with a custom duration:

```
nohup time ./orion -run advanced -testname test1 -num_disks 10 \
  -size_small 8 -size_large 1024 -type rand \
  -simulate concat -write 0 -duration 7 \
  -matrix detailed &
```

Enter the command carefully because a value other than 0 for the `-write` argument results in random data being written to the specified files or disk volumes.

Using Disk-to-Disk dd

The simplest of the common performance testing tools is dd. Available in every Linux distribution base install, dd provides an effective and simple method of I/O benchmarking. The tool is a legacy UNIX utility for dumping raw data from one device to another. With dd, the user can write to either a file system or a raw device. However, note that despite the ubiquitous nature of dd and extremely simple appearance, there is a plethora of options that can easily be incorrectly used, leading to results that can in turn be misinterpreted.

TIP

Thoroughly double-check the dd syntax. This utility writes data wherever the output file is directed and for as many bytes as it is told to write. If the command is mistyped, it can corrupt data, application executables, or the operating system itself.

Tests can be run from the VMware Management Assistant (vMA) using the remote console of an ESX/ESXi host. However, the remote console is a specialized VM with one vCPU and a maximum of 800MB of memory. The dd results from the remote console are not typically indicative of the I/O that a VM experiences on the same ESX/ESXi host. A more accurate I/O benchmark is performed on an ESX/ESXi host from a guest VM.

Running a dd Test on Linux

To run a dd test on Linux, complete the following steps:

1. Locate a file system with sufficient available space to contain the resulting test file.

2. Determine the total number of bytes to write during the test. Divide the target total bytes by the block size (bs parameter) to determine the count parameter, which is the number of blocks that dd writes. Figure 8-43 shows an example of the commands.

```
linux:~/io-benchmark$ dd if=/dev/zero of=/dev/null bs=8192 count=1048576
1048576+0 records in
1048576+0 records out
8589934592 bytes (8.6 GB) copied, 1.32734 s, 6.5 GB/s
linux:~/io-benchmark$ []
```

Figure 8-43 dd commands

3. Calculate carefully, because an error can result in unpredictable results. When testing using raw devices, if an inadvertent dd operation writes more than the size of the raw device specified as the output file, dd might continue writing over whatever is physically next on the disk, potentially destabilizing or taking down the node in the process.

TIP

To test write speed, direct dd to read from /dev/zero and write to the file or raw device specified. Before performing a write test with dd, test to verify that the system can read from /dev/zero fast enough to push the I/O subsystem to its limit.

Running the Linux dd Pretest

Run the following command to test /dev/zero. The write test to /dev/null is expected to be very fast. The test displayed in Figure 8-44 shows that in 1.3 seconds 8GB was written.

```
linux:~/io-benchmark$ dd if=/dev/zero of=/dev/null bs=8192 count=1048576
1048576+0 records in
1048576+0 records out
8589934592 bytes (8.6 GB) copied, 1.32734_s, 6.5 GB/s
linux:~/io-benchmark$ []
```

Figure 8-44 dd pretest example

Running the Linux dd Write Test

Figure 8-45 shows running the command to copy bytes with 0s to an output file. This test wrote 8GB of data at 65.3MBps.

```
linux:~/io-benchmark$ dd if=/dev/zero of=8GB.bin bs=8192 count=1048576
1048576+0 records in
1048576+0 records out
8589934592 bytes (8.6 GB) copied, 131.544_s, 65.3 MB/s
```

Figure 8-45 dd write test example

Running the Linux dd Read Test

The read test is performed by reading back the file that was written in the write test. This example uses the 8GB.bin file. The file is read and then dumped to /dev/null. Figure 8-46 shows the commands.

```
linux:~/io-benchmark$ dd if=8GB.bin of=/dev/null bs=8192 count=1048576
1048576+0 records in
1048576+0 records out
8589934592 bytes (8.6 GB) copied, 139.693_s, 61.5 MB/s
```

Figure 8-46 dd read test example

A read test is expected to be faster than the corresponding write test, but this example contradicts that point. This situation is typically reflective of problems within the storage subsystem, such as storage configuration issues or storage cache saturation. In this case, the problem was caused by heavy disaster recovery related traffic the day of the test. The SAN cache is likely inadequately sized. Typically, a read test such as this example should achieve at least 125% of the write test.

Storage IO Control

Storage I/O Control (SIOC) is a feature for maintaining I/O performance for heavy workloads within an ESXi cluster such as Oracle workloads. It was introduced in vSphere 4.1 and allows for prioritized storage throughput between hosts by using shares much like CPU and memory shares. There are two practical uses for SIOC for Oracle workloads.

SIOC enables administrators to throttle I/O-intensive workloads such as development projects, for the protection of other prioritized workloads on the same LUN.

SIOC has no effect when two VMs are running on the same host because normal resource pools can be used to address that prioritization of storage access from a single host. When the VMs are running on different hosts within an ESXi cluster, SIOC can be used to prioritize storage access. Only when a predetermined threshold is exceeded will SIOC throttle the lesser-priority VM's access to the shared datastore by restricting the storage access through the HBA on that host.

Basically, this is grant to a VM of a higher priority than other VMs accessing the same datastore. A potential application of SIOC high I/O priority is for a Quality Assurance (QA) node during business user functional testing. For more information, refer to *Storage I/O Control Technical Overview and Considerations for Deployment*, which you can find on VMware's website.

www.vmware.com/files/pdf/techpaper/VMW-vSphere41-SIOC.pdf

Figure 8-47 shows two I/O-prioritized workloads, Oracle Prod and Oracle QA, with I/O bandwidth privilege beyond their reservations. However, the two deprioritized I/O workloads, Oracle Dev and Oracle Test, are not permitted to consume I/O bandwidth to interfere with the I/O-prioritized workloads' reservation, even if the I/O bandwidth is available.

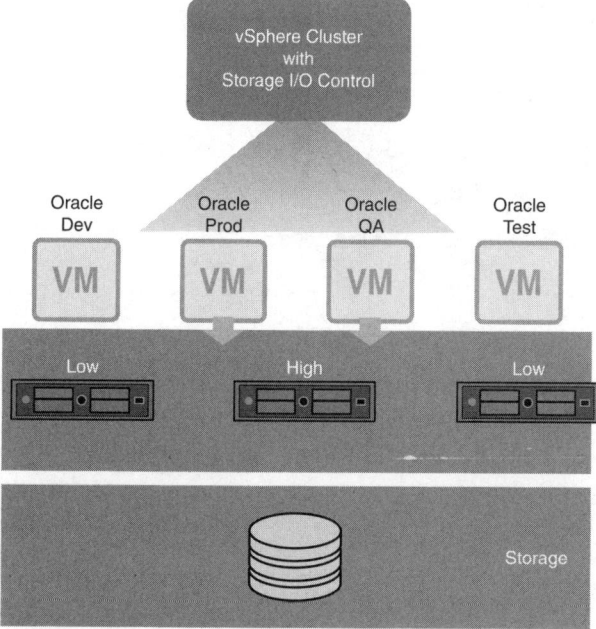

Figure 8-47 Storage I/O Control

SIOC monitors datastore latency on the cluster, not only on each separate ESX/ESXi hosts. It can be described as SAN/NAS *array aware*. If the average disk latency reaches (the default which can be adjusted) 30ms for a specified period, SIOC starts to prioritize workloads based on disk shares. SIOC is configured by enabling SIOC for the datastore and enabling disk shares for the VMs.

To configure SIOC, follow these steps and see Figure 8-48:

1. Display the Properties dialog box for the datastore.

2. In the Storage I/O Control section, select **Enabled**.

3. Click **Advanced** to edit the Congestion Threshold. The default latency is 30ms.

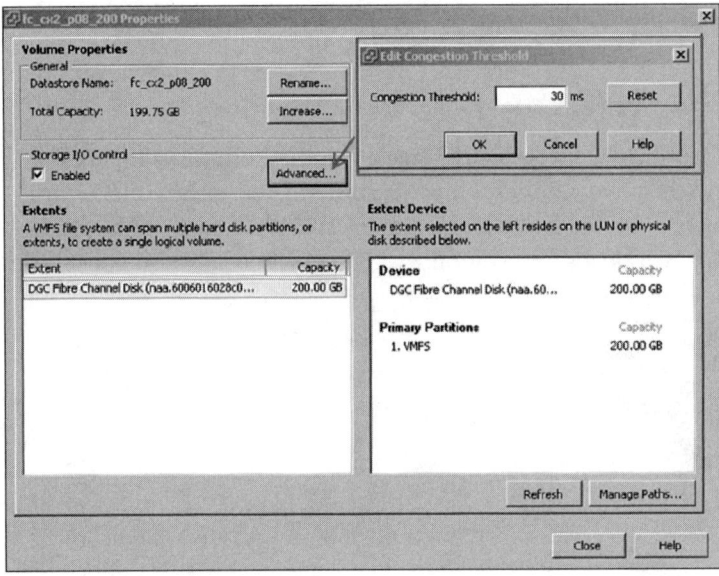

Figure 8-48 Setting SIOC

TIP

SIOC supports block devices, iSCSI, and Fibre Channel. It does not support NFS, raw device mapping (RDM), or datastores with multiple extents.

Configuring the Disk Shares

To configure the disk shares, click **Edit Settings** for a VM and enable disk shares on each desired VMDK. See Figure 8-49 for details.

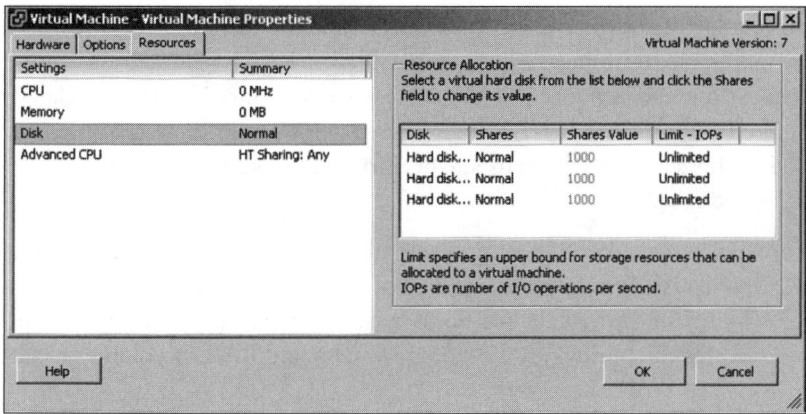

Figure 8-49 Setting SIOC shares

RAID Selection

In 2014, few modern arrays allow administrators to configure the Redundant Array of Independent Disks (RAID) level. It has become an accepted proactive approach on the part of the array vendors to preconfigure all aspects of redundancy. Concepts such as RAID 6 and RAID 3D, along with a plethora of variations of autostorage tiering, dominate the storage market. However, it is extremely useful for Oracle professionals and their vSphere counterparts to understand the fundamental concepts behind storage redundancy. Remember that the main pillar behind the proposition of Oracle on vSphere is that no fundamental distinctions exist between the virtualized and nonvirtualized stacks.

The specific RAID types are of less importance than the storage access metrics of latency, throughput, and IOPS when planning vSphere datastores. Modern SANs and NAS devices move around hot blocks in response to usage metrics. With sufficient storage cache, Tier 1 performance can be achieved on many types of storage hardware. Many storage solutions can move hot blocks to more optimal disks. Benchmark results can vary depending on whether data blocks have been moved from one storage device to another. For enterprise-level SANs, the RAID type is not necessarily the bottleneck, because slow performance can result from poor storage design or driver issues.

To improve cost and performance, storage vendors have introduced hardware-based RAID 5 calculation, RAM caches, and intelligent controllers. Today, RAID 5 and RAID 6 are viable mechanisms for providing redundant storage capacity that is reasonably fast without doubling raw storage capacity as RAID 10 or RAID 0+1 requires.

With the majority of modern enterprise SAN systems available today, RAID 5 is a reasonable option. Most midrange customers run successfully with RAID 5 storage systems. However, if the cache is "pierced" (that is, if heavy write activity cannot be accommodated by the SAN cache), RAID 5 performs poorly. Enterprise systems can offer mechanisms to reduce the likelihood of this scenario when storage performance would otherwise be suddenly and dramatically reduced.

A mix of RAID 10 or solid state disk (SSD) is recommended and available on many modern storage systems. Oracle redo logs should be placed on the higher write performance storage volumes. This offers the immediate benefit of hardware performance for critical or heavy-write files and reduces the burden on the storage system and RAID 5 volumes.

Storage Path Selection

The following native storage path selections are available in ESX/ESXi 5.X:

- Most Recently Used (MRU)
- Fixed (Fixed)
- Round Robin (RR)
- Fixed Path with Array Preference (VMW_PSP_FIXED_AP)

For optimal performance, consult the storage vendor's documentation for configuration best practices. Some vendors recommend Round Robin rather than MRU as the best practice, and some support Asymmetric Logical Unit Access (ALUA) for active/passive SAN such as the EMC CLARiiON/Celerra. CLARiiON LUN access is allowed through paths not owned by the controller. Refer to the EMC Applied Technology guide EMC CLARiiON Integration with VMware ESX. You must first obtain and EMC login to access this paper.

www.emc.com/collateral/hardware/white-papers/
h1416-emc-clariion-intgtn-vmware-wp.pdf

Round Robin and ALUA work well together, providing better performance and availability. ALUA effectively allows for active/active path connectivity. VMware states "Switching to Round Robin from MRU or Fixed is safe and supported for all arrays". Consult VMware KB 1011340 article, *Multipathing policies in ESX/ESXi 4.x and ESXi 5.x.*

Raw Device Mapping

Raw device mapping (RDM) can be used for a number of different legitimate reasons, but often the reasoning behind the use of an RDM is either a long-since-obsolete legacy notion or an emotional barrier. RDMs can be used in virtual compatibility mode (RDM-V) or physical compatibility mode (RDM-P).

RDM-V: Raw Device Mapping Virtual Mode

RDM-V specifies full virtualization of the mapped device. In RDM-V mode, the hypervisor is responsible for SCSI commands. With the hypervisor as the operator for SCSI commands, full virtualization tooling is available.

RDM-P: Raw Device Mapping Physical Mode

In RDM-P, the SCSI commands pass directly through the hypervisor unaltered. This allows for SAN management tooling of the LUN. The cost of RDM-P is losing vSphere snapshot-based tooling and losing vMotion.

Reasons Not to Use RDMs

VMware's stated direction is to support all new features with Virtual Machine File System (VMFS) without consideration of RDM.

RDM is more difficult to configure, operate, and maintain than VMware vSphere VMFS.

Each RDM uses a simple link file very similar to a UNIX/Linux symbolic link. In a re-platform to native, it might be advisable to remove these links to minimize the threat of applications inadvertently accessing the storage through them. You can script this to automatically remove the link files. RDM link files can be added and removed with power shell scripting (or using `vmware-cmd` on earlier ESX versions).

To be accessed by cluster-aware software, such as Oracle RAC, inside VMs spread across multiple ESX/ESXi hosts, RDMs can be configured in either physical or virtual compatibility mode.

When using Oracle RAC, it is possible to use RDMs in virtual compatibility mode, which should be configured without SCSI bus sharing and with the multi-writer flag set. When configured this way, this mode allows VMware vSphere vMotion operations. If RDM physical compatibility mode is used, vMotion cannot be used in a supported fashion.

Using RDM was, historically, the preferred mechanism for applications that required fast I/O. However, improvements in VMFS and VMDK performance now make VMDKs preferable to RDMs. There is no longer any significant impact to performance with VMDKs.

The following list constitutes the reasons to consider using RDMs:

- RDM maintains some of the storage tooling at the SAN layer and the vSphere layer. Sometimes it is easier to use vendor-based snapshotting tools with RDMs than with VMFS.

- Cluster systems that use SCSI reservations require the use of RDMs such as Microsoft Cluster Services/Windows Failover Clustering.

- Slight performance increase over the use of VMFS.

TIP

Use the REPORT LUN command for LUN ownership isolation, as documented in *RDM Virtual and Physical Compatibility Modes*. See KB article 2009226 as well as the link listed here:

http://pubs.vmware.com/vsphere-51/index.jsp?topic=%2Fcom.vmware.vsphere.storage.doc%2FGUID-4B2479B1-541D-4FF4-865E-2EE711294478.html

---

A common implementation for use of a RDM-P is for SCSI reservation technologies like Microsoft Clustering. A SCSI reservation is a way for a host to reserve exclusive access to a LUN in a shared storage configuration.

Oracle Grid Infrastructure does not use SCSI reservations. Instead, Oracle relies on its own software mechanisms to protect the integrity of the shared storage in a RAC configuration. VMware recommends RDM-V over RDM-P for Oracle RAC configurations for those shops that choose not to follow the VMDK recommendation.

RDM-P allows SAN tooling unfettered access to the storage. For this reason, shops that heavily leverage such tooling might be tempted to configure RDM-P even given its sacrifice of a significant amount of VMware-level tooling capabilities. Table 8-4 compares both modes of RDMs.

Table 8-4 RDM-V and RDM-P Supported Features

vSphere Feature	RDM-V	RDM-P
vMotion	Yes	No
DRS	Yes	Yes
VMware vSphere High Availability (HA)	Yes	Yes

vSphere Feature	RDM-V	RDM-P
Snapshot	Yes	No
VMware vSphere Storage vMotion	Yes	Yes
Storage I/O Control	No	No
VMware vCloud Director	No	No
VMware vSphere Fault Tolerance (FT) (KB article 101631, *Turn on Fault Tolerance option is disabled*)	Yes	No
VMware vCenter Site Recovery Manager (SRM)	Yes	Yes
SAN tooling	Limited	Full

TIP

Although nonclustered workloads might appear to execute vMotion without issues under RDM-P, vMotion is not supported in this configuration.

Other Implications of RDMs

Creating an RDM results in the creation of a special file that is used by VMs to access the physical LUN. This link is, effectively, a link to the physical LUN. If the link is no longer needed by VMs, remove it to prevent unplanned access to the storage. See Figure 8-50 for details.

Other shared or clustered storage mechanisms can be accessed directly by both physical and virtual machines, such as iSCSI, and NFS that do not prohibit or reduce the capabilities of VMware features. All these are in-guest mechanisms and do not prevent a vMotion operation of the VM itself. Direct-mounted NFS is also known as in-guest NFS. See Figure 8-51 for details.

TIP

It is possible to use NFS to mount directly to the ESXi host. From that point, the user can create and use NFS datastores.

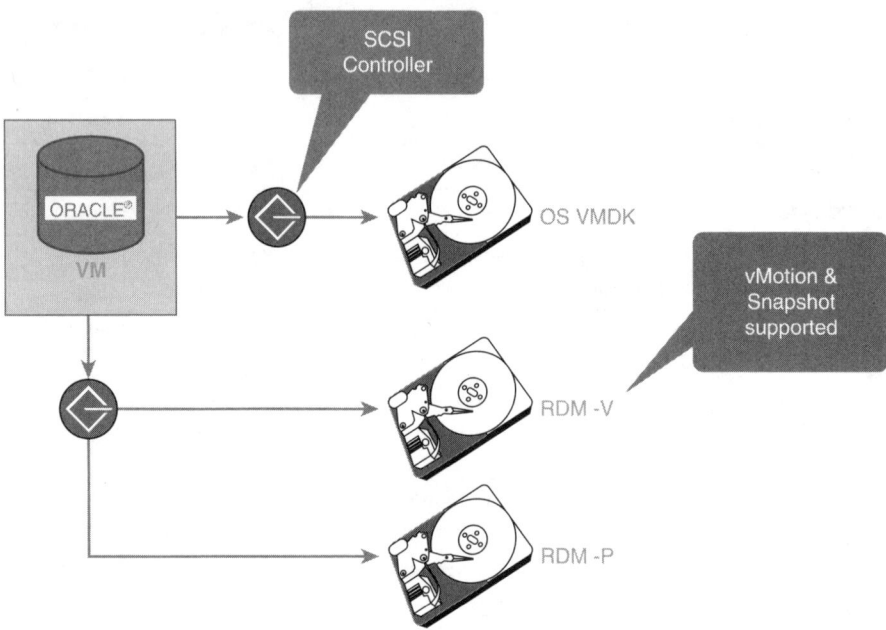

Figure 8-50 RDM implications

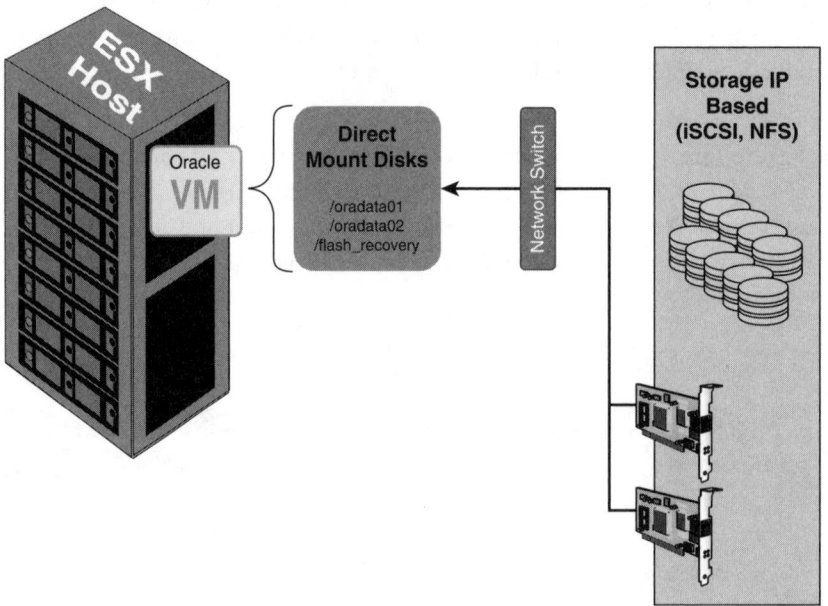

Figure 8-51 Direct-mounted IP-based storage

Oracle Direct-NFS

With Oracle Direct-NFS (dNFS), the Oracle Server becomes an NFS client. Beginning in Oracle Database 11g, you can use Oracle dNFS for Oracle data files, as described in *Oracle Database 11g Direct NFS Client*, which can be found at Oracle's website. Oracle dNFS uses NFS protocol to talk directly with NFS storage devices. The mount of the NFS device is handled directly by the Oracle kernel and not the GOS or ESX/ESXi host. To implement Oracle dNFS, the NFS mount is presented directly to the GOS. Figure 8-52 shows a graphical display of dNFS.

Oracle dNFS has the following benefits:

- Direct I/O bypasses any operating system level caches

- Eliminates write-orders locks from the operating system

- Eliminates double caching, where Oracle is cached in both the operating system file system cache and the Oracle SGA

- Supports up to four concurrent multipath connections (separate VM networks)

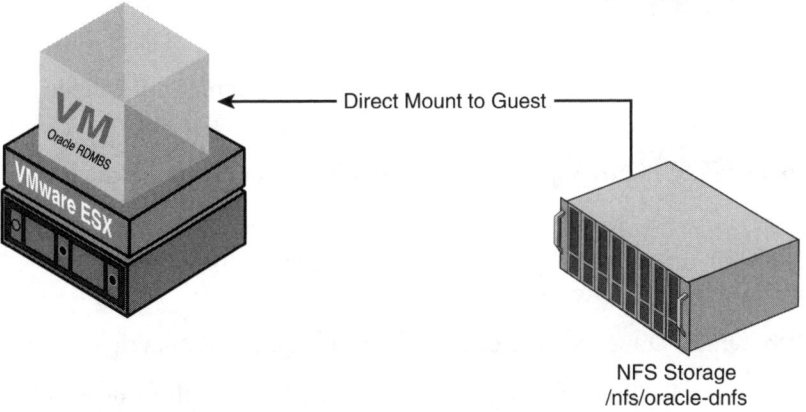

NFS Storage
/nfs/oracle-dnfs

Figure 8-52 dNFS storage directly mounted to the Guest OS

Traditional operating system NFS is not optimized for Oracle data file I/O, and it does not perform as well as Oracle dNFS. dNFS uses concurrent direct I/O to access Oracle data files. This means that it can use multipath I/O, with enough bandwidth and Ethernet interfaces. With direct I/O, the undesirable behavior of double caching is eliminated. Double caching, in a nondirect I/O environment, reads data into the Oracle SGA and the operating system file system cache. The operating system file system cache provides no value to Oracle, creating a double-caching effect. Direct I/O eliminates the file system caching by reading data directly into the Oracle SGA. It also reduces superfluous CPU usage and interrupts, and aids in the effort in following best practices for a virtual environment. Different storage presentations were benchmarked to compare them to dNFS. Figure 8-53 shows the results.

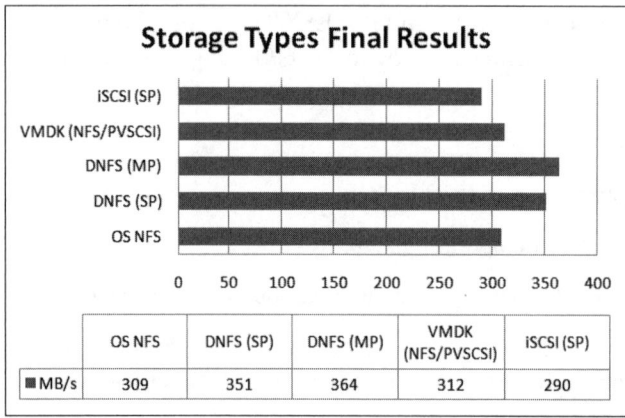

	OS NFS	DNFS (SP)	DNFS (MP)	VMDK (NFS/PVSCSI)	iSCSI (SP)
■ MB/s	309	351	364	312	290

Figure 8-53 Oracle dNFS comparison

The tests were conducted over an HP Flex 10GbE interface traffic shared with 4Gb dedicated to storage:

- **iSCSI single path:** iSCSI to NetApp using a single-path iSCSI initiator on the Red Hat guest

- **VMDK (NFS/pvSCSI):** Traditional NFS presented to the guest with the VMware PVSCSI driver load in the Linux guest

- **dNFS multipath:** Oracle Direct NFS directly to the Linux guest with multiple paths

- **dNFS single path:** Oracle Direct NFS directly to the Linux guest with a single path

- **Operating system NFS:** Traditional NFS directly to the Linux guest

Oracle dNFS performs well in a virtual environment. In addition to the I/O performance gain from dNFS, there is also a reduction in the CPU utilization compared with traditional NFS. This is attributed to the way Oracle makes the NFS calls to the Linux kernel with dNFS. The Oracle whitepaper *Oracle Database 11g Direct NFS Client* records this at 25% reduction in CPU of a two-CPU workload.

NFS Setup Notes for Benchmark Test

The published Oracle recommendations for operating system NFS were used as published in MyOracleSupport (MetaLink Note) *How to Optimize NFS Performance with NFS options*, Doc ID 397194.1, and *Mount Options for Oracle files*, Doc ID 359515.1.

Use the following parameters for Oracle over NFS:

- `rw,bg,hard,nointr,rsize=32768,wsize=32768,tcp,nolock,vers=3,`
  `timeo=600`

- `actimeo=0 directs the operating system to bypass file attribute`
  `cache.`

Oracle dNFS Guest Configuration

To configure a dNFS client, follow these steps:

1. Mount NFS through the traditional methods by using an entry in /etc/fstab.

2. Set up /etc/oranfstab.

3. Configure Oracle to use the Client Oracle Disk Manager (ODM) library.

To use a dNFS client, the NFS file systems must first be mounted and available over standard NFS mounts. The mount options used in mounting the file systems are irrelevant, because the dNFS client manages the configuration. For more information, refer to *Oracle Database 11g Direct NFS Client* whitepaper on the Oracle "technet" website. www.oracle.com/technetwork/articles/directnfsclient-11gr1-twp-129785.pdf

dNFS uses an fstab file similar to the Linux /etc/fstab. Choose from the following files for mount entries:

- $ORACLE_HOME/dbs/oranfstab

- /etc/oranfstab

- /etc/mtab

Oracle searches for them in the order listed, starting with $ORACLE_HOME/dbs/ oranfstab. The $ORACLE_HOME/dbs file is unique because it can be used only for a single instance. Therefore, if multiple databases are running on one node but dNFS is running for only a single database, use the $ORACLE_HOME/dbs file. The following is a sample /etc/oranfstab file:

```
[oracle@oel55-64-11g lib]$ cat /etc/oranfstab
server: DBA_NAS01
```

```
local: 10.90.84.28
path: 10.90.84.10
dontroute
export: /vol/DBA01/data_NFS mount: /data_NFS
```

TIP

The entry dontroute specifies that the dNFS kernel not route NFS traffic. The 4Gb NFS network is all on one subnet. This informs Oracle of the redundancy and throughput of a multipath setup without the extra complexity of adding more subnets.

Enable dNFS ODM library by linking libodm11.so to libnfsodm11.so. Do this with the following commands:

```
cd $ORACLE_HOME/lib
mv libodm11.so libodm11.so_bak
ln -s libnfsodm11.so libodm11.so
```

Verify Oracle Direct NFS

To verify Oracle dNFS, restart the Oracle database and examine the alert log looking for the entry "Oracle instance running with ODM: Oracle Direct NFS ODM Library," as shown in the following log extract. This verifies only that the NFS ODM library is loaded, but it does not verify that Oracle reads the oranfstab correctly. To verify that the oranfstab loads correctly, look for the following entries in the Oracle alert log, as shown in Figure 8-54. The figure shows the two lines that reference "Direct NFS." but the last line displayed here indicating that the Oracle instance is running with ODM—although not in the figure—will appear in the alert long.

```
Direct NFS: channel id [0] path [10.90.84.10] to filer [DBA_NAS01] via
local [10.90.84.28] is UP
Direct NFS: channel id [1] path [10.90.84.10] to filer [DBA_NAS01] via
local [10.90.84.28] is UP
Oracle instance running with ODM: Oracle Direct NFS ODM Library Version 2.0
```

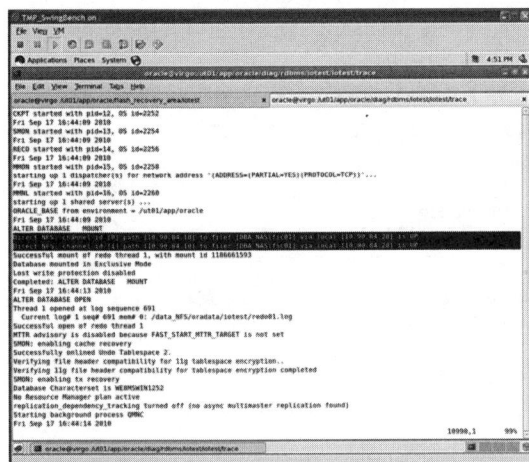

Figure 8-54 Verify Oracle dNFS

Verify Oracle dNFS Using `netstat`

Oracle dNFS can also be verified by running `netstat -an | grep 2049`. Figure 8-55 displays that a single path is being used when Oracle dNFS is running correctly.

```
[oracle@oel55-64-11g trace]$ netstat -an | grep 2049
tcp        0        0 192.168.209.20:1005        192.168.209.21:2049        ESTABLISHED
[oracle@oel55-64-11g trace]$
```

Figure 8-55 Verify Oracle dNFS using `netstat`

Comparing Storage Types

We have discussed many different types of virtual storage that can be used for Oracle database server stacks. Figure 8-56 shows a comparison of the different storage considerations and their respective capabilities.

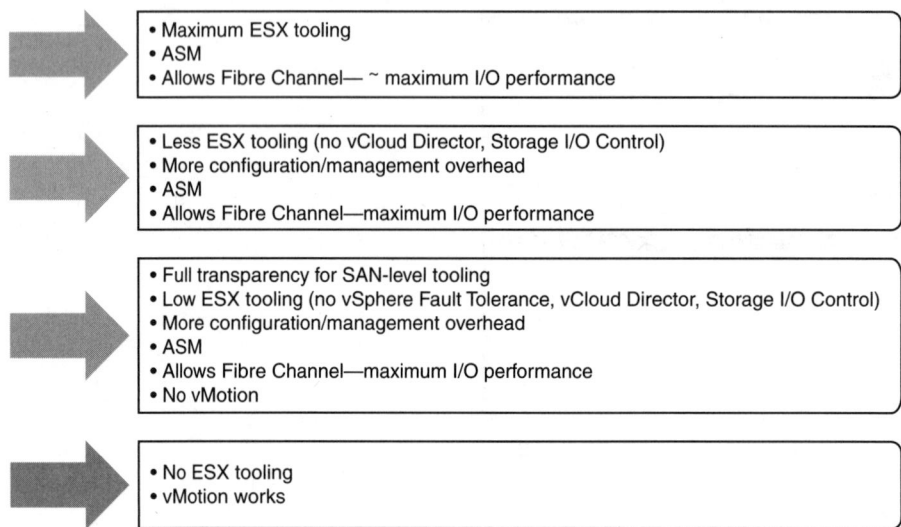

Figure 8-56 Comparing storage types

Block Alignment

Misaligned file systems can cause poor performance in all systems. High-intensity work-loads, which are typical in Oracle environments, are especially vulnerable to these potential devastating effects. Rudimentary performance analysis will reveal that the impact can rise to 50% degradation. When you consider the problem of block alignment, three layers affect performance: chunks, blocks, and clusters.

LUNs are created with chunks or stripes. This is the first layer involved in block alignment and is normally defined by the SAN vendor. VMware recommends using the SAN vendor defaults. Typically, no action needs to be taken at this layer. The vendor has done extensive testing to find the optimal chunk or stripe size.

The second layer is the VMFS file system layer; this layer uses blocks for allocation. As of ESX 3.x and later, the second layer is automatically aligned. VMFS-3 volumes are aligned to 64KB during creation when using the vSphere Client.

The final layer exists in the VM and is defined by the operating system disk management tool. This layer refers to the allocation as clusters. This is the layer that can have misalignment issues. For an example of misalignment, refer to *Recommendations for Aligning VMFS Partitions* at the VMware website.

www.vmware.com/pdf/esx3_partition_align.pdf

Figure 8-57 shows the various levels of alignment.

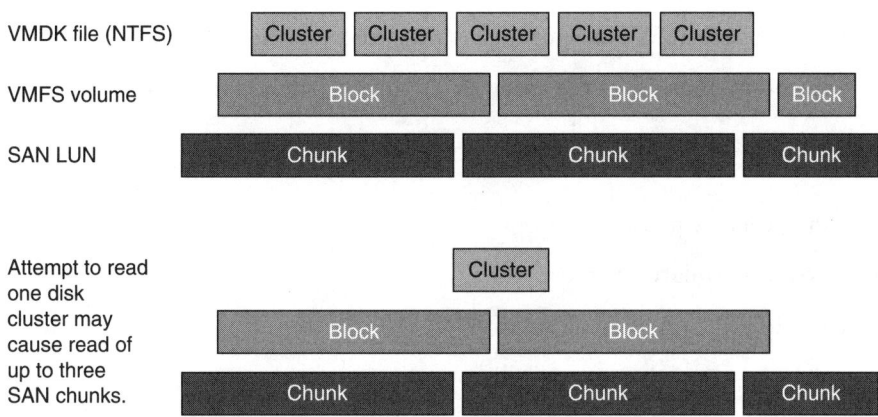

Figure 8-57 Recommendations for aligning VMFS partitions

If data is misaligned, this can cause multiple reads for each block of data. This can occur because the cluster in the operating system's file system is stored in multiple chunks. File alignment, performed correctly, avoids unnecessary I/O. Figure 8-58 shows a properly aligned VMFS.

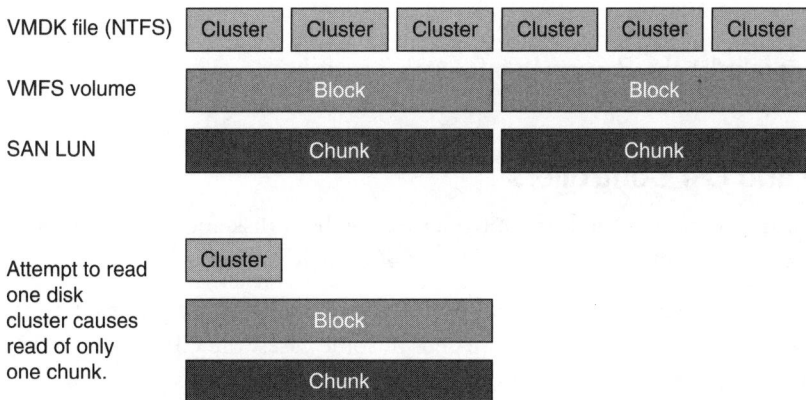

Figure 8-58 VMFS partition alignment

For Intel-based systems, the virtual disks from a VMFS volume must be aligned at the VM level.

Follow these steps to create ASM disk aligned partition using `fdisk`:

1. At the command prompt, enter the following command, where <x> is the device suffix:

   ```
   fdisk /dev/sd<x>
   ```

2. Press **n** to create a new partition.

3. Press **p** to create a primary partition.

4. Press **1** to create partition number 1.

5. Select the defaults to use the complete disk.

6. Press **t** to set the partition's system ID.

7. Press **fb** to set the partition system ID to `fb`.

8. Press **x** to go into expert mode.

9. Press **b** to adjust the starting block number.

10. Press **1** to choose partition 1.

11. Enter **2048** to set the starting block number to 2048 for a 1MB disk partition alignment.

12. Press **w** to write the label and partition information to disk.

Using pvSCSI and LSI Controllers

For the base operating system, use the LSI controller for the boot disk and operating systems. VMware generally recommends the use of the pvSCSI driver for the ASM drives.

The paravirtual driver enhances I/O throughput in many situations. More significant is that the CPU cost of servicing the I/O is decreased. In some cases, the CPU cost is reduced by up to 30%. This can have a significant impact on an enterprise's processor-based licensing. For more information, refer to *PVSCSI Storage Performance* paper available on VMware's website.

http://www.vmware.com/pdf/vsp_4_pvscsi_perf.pdf

> **TIP**
>
> Under rare circumstances, consider not using the pvSCSI driver for extremely latency-sensitive operations. For some highly latency-sensitive applications, the pvSCSI *adapter*, although highly efficient in that it reduces overall CPU overhead for each individual I/O operation, can cause extra latency because the individual I/Os may be processed as batches. It is very important to doubly qualify this advice as only pertaining to extreme latency-sensitive situations. The great majority of Oracle implementations will perform optimally when using the pvSCSI drivers for all VMDKs containing database files of all kinds.

Figure 8-59 shows the selection of the pvSCSI controller.

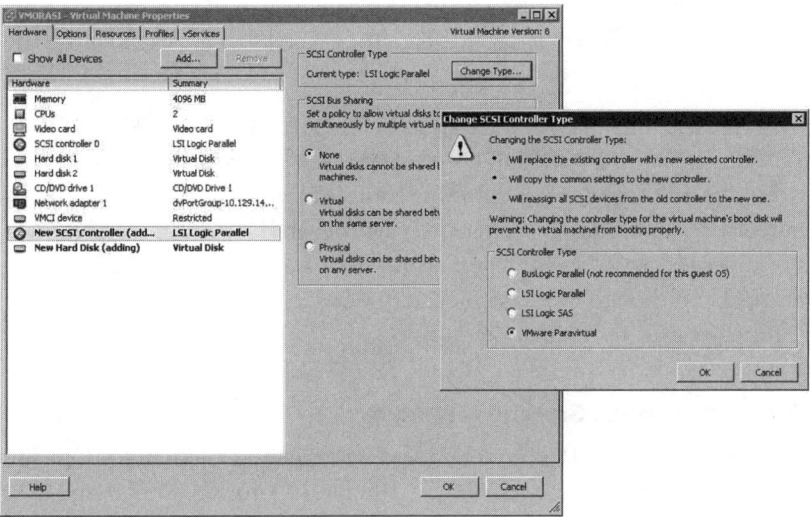

Figure 8-59 pvSCSI controller

Dynamic Expansion of VMFS Volumes

In general, you can dynamically extend a VMFS volume by following the configuration guide appropriate for the version of ESXi in use. Refer to the KB 1752 article, *Extending a VMFS volume to use new LUN space after expansion*.

Adding Extents to the Datastore

Adding an extent has historically been the only way to increase the size of a VMFS, and it has served adequately through version 3. Customers have reported a variety of issues working with "extended" VMFS datastores. Although VMware allows up to 32 extents per datastore, avoid adding extents unless you have no other options available.

Growing a Datastore

Beginning with vSphere 4, you have the option of growing existing extents within a VMFS datastore. You accomplish this by first changing the underlying LUN using SAN tools to increase the size and creating additional unused space at the back of the LUN. Subsequent use of the vSphere Client or the command-line interface to direct vSphere to rescan the HBA will reset the extent size. The datastore properties dialog now indicates that the datastore is Expandable. Finally, direct the vSphere Client to grow the datastore to the size of the extended LUN by selecting **Maximize Capacity**.

Understanding Logical Volume Manager

Because the storage volumes presented to a guest can usually be resized (whether VMDK, RDM, iSCSI, FCoE, or other), you may take advantage of the increased size. Recognizing and using the additional storage most often requires additional steps to be taken within the guest itself.

For that reason, VMware recommends using the Logical Volume Manager (LVM) of the GOS to aggregate storage with the guest. The LVM offers the cleanest way to manage storage volumes within the guest, and offers the most choices in how the storage is utilized. The LVM comes with no performance penalty whatsoever. This recommendation to use the guest's LVM stands regardless of whether the customer anticipates the need to resize a storage volume. Even though there is no current need to resize a storage volume, there might be a requirement for resizing in the future.

Understanding Oracle Automatic Storage Manager

Automatic Storage Management (ASM) is an RDM and disk container system for Oracle database files and therefore adds no latency to Oracle data file I/O during normal operations (that is, if ASM is not rebalancing due to the hot add or hot drop of a storage device). ASM is strongly recommended for both single-instance Oracle and for Oracle RAC. ASM works with the following storage presentations in virtual environments:

- **VMDK backed by either VMFS or NFS:** The ESX/ESXi kernel presents ASM with what appears to be raw device slices.

- **RDM:** The actual physical storage raw devices are transparently visible to and mounted by ASM.

- **In-guest NFS:** Create block devices using the dd command.

TIP

In architecting Oracle database on ASM, the same constraints apply with VMware as apply with native hardware implementations.

ASM Is Comparable to an LVM

Increasing the size of a storage volume (configured as an ASM disk) under ASM is allowed, and the ASM command syntax has commands to allow Oracle to dynamically use the additional space by altering the ASM disk group.

Understanding Thin Provisioning VMDKs

Because it is often unknown in advance how much storage will need to be allocated to the VMDK, thin provisioning provides for additional space that is not allocated but is immediately and automatically available if needed.

VMware recommends using thin provisioning at the SAN storage volume level for non-database volumes. Do not thin provision at more than one layer in the stack.

However, if thin provisioning is not an option at the SAN, consider using it on the VMFS level to reduce the amount of wasted storage in the environment. However, thin provisioning carries a performance penalty when it extends the allocation. The overhead of extending a VMDK is usually higher than that of the SAN. This effect is most often referred to as the *first write penalty*.

Although this technique can prove useful for non-database volumes and test/development environments, use it with caution with production and particularly Tier 1 workloads.

Follow these general rules for SAN-based provisioning:

- Use thick or zeroed thick provisioning for VMDKs.
- Do not use multiple thin-provisioning mechanisms at the same time.

Understanding Eager-Zeroed Thick Disk

The default virtual disk or VMDK is a thick lazy-zeroed disk. The thick disk has its space fully allocated at creation time. The lazy-zeroed disk does not zero the blocks before the first write, and an eager-zeroed disk zeroes the blocks at the time of the VMDK creation. Creating an eager-zeroed disk takes longer because of the zeroing process during its creation. The result is a better performing VMDK, as documented in the *Performance Best Practices for VMware vSphere* guides, which you can find on the VMware website.

http://www.vmware.com/pdf/Perf_Best_Practices_vSphere5.5.pdf

VMware recommends that Oracle data VMDKs be created as thick eager-zeroed disks, including ASM disks. Regardless of the storage type (NFS, iSCSI, or Fibre Channel), this improves performance by avoiding the first write penalty associated with a typical lazy-zeroed thick disk.

For the ASM disk, check the **Support clustering features such as Fault Tolerance** check box for an eager-zeroed disk. Perform this step during the VMDK creation and see Figure 8-60.

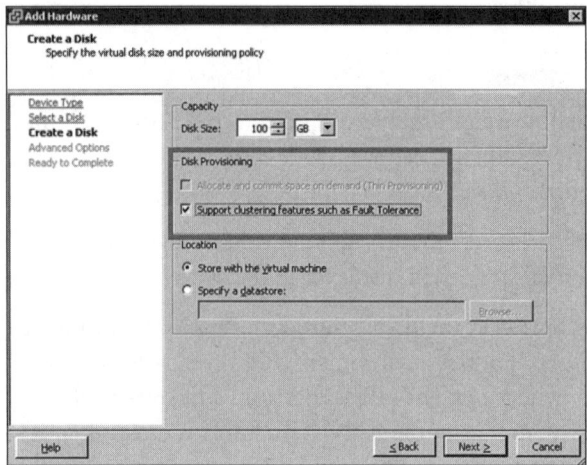

Figure 8-60 Adding clustering features

Understanding VMware VAAI

Whenever VMware uses the acronym VA, the reference is to VMware API. In this case, VAAI refers to VMware API - Array Integration, or more completely to VMware vSphere Storage APIs - Array Integration (VAAI). VAAI offloads tasks normally performed on the ESXi host to the support storage device. The offloading of these tasks reduces I/O operations and decreases memory and CPU consumption. Not all storage vendors support VAAI with their arrays. Check the VMware hardware compatibility list (HCL) and the storage vendor's documentation for details on this capability. Refer to the KB 1021976 article, *Frequently Asked Questions for vStorage APIs for Array Integration*.

Currently VAAI offloads the following tasks:

- Full Copy
- Hardware Assisted Locking
- Block Zeroing

Figure 8-61 shows basic VAAI functionality.

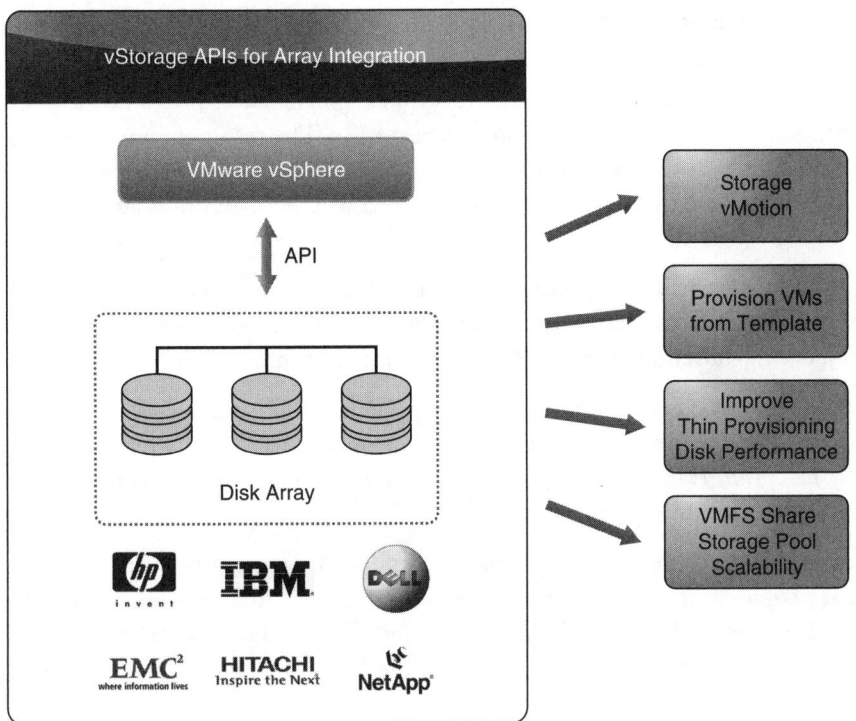

Figure 8-61 VAAI functions

Full Copy

Traditional Storage vMotion and cloning first read all the blocks and then write them back out, passing the traffic through the hypervisor. Full Copy improves Storage vMotion by offloading the entire task to the storage array.

Hardware Assisted Locking

Certain operations cause the hypervisor to lock the LUN. With Hardware Assisted Locking, only the blocks that must be locked are locked.

Block Zeroing

Block Zeroing offloads the zeroing tasks from the ESXi host. The hypervisor specifies the blocks to be zeroed, and the array performs the operation.

Understanding VMware Snapshots

VMware snapshots are problematic for Oracle RDBMS nodes because they can cause performance problems. They also tend to grow very quickly on database nodes due to the nature of I/O (inserts, updates, and deletes) on database VMs. The result of an old snapshot or rapidly growing snapshot can overrun the datastore space, risking snapshot data corruption. The DBA should establish alerts to be notified whether datastores approach their capacity.

Two common scenarios for using snapshots are backups and quick snapshots for operating system updates or software upgrades. In either case, limit the lifetime of the snapshot. In a backup scenario, backup duration determines how much space is required for a snapshot.

A VMware KB search for "snapshot problems" reveals a large number and variety of problems, ranging from slow performance in the guest to host instability. The VMware KB 1025279 article, *Best practices for VM snapshots in the VMware environment*, describes limitations and best practices to minimize problems.

If snapshots are used with database storage from any vendor, there are issues with hot backups and fuzzy copies of the files that can result in both inconsistent and unrecoverable image copies. VMware recommends making data volume VMDKs *independent*, meaning that they are excluded from any snapshots created for the VM.

Understanding the Oracle Enterprise Manager vCOPS Adapter

Oracle Database server metrics can be obtained through a number of mechanisms, but here we discuss vCenter Operations Manager, which can accumulate Oracle data by the following methods:

- **Oracle Enterprise Manager (OEM) adapter:** The OEM adapter is an embedded adapter for vCenter Operations Manager (vCOPS). The adapter collects data from OEM database management tables. Beginning in late 2013, the development of this adapter has been assumed by Blue Medora Corporation. Interestingly, Blue Medora now produces the OEM 12c plug-in for VMware (mentioned earlier) and the vCOPS adapter for OEM.

  http://blogs.vmware.com/management/2013/12/introducing-the-blue-medora-vc-operations-management-pack-for-oracle-enterprise-manager.html

  www.bluemedora.com/product/vcenter-operations-management-pack-oracle-enterprise-manager

- **Adapter for Hyperic – Oracle Plug-in:** Hyperic has an Oracle plug-in that discovers and monitors Oracle metrics. Hyperic Oracle metrics can be used for basic administration, but for detailed analysis, such as investigating Oracle wait events, the OEM adapter from Blue Medora is required.

The Oracle Database monitoring example described in this chapter is based on metrics obtained from Oracle Enterprise Manager plug-in. The OEM adapter is an embedded adapter for vCenter Operations Manager Enterprise. The adapter collects data from OEM database management tables. It supports both manual discovery and autodiscovery. The OEM adapter is compatabile with Oracle Enterprise Manager versions 10g, 11g, and 12c.

The OEM adapter requires a Java Database Connectivity (JDBC) connection to the OEM database. The OEM adapter connection has certain requirements:

- You must open an Oracle JDBC port on the firewall. The default port number is 1521.

- You must use a valid Oracle JDBC connection uniform resource locator (URL). The default URL format is jdbc:oracle:thin:@<host>:1521:<SID>.

- Credentials must allow reading from the following OEM database management (SYSMAN) tables:

  ```
  MGMT$TARGET
  MGMT$METRIC_CURRENT
  MGMT$AVAILABILITY_CURRENT
  MGMT$METRIC_DETAILS
  ```

Figure 8-62 describes the high-level architecture of the vCOPS OEM adapter. Note that the adapter is delivered in the form of a virtual appliance (vAPP) and that the data from OEM is "passed through" to the OEM adapter for default or customized dashboard display. In the future, the OEM data will be used by the innate vCOPS performance analytics capability to generate various forms of predictive analytics.

At this point, let's transition from the acquisition and display of the metrics to the use of those metrics.

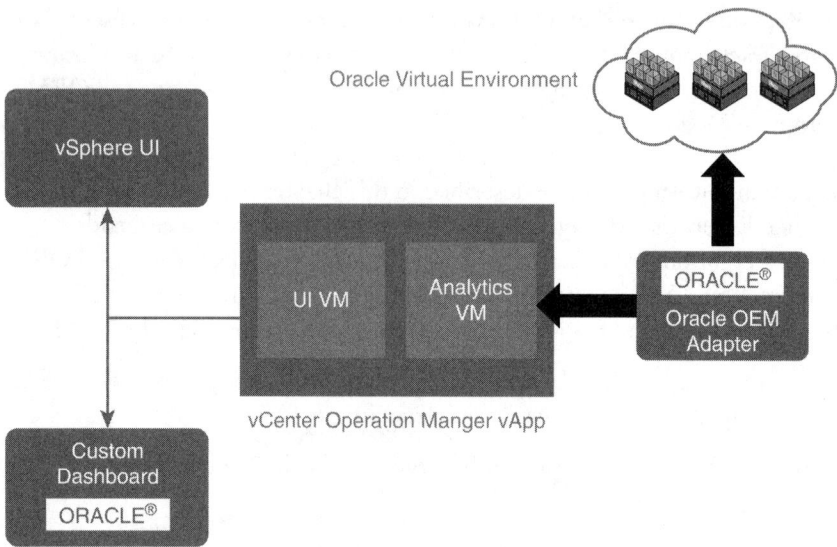

Figure 8-62 Oracle Enterprise Manager adapter: high-level architecture

Using Oracle Database Server Metrics

Table 8-5 provides a partial list of some useful Oracle Database server metrics. Some of these metrics are leveraged in the dashboard example described later in this chapter.

Table 8-5 Some Oracle Database Server Counters (Incomplete List)

Counter	Description
Load CPU Utilization (%)	Monitors the CPU utilization as a percentage.
Load Run Queue Length (5-minute Average)	5-minute average run queue length.
Load CPU in I/O wait (%)	Monitors the CPU in I/O wait time percentage.
Load Memory Utilization (%)	Monitors memory utilization as a percentage.
Load Swap Utilization (%)	Monitors swap utilization.
Network interface Collisions (%)	Monitors network interface collisions for a particular network interface.
Network interface Read (MB/s)	Monitors network interface read in MBps.

Counter	Description
Network interface Write (MB/s)	Monitors network interface write in MBps.
Physical Read per Minute	Monitors the storage physical reads per minute.
Physical Writes per Minute	Monitors the storage physical writes per minute.
SQL Response Time	Represents the SQL response time.
Wait Time (%)	Represents the percentage of time spent waiting, instance-wide, for resources or objects during this sample period.
Listener – Connections Established (per Min.)	Represents the average number of connections per minute that were established with the listener.
Active Sessions Waiting : I/O	Database-level metric that represents the active sessions waiting for I/O.
Database Time Spent Waiting (%)	Represents the percentage of time that database calls spent waiting for an event.
Average Users Waiting Count	Represents the average number of users who have made a call to the database and who are waiting for an event, such as an I/O or a lock request, to complete. If the number of users waiting on events increases, it indicates that either more users are running, increasing workload, or that waits are taking longer (for example, when maximum I/O capacity is reached and I/O times increase).
Data Guard Status	Use the Data Guard Status metric to check the status of each database in the Data Guard configuration.

You can see a detailed list of metrics at Oracle's website. Figure 8-63 shows the available metrics from Oracle Enterprise Manager. All these metrics can be imported into vCenter Operations Manager via the OEM adapter.

http://docs.oracle.com/cd/E11857_01/em.111/b25986.pdf

TIP

Only some metrics are available if you use database (DB) control. To acquire the complete set of metrics, you need Oracle Grid Control and the correct license. OEM adapter supports Oracle Database 10g, 11g, and 12c.

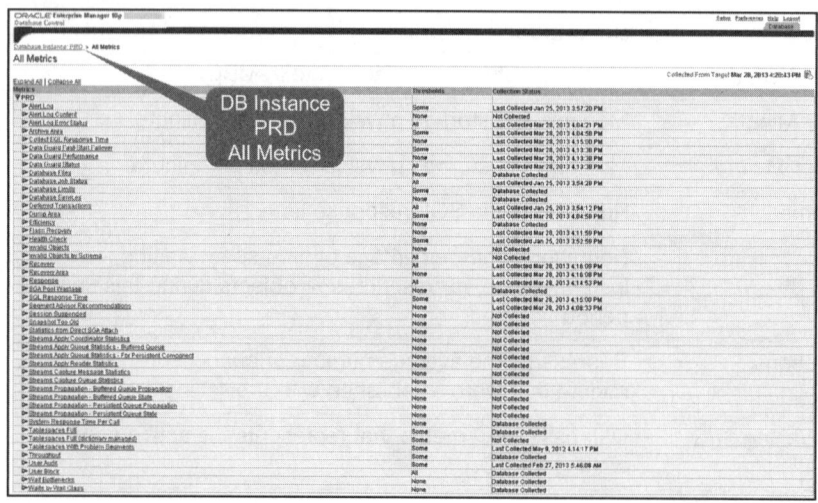

Figure 8-63 Oracle Enterprise Manager: all metrics

Installing Oracle Enterprise Manager Adapter

You can find the OEM adapter installation and configuration details in a number of locations. Make sure to pay attention to release notes for each version so that the installation is properly done as per the chosen version. Figure 8-64 describes the OEM adapter install, configure, and validate process.

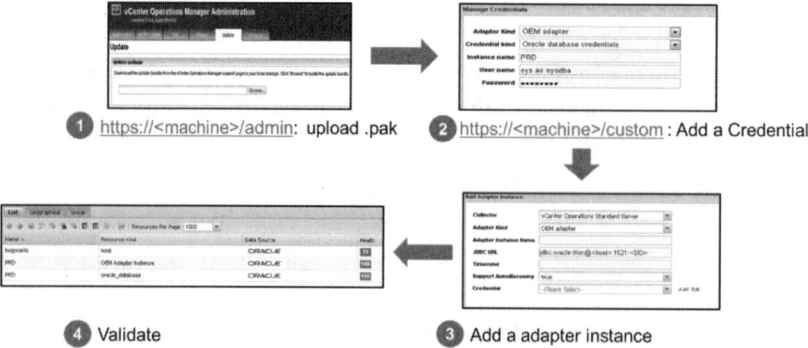

Figure 8-64 Oracle Enterprise Manager adapter: install, configure, and validate

Validating the OEM Adapter

After you add an adapter instance for the OEM adapter, verify that resources are created and that metrics are collected through the adapter instance in vCenter Operations Manager, as follows:

1. Log in to the Custom user interface as an administrator.

2. Select **Environment > Environment Overview** and examine the resources on the Environment Overview page.

3. Verify the details for each resource:

   a. Select the resource on the List tab and click the **Show Detail** icon. The Resource Detail page appears for the resource.

   b. Examine the metric graph and compare the values to the source values. You can view the source data in the Oracle Enterprise Manager console.

Creating Oracle Database Custom Dashboard

This section describes the creation of an Oracle Database dashboard. The dashboard is simply a customized screen constructed through a vCOPS-provided widget that contains a subset of the available metrics with a customized display.

Follow these steps and see Figure 8-65 to create a dashboard:

1. Log on to the custom user interface in a web browser, https://<machine->/ vcops-custom.

2. The tabs near the top of the Home page are your dashboards. You can switch to a different dashboard by clicking its tab or selecting it from the Dashboards menu. To create a new dashboard, click the plus (+) sign to the right of the last dashboard tab. You will enter the dashboard editor, as shown in Figure 8-65.

vCenter Operations Manager – Dashboard Editing Tab

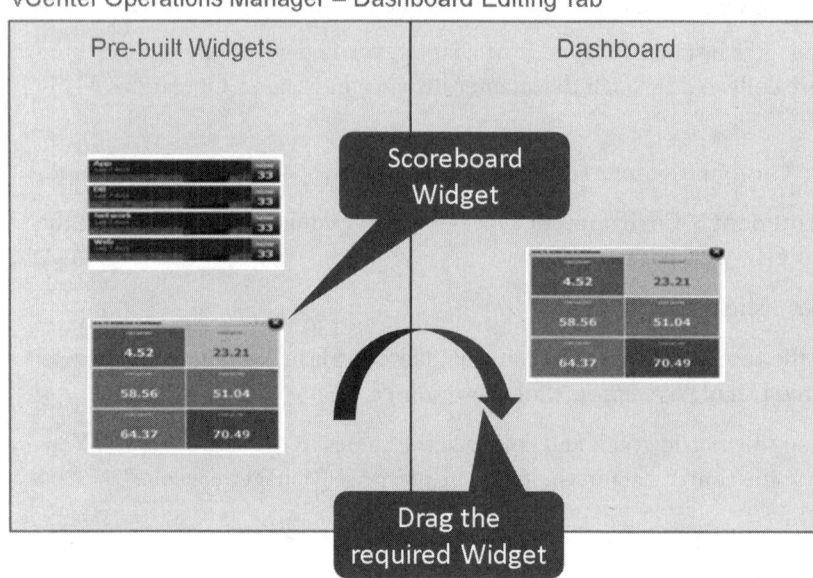

Figure 8-65 Creating an Oracle Database dashboard

3. In Figure 8-65, all the predefined widgets are available on the left pane, and the required widgets are dragged to the right pane. Each selected widget generates a separate pane in the final dashboard. The widgets selected for this dashboard are as follows:

- **1 x Heath Tree Graph:** This widget shows the resource hierarchy of the Oracle application container construct (this was manually created under Environment > Application Overview).

- **1 x Metric Graph:** This widget shows a graph of the recent performance and predicted future performance of a metric. It is possible to show multiple metrics in separate graphs or have them merged into a single graph for easier comparison.

- **3 x Metric Graph (Rollover View):** This widget shows a graph of the recent performance and predicted future performance of a metric. You could have multiple metrics roll over one by one with the assigned timing.

- **1 x Generic Scoreboard:** This widget shows the current value for each metric that you select. Each metric appears in a separate box. The value of the metric determines the color of the box. You define the values for each color when you edit the widget.

After the widgets have been selected and the dashboard is displayed, you then need to edit the widget to assign the required metrics. You can customize a widget by editing its configuration options. Some widgets do not show data until you configure them, as shown in the next section on how to configure the widgets.

Configuring a Metric Graph (Rollover View) Widget

The dashboard will contain a customized view and presentation of the selected metrics. This section shows how to assign metrics to one of the metric graph (rollover view) widgets. Figure 8-66 displays the initial steps to construct the dashboard. Log in to the custom user interface, https://<machine->/vcops-custom:

1. Click the tab for the dashboard that contains the widget to edit.

2. Click the Edit Widget icon on the widget's toolbar.

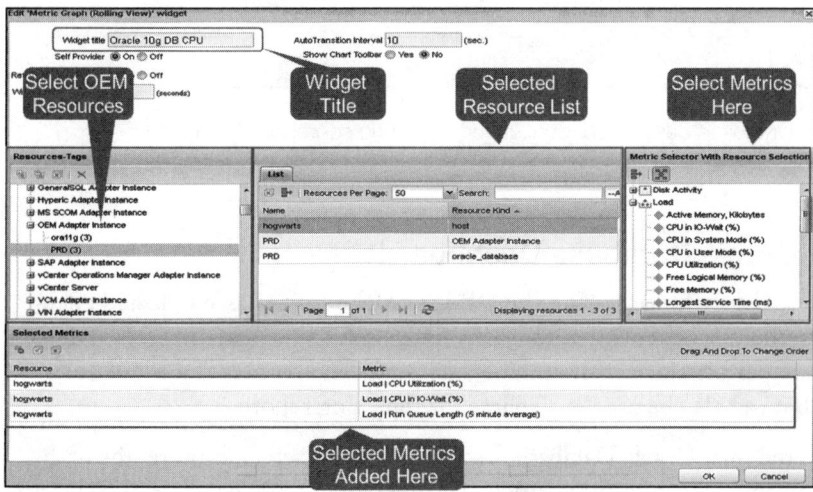

Figure 8-66 Oracle Database dashboard: configuring a metric graph (rolling view) widget

Configuring a Generic Scoreboard Widget

Now we need to consider the steps to take to define a scoreboard widget in greater detail, as shown in Figure 8-67, to complete the population and display format of the dashboard. So, we need to assign metrics to one of the generic scoreboard widgets and log in to the custom user interface, https://<machine->/vcops-custom, as follows:

1. Click the tab for the dashboard that contains the widget to edit.

2. Click the **Edit Widget** icon on the widget's toolbar.

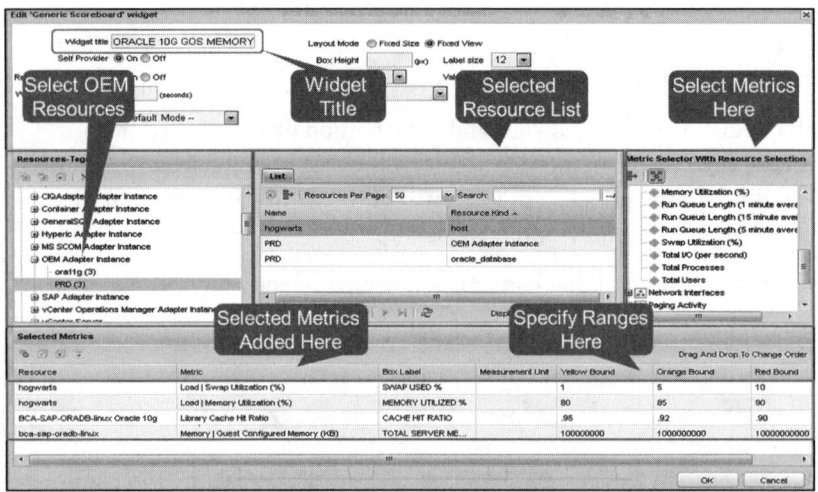

Figure 8-67 Oracle Database dashboard: configuring a generic scoreboard widget

Finalizing the Oracle Database Dashboard

Finally, we complete the dashboard. Now the DBA (or VMAdmin) has simple and effective visual access to the specific data that the DBA finds useful when executing the everyday tasks involved in performance analysis. The data is now in a format that is not only familiar to DBAs but can also be used as a source for repeating reports.

Figure 8-68 shows the final Oracle Database dashboard. In this screen capture, the dashboard is monitoring an SAP application workload against Oracle 10g database. The workload has been consistently running for multiple days and can be regarded as a baseline. The workload is I/O read intensive.

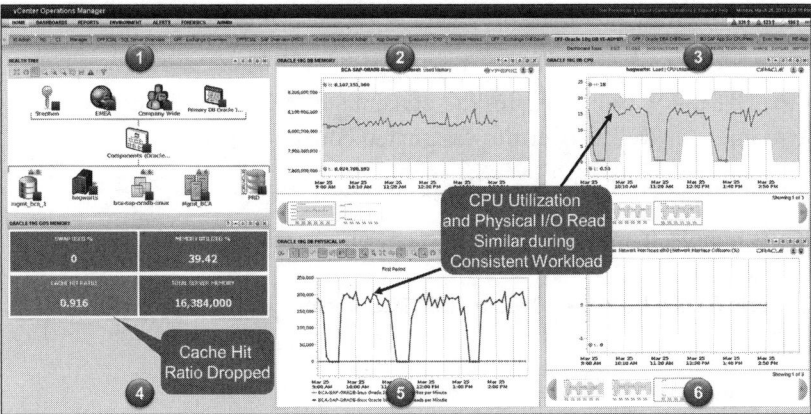

Figure 8-68 Final Oracle Database dashboard

The six widgets comprising the dashboard shown in Figure 8-68 are numbered as 1 to 6. The list that follows describes the contents of each widget.

- **Widget 1 – Health Tree:** The Health Tree shows the health of various resources Oracle Database depends on, as follows:

    - **Mgmt_bca_1:** Datastore, source vSphere adapter

    - **Hogwarts:** Source OEM adapter (automatically discovered and created)

    - **Bca-sap-oradb-linux:** Source vSphere adapter

    - **Mgmt_BCA:** Cluster name, source vSphere adapter

    - **PRD:** Oracle Database instance, source OEM adapter

- **Widget 2 – Metric Graph (Rollover View) – "Oracle 10G DB Memory":** Counters are as follows:

    - **Used Memory:** Indicates the amount of OS memory being used. If vSphere memory reservations are set, you can infer that the VMware balloon driver will not be using any of this memory and that memory is being utilized by the Oracle Database server application in the GOS.

    - **Guest Configured Memory:** Total number of processes per second waiting for a workspace memory grant. Numbers higher than zero indicate a lack of memory.

- **Widget 3 – Metric Graph (Rollover View) – "Oracle 10G DB CPU":** Counters are as follows:

  - **Load CPU Utilization (%):** Indicates the percentage of CPU utilization at a specific moment as well as over the designated collection period.

  - **Load CPU in I/O wait:** Shows the CPU time in I/O wait.

  - **Run Queue Length (5 min. Avg.):** Time spent on run queue, 5-minute average.

- **Widget 4 – Generic Score board – "Oracle 10G GOS Memory":** Counters are as follows:

  - **Swap Utilization (%):** This should be zero.

  - **Cache Hit Ratio:** Monitors the percentage of data requests answered from the buffer cache since the last reboot. Pay attention if the value is regularly below 90.

  - **Memory Utilized:** Shows the amount of memory that the Oracle Database server is using. Because vSphere memory reservations are recommended for BCAs, this value can help to show how the memory is being used by the actual application.

  - **Total Server Memory:** VM configured size.

- **Widget 5 – Metric Graph (Rollover View) – "Oracle 10G DB Physical I/O":** Counters are as follows:

  - **Physical Read per Minute:** This metric represents the number of data blocks read from disk per minute during this sample period.

  - **Physical Writes per Minute:** This metric represents the number of data blocks written from disk per minute during this sample period.

- **Widget 6 – Metric Graph (Rollover View) – "Oracle 10G DB Network":** Counters are as follows:

  - **Network interface Collisions (%):** This metric shows the collision in % for a particular network interface.

  - **Network interface Read (Mb/s):** This metric shows the reads in megabits per second for a particular network interface.

  - **Network interface Write (Mb/s):** This metric shows the writes in megabits per second for a particular network interface.

Summary

Performance analytics can be a daunting task for the entry-level DBA. Oracle metrics and statistics have exotic-sounding names that often do not reflect the actual idea that the name suggests. After all, is anyone really sure what causes the accumulation of a db_file_sequential_read as *compared* to a db_file_scattered_read? Anyone having completed an Oracle University's Performance Tuning class or anyone who has read the definition of these somewhat well-known metrics from Oracle documentation would provide a reasonable answer. But that answer is most likely incomplete because many of the Oracle metrics have multiple (some not published) factors that contribute to their ultimate aggregate.

The essence of the point is not to dissuade anyone from using these metrics but to help DBAs understand that the actual number that you read associated with a particular metric is less important than how that value changes over time and how that value compares to other metrics. An AWR report will notably list the "Top 5 wait events" to draw the attention of the DBA.

Performance tuning is both an art and a discipline. Yet some claim that performance tuning is a science because the detailed understanding that is required challenges the technical acumen of the most talented computer scientist. But real tuning involves more interpolation than calculation. It requires a "landscape" perspective, which allows the vDBA to view the "big picture," which is the total system, end to end. If a DBA becomes fixated on any one particular metric, the effort may devolve into an irrelevant waste of time. A highly disciplined DBA will know which metrics and parameters matter under which circumstances and adjust those to achieve a desired aggregate result. Performance tuning a business-critical database is not an academic exercise; it is an effort to maximize the effectiveness of the most important asset of any organization.

This chapter discussed the fundamental principles of the performance of Oracle running on vSphere. You also learned various techniques and approaches to tuning. Some of the practices presented have been used and developed by VMware PSO and by VMware's trusted partners, such as HOB. You also learned about advanced features and capabilities of vSphere, such as hot-add, vNUMA, memory reservations, and hyperthreading. Each of these tools helps the vDBA customize and optimize the virtualized environment for all BCAs.

Any effective tool will allow for adequate customization of the display while still highlighting the most important data to be displayed. This is the real purpose of all the performance monitoring tools. The vCOPS OEM adapter has been designed primarily to work as an add-on to vCOPS for the purpose of displaying the relevant OEM data in a form both familiar and riveting to the DBAs (present and future).

Ultimately, this same OEM data will be incorporated into the greater vCOPS framework for the purpose of incorporating the Oracle metrics into the vCOPS performance analytics engine. For now, however, the adapter serves the tremendously effective purpose of both including the DBAs in the management of the virtualized environment and educating the DBAs as to how to navigate within the modern infrastructure.

## Chapter 9

Business Continuity and Disaster Recovery

In everyday life, disasters never happen until they do. With modern engineered super-systems, we can guarantee zero data loss and zero downtime, respectively known as a recovery point objective (RPO) and recovery time objective (RTO) of zero. In all disaster scenarios less severe than a comet hitting the Earth, the system can be engineered to meet this lofty aspiration if the adequate time and resources are allocated to the design, implementation, and the maintenance of the system. We're quite sure that blissful dinosaurs at the moment of the Cretaceous–Tertiary (KT) boundary had no comprehension that the planet was about to be so radically altered that the furry little creatures that scurried beneath their leathery feet would soon rule the planet. But it did happen. And so, too, will less "earth-shattering" disasters occur in the professional careers of every information technology (IT) professional.

This chapter revisits the overall theme of this book: the four V's, covering specifically the value and versatility factors. The extension of vSphere through VMware Site Recovery Manager (SRM) allows seamless integration of storage replication and the virtual machines (VMs). The coordination of the VM failover and the storage failover when a disaster occurs is of tremendous added value to the overall proposition. The fact that the storage vendors use the open application programming interface (API) for SRM and write the storage replication adapters (SRAs) for their individual replication products highlights the versatility. Figure 9-1 shows the four V's.

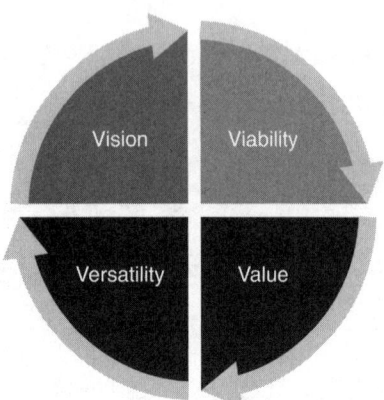

Figure 9-1 Four V's approach

Chapter 10, "Backup and Recovery" covers the ideas and concepts of backing up and recovering a database, but here in Chapter 9, we step out further into the world of true downtime. The loss of a datacenter, the loss of the building that the datacenter is housed within, the loss of the city block that the building previously existed upon, or something even bigger may constitute a rather dramatic disaster scenario. We have all seen the rise of the remote datacenter over the past decade. Places such as Jersey City, New Jersey (about 5 miles across the Hudson from lower Manhattan), or even farther away from New York City in western New Jersey, have become favored locations for the disaster-conscious data-driven executive. We have all also experienced the silly and sometime hilarious disaster plans such as the disaster recovery (DR) center a floor below the main production facility. Consider the DR location 3 miles away from the production facility where both are within a few miles of a known earthquake fault line. Often, there are more disaster scenarios and plans than there are respective production systems. However, all these plans are meaningless without diligent preparation and testing, which is so often left out of the project's list of critical activities. The DR plan, relegated to the futile solitude of nicely printed runbooks, is as worthless as the paper that it is printed on (which is probably burning when an actual disaster occurs).

However, all this compelling drama aside, the great majority of the disasters that IT professionals encounter have little to do with hurricanes, volcanoes, earthquakes, man-caused disasters, renegade asteroids, or even the buffoonish janitor spilling his nightly caffeinated drink in the most inopportune place at the worst possible time. The great majority of disasters occur when storage fails. Yes, simple disk failure is the main reason that we need DR systems in place. Of course, not a single disk failure, because most arrays can handle that failure, but a catastrophic failure of an entire storage array or even a subtle and undetected corruption may effectively constitute a disaster.

This chapter describes a number of different approaches to addressing the challenge of an IT disaster. All of them involve the use of VMware's Site Recovery Manager (SRM). We discuss the use of storage-based replication as well as the Oracle relational database management system (RDBMS) capability of hedging against disaster with its log streaming technologies. But each recommendation we propose involves the only system in the industry that effectively coordinates the storage and server-level failovers: SRM.

VMware vCenter Site Recovery Manager

Preparedness for business continuity and DR planning is required to support users from alternate locations with access to business-critical applications such as Oracle databases and applications. Failover of the business-critical applications from the primary datacenter to an alternate datacenter is needed to confirm that business-critical applications are available in case of a disaster at the primary datacenter. vCenter SRM helps to address these needs in the following ways:

- Applications hosted on vSphere can fail over from a primary site to a DR site.

- Applications failed over to a DR site can be failed back to the primary site.

- Failover testing can be performed without affecting production.

- Failover testing can be performed often and reliably to verify that the DR plan works if there is an actual disaster.

- Reports can be generated from the failover testing to meet audit and regulatory requirements.

- Corporate acquisitions, mergers, and relocations require a solution to migrate datacenter resources from one datacenter to another. vCenter SRM addresses the need to migrate applications that are running on vSphere.

The solution to support DR of the workloads running on VMware vSphere contains various components that must be integrated to make them work well together. These components range from networking devices, infrastructure services, and storage-area network (SAN) devices to vSphere and applications. Each of these components has a large number of potentially valid configurations, but only a few of these configurations result in an integrated, functional system that meets the specified business and technical requirements for true business continuity.

The vCenter SRM architecture addresses a two-site solution. Figure 9-2 shows a high-level view of that basic architecture.

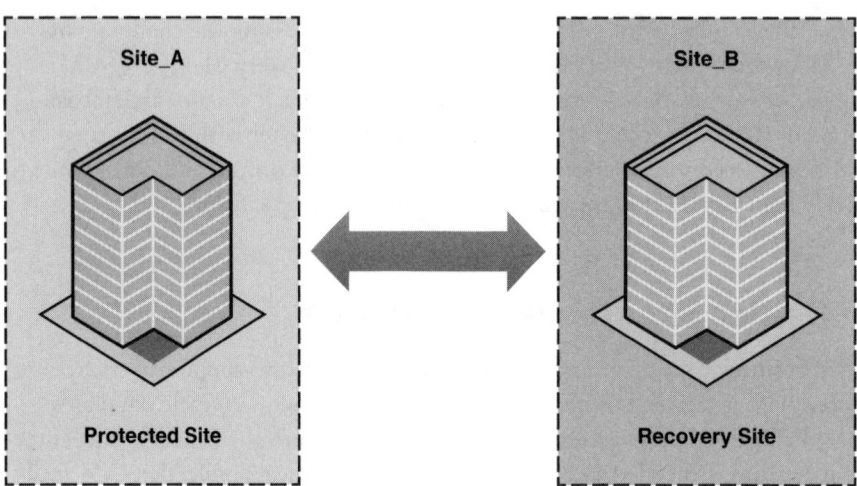

Figure 9-2 High-level overview

VMware vCenter SRM is a DR solution and workflow system that provides automated orchestration, coordinated failover, and nondisruptive testing of centralized recovery plans. SRM provides centralized recovery plans and steps to

- Create and manage recovery plans directly from VMware vCenter Server
- Automatically discover and display VMs protected by vSphere Replication or array-based replication
- Map VMs to appropriate resources on the failover site
- Extend recovery plans with custom scripts
- Control access to recovery plans with role-based access controls

For more details, refer to the VMware website and the SRM section.

http://www.vmware.com/products/site-recovery-manager

SRM provides two replication solutions: vSphere replication and storage-based replication, as shown in Figure 9-3. The figure shows a number of different facets and options of the comprehensive SRM architecture. We start with two sites, A and B. Notice that each site has a separate installation of both vCenter and SRM. A simple physical and virtual infra-structure is included in the diagram. Most important, both general replication options, vSphere and storage replication, are depicted.

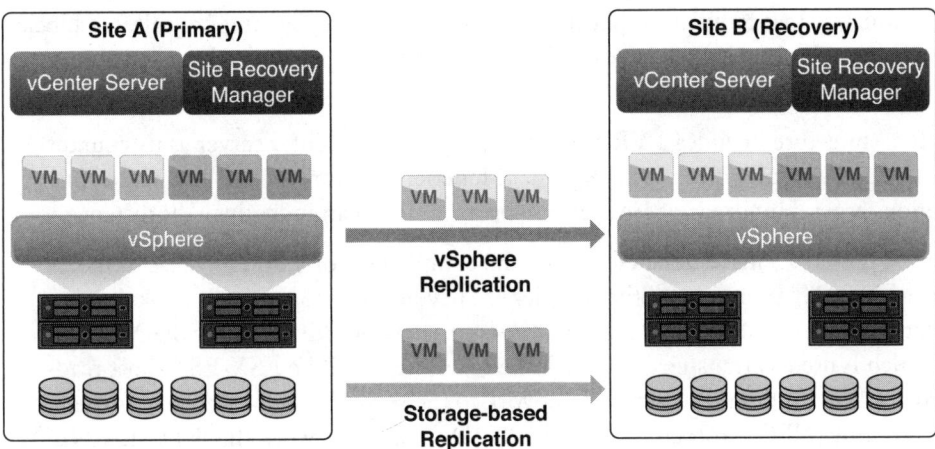

vSphere Replication
Simple, cost-efficient replication for Tier 2 applications and smaller sites

Storage-based Replication
High-performance replication for business-critical applications in larger sites

Figure 9-3 vSphere SRM overview

vSphere Replication

vSphere Replication (VR) is a deeply integrated component of the vSphere platform. It is the only true "hypervisor-level" replication engine available today. Changed blocks of the VM disks (VMDKs) being used by a running VM are sent to a secondary location, where they are received by a virtual appliance that writes them to an on-disk redo log. Only when that redo log is complete and all blocks in a given replication set are received is that set of data applied to the VMDKs for the offline (protection) copy of the VM. The entire set of replicated data for the source VMDKs must be successfully applied to the target for any of the replication set to be complete. If the replication set is not completely applied for any reason, the target site will be reset to the state prior to that particular replication operation.

TIP

At the time of this writing, for reasons primarily related to the default 15-minute RPO, VR is not recommended for use with live databases.

VR is an innately low-footprint replication protocol. When replicating only altered blocks on a continuous basis, network bandwidth usage can be reduced, and acknowledgment times minimized.

The VR architecture includes a VR appliance and a single vCenter server as its counterpart. The appliance provides the management functionality for VR and also acts as the replication target. Hundreds of VMs can be protected with an individual VR instance.

Figure 9-4 presents a more detailed view of the components of VR. The ideas of the "LAN" and "SAN" transport methodologies are beyond the scope of this book, but it is important to understand the basic idea of "VMware network file copy" or the *NFC* protocol, which is used to transport the blocks being replicated. The ESX/ESXi host reads data from storage and sends it across a network to the second host. VMware uses the Network File Copy (NFC) protocol to read the VMDK using Network Block Device (NBD) transport mode. One NFC connection for each VMDK file being replicated is required. Although version dependent, a limit applies to the number of NFC connections that can be made per ESXi/vCenter server.

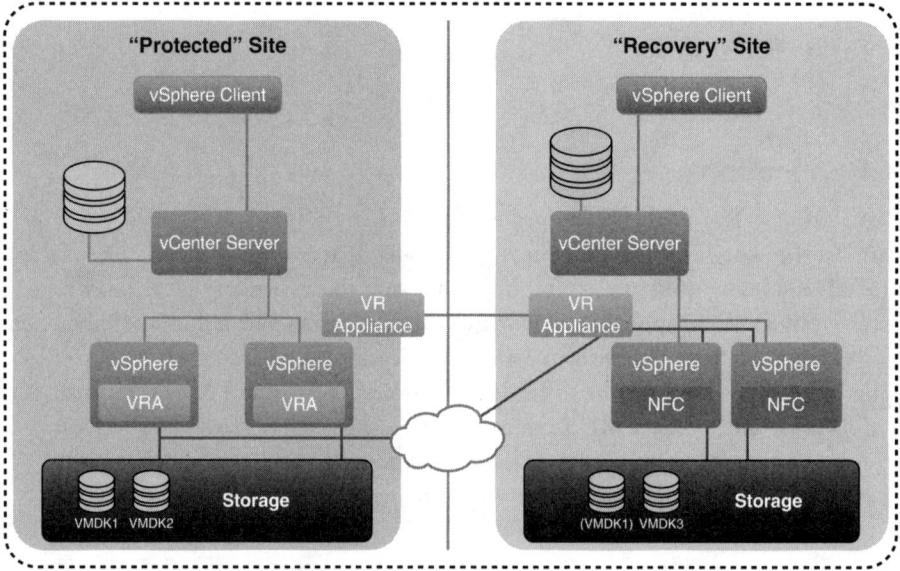

Figure 9-4 VR overview

Storage Array-Based Replication

When you use array-based replication, one or more storage arrays at the protected site replicate data to peer arrays at the recovery site. When using storage replication adapters (SRAs), each of which are developed by the individual storage vendor and integrated into SRM through the open API provided by VMware, you can integrate SRM with a wide variety of arrays.

To use array-based replication with SRM, you must configure replication first before you can configure SRM to use it.

Storage Replication Adapters

SRAs are not included in any release of SRM. Each array vendor develops and supports them. You can download SRAs and their documentation from the vendor's website. Also, VMware does not support SRAs, because they are the intellectual property of the storage vendor. The SRA must be installed and configured specifically for each array. The SRA must also be installed on each individual host involved in the replication effort. SRM supports the use of multiple SRAs on a single individual ESXi host. Refer to VMware.com and the various storage vendors for the documentation-specific information about the individual SRA. Figure 9-5 shows the inclusion of SRM on a set ESXi hosts with storage replication being used between them.

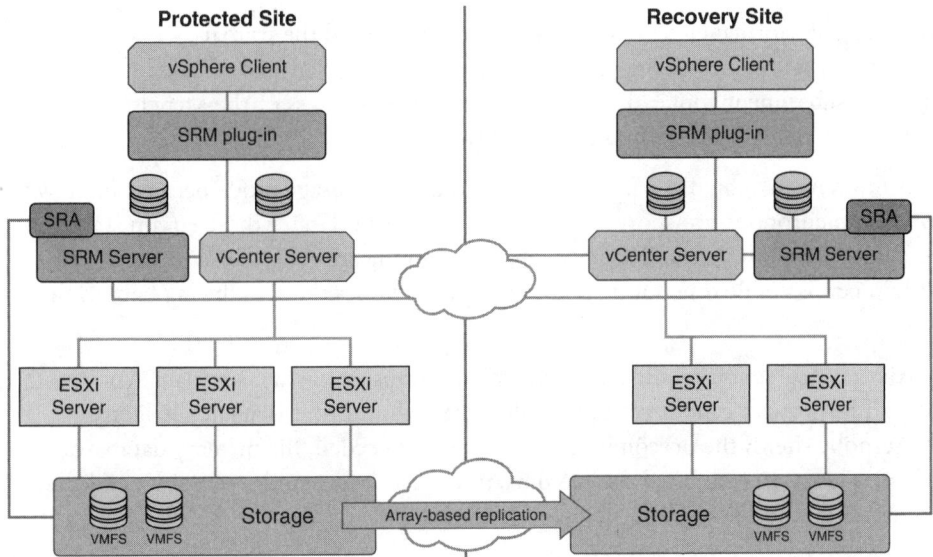

Figure 9-5 vSphere SRM array-based replication overview

Application-Based Replication

Now we will transition the discussion to the realm of replication being accomplished by the application. In this case, the replication will be done by the Oracle RDBMS.

Oracle Data Guard

Oracle Data Guard (DG) provides the management, monitoring, and automation software infrastructure to create and maintain one or more standby databases to protect Oracle data from failures, disasters, errors, and data corruptions. A "standby database" is a database copy that is in a constant state of recovery. The standby database will be a near-real-time replica of the primary database, which is the standby's source. Data can be transported to the standby through two basic methodologies. First, the archived redo logs can be copied to the standby site and subsequently applied to the standby database. Otherwise, data can be transmitted through the network transport method, which transports the individual change vectors of the redo log stream. After the transport, the redo logs are applied through the continuous recovery process.

DG is unique among Oracle replication solutions in supporting both synchronous (zero data loss) and asynchronous (near-zero data loss) configurations. To maintain high availability (HA) for mission-critical applications, administrators can choose either manual or automatic failover of production to a standby system if the primary system fails. A Data Guard system can be set up in one of three modes:

- Maximum Performance allows the standby to lag behind the primary so as to never affect the performance of the primary. It uses either the transfer of individual archive logs and subsequent application during the recovery process or the asynchronous copy of the change vectors in the redo stream.

- Maximum Availability is by far the most common DG usage mode because it allows for the synchronous transportation of the redo stream. Under these circumstances, no data will be lost, because the primary and standby are always in sync. Only if a certain configurable timeout threshold is exceeded does the standby lag behind the primary.

- Maximum Protection requires the redo stream transfer to always remain synchronous. The primary cannot continue unless the redo transfer is acknowledged at the standby site. If the preconfigured lag time is exceeded, the primary database "crashes" so as to guarantee that no deviation exists between the standby's and the primary's log stream.

Figure 9-6 shows a detailed diagram of the DG architecture.

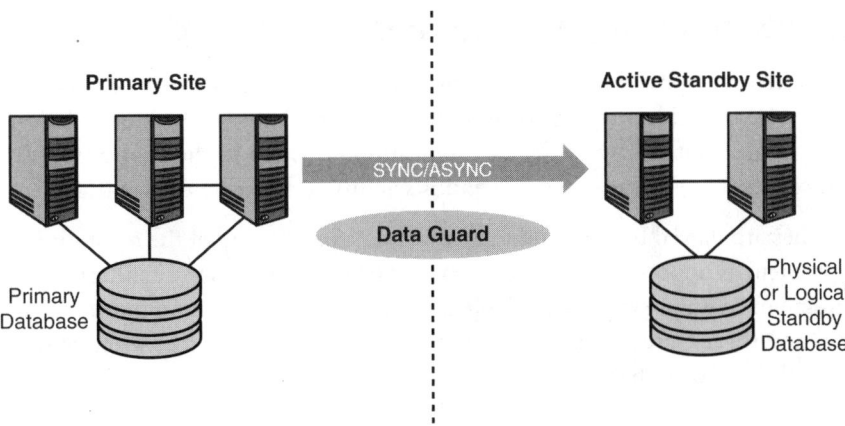

Figure 9-6 Oracle DG overview

Repairing Logical Data Block Corruption with Oracle Data Guard

Although a rare occurrence, an Oracle data block can become logically corrupt. Strangely, this phenomenon can occur and go unnoticed for long periods of time by the storage replication mechanisms, the DBA, or even the application. Then one day, for some random reason, some process attempts to read that offending data block. It would be an exaggeration to imply that this set of unfortunate circumstances is common, but it is possible. However, those intrepid architects who had the foresight to include a single standby database in their DR system will most likely be able to tell the DBA to use the Oracle Recovery Manager (RMAN) tool to simply extract the offending block from the standby and recover the data block in the primary database.

The set of circumstances that caused the original data block to become corrupt may not have affected the change vectors in the log stream. Although it seems strange that the storage replication may not have detected the logical data block corruption, it is possible because the storage replication is concerned with the storage blocks not the logical Oracle data block. And because it is probable that the data block in the standby remained entirely unaffected, the recovery of the corrupted block can be completed. This is a very simple and elegant solution to a potentially catastrophic problem.

Combining vSphere Replication and Data Guard

There are many different approaches to developing and implementing comprehensive DR architectures. Some involve solely the use of storage replication; others rely only on host-based replication. Some solutions primarily use replication provided by the application vendors, whereas others trust in the database vendor's ability to replicate the data.

All these approaches are flawed because they are based on a philosophy of the solution applied to the problem as opposed to the approach that first determines the application's DR SLA requirements and then applies available technology to meet those requirements. More often than not, the architect discovers that the best approach combines some of the best attributes of all the approaches available.

This solution combines both vSphere Replication for protecting a set of SAP application VMs and Oracle DG to protect Oracle database VMs. The SAP-specific data is protected by vSphere Replication, whereas the database data is protected by DG using the Maximum Availability DG mode. Figure 9-7 presents the basic approach to this combination DR solution.

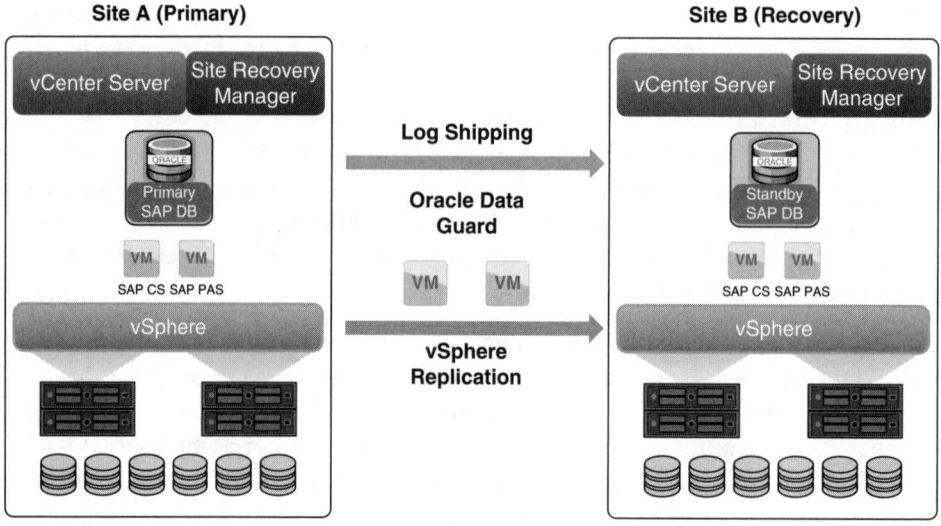

Figure 9-7 Oracle DG and VR solution overview

This solution elegantly integrates vSphere Replication with DG by allowing SRM to remain the controlling application. When the simulated DR event occurs, SRM is used to orchestrate the entire system failover. The standby database is failed over first as an embedded "callout" script is used to execute the appropriate DG commands to perform the "switchover" of the primary to the standby. After the database switchover is complete and the "callout script" exits, the next step in the orchestration occurs, which is the failover of the VMs that run the SAP application.

The beauty of this orchestration is that under the circumstances that any step within the orchestration fails, the entire workflow reverses course. Because DG used a "switchover" as opposed to a "failover," even the database role reversal will smoothly return to the original state.

> **TIP**
>
> Always use the switchover when transitioning from a primary to a standby when possible. Failover should be used only when the primary has been lost.

Testing SRM vSphere Replication

When testing the SRM VR and Oracle DG solution, follow these steps:

1. Initially, the Oracle primary database is at Site A and the standby database is at Site B with the DG setup.

2. The SAP application is connected to the primary database at Site A.

3. The SAP application and central services VM are replicated to Site B using VR.

4. When the simulated DR event occurs, the DBA will switch over Oracle standby to a primary using an SRM callout script from the SAP application VM or the VR server at Site B.

5. Connect/Resume the SAP application to the Oracle database at Site B.

Figure 9-8 shows the callout script used in the combined VS/DG failover solution.

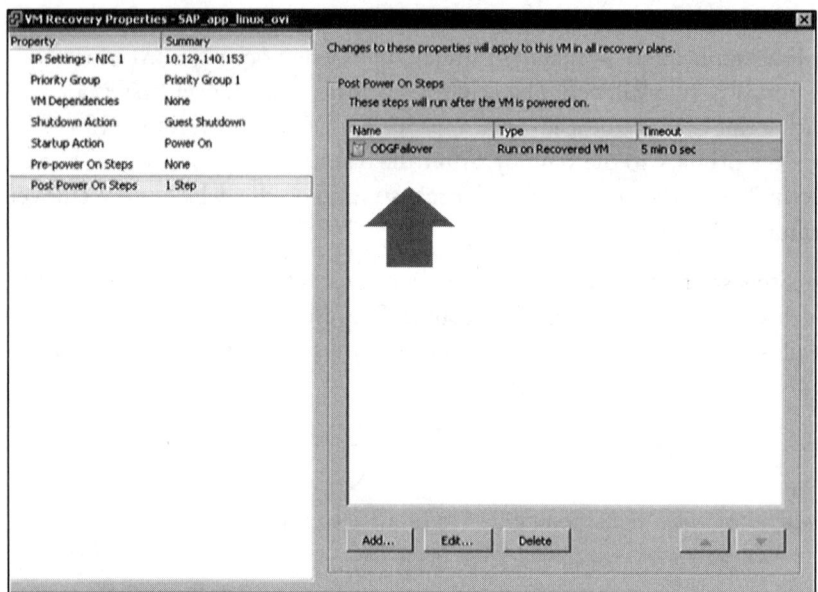

Figure 9-8 SRM: Callout script

The following is the actual script used to perform the database switchover:

```
~ # cat odgfail.sh
#! /bin/sh
#########################################################################
#     file name    : odgfail.sh
#     location     : /scripts
#     called from  : Application VM/VR server on Site B
#########################################################################
echo  "Job 'basename $0': started at 'date'"
#
# Set up standard ORACLE environment variables
ORACLE_SID=stdby; export ORACLE_SID
ORACLE_BASE=/oracle; export ORACLE_BASE
ORACLE_HOME=/oracle/PRD/102_64; export ORACLE_HOME
PATH=/oracle/PRD/102_64/bin:.:/oracle/PRD:/usr/sap/PRD/SYS/exe/run:/usr/
kerberos/bin:/usr/local/bin:/bin:/usr/bin:/usr/X11R6/bin;export PATH
LD_LIBRARY_PATH=/usr/sap/PRD/SYS/exe/run:/oracle/client/10x_64/
instantclient; export LD_LIBRARY_PATH
#
# Failover to Standby
```

```
$ORACLE_HOME/bin/sqlplus /nolog <<EOFarch1
connect / as sysdba
--shutdown Primary database(in case of RAC, shutdown all RAC instances)
--Initiate failover to Standby Database:
ALTER DATABASE RECOVER MANAGED STANDBY DATABASE FINISH FORCE;
--Convert the physical standby database to the production role:
ALTER DATABASE COMMIT TO SWITCHOVER TO PRIMARY;
--Comment/Uncomment either of the 2 sets of commands below
--If the database was never opened read-only since the last time it was
started,
--open new production database via:
ALTER DATABASE OPEN;
--If the physical standby database has been opened in read-only mode since
the last time it was started,
--shutdown standby database and restart it
--SHUTDOWN IMMEDIATE
--STARTUP pfile=initSTDBY.ora
exit
EOFarch1
echo  "Job 'basename $0': ended at 'date'"
######################### end of script
~ #
```

Application needs for DR are unique to the company and the reason that the particular application is being used. Some applications do not need to be part of a DR plan, but others have the need for zero recovery point and zero recovery time.

The DR discussion is similar to the discussion concerning HA, but the two should never be confused. These discussions, although often sheathed in soaring and inflammatory rhetoric, should almost always be focused on the most mundane failures. Simply put, HA refers to server-based failure, and DR refers to storage-based failure.

Using Storage Array-Based Replication with vSphere

There are many permutations for solutions when using a virtualization platform employing VMware vCenter SRM as your DR orchestration and workflow system. For example, integration of the EMC tool, RecoverPoint Continuous Remote Replication (CRR), and VMware SRM enables automated failover of the Oracle database from the production site to the recovery site and ensures that data replicated to the recovery site is available to the recovery site servers.

Figure 9-9 focuses on a DR solution between heterogeneous arrays to include a Symmetrix VMAX 10K and an EMC VNX5700, which is enabled by RecoverPoint CRR and the RecoverPoint splitter. For more details refer to the EMC website.

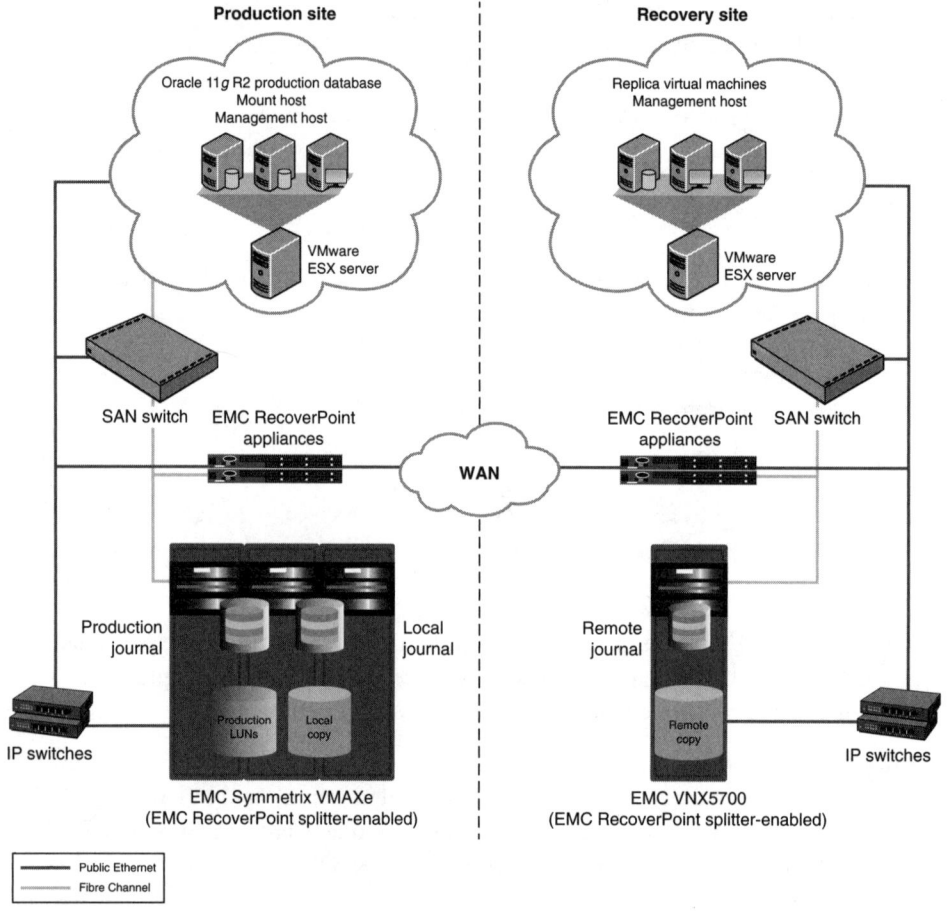

Figure 9-9 Oracle database and vSphere EMC array replication solution overview

EMC RecoverPoint provides continuous data protection for operational recovery and DR. It enables any-point-in-time recovery for disparate storage systems both within and between datacenters. This solution demonstrates the local protection and DR capabilities of the EMC Symmetrix VMAX 10K with Enginuity, which provides the storage platform at the production site. Storage at the recovery site is provided by an EMC VNX5700 array, demonstrating RecoverPoint support for heterogeneous storage platforms. SRM, which is integrated to RecoverPoint through an SRA developed by EMC, is used as the orchestrator of the DR system.

Figure 9-9 shows the splitter. Host-based write splitting is done using a driver that is installed on the server that has access to the storage. The splitter allows replication of non-EMC storage. However, splitters are not available for all operating systems and versions. The purpose of a splitter is to split the I/O to guarantee that the recovery point appliance (RPA) and the storage receive a copy of the write while maintaining write-order fidelity.

Virtual Provisioning for Oracle ASM Disk Groups

The Oracle database for any application should have separate ASM disk groups for data files: redo logs, fast recovery area (FRA), and temp files. Separate VMFS volumes are presented to the VMs on dedicated datastores for each ASM disk group.

The +DATA, +TEMP, and +REDO ASM disk groups are deployed on thin-provisioned devices bound to a virtual pool composed of Fibre Channel (FC) devices with RAID 5 (3+1) protection. This pool provides the high performance required by these devices.

The thin device provisioned for the +REDO logs was fully provisioned at the time of deployment; that is, all physical storage was assigned up front. The VMFS datastore for the +REDO log file was also provisioned to request all storage from the outset.

The +FRA device is bound to a virtual pool composed of high-capacity SATA devices with RAID 6 (6+2) protection. Flash recovery area (FRA) devices typically do not have the same high-performance demands as data files and redo logs, so SATA devices provide an efficient deployment for this data. Figure 9-10 shows a classic disk layout for an Oracle database using ASM disk groups as recommended by EMC.

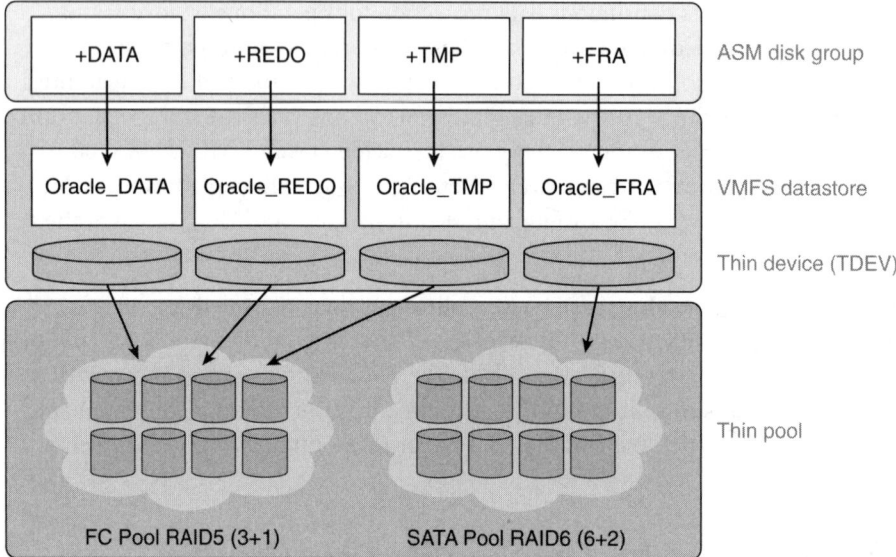

Figure 9-10 Oracle database ASM disk groups and thin pools

Solution Findings

Here are the findings and benefits of this solution:

- Integration of RecoverPoint with vCenter SRM enables DR testing to be carried out in isolated environments on the recovery site so that production can remain active and replication can continue uninterrupted. SRM also documents the recovery process.

- RecoverPoint enables replication of entire virtualized Oracle environments between datacenters for DR.

- The RecoverPoint splitter supports replication across heterogeneous storage platforms.

- Integration of RecoverPoint with vCenter SRM enables DR testing to be carried out in isolated environments on the recovery site so that production can remain active and replication can continue uninterrupted.

Creating a Disaster Recovery Plan

This section identifies common steps when considering, designing, and configuring a DR plan. This is not a comprehensive list, nor does the list constitute a set of required steps or procedures. This is simply a set of recommended considerations when using VMware vCenter SRM for your DR solution.

Configure Connections

1. Log in to the VMware vSphere Web Client and connect to the VMware vCenter Server for either the protected or recovery site.

2. Launch the vCenter SRM application.

3. Select the **Sites** panel in the left pane, and then select the **Summary** tab.

4. Select **Configure Connection** from the Command pane.

5. Enter the IP address for the remote vCenter Server.

6. Enter the port for the remote vCenter Server.

7. Click **Next**.

8. At the Completed Connections screen, click **Finish**.

Break the Connection

1. Log in to the vSphere Web Client and connect to the vCenter Server for either the protected or recovery site.

2. Launch the vCenter SRM application.

3. Select the **Sites** panel in the left pane, and then select the **Summary** tab.

4. Select **Break Connection** from the Command pane.

5. When prompted "Are you sure you want to break the connection...," click **Yes**.

Export System Logs

1. Log in to the vSphere Web Client and connect to the vCenter Server for either the protected or recovery site.

2. Launch the vCenter SRM application.

3. Select the **Sites** panel in left pane, and then select the **Summary** tab.

4. Select the **Export System Logs** from the Command pane.

5. Click **Browse** to select the download location, and then click **OK**.

6. When the system log bundles have been downloaded, click **Close**.

Using Array-Based Replication

Protect New Virtual Machines in the Existing Datastore

1. Log in to the vSphere Client and connect to the vCenter Server for either the protected or recovery site.

2. Launch the vCenter SRM application.

3. Select **Protection Group** in the left pane, and then select the **Virtual Machines** tab.

4. Select the protection group from the Protection Groups pane. This is the protection group with the datastore that contains the new VMs.

5. Select the **Virtual Machines** tab.

6. Right-click the VM that has a status of Mapping Missing.

7. Click **Configure Protection**.

8. Select the appropriate VM properties where an exclamation mark appears and choose the appropriate setting.

9. Click **OK**.

Protect New Virtual Machines in the New Replicated Datastore

1. Log in to the vSphere Client and connect to the vCenter Server for either the protected or recovery site.

2. Launch the vCenter SRM application.

3. Select **Array Managers** in the left pane, and then select the array where the replicated LUN exists.

4. Click the **Devices** tab.

5. Validate that the new replicated datastore is listed, and if it is not present, click **Refresh**.

6. Select **Protection Group** in the left pane.

7. Click **Create Protection Group**.

8. Configure properties for the new VMs.

Using vSphere Replication and Configuring a New Virtual Machine

1. Log in to the vSphere Web Client and connect to the vCenter Server on the protected site.

2. Select **vCenter**, and then select **VMs and Templates**.

3. Select the VM that you want to replicate.

4. Right-click and select **All vSphere Replication Action**, and then select **Configure Replication**.

5. Select **Recovery site vCenter**.

6. Leave the default setting and click **Next**.

7. Select the target destination datastore where you want the VM to be replicated and click **Next**.

8. Enable the **quiesced** option (VMware tools required) and click **Next**.

9. Adjust the **Recovery Point Objective** if the default setting is not sufficient, and enable the **Point in time instances** feature if the data replicated requires more granularity.

10. Select **Next**, and then click **Finish**.

Protecting a New Virtual Machine

1. Log in to the vSphere Client and connect to the vCenter Server on the protected site.

2. Launch the vCenter SRM application.

3. Select **Protection Group** in the left pane, and then select the protection group in which you want to place the new VM.

4. Select **Edit Protection Group**, and then click **Next**.

5. Select the VM that you want to add to the protection group.

6. Click **Next**, and then click **Finish**.

Unprotecting a Virtual Machine

1. Log in to the vSphere Client and connect to the vCenter Server for either the protected or the recovery site.

2. Launch the vCenter SRM application.

3. Select **Protection Group** in the left pane, and then select the protection group that contains the VM that must be unprotected.

4. Click the **Virtual Machines** tab.

5. Right-click the VM and select **Remove Protection**.

Removing the Virtual Machine

1. Log in to the vSphere Client and connect to the vCenter Server for either the protected or recovery site.

2. Launch the vCenter SRM application.

3. Select **Protection Group** in the left pane, and then select the protection group that contains the VM that needs to be unprotected.

4. Click the **Virtual Machines** tab.

5. Right-click the VM and select **Remove Protection**.

6. Right-click the VM and select **Remove VM**.

7. When prompted "Do you want to remove the selected virtual machines from the protection group?", click **Yes**.

Recovery Plan Procedures

Create a Recovery Plan

1. Log in to the vSphere Web Client and connect to the vCenter Server for either the protected or recovery site.

2. Launch the vCenter SRM application.

3. Select **Recovery Plans** in the left pane.

4. Click **Create Recovery Plan**.

5. Select **Protected Site** or **Recovery Site**.

6. Select the protection groups to include in the plan.

7. Select the test network to use during the recovery plan tests.

8. Enter the name and description of the recovery plan, and then click **Next**.

9. Click **Finish** to save.

Editing a Recovery Plan

1. Log in to the vSphere Client and connect to the vCenter Server for either the protected or recovery site.

2. Launch the vCenter SRM application.

3. Select **Recovery Plans** in the left pane, and then select the recovery plan you want to edit.

4. Click **Edit Recovery Plan**.

5. Modify the recovery plan, and when you are done, click **Finish** to save it.

Removing a Recovery Plan

1. Log in to the vSphere Client and connect to the vCenter Server for either the protected or recovery site.

2. Launch the vCenter SRM application.

3. Select **Recovery Plans** in the left pane, and then select the recovery plan you want to remove.

4. Right-click the recovery plan and select **Delete Recovery Plan**.

5. When prompted "Do you want to remove the recovery plan?", click **Yes**.

TIP

Removing a recovery plan permanently deletes the plan from vCenter SRM. You cannot retrieve a recovery plan after it is deleted.

Configuring Virtual Machines in a Recovery Plan

1. Log in to the vSphere Client and connect to the vCenter Server for either the protected or recovery site.

2. Launch the vCenter SRM application.

3. Select the **Recovery Plans** panel in the left pane.

4. Select the recovery plan in the Inventory list.

5. Click the **Virtual Machines** tab, and then click **Edit**.

6. Select the VM you want to configure, and then click **Configure Recovery**.

7. Select **IP Settings** for the VM.

8. Select **Priority Group** for the VM.

9. Define **VM Dependencies** for the VM.

10. Select **Shutdown Actions** for the VM.

11. Select **Start Up Actions** for the VM.

12. Create **Pre-Power on Steps** for the VM.

13. Create **Post-Power on Steps** for the VM.

Testing a Recovery Plan: Failover Test

1. Verify that all the prerequisites for a failover test have been completed.

2. Log in to the vSphere Client and connect to the vCenter Server for either the protected or recovery site.

3. Launch the vCenter SRM application.

4. Select **Recovery Plans** in the left pane.

5. Select the recovery plan in the Inventory list that you want to run a test recovery on.

6. Click **Test**.

7. Monitor the recovery progress and verify that all steps completed successfully.

Testing a Recovery Plan and Cleaning Up After a Recovery Test

1. Verify that all the prerequisites for a failover test have been completed.

2. Log in to the vSphere Client and connect to the vCenter Server for either the protected or recovery site.

3. Launch the vCenter SRM application.

Running a Recovery Plan: Failover

1. Make sure that the prerequisites for a failover have been completed, including DNS updates.

2. Log in to the vSphere Client and connect to the vCenter Server for either the protected or recovery site.

3. Launch the vCenter SRM application.

4. Select **Recovery Plans** in the left pane.

5. In the Inventory list, select the recovery plan on which you want to run a recovery.

6. Click **Recovery**.

7. Click **I understand that this process will permanently alter the virtual machines and infrastructure of both the protected and recovery datacenters**, and then select the recovery type **Disaster Recovery**.

Running a Recovery Plan Followed by the Subsequent Reprotect

1. Log in to the vSphere Client and connect to the vCenter Server for either the protected or recovery site.

2. Launch the vCenter SRM application.

3. Select **Recovery Plans** in the left pane.

4. Select the recovery plan in the Inventory list that you want to reprotect.

5. Click **Reprotect**.

Running a Recovery Plan and Planned Migration

1. Make sure that the prerequisites for a failover have been completed, including DNS updates.

2. Log in to the vSphere Client and connect to the vCenter Server for either the protected or recovery site.

3. Launch the vCenter SRM application.

4. Select **Recovery Plans** in the left pane.

5. In the Inventory list, select the recovery plan on which you want to run a planned migration recovery.

6. Click **Recovery**.

7. Click **I understand that this process will permanently alter the virtual machines and infrastructure of both the protected and recovery datacenters**, and then select the recovery type **Planned Migration**.

Exporting Recovery Plan Steps

1. Log in to the vSphere Client and connect to the vCenter Server for either the protected or recovery site.

2. Launch the vCenter SRM application

3. Select **Recovery Plans** in the left pane.

4. In the Inventory list, select the recovery plan that you want to export.

5. Click the **Recovery Steps** tab.

6. Click **Export Steps**.

7. Save the file in a directory using a filename of your choice. The report exports to XML, .doc, XLW, HTML, or CSV format.

Export Recovery History Results

1. Log in to the vSphere Client and connect to the vCenter Server for either the protected or recovery site.

2. Launch the vCenter SRM application.

3. Select **Recovery Plans** in the left pane.

4. Click the **History** tab.

5. Select the recovery plan to export and click **Export**.

6. Save the file in a directory using a filename of your choice. The report exports in XML, .doc, XLW, HTML, or CSV format.

Summary

Each and every DR plan will differ because each system has different service level agreements imposed on it by a combination of the often unrealistic expectations of executives and application owners but tempered by the more realistic IT administrators. It is always important to understand the distinct line between HA and DR, and unless the conversation is focused on a storage virtualization product, that line should not be blurred. HA events can and should be managed automatically; whereas DR events can be automated but should always be initiated via intelligent human intervention. (Apologies to those who created the fast_start_failover option.)

Comprehensive DR systems and plans consider all possible disaster scenarios, including the dramatic and the mundane. True viability of the system, virtualized or nonvirtualized, is not achieved until these questions are addressed and the preparation is complete, because some form of disaster is inevitable. DR plans should consider subtle corruption and how a database block that was corrupted months earlier yet went undetected will be recovered. The conclusion may be that the storage-based replication system should be augmented with a standby database. Obviously, this is an old-school approach, but it might be the right answer in some circumstances.

Remember, prepare like it is the last important thing that you will do in your professional career, because someday it may be just that.

## Chapter 10

Backup and Recovery

The viability of the overall system, the database, the jobs of all information technology (IT) personnel, especially the database administrator (DBA), as well as the future existence of a company may depend on the DBA's ability to recover a critical database.

Our journey through the four V's takes an abrupt turn toward luminescent clarity in this chapter. The only facet of our quad-pronged theme addressed in this chapter is viability. The chapter is purposefully short because there is very little in the subject area of backup and recovery that is specific to vSphere. Most of the conversation centers on backup tools and methods that work on the database inside the virtual machine (VM) or storage-based tools that work in the exact same way as they would in the nonvirtualized environment. As stated throughout this book, a main pillar of the "Oracle on vSphere" proposition is that very little of substance changes between the virtual and the nonvirtual environments. Figure 10.1 shows the four V's approach.

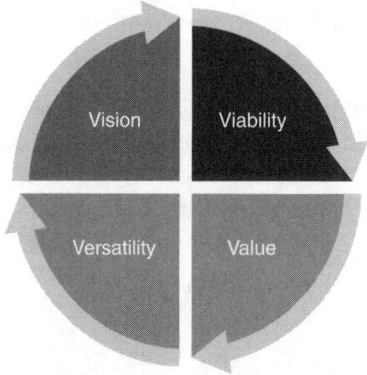

Figure 10.1 Four V's approach

From experience, the best advice for a DBA confronting a critical restore/recovery situation is to "get a cup of coffee." The point being that the DBA should stop and carefully assess the situation and relax. There will be pressure from every angle to fix the problem immediately. But the DBA is in charge and must make the right decision, and without careful consideration of all aspects of the usually dire circumstances, the situation can often deteriorate quickly. Experienced DBAs approach every move with caution and only act when they are as certain as humanly possible. Measure ten times and cut once!

The point of this cogent advice is to stay calm and dig in for the long haul, because regardless of the number of executives who sign your paycheck, they will hound you during that period because you are in charge of everything. Recovering and restoring an Oracle database can be a complicated and arduous process. However, most of the time, the notion of Occam's razor should be adhered to, which means that the simplest, most succinct answer is most often the correct answer. In the 1990s, the DBA would copy a data file from the most recent backup and type on the keyboard "recover database." Around the year 2000, the DBA would simply use some version of Recovery Manager to accomplish essentially the same thing.

There are a few essential components of the backup and recovery process (using third-party tools):

1. Know where the backups live.

2. Be prepared (based on testing and practice as opposed to hope and luck) to fix or replace the damaged components of the database.

3. Have the confidence of a battle-tested sergeant and the arrogance of an emergency room surgeon.

And there are a few undeniable facts:

- DBAs may do very little for a long time, but this is where you earn your money.

- During a critical database restore/recovery, the DBA is the most important person in the company.

- The Oracle University Backup and Recovery Workshop is the best class in the history of technology education to prepare an individual to deal with these challenges.

It is a sobering fact that many companies have liquidated because of the loss of critical databases. Although we run the risk of sounding like we are employing overreaching rhetoric, the junkyard of IT history is riddled with companies that did not properly heed these warnings.

In 2014, the database may be made up of many different and unwieldy components. Respectively, there are many tools and systems to allow for what is effectively the copying of database files for backups and restores. This chapter lists only a few specific tools and techniques, but you are admonished as to the main pillar of the Oracle on vSphere proposition: Oracle does not change when run on vSphere. And therefore, the ideas, notions, techniques, and systems for the most part do not change either.

DBAs are responsible for developing, implementing, and periodically testing a backup and recovery plan for the databases they manage. Even in large shops where a separate system administrator performs server backups, the DBA has final responsibility for making sure that the backups are being done as scheduled and that they include all the files needed to make database restore and recovery possible after a failure. When failures do occur, the DBA needs to know how to use the backups to return the database to operational status as quickly as possible, without losing any transactions that were committed.

DBAs understand the idea of the ACID properties of a true relational database management system (RDBMS). ACID stands for atomic, consistency, integrity and durability. If a database management system is compliant with ACID properties, its natural state will be that it will be fully recoverable upon failure. The only real absolute requirement of a DBA is to be able recover databases to the point that the service level agreement (SLA) has been satisfied.

The database can fail in several ways, and the DBA must have a strategy to recover from each possibility. From a business standpoint, a cost applies to doing backups, and the DBA makes management aware of the cost/risk trade-offs of various backup methods. Professional DBAs use techniques, such as online backups, clustering, replication, and standby databases, to ensure an adequate higher level of availability to meet the requirements of the SLA and provide the most effective backup strategy feasible.

Backup and Recovery Principles

You should give the same amount of attention and diligence to backing up a database on a VM as when backing up a database on a physical server. The principles are the same. When deployed in a virtual environment, all the native backup tools included by database vendors are supported. VMware and VMware partners provide other options for protecting entire VMs.

Every method that the DBA has used and every skill that the DBA has learned with regard to backups over many decades translates exactly to the virtualized environment. Although vSphere provides capabilities that do not exist in nonvirtualized environments, the essential approaches to Oracle backups remain the same.

Backing Up Data Using In-Guest Software Solutions

The guest operating system (GOS) operates autonomously and abstracted from the virtualization layer. It is possible to attach storage to the guest by using various network storage methods, such as Network File System (NFS), to directly attach that storage to the OS. This is called *in-guest storage*. With NFS, the system administrators or the DBA simply mount the NFS storage directly to the OS.

Oracle Direct-NFS (dNFS), discussed in Chapter 8, "Performance Management and Monitoring," is an advanced form of NFS. NetApp storage uses two different types of NFS mounts: in-guest, which is usually recommended for Oracle databases being run on NetApp; and NFS datastores, as discussed later in this chapter.

Similar to backing up a database on a physical server, all the native backup tools included by database vendors and any supported third-party backup solutions by database vendors can be used the same way in the VM environment. Backup administrators can continue to deploy and manage the backup agents, jobs, and restores as though they are running on physical systems. DBAs do not need to be concerned with additional components of complexity introduced by the virtualization layer. Simply put, the system is logically congruent to the nonvirtualized system.

Oracle Database Backup Methods

Over the decades, many attempts have been made to simplify Oracle backups. However, each of the many approaches has its own innate validity. Hot backups were declared dead when Recovery Manager (RMAN) was introduced. The legion of third-party backup vendors all declared victory in the backup battles many times as well. Storage vendors introduced snapshots and tremendously sophisticated techniques to "split the mirror" and render all other backup methods antiquated. It does seem, however, that each and every approach to backups for Oracle databases has its own unique place in this industry, and even with the addition of a new set of technologies that "make backups better," each of these methods has a deep-rooted place in the industry and certainly in the hearts of some DBA somewhere. Therefore, this section touches on them all.

Classic Oracle Database Backups

The following list describes classic Oracle backup methodologies and techniques:

- **Cold/offline backups:** Shut down the database and back up *all* data, log, and control files. Figure 10.2 describes the cold backup process.

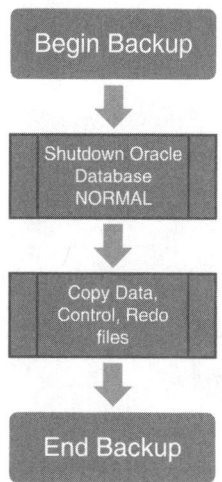

Figure 10.2 Oracle cold backup process

- **Hot/online backups:** If the database is available and in ARCHIVELOG mode, set the table spaces into backup mode and back up their files. Also back up the control files and archived redo log files.

- **RMAN backups:** While the database is offline (mounted)/online, use the RMAN Oracle utility to back up the database. Figure 10.3 describes the RMAN backup.

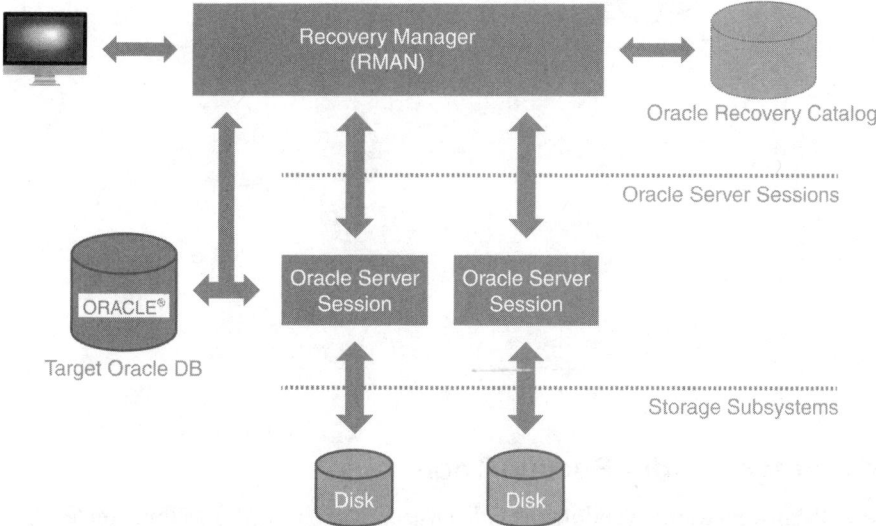

Figure 10.3 Oracle RMAN backup

- **Data pump/export/import:** Data pump/exports are *logical* database backups; they extract logical definitions and data from the database to a file. Figure 10.4 shows the Oracle data pump/export/import process.

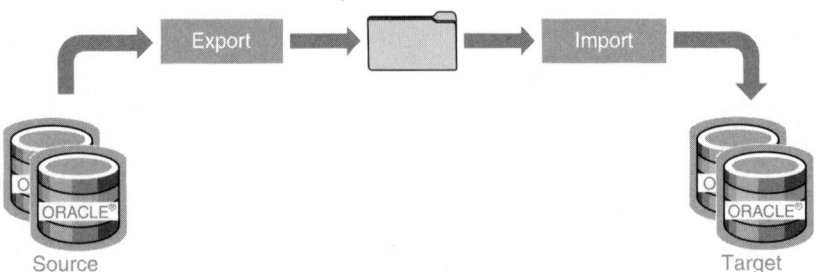

Figure 10.4 Oracle Data Pump

- **Oracle Flashback:** The DBA can use the Flashback Area (FRA) to return a database to a significantly earlier point in time. Figure 10.5 shows the Oracle database Flashback process. Note that the background process known as the Flashback Writer (RVWR) is unique to the Flash Recovery feature.

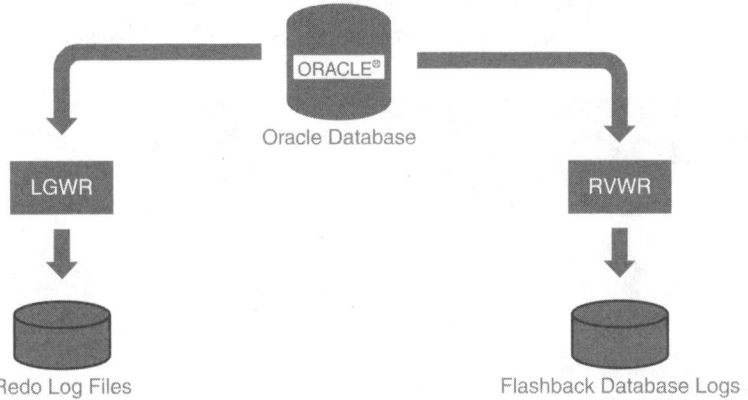

Figure 10.5 Oracle Flashback database

Listing of Storage Vendor Backup Tools

Many of the well-known storage vendors provide customized backup tools for Oracle. Each vendor intends on creating a complimentary relationship between their product and

Oracle by aspiring to produce a backup product that is both effective and efficient as well as seamless in terms of usability. Here is partial list of well-known vendor backup systems for Oracle.

- EMC NetWorker—Unified backup and recovery software.

- EMC TimeFinder—Provides local storage replication and mirror splitting capability.

- EMC Replication Manager—Automates data replication processes through a single console.

- EMC Avamar—Provides efficient backups through the use of deduplication.

- NetApp SnapManager for Oracle—Backup, restore, and cloning as well as data protections.

- NetApp Snap Creator—Provides plugins to integrate with Oracle.

- Pure Storage Zero Snap—Clone databases instantly. Snapshots are crash consistent across volumes.

Other Backup Tools

- **VMware Data Protection Advanced (VDPA):** Presently not supported for Oracle backups, but will be at some point in the future.

- **NetBackup:** Symantec backup tool that can perform hot and cold backups of Oracle databases.

Storage Vendor Backup Solutions

As in the case of the in-guest solutions, array-based solutions provided by many of the leading storage vendors are effective with databases running VMware vSphere. Array-based backup solutions for Oracle can produce near-instant application-aware clones or snapshots of databases. These local clones or snapshots can then be backed up to disk or tape or cloned offsite for disaster recovery purposes.

TIP

Before backing up, consult your storage vendor for guidance on array-based backup support in a virtualized environment.

DBAs and IT organizations face the challenge of backing up large-scale databases whether or not they are running on virtualized infrastructure. Database backup and recovery can be a demanding task that consumes considerable time, effort, and resources. In some cases, the backup and restore task constitutes the majority of a DBA's daily activities.

Working with NetApp Backup Solutions

For these reasons, it is clear that the ability to quickly back up or restore a database that has been virtualized adds value to the DBA and IT organizations and to the customers that are consumers of the database applications. Customers can deploy Oracle 11g Release 2 databases, using VMware virtualization, and leverage technologies such as NetApp Snapshot to safely and efficiently complete regular backup operations.

You can create a NetApp Snapshot copy of a volume in a single second, regardless of the volume size, which makes it a complementary solution to be deployed with VMware. The two technologies combine to deliver an extremely simple and space- and time-efficient database and respective backup. This is an effective protection methodology for the virtualized Oracle database solution.

A non-RMAN database backup is usually classified as either a cold backup or a hot backup. A cold backup, also known as an offline backup, refers to a backup that is taken when the database is down (or has been shut down). A hot backup, or online backup, can be performed while the database is open and available for use. To use the hot backup method, the database must be in ARCHIVELOG mode. Hot backups are required for production environments because such databases cannot be shut down unless the backup is performed during planned downtime.

NetApp Backup and Restore Solution Overview

This section describes how to use NetApp clustered Data ONTAP to quickly back up an Oracle database using NetApp Snapshot and walks you through a way to back up a virtualized Oracle database with NFS datastores and in-guest NFS mounts and ultimately restore an Oracle database using NetApp Snapshot capabilities.

Integrating NetApp with vSphere

The NetApp storage OS, clustered Data ONTAP, enables users to quickly back up an Oracle database. Data ONTAP includes functionality that allows for the execution of a quick backup and restore of storage components that contain an Oracle database. Just as VMware delivers a virtual server infrastructure, NetApp delivers the same agile infrastructure for data and storage. NetApp provides storage flexibility and virtualization with a pool of storage that frees virtual servers and the applications running on them from having to manage or be tied to underlying physical storage systems.

At the core of NetApp integrations with VMware ESXi is the Virtual Storage Console (VSC) plug-in. It is an all-encompassing vCenter plug-in that provides end-to-end storage management within the virtualized environment. VSC allows your VMware administrators to access and execute these functions from vCenter. Using the built-in role-based access control (RBAC), the VMAdmin can control permissions, enhancing server and storage efficiencies without affecting the storage administrators' established policies.

As a vCenter plug-in, all vSphere Clients that connect to vCenter can access it. This availability differs from a client-side plug-in that must be installed on every vSphere Client.

Working with NetApp Snapshot

NetApp Snapshot technology is a point-in-time snapshot capability that offers unique advantages to include unparalleled simplicity in the snapping process, built-in Oracle-specific capabilities, and advanced snapshot version management. NetApp Snapshot is a low-overhead, scalable, high-performance snapshot technology that provides an efficient backup and restore capability for Oracle databases.

A Snapshot copy is a point-in-time file system image that is facilitated by the NetApp clustered Data ONTAP operating system. The NetApp Snapshot copy takes only a few seconds to create, regardless of the size of the volume or the level of activity on the NetApp storage system. This makes NetApp Snapshot technology a very fast and efficient method for backing up and restoring NetApp FlexVols, which are used for an Oracle database. NetApp also enables you to do a Single File Snap Restore (SFSR), which allows you to restore a standalone virtual machine disk (VMDK).

Backing Up a Virtualized Oracle Database with NetApp Snapshot

Oracle DBAs working in virtualized environments continue to have issues executing necessary backup and restore operations on the storage used for an Oracle database. The DBA can derive a backup and restore methodology to solve many problems faced by the DBA community when using NFS datastores for the ESXi cluster as containers for VMDKs used by Oracle databases.

Although the primary storage configuration recommendation for all network-attached storage (NAS) solutions for Oracle on vSphere is to use in-guest NFS mounts, the approach of presenting the NFS mount directly to ESXi is valid as well. An NFS datastore is built by NFS mounting storage directly to the ESXi host, as opposed to the method of NFS mounting directly to the GOS. Refer to the vSphere administration guide found at the main VMware website for details on the configuration specifications for NFS datastores.

http://pubs.vmware.com/vsphere-55/topic/com.vmware.ICbase/PDF/
vsphere-esxi-vcenter-server-55-virtual-machine-admin-guide.pdf

One solution available to those virtualizing databases is to define appropriate NFS datastores for the ESXi cluster, which would then be used for the VMDKs that would serve as disk devices for those databases. Consider the key components that make up a database, especially those required for a complete database recovery. The DBA can simply provide an NFS datastore to the ESXi cluster for each of those components of an Oracle database (that is, data, archive logs, redo logs, and control files). In this case, the datastores are allocated to the ESXi cluster and dedicated to specific components of an individual Oracle database. In addition, it is possible to include multiple database virtual disks within the same datastores.

In other variations, you could have multiple databases where the respective data components of each database would share the same datastore, and the same for the other components of a database. This allows for fewer NFS datastores, yet still provides a user with the capability of performing advanced restores to still take advantage of capabilities and efficiencies of the technology. See Chapter 8 for a complete discussion about storage configuration for Oracle databases run on vSphere.

Tools Available for Backups of Oracle Using NetApp

- **SnapManager for Oracle (SMO):** SnapManager for Oracle is a GOS-based backup, restore, and cloning solution that is raw device mapping (RDM) aware. When running Oracle on in-guest NFS mounts, SMO is a capable tool for performing backups and restores. SMO can also identify the underlying storage used for the database when RDMs are part of the deployment. However, SMO cannot identify the underlying storage of the VMDKs used for an Oracle database.

- **Snap Creator Framework:** Snap Creator is a GOS-based backup and restore solution that allows the end user to identify the underlying storage used for the database that contains the VMDKs. Along with SMO, Snap Creator can provide the capability of a Single File Restore (SFR) of a VMDK file when using NFS datastores.

  https://communities.netapp.com/docs/DOC-4865

Step-by-Step Solution for Backing Up a Virtualized Oracle Database with NetApp Storage and NFS Datastores

1. Verify that the NFS datastores have NetApp storage FlexVol allocated via the VCS plug-in to ensure proper setting and provisioning details

2. Provision storage using vCenter and create the VMDKs. Then create the database named DB1. Make certain that the database has been built within the VM to correspond to storage layout best practices. The database structure will be contained within the VMDKs that have been created to hold specific components, including data, redo, and archive of the Oracle database on the NFS datastores. Now there is a VM, with an operational database whose database VMDK components (data, archive, redo, control) are provisioned with VMDKs within the respective NFS datastores. (For example, the Data VMDK is in the Data NFS datastore.)

3. The DBA can now leverage the technology to make backups of this database by using Snap Creator.

TIP

Snap Creator can be used to create custom scripts, or the Snap Creator Framework can be used with vSphere integration. Note that the DBA must continue to make certain that the database is placed in backup mode if the backup is to be taken without the database being shut down.

---

4. The DBA can create a backup of the datastores used for the VMDKs of the DB1 database. This creates a NetApp Snapshot copy of the NFS datastores. In addition, Snap Creator would handle the requirement of ensuring that an application-consistent backup of the database is created.

5. An alternative solution is to back up the entire VM with Snap Creator using the Snap Creator vSphere integration. This way, the DBA can produce a VM snapshot that is integrated with the databases within the VM to get a consistent backup.

6. Use the Snap Creator Framework tool along with NetApp clustered Data ONTAP to provide backups of a virtualized Oracle database within the ESXi infrastructure.

Restoring a Database Using NetApp Snapshot

A function that all DBAs will need to do at some point with a database is to restore and recover the database. As with creating a time-efficient backup using the NetApp Snapshot copy, the DBA can also quickly restore the database from that backup. When using clustered Data ONTAP and Snapshot copies along with the NFS datastores, you can restore the appropriate NetApp FlexVol containing the appropriate VMDKs. In more complex configurations, a DBA may be required to perform a "single file restore" of the VMDK file used for the database requiring the restore and recovery. This is a feature of newer versions of clustered Data ONTAP. You can also use the Snap Creator Framework to perform the file restore, or a storage administrator can perform the restore using the command-line interface with the storage.

TIP

When backing up VMDKs, be sure to identify the proper VMDK that you would require for a successful restore and recovery of an Oracle database. It is recommended to not use VM snapshots because that will provide a level of abstraction for the proper file to restore when using VMDKs.

Backup and Restore Use Case with Snap Creator

One of the tools available for DBAs to back up and restore the components of the database is the Snap Creator Framework. It provides a graphical user interface (GUI) or command-line interface (CLI) that will integrate with the Oracle database as well as with the NetApp storage, providing users with a layer of abstraction where they do not need to know all the Oracle or storage commands. The user only needs to understand the workflow of backing up an Oracle database. Figure 10.6 depicts a use case example and provides a diagram where a database has each VMDK for the respective database components allocated within the specific datastores. You can see each NFS datastore. In this example, one datastore exists for the archive logs, data files, control files, and redo logs. Snap Creator Framework is a simple tool, which is easy to use, that can back up and restore the appropriate storage components based on the configuration of the workflow.

The efficiencies of the NetApp Snapshot copy allow a DBA to quickly make a backup, as well as restore the Snapshot copy to a previous point in time (and thus allowing DBAs to perform the necessary recovery commands quickly as required in their situation).

As part of any backup and recovery solution, thorough tests should be completed to ensure that the selected procedure meets the requirements of the SLA for the recovery time objective (RTO) and recovery point objective (RPO) for the application database.

Figure 10.6 depicts the usage of Snap Creator for the purpose of directly taking a snapshot of the VMDKs and storing them in the predesignated snapshot area on the storage. Notice that the ESXi and NetApp cluster layers are purposefully bypassed in the graphic.

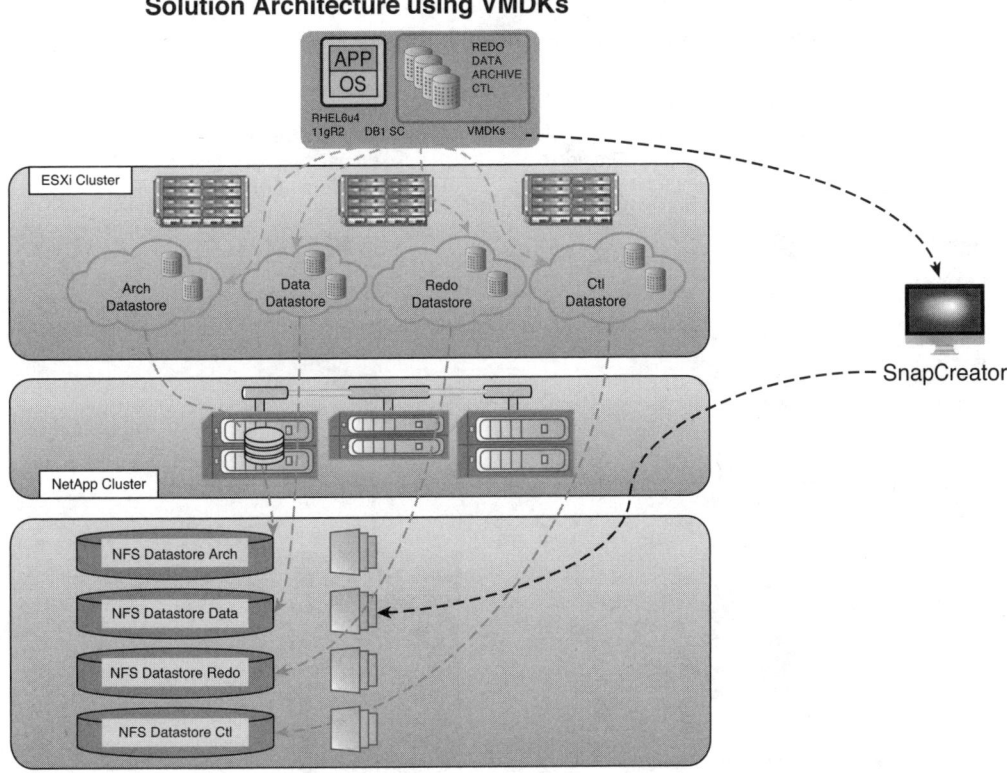

Solution Architecture using VMDKs

Figure 10.6 NetApp virtualized Oracle backup solution

For more details on this solution, refer to the document *Oracle Database Dev/Test Reference Architecture Using Data Guard and SnapManager for Oracle Deployment Guide.* Found on the Netapp website and listed here.

http://www.netapp.com/us/media/ra-0002.pdf

EMC Avamar Backup and Restore Solution Overview

The Avamar plug-in for Oracle works with Oracle and Oracle Recovery Manager (RMAN) to back up an Oracle database, tablespace, or data files to an Avamar server or a data domain system. The Avamar plug-in for Oracle serves as a backup module, and the Avamar server and/or data domain system serves as a storage device.

RMAN initiates the backup and recovery operations. The Avamar plug-in for Oracle interprets RMAN backup and recovery commands, and then routes the commands to the

Avamar server. The Avamar server sends commands to the Avamar plug-in for Oracle to perform the backup and restore activity, as shown in Figure 10.7.

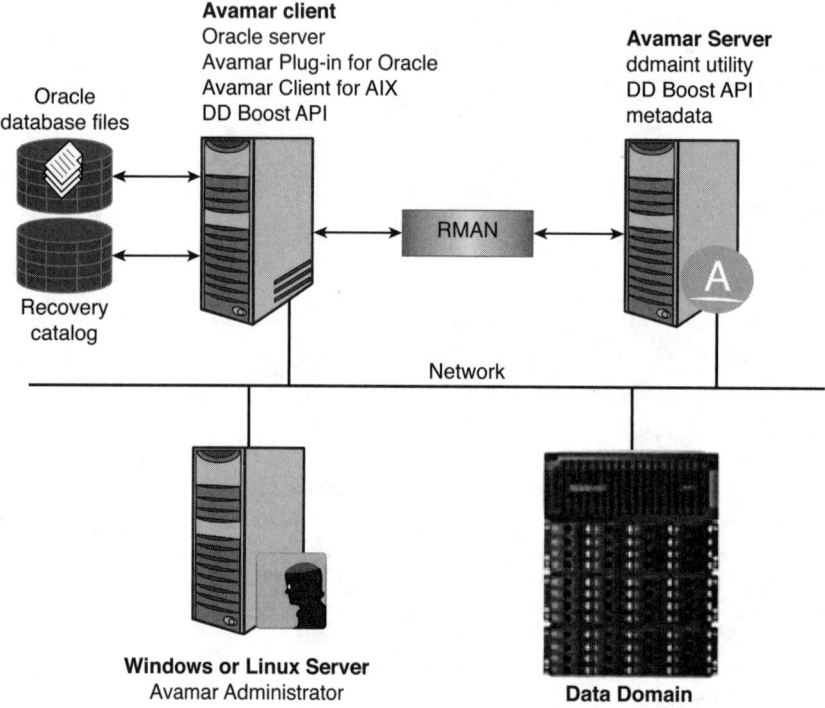

Figure 10.7 Avamar server and Avamar plug-in for Oracle

Backing Up the Oracle Database

When running a backup of an Oracle database, the DBA must fully understand the capabilities and limitations of the specific storage tool. Some tools can perform any type of an Oracle backup with minimal configuration or effort. Some tools, however, simply copy logical files and may require significant effort to be legitimately considered an Oracle backup tool.

Avamar, for example, has been instrumented to perform many types of Oracle backups with minimal extra configuration. To perform a simple Oracle database backup, follow these steps:

1. To run a backup from the Avamar Administrator interface, click Backup to start the backup process. While the backup is running, use the Activity Monitor screen to monitor the backup process. After a backup job completes, the job status indicates Completed.

2. Upon backup completion, view the Activity Monitor screen, select a completed backup job, review the number of datasets that were backed up, and then check the deduplication ratio of the backup dataset.

Restoring the Oracle Database

Restoring the Oracle database is also a simple process. It is always essential for the DBA to prove that the restore/recovery process actually works. The DBA's most important day-to-day task is to make certain that valid backups have been taken. However, the only intrinsic value of an individual backup is its innate ability to be used in a real recovery. And the only way to be sure that the backup is "valid" is to use that backup in a simulated recovery operation. Of course, one could argue that the DBA could simply wait for the restore/recovery situation to present itself and at that time the legitimacy of the backup will become self-validating. Validation could actually become a fifth V, but our heartfelt recommendation is to test the backups constantly and thoroughly, if only for peace of mind, as follows:

1. After the Oracle database is backed up successfully, the DBA can change the database to correspond to the test plan.

2. To simulate recovering an entire database to its last full database backup, use the Avamar Administrator **Select for Restore** option in the Backup and Restore panel.

For more details on this solution, refer to the document at www.emc.com/collateral/technical-documentation/h11445-vspex-virtualized-oracle-ig.pdf.

TIP

There are many different vendor-specific backup tools that we choose not to concentrate on in this text. Throughout the rest of this chapter, we discuss the capabilities of the VMware-specific methods.

VMware Data Protection Advanced

VMware Data Protection Advanced (VDPA) protects your data at the VM level, capturing application and system data as a full VM image. VDPA runs at the ESXi host level as a virtual appliance to provide streamlined deployment and full integration with VMware vCenter Server. VDPA stores multiple restore points for each VM using deduplication technology, which reduces the total backup sizes by referencing duplicate blocks as opposed to generating multiple copies of the same block. In this way, VDPA not only provides point-in-time restore capabilities, but also efficiently uses available disk space. Although VDPA is a recommended tool for many VM use cases, it is not presently supported for live Oracle databases. Figure 10.8 describes the VDPA components.

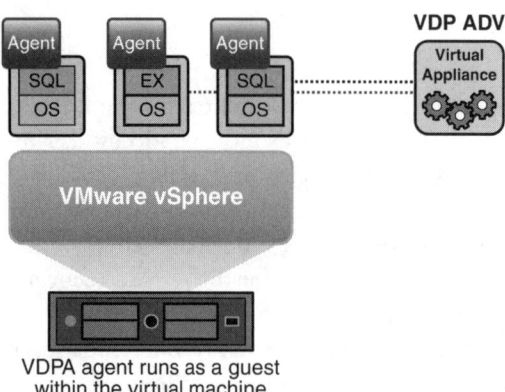

Figure 10.8 VMware Data Protection Advanced

As most DBAs know, the use of a database-aware backup agent provides database health checking and log truncation. Though VDPA can use the Microsoft Windows feature Volume Shadow Copy Service (VSS) framework to back up guest VMs, it does not contain the required database VSS requestor to properly back up and restore an Oracle database. You may write custom scripts to involve the appropriate database VSS writer. VSS writer is supported only on Microsoft Windows. This solution is optimal for small Oracle databases running on a Windows operating system.

Comparing VMFS and RDM

The use of Virtual Machine File System (VMFS) versus the use of raw device mapping (RDM) was addressed in Chapter 8 in terms of the performance question. The question of VMFS or RDM in terms of the suitability for backup efficiency differs slightly and is addressed in this section. The question of VMFS versus RDM is asked in one of two contexts:

1. Which performs better?
2. Which is more efficient for performing backups?

To answer the performance question, both VMFS and RDM volumes can provide similar transaction throughput (as described in Chapter 8). For more details, refer to the document *Performance Characterization of VMFS and RDM Using a SAN* (www.vmware.com/files/pdf/performance_char_vmfs_rdm.pdf).

Backups

In terms of backups, it is fair to say that RDMs may facilitate the use of third-party backup Snap tools, whereas VMFS often complicates the issue. RDMs intrinsically provide a one-to-one relationship between RDM and logical unit number (LUN), making the mapping of the physical storage to be snapped quite simple. The use of VMFS does not prohibit the use of storage-level snaps. However, the DBA must realize that the entire LUN/datastore will be part of the snapshot, meaning that all the objects (VMDKs) within the LUN/datastore will be part of the snapshot. In terms of practicality, this practice would limit each datastore to a single VMDK. Although this is a solution, it is one that imposes the restriction of limiting the number of devices that can be connected to an ESXi host, which in vSphere 5.5 is 256. For completeness, the number of paths per host in vSphere 5.5, which is 1,024, should also be mentioned, although that is not normally a restricting factor. It is, however, the simplicity of use that motivates certain storage vendors to recommend RDMs over VMDKs.

It is also useful to note that VMware supports two modes of RDMs: physical compatibility mode, used for sharing between physical hosts; and virtual compatibility mode, usually used for sharing between VMs on the same host.

Physical compatibility mode (RDM-p) is the sharing methodology for RDMs between hosts that use SCSI bus sharing. Virtual compatibility mode (RDM-v) is the sharing methodology for storage between VMs running on the same host.

RDM-p requires the use of SCSI bus sharing, which negates official (GSS) support for vMotion. So, if the customer chooses to use RDM-p to facilitate the use of physical snapshots, they will be forgoing the proper use of vMotion. However, in an ironic twist, it is possible to use RDM-v across physical hosts. Although this is counterintuitive, the exploitation of this nuance will allow the customer to leverage to the simplicity of RDM for snapshots but also use vMotion, because vMotion when using RDM-v is supported specifically when using the SCSI multi-writer flag (SMWF).

Understand the Functionality of VMFS Versus RDMs

By default, VMware recommends the use of VMFS. In some situations, however, RDMs can be preferred or even required. Table 10.1 summarizes some of the options and trade-offs between VMFS and RDM. The inclusion of SCSI reservation cluster technologies such as Windows Failover Clusters requires the use of RDM-p, and the use of EMC snapshots in general is often made simpler when using RDMs (in this case, either RDM-p or RDM-v).

For a more complete discussion, see the vSphere storage guide on the VMware website.

http://pubs.vmware.com/vsphere-50/topic/com.vmware.ICbase/PDF/
vsphere-esxi-vcenter-server-50-storage-guide.pdf

Table 10.1 VMFS and Raw Disk Mapping Trade-Offs

VMFS	RDM
Volume can host many VMs (or can be dedicated to 1 VM).	Maps a single LUN to 1 VM, so only 1 VM is possible per LUN.
Increases storage utilization, provides better flexibility and easier administration and management.	More LUNs are required, so it is easier to reach the LUN limit of 256 that can be presented to an ESX host.
Can potentially support clustering software that does not issue SCSI reservations, such as Oracle Clusterware. To configure VMFS, follow the VMware KB 1034165 article, *Disabling simultaneous write protection provided by VMFS using the multi-writer flag.*	RDM may be required to leverage third-party storage array-level backup and replication tools.
Oracle RAC vMotion possible. This eliminates downtime for hardware maintenance and allows for flexibility in terms of the VMs using all the nodes within the ESXi cluster through Distributed Resource Scheduler (DRS).	RDM volumes can help facilitate migrating physical Oracle databases to VMs. Also enables quick migration to physical in rare Oracle support cases.
VMFS is supported by VMware for all present functionality and is guaranteed to be supported for future features and functions. VMFS is the recommended storage approach by VMware.	RDMs are not guaranteed to be supported for future features and functions.

Oracle Data Guard for Backup

One of the challenges of traditional database cloning and application test preparation is that it is very time-consuming. Frequent releases and patches from software vendors pressure administrators to upgrade their applications often, creating a need for rapid development and testing. However, the lengthy test preparation processes for dev/test environments often preclude rapid deployment, causing fewer new releases than are desirable. As a result, application functionality, quality, performance, and organizational competitiveness can suffer.

Another challenge with traditional cloning methods is that they require 100% storage capacity overhead. For example, cloning a 1TB production database volume results in the reservation of 2TB of data storage. Because testing often requires creation of multiple clones, it is not unusual for environments to consume a very large amount of storage capacity for their dev/test systems, resulting in much higher infrastructure costs and higher database administration and maintenance costs.

DBAs have the option to *switch over* to the standby site as opposed to performing a *failover* to the standby site, which would render useless the original primary database. In this sense, the standby database is actually a backup that can be used upon a failover and the subsequent activation as the primary. The standby can also be used as a source of single data blocks to be copied from in the event of an anomaly of data block corruption. The standby database is, however, often used for the mundane purpose of serving as the source from which to generate a backup.

Figure 10.9 shows the reference architecture where Oracle Data Guard is used between a primary and standby site. A clone database is created from the Data Guard physical standby database. There are multiple ways to create development or test databases from the physical standby database with or without third-party vendor tools.

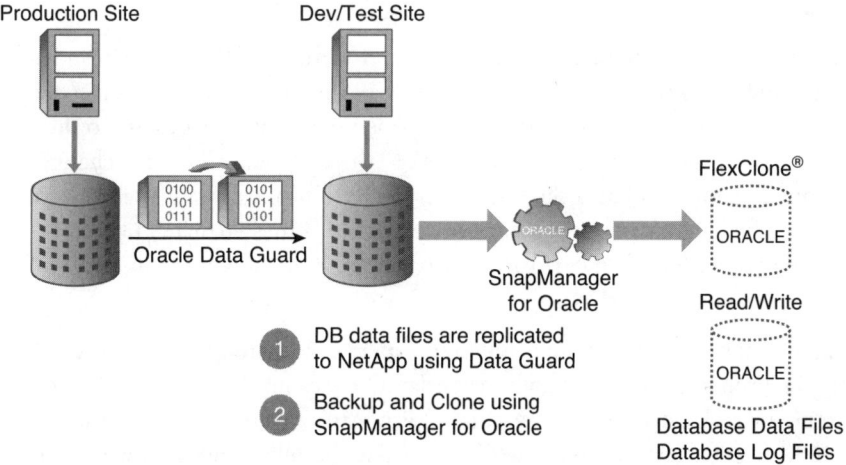

Figure 10.9 Oracle Data Guard and SnapManager for Oracle

We will use NetApp as an example of how to leverage vendor tools to perform backups when running Data Guard. When using NetApp, a DBA may use SMO or Snap Creator Framework or a proprietary process. Notice the various sections of the graphic. First, Oracle Data Guard creates and manages an Oracle standby database. Second, NetApp SMO builds the NetApp FlexClone from the standby and subsequently generates an operational database for the DBA.

This configuration has multiple beneficial facets. The standby can be used for many different functions, including offloading read-only nodes and individual corrupt data block recovery. It is primarily used within a disaster recovery plan for the database. Also, the standby infrastructure can be used to easily provide production-like copies of a database for development or quality-assurance (Q/A) purposes.

For more details on this reference architecture, see the *Oracle Database Dev/Test Reference Architecture Using Data Guard and SnapManager for Oracle Deployment Guide* (www.netapp.com/us/media/ra-0002.pdf).

Oracle Database Backup Strategy Matrix

The Oracle database backup strategy matrix in Figure 10.10 lists various backup methods and how they are used as per their functionality.

Summary

From the outset, the core recommendation of this chapter is for the DBA to perform backups in the same manner with the same tools as was done in the nonvirtualized infrastructure. Although there are some minor caveats that must be understood that relate to the virtualized infrastructure, such as the use of the SMWF, these deviations do not change the basic discipline. The main pillar of the Oracle on vSphere proposition is that nothing really changes when the database environment evolves and becomes virtual. There are a plethora of useful tools to help you perform your backups, some of which this chapter discusses.

Ultimately, the only sound advice that any supposed expert can relate to any unseasoned DBA is to always be prepared to restore and recover at all times under all circumstances. For a DBA, paranoia is not a disorder of the mind, it is a feature of the soul. You cannot be an effective DBA without expecting the worst every day, because one day it will be true. Just remember that you are not truly paranoid if they really are "out to get you."

Database Backup Strategy	Granularity	Storage Type	File Type	Oracle RAC	vSphere HA	vMotion	Site Recovery Manager	RPO-DataLoss	RTO-Downtime	Notes
Oracle Data Guard as the backup	Database	LOCAL/SHARED	VMFS, RDM	Y	Y	Y	Y	The backup is the Standby database which will usually be up to a single archive log behind	The length of recovery time for a single archive log or less	Must Switch over manually
Backups taken of a Standby Database	Database	LOCAL/SHARED	VMFS, RDM	Y	Y	Y	Y	The backup is taken from the Standby database which will usually be up to a single archive log behind	The length of recovery time for a single archive log or less	
Recovery Manager (RMAN)	Database	LOCAL/SHARED	VMFS, RDM	Y	Y	Y	Y	Full recovery possible if the current redo logfile is available	Depends on the amount of recovery necessary-All Oracle database recoveries start at the most recent checkpoint SCN and continue through all the available redo	The standard for all Oracle backups
Hot Backups	Database	LOCAL/SHARED	VMFS, RDM	Y	Y	N	Y	Full recovery possible if the current redo logfile is available	Depends on the amount of recovery necessary-All Oracle database recoveries start at the most recent checkpoint SCN and continue through all the available redo	The classic Oracle backup methodology. Only possible when the Database is in Archive log mode
Storage Level Snapshot (PC, NAS)	Lun/Datastore	LOCAL/SHARED	VMFS, RDM - When taking a snapshot of a LUN/Datastore all vmdks/database files within the LUN/DS will be included in the Snap. For this reason many storage vendors recommend using RDMs	VMFS/RDM - Use of the SCSI MultiWriter Flag (MWF) for VMFS. The MWF prohibits the use of storage level snapshots which is a reason that RDMs may be a viable option. RDM-v with the MWF allows for the use of storage snapshots and does not prohibit vMotion.	Y	Y	Y	Dependant on the frequency of the Snapshot	Dependant of the frequency of the snapshot	Some storage vendors such as Netapp have sophisticated tools which automatically place databases in backup mode prior to the snapshot.
Mirror Split	Lun/Datastore	LOCAL/SHARED	VMFS, RDM	Y	Y	Y	Y	Instance recover time only as this is a "Crash Consistent" Methodology	Instance recover time only as this is a "Crash Consistent" Methodology	
VMware Snapshot**	VM Level	LOCAL/SHARED	VMFS	N	n/a	n/a	n/a	n/a	n/a	Manual (Not Recommended for database backup)
Oracle Data Pump (Export/Import)	Database/Schema/Table	LOCAL/SHARED	VMFS, RDM	Y	Y	Y	Y	Dependant on the frequency of the DP operation	Dependant on the frequency of the DP operation	

Figure 10.10 Oracle database backup strategies

** Not Recommended as a Backup Strategy for a Oracle Databases

## Chapter 11

Provisioning and Automation

As we continue the journey toward complete and comprehensive virtualization and we traverse the four V's, we move into the provisioning and automation arena. The vision and versatility are highlighted in this chapter and depicted in Figure 11-1. There can be little doubt that any improvement in the process of provisioning provides tremendous value to the Oracle database administrator (DBA). The role of the DBA is evolving exponentially. The DBA's responsibilities have been extended over the years well beyond simple management of the relational database management system (RDBMS). The networking that intricately affects the complete applications systems became part of the DBA's duties, and those same concerns were later extended into the province of the storage administrator. Most recently, it has become obvious that the DBA needs to elongate those classic information technology (IT) skills into the arena of virtualization.

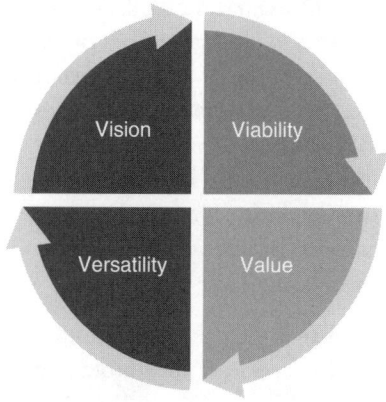

Figure 11-1 Four V's approach

The era of the virtual DBA (vDBA) or the virtual Real Application Clusters DBA (vRAC-DBA), or the CloudDBA is upon us. In prior years, the DBA could be professionally satisfied and remain gainfully employed with a skillset that did not extend beyond the physical components of the compute stack. In the present day, a highly skilled DBA must understand technologies that not only encompass the intrinsic abstractions of virtualization but also the physical disconnection of the Cloud. IT Clouds come in many forms, including public, private, and hybrid.

The public Cloud may be provided by a third party. A private Cloud may have all the ephemeral attributes of a Cloud but be totally managed, monitored, provisioned, and controlled internally by a group that the DBA belongs to. Most likely, the modern DBA will have, at some point, some responsibility over the combination of a public and private Cloud called a hybrid Cloud. A hybrid Cloud is either the best or the worst of both worlds depending on your perspective. Regardless of whichever particular viewpoint one possesses, these new technologies call for new categorizations of professionals, which is why we see the rise of the terms vDBA, vRAC-DBA, and Cloud-DBA in recent years from somewhere within the vast expanse of the internet.

A more narrow set of responsibilities will still fall to the classic DBA regardless of whether that individual decides to cloak himself or herself in the more modern and lofty titles. Those duties revolve around the basic fundamental and often extremely mundane tasks that continue to dominate the everyday work of the Oracle professional. Nothing could illustrate this point better than the chore of provisioning. A server must be allocated, the operating systems loaded, the kernel parameters shifted, RPMS embedded, the software allocated, the database created, and the application installed and configured. And then it all needs to be done again and again and again.

Fortunately, this brave new world of the Cloud that has descended upon us includes a plethora of tools and methodologies that allow the modern DBA to meet the new demands. The modern DBA (shall we say the CloudDBA or vDBA) has the skillset to employ VMware provisioning techniques on many different levels. The simple act of saving the virtual machine (VM) as a template is a great start, and cloning of all types has been a great friend to the DBA for many years. The term *clone* has been used over the decades in many different manners to include the simple copying of the Oracle database datafiles and re-creation of the controlfile or to the copying of the storage volumes containing the database files on a storage level to effectively copy the entire database. The words *snapshot* and *clone* have often been confused and used in the same context, but we will allow those confusing and clever distinctions to be sorted out by the various vendors.

All this interesting history aside, the truly modern vDBA uses true Cloud provisioning tools. This DBA does no provisioning at all! This is because the users use the automated systems to perform the provisioning themselves. The DBAs will set up automation methods, create standards and policies that must be adhered to, and they will allow the requestor of a database or an entire application/database environment to apply for those resources and services. This is the notion of *database-as-a-service* (DBaaS), which is the true underpinning of Cloud architecture. As we go forward in this chapter, we will discuss the notion of DBaaS and extend that idea to the more specific idea of Database-server-as-a-Service as well as application-as-a-service.

A wise man once asked a CEO, *"What is your most valuable resource?"* The CEO, responded, *"Well, my people, sir."* The wise man looked back at him and explained, *"It's your data, sir; you would lay off your people in a moment after a bad earnings report, but you will never let your data out of sight."* However, despite the wise man's prescient, albeit uncouth, advice, he did not deliver the CEO any real advice as to how to manage that data. The problem with data is that it behaves badly. The data that is needed at any particular moment is elusive. The most important data can be extremely sensitive and easy to compromise and trivial to lose. Worse yet, the data can be very fickle, and therefore easily altered. The best DBAs are always looking for better ways to provide access to important and useful data while simultaneously protecting it from loss, alteration, or even unauthorized access.

The VMware software tools described throughout this chapter help the vDBA to provide that near-real-time access to entire systems through Cloud provisioning methodologies while maintaining the security of the most critical attributes of that data through filtering and masking features. Selected reference architectures will show how to provision entire mixed workload systems or a single VM with a single database. For example, it may be necessary to set up an entire army of new developers, each of whom needs newly refreshed database/application systems each week. This chapter covers how to eliminate the stress and struggle so long associated with these daunting tasks by examining the techniques that virtualized infrastructure provides. The example worked through in this chapter migrates multiple Oracle databases from a physical environment to a virtual environment.

Migrating Oracle Database from a Physical to Virtual Environment

To virtualize Oracle databases running on physical servers, Oracle databases must be migrated from a physical to a virtual environment (P2V). There may be multiple databases running on a physical server, which can be separated into their own dedicated database servers in the virtualized environment. Based on the database endian or byte order format, which differs between x86- and RISC-based systems, you can use different migration methods to complete the migration.

Those tools include the popular Oracle tools Data Guard, Data Pump, Golden Gate, Recovery Manager, and Transportable Tablespaces. For this use case, we have chosen Oracle Data Pump as the migration tool. Data Pump provides the classic export/import capabilities that have been used for decades to perform logical transfers of Oracle data. Although not the most efficient or the fastest method, it is certainly the simplest. And when the dataset is sufficiently small, Data Pump is often the most sensible approach. This is in no way an endorsement of any particular approach to migration over another.

Typically, the migration process using Oracle Data Pump requires many manual steps. Automating this process will help alleviate unnecessary manual steps and enable DBAs to save time and migrate to a virtual environment seamlessly. You can achieve this by using a number of VMware solutions, such as VMware vCloud Automation Center (vCAC), shown in Figure 11-2, and vCenter Orchestrator (vCO), shown in Figure 11-3.

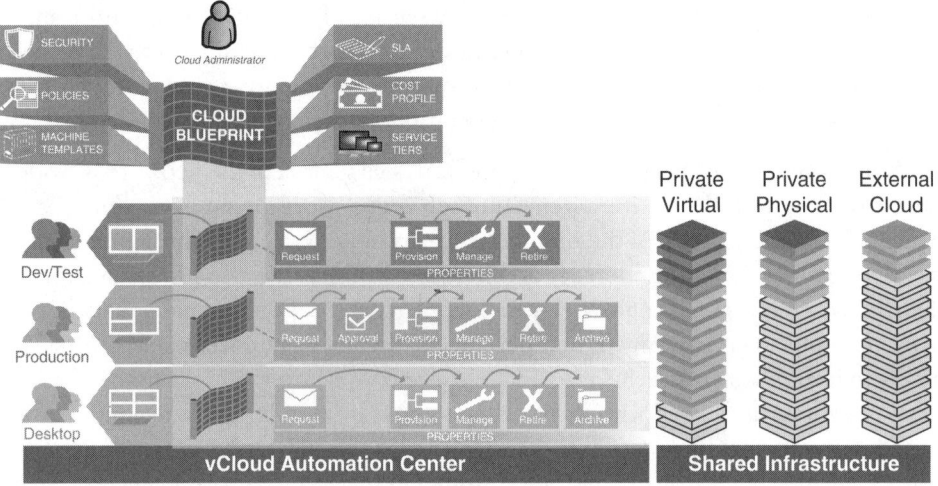

Figure 11-2 VMware vCloud Automation Center

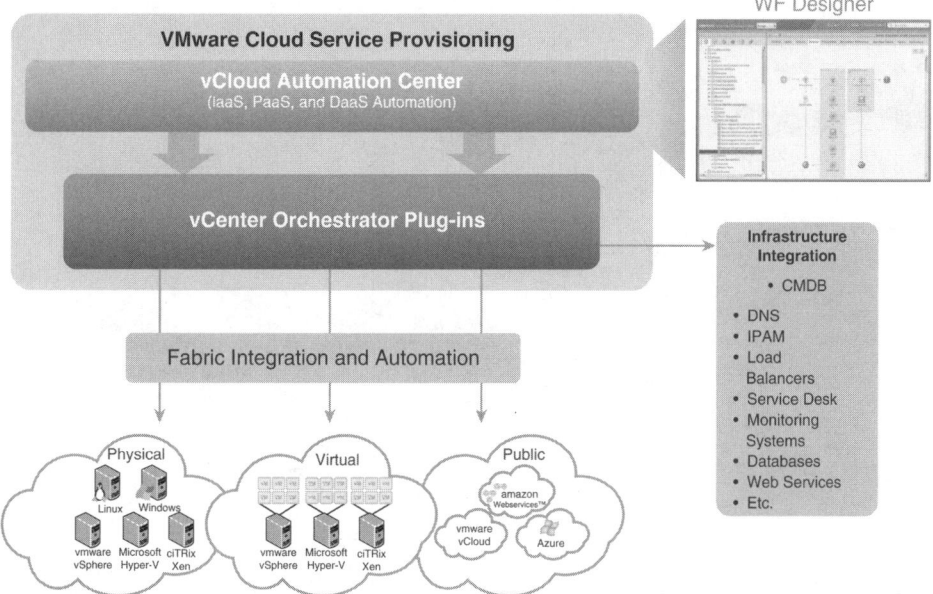

Figure 11-3 VMware vCenter Orchestrator

Viewing Oracle Migration from a Physical to Virtual Solution

A solution is demonstrated through a specific use case in the section titled "Facilitating Deployments" and depicted in Figure 11-4. The concept is the automation of the migration of two databases running on a single physical or virtual server to two separate virtual Oracle database servers. This use case is based on the following:

- Completely automated solution for migrating Oracle databases from a single physical or virtual server with multiple databases to many VMs, each with one database

- Utilization of Oracle database scripts to migrate the databases and coordination with VM creation processes to separate databases among the appropriate number of VMs

- vCenter Orchestrator workflows that provision Oracle database VMs based on the number of databases on the source and migrate each database to its individual Oracle database VM

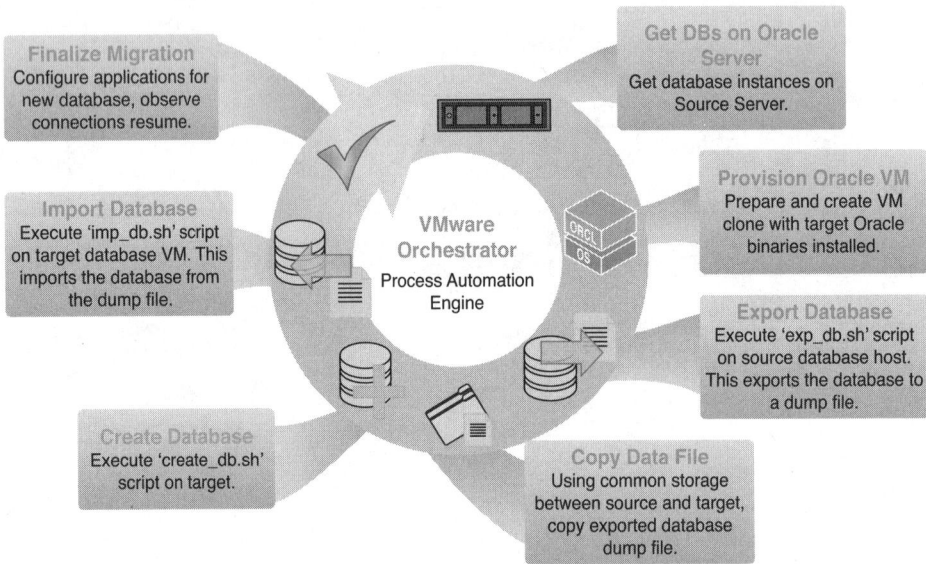

Figure 11-4 Oracle database migration process

Facilitating Deployments

To begin this section, we should describe how VMware products, in their present state, at the time of the writing of this book, facilitate the development of completely automated systems for provisioning, allowing for simplified Oracle database physical/virtual to virtual migration. The following discussion provides a base set of configuration guidelines, vCenter Orchestrator workflows, and Oracle scripts that can be leveraged for further projects.

In the following example, depicted in Figure 11-5, both the source and target systems are Oracle database servers running Linux using the Secure Shell (SSH) plug-in for vCenter Orchestrator; both systems can be easily interacted with to execute commands at the appropriate steps of the workflow.

Understanding the Business Scenario

The business scenario for the use case described in this section is as follows:

The source Oracle database server has two databases running on legacy hardware, each of which needs to be migrated to two separate virtual servers with its own Oracle database.

To migrate Oracle databases from physical/virtual to virtual, follow these steps:

1. Determine the numbers of databases and database names from the physical server by inspecting /etc/oratab.

2. Provision Oracle database VMs from prebuilt templates, which have Oracle binaries preinstalled.

3. Export each Oracle database using shell script, which utilizes the Oracle Data Pump utility.

4. Copy the export dump file to the target server or common file share.

5. Create a database on each deployed Oracle database VM using Oracle SQL scripts.

6. Import each Oracle databases to respective Oracle database VMs using the Data Pump utility.

7. Finalize the migration checking by connecting the application with Oracle database on the VMs.

Lab Architecture

To further illustrate the capabilities of both vSphere as the target for the migration and the ability of vCO to facilitate that migration, Figure 11-5 shows the lab architecture with vCO with an Oracle database virtual environment.

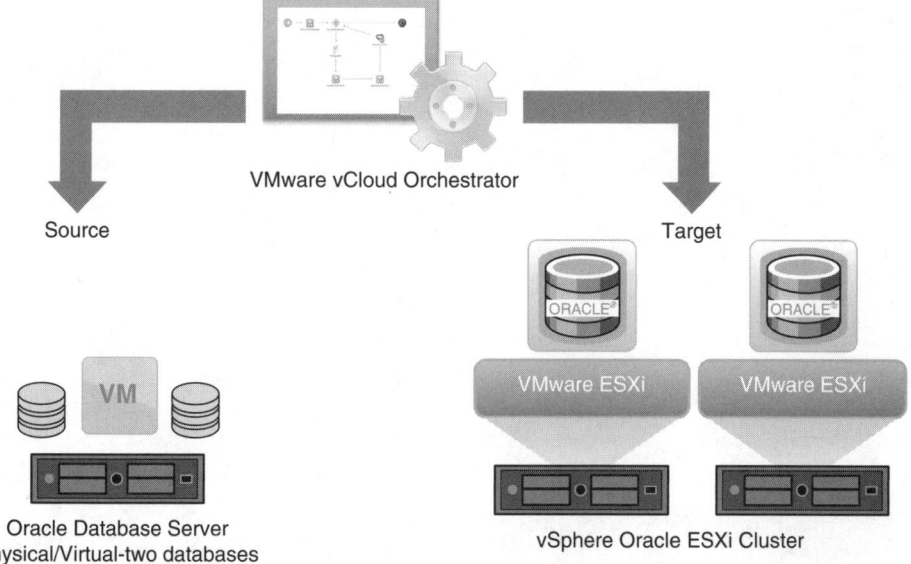

Figure 11-5 Oracle database lab architecture

The architecture includes the following components:

- **Source environment:** The Source environment consists of either a physical or virtual server with two Oracle databases running on a single server; two different applications are connected to its respective databases.

- **Target environment:** The Target environment consists of VMware vSphere environment with ESXi clusters where two Oracle Database VMs with separate Oracle databases migrated from the source.

- **vCenter Orchestrator:** VMware vCO simplifies the automation of complex IT tasks and adapts and extends service delivery and operational management, thereby effectively working with existing infrastructure, tools, and process. This workflow engine manages design and execution of Oracle database migration workflow.

Migrating Oracle Database from Physical to Virtual

The workflow outlined in Figure 11-6 shows a design example for Oracle database migration. It includes steps that you can automate with vCO.

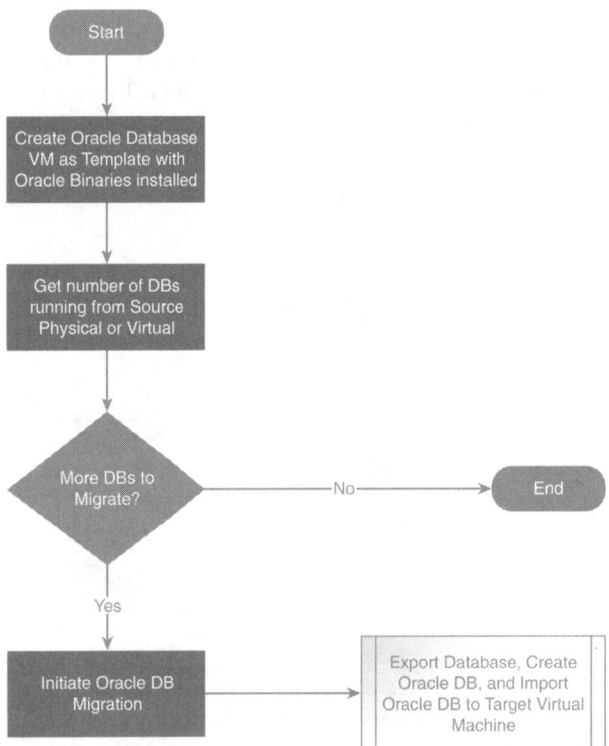

Figure 11-6 Oracle database physical to virtual migration workflow

For the purpose of demonstrating the functionality of vCO and Oracle scripts, the work-flow shown in Figure 11-7 was validated in the lab. The vCO workflow shows the Get Oracle Database process, which runs a shell script to retrieve the number of databases in the source system. Based on the number of databases, the workflow initiates the migration and creates the Oracle DB server as a VM from the pre-created template using the Create Oracle Serve process. Then the workflow initiates the Migrate Oracle Data process to migrate the database from physical to virtual. These are high-level steps; you'll learn more about each process as you progress through this section.

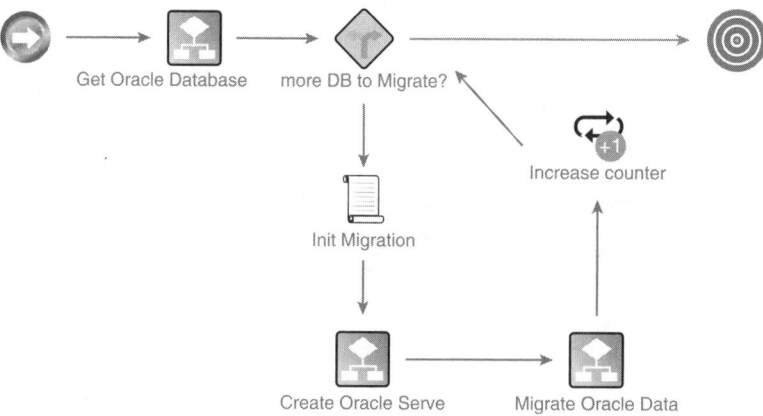

Figure 11-7 Workflow validated in lab using vCO

Retrieving Oracle Database (Workflow): Get Oracle Databases

The Get Oracle Database process retrieves the Oracle database instances listed in /etc/oratab on the source host and sets the databaseNames property to the list of databases. Figure 11-8 shows the details of Get Oracle Database process where the shell script is executed to retrieve the number of databases and its names.

Figure 11-8 Get Oracle Database process workflow

Migrating More Database and Increase Counter Workflows

After you complete the Get Oracle Database process workflow, the workflow in Figure 11-9 will run the migration for each database in the list of database names retrieved in the previous step.

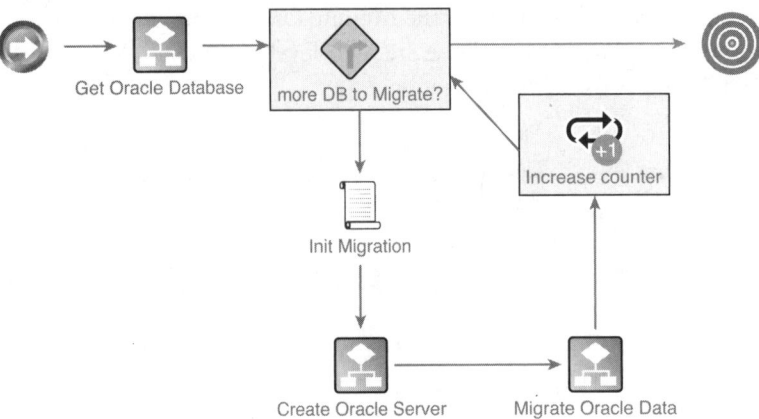

Figure 11-9 More DB Migration process workflow

1. **More DBs to Migrate conditional task:**

   The Scripting section of the task includes code for checking that there exists at least one database on the source system and that the loop has processed all database names:

   ```
   if (databaseNames == null ) {
           System.log("No database found on source host - exiting!");
           return null;
   }
   return (databaseLoopCounter < databaseNames.length ) {
   ```

2. Increase Counter Scriptable task:

   The Scripting section of the task increments the counter:

   ```
   counter = counter + 1;
   ```

3. Init Migration task:

   Prepares properties for use within the loop. The `Scripting` section is as follows:

   ```
   currentDatabaseName = databaseNames[databaseLoopCounter];
   currentTargetIP = ipAddressPool[databaseLoopCounter];
   targetVMName = targetVM_NamePrefix + "-" + currentDatabaseName;
   ```

Creating Oracle Server (Workflow)

The step displayed in Figure 11-10 depicts a clone of a new target VM from a VM template that has Oracle preinstalled. The users will use the appropriate built-in workflow for each individual environment (cloned from the template, guest options, and so on).

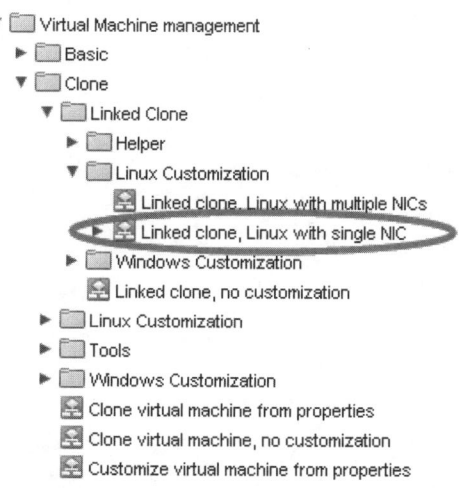

Figure 11-10 Creating an Oracle database VM from a clone

Migrating Oracle Data (Workflow)

The migration workflow diagram shown in Figure 11-11 displays the management of the movement of the data from the source database on the host system to the target system. As it is used in the main workflow, the target system is a newly created VM.

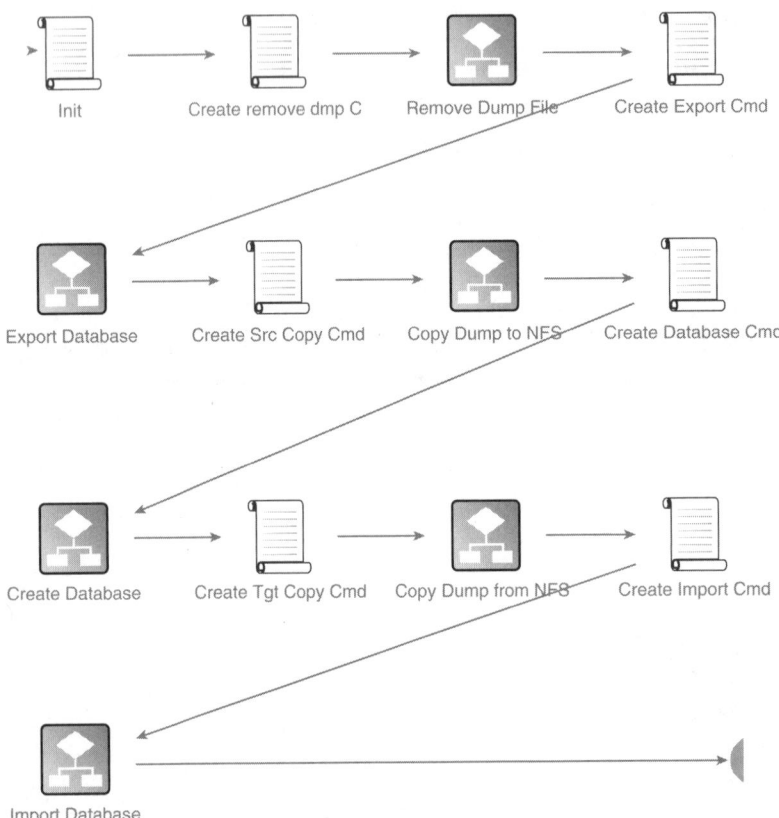

Figure 11-11 Oracle database migration workflow details

The workflow consists of both creating and running the commands on the hosts with Secure Shell (SSH). The following are the commands used within the script executed with SSH:

- Scriptable task elements in the workflow prepare the appropriate command for similarly named SSH execution workflow items. The scripting is embedded within the "Create Src Copy Cmd" element referenced in Figure 11-11. Note the constructed command is stored in the `source_copyDump_cmd` attribute:

```
var retval_cmd = "cp -f "  + dpDump_Path + " " + common_dbDump_Path;
//source_copyDump_cmd = "hostname; echo Would Exec: " + retval_cmd;
source_copyDump_cmd = retval_cmd;
//System.log("source_copyDump_cmd: '" + source_copyDump_cmd + "'");
```

- SSH workflow elements in the workflow show in Figure 11-12 execute the prepared commands. With regard to the Copy Dump to NFS workflow visual binding, notice that the CMD binding is associated with the `source_copyDump_cmd` attribute constructed previously.

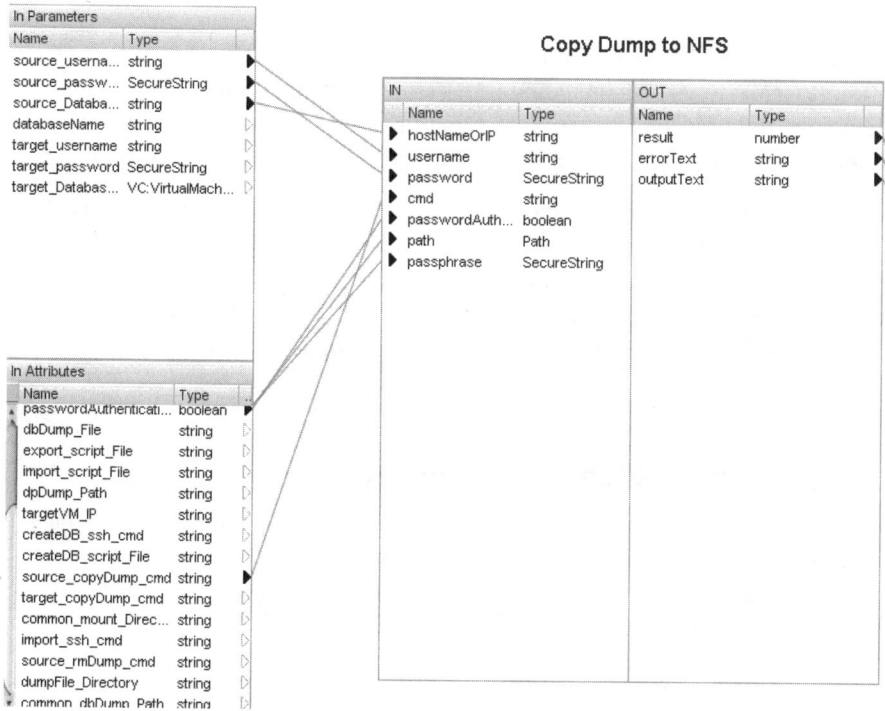

Figure 11-12 Oracle database migration workflow elements

- For this example, the exp_db.sh and imp_db.sh scripts executed are accessible locally on the source and target VMs. A production version would store the scripts as vCO resources per the documentation (http://pubs.vmware.com/vsphere-55/topic/com.vmware.vsphere.vco_dev.doc/GUID-A94A6C16-1439-46AF-BD21-0188DB087907.html).

  - **exp_db.sh:** The primary command used in the exporting a database to a dump file using Oracle Data Pump:

    ```
    $ORACLE_HOME/bin/expdp  \'/ as sysdba\' DUMPFILE=DATA_
    PUMP_DIR:${expfile} LOGFILE=DATA_PUMP_DIR:${logfile} JOB_
    NAME=${dbname}_expdp_full_${datestamp} FILESIZE=30G STATUS=15
    FULL=Y COMPRESSION=ALL ENCRYPTION=ALL ENCRYPTION_MODE=PASSWORD
    ENCRYPTION_PASSWORD="vmware123" ENCRYPTION_ALGORITHM=AES256
    CLUSTER=N 2>&1 > $logfile
    ```

- **imp_db.sh:** The command used in the importing a database from a Data Pump dump file:

```
$ORACLE_HOME/bin/impdp  \'/ as sysdba\' DUMPFILE=DATA_
PUMP_DIR:${expfile} LOGFILE=DATA_PUMP_DIR:${logfile} JOB_
NAME=${dbname}_impdp TABLE_EXISTS_ACTION=REPLACE PARALLEL=1
STATUS=15 ENCRYPTION_PASSWORD="vmware123" 2> /tmp/log.out
```

vCO enables creation of workflows to automate the entire Oracle database migration process from physical/virtual to virtual, including provisioning Oracle database VMs. The workflow example tested here demonstrates the functionality of VMware vCO. A final production solution may include more workflow steps and logic as per business requirement.

Integration between Oracle Data Pump and vCO allows vCO workflows to be triggered by the number of Oracle databases on source, thus enabling automatic migration of databases to individual Oracle database VMs. For each database on the source, a vCO workflow triggers Data Pump to execute export and import of database, which constitutes the migration process. These configuration details, workflows, and Oracle Script examples can be used as a foundation of further automation projects.

Configuring Application Blueprints Using vCAC

Application blueprints shown in Figure 11-13 enable the concept of design once—deploy anywhere. The various components of application blueprints include operating systems, application services and components, component dependencies, property bindings, lifecycle scripts, and networks and storage.

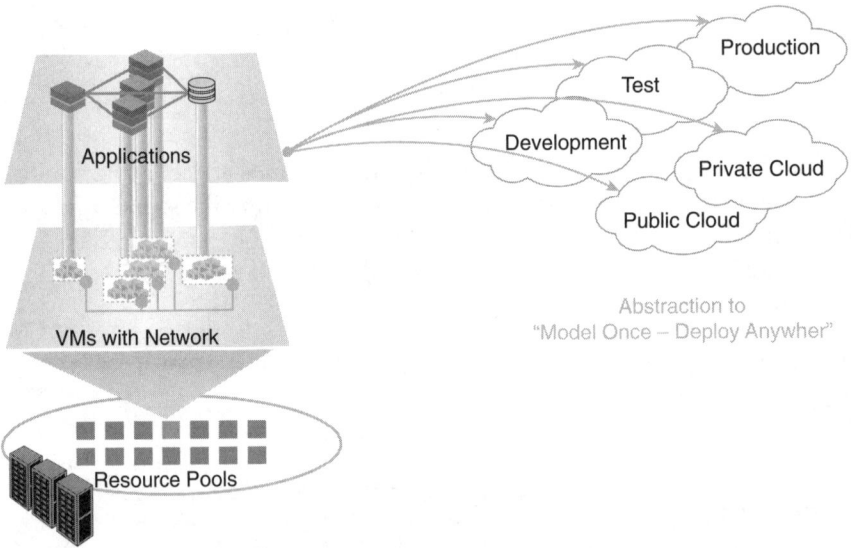

Figure 11-13 Application blueprint

Now, let's delve into an example of how to build an application blueprint using vCAC:

1. **Creating a blueprint:** We will create a multitier application blueprint, as shown in Figure 11-14, with a load_balancer, JBoss appserver, and a MySqL (or any other) database. Note that this blueprint is an abstract model. The components in this blueprint are instantiated using the available components in the Cloud. For example, even if the logical template in the blueprint is CentOS v6.3, it can be instantiated to a CentOS v6.4 VM by the application admin.

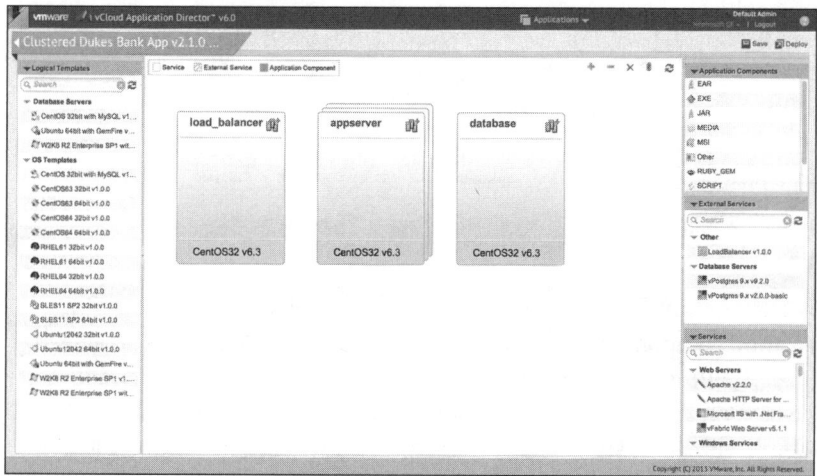

Figure 11-14 Creating an application blueprint

2. **Adding services:** Next, we add the services, as shown in Figure 11-15, from the catalog to each node in the blueprint. First, we add the Apache service to the load_balancer. Drag and drop Apache v2.2 to the load_balancer node and rename it to **Apache_LB**. Similarly, we add a JBoss service to the appserver node and a MySQL service to the database node. Add JBoss on Linux v5.1 to the appserver node. Rename it to **JBossAppServer**. Add MySQL 5.0 to the database node and rename it to **MySql**.

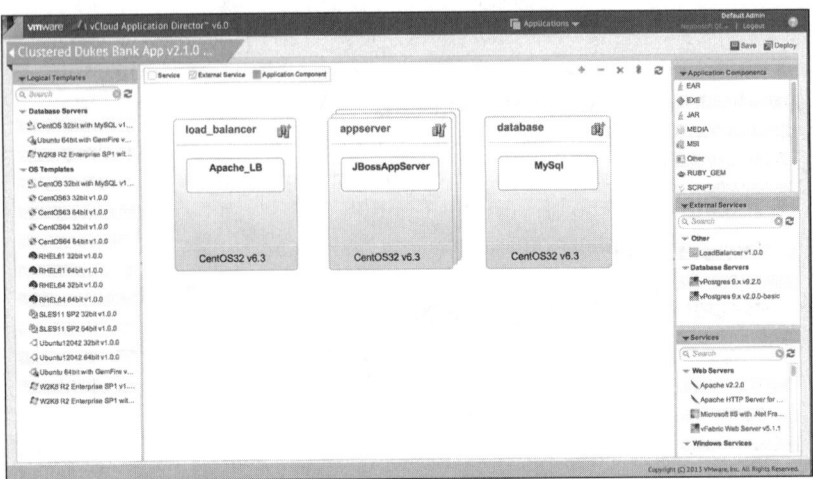

Figure 11-15 Adding application services

3. **Adding application components:** Next, since we have the server nodes set up, we will add application components to the appserver and the database nodes, as shown in Figure 11-16. Application components must be compatible with the relevant service, so the user cannot drop a SQL script on the JBoss service or drop a war file on the MySQL service. We will drop a SQL script to the MySql service. Following the example, we drag and drop SQL script to the MySQL service and rename it to **initialize_db_script**. Next, drag and drop a war file to the JBoss service and rename it to **Dukes_Bank_App**. For scaling deployments, the user may need to deploy multiple VMs or a cluster for a particular node and use a load balancer to manage each. In this blueprint, we transform the application server into a cluster. Click the cluster icon and increase the cluster size to 3.

Figure 11-16 Adding application components

4. **Adding dependencies:** Dependencies are added in the blueprint to define an order
   in which the deployment tasks must be performed. Creating a dependency link from
   one item to another, such as a service or application component, guarantees that the
   task of creating the first item finishes successfully before a second task begins. For
   example, a load balancer usually cannot be configured until the application is up and
   running. Next, we add a dependency, as shown in Figure 11-17, from the Apache
   service to the war file on the JBoss server. Then, we add a dependency from Apache
   service to the Dukes Bank war file. A blue dotted line appears and points to the
   dependent component. Similarly, we will add a dependency from the war file to the
   SQL script in the database node.

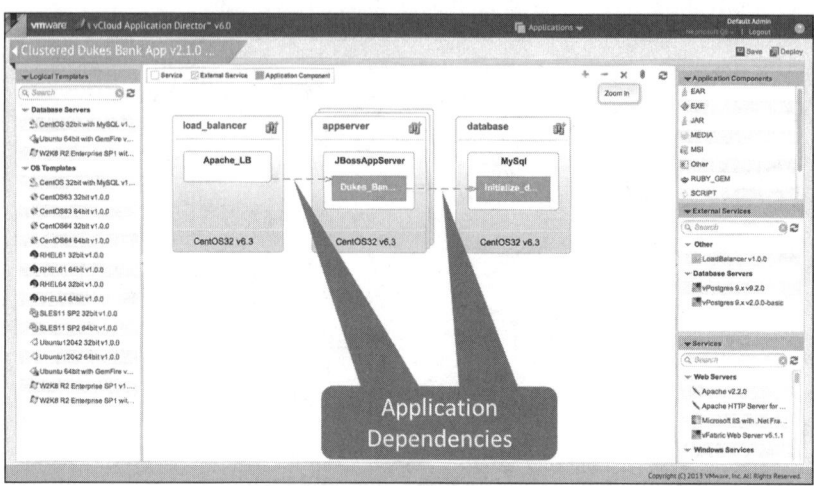

Figure 11-17 Adding application dependencies

5. **Binding properties:** As shown in Figure 11-18, click the Apache_LB service. Show the http_node_port property of the load balancer. Now that we have all the components set up in the blueprint, let's look at some details. Property binding is a very important feature in blueprints. Binding to another property lets you customize a script based on the value of other node's runtime property values. In this example, the http_node_port property is bound to the port number of the JBoss app server. So, if the port number on the JBoss number changes, the property http_node_port in the scripts of the load balancer will receive the latest value. This is set by using the Edit Property dialog box and clicking the edit icon against each property. Properties for each service and component receive the value set during service creation, if any. If the catalog administrator who created the service has not marked a property as not overridden, the property values can be overridden at the time of creating the blueprint. The app architect can mark a property as not overridden if the admin does not want a value to be changed during deployment time. This provides flexibility in setting property values and lets the best person in the chain make the decision on what a good value is for each property.

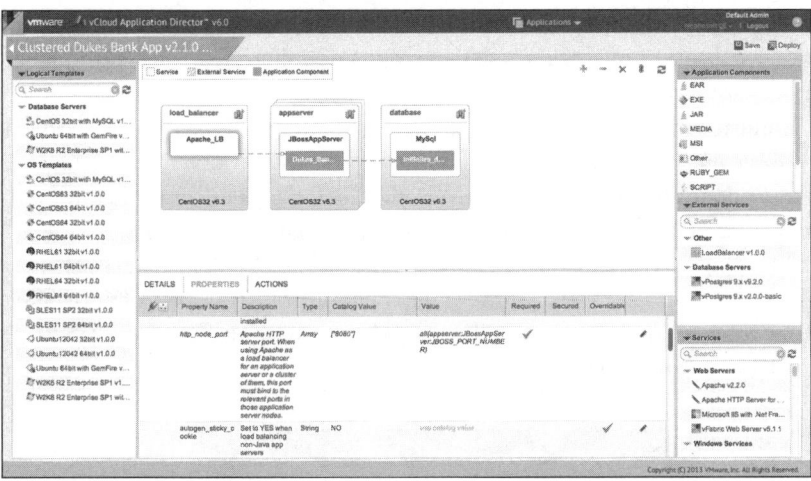

Figure 11-18 Property binding

6. **Working with actions:** Click the SQL script in the MySql node, and then click the Actions tab, as shown in Figure 11-19. Each component in the blueprint has multiple lifecycle stages: install, configure, start, update, rollback, and teardown. The service creator can define scripts for each lifecycle stage. If a script is present, the deployment engine executes it at the appropriate time. The script of dependent components is executed first, and then property values are passed to the scripts of the depending component.

Figure 11-19 Working on actions

7. **Adding multiple NICs:** As shown in Figure 11-20, click the load_balancer VM. In most deployments, a subset of servers is deployed to a demilitarized zone (DMZ), and other servers are deployed to a network protected by a firewall. In the Clustered Dukes Bank application, the load_balancer node is the only node that can be accessed from a public network. The database and application server (appserver) nodes must be deployed in a private network behind a firewall. The load_balancer node must also have access to the database and appserver nodes. To handle this situation, the admin can define two network interface cards (NICs) on the load balancer. Each NIC must specify a logical network name. At deployment time, the logical network is mapped to an actual Cloud network. When a VM is created, the number of NICs for the VM is derived from the node.

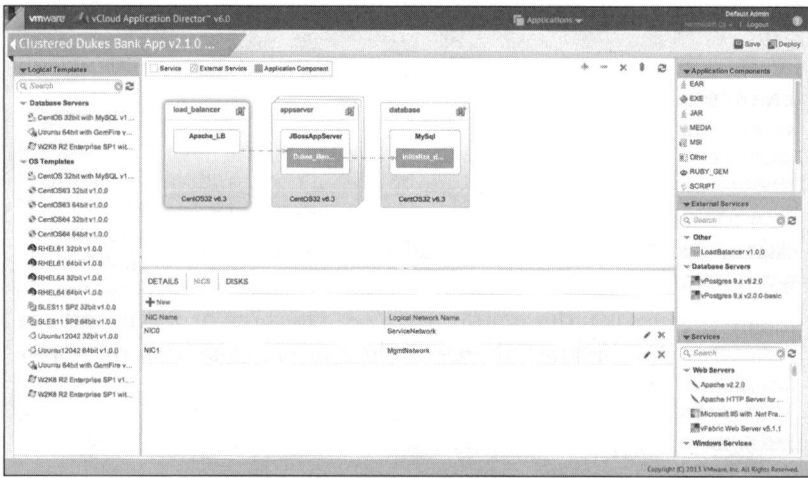

Figure 11-20 Adding multiple NICs

8. **Working with disk profiles:** Click the database node, as shown in Figure 11-21. Then select the Disks tab. Notice in the Disks tab of the database node that this blueprint has multiple disks configured. Flexible disk layout enhances the storage flexibility and lets the admin add additional disks to a node when creating an application blueprint. The disks are created dynamically during provisioning and added to the node. The admin can also manage placing the disks on different datastores. Once the user defines the flexible disk layout for nodes in the blueprint, the application admin can further customize the deployment.

Figure 11-21 Disk profiles

9. **Adding an external service:** Finally, click Dukes Bank v 2.5 and load its blueprint. The admin can add basic or advanced external services to the blueprint, as shown in Figure 11-22. The external service has been installed separately from the application. External services are commonly used because these services are not provisioned as part of the blueprint but the application still needs the external service in order to work.

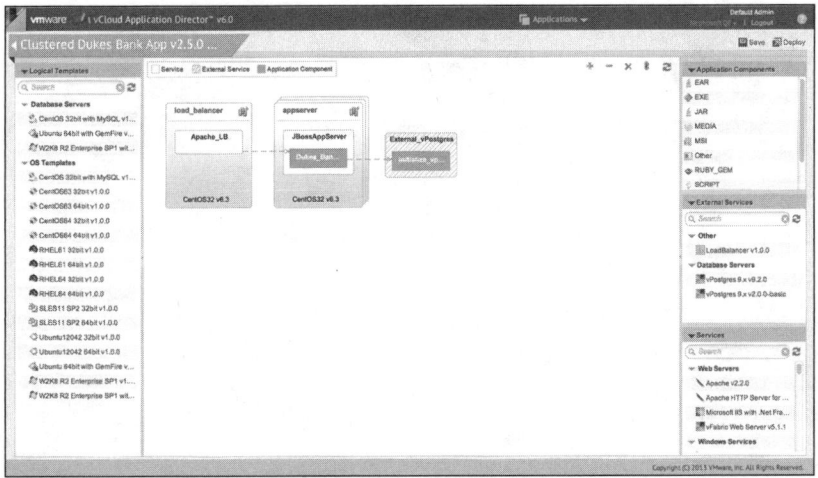

Figure 11-22 Adding external services

Once an application blueprint is built, it can be used to deploy at many environments. You can automate and provision the whole deployment process with the click of a button. As shown in Figure 11-23, an application and its changes are always deployed using dev, test, and production environments. It takes considerable effort to stand up those environments, and often each application has ten or more environments. Using application service models, consistent applications (that is, applications with standardized configurations) can now be deployed over and over again across Clouds. It is possible to deploy a dev environment into the public Cloud in Amazon and a production environment into a vSphere-based private Cloud. Of course, it is possible to adapt configurations at deployment time to meet specific environment-specific requirements. Applications see constant change. We can also promote a consistent set of changes across applications from dev to test to production. This allows us to not only stand up consistent environments but also to keep those consistent to a large extent during their lifetime. Those capabilities combined allow automation of the application release process and acceleration of application system development lifecycle.

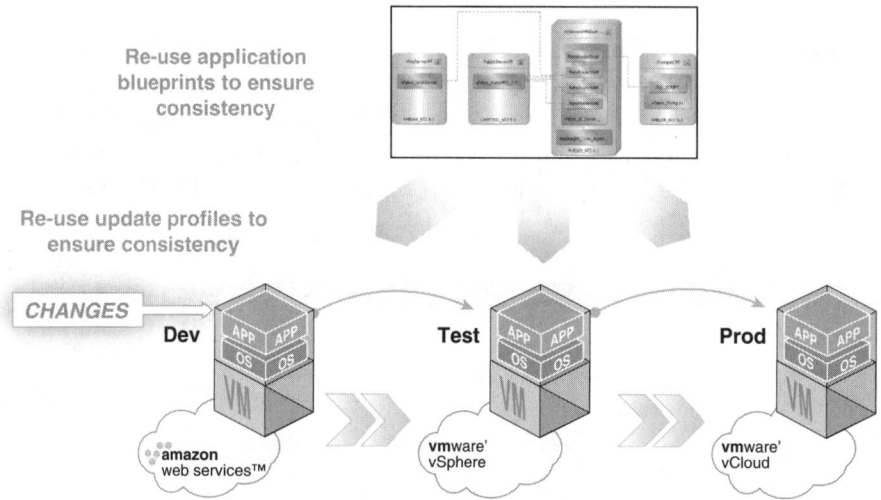

Figure 11-23 Rapid provisioning using blueprints

Building a Database-as-a-Service Platform

There are many different definitions of database-as-a-service (DBaaS). Some definitions concentrate solely on the provisioning of the database itself. The Oracle 12c capability of the Container and Pluggable database fits this paradigm. It is just as valid to define DBaaS as database-server-as-a-service, which is what we do in this section.

To begin with, we should at least offer a definition for DBaaS: The ability to manage, monitor, and provision database resources on demand through self-service catalogs with minimum requirement for installation and configuration of hardware or software upfront with minimal dependency on the physical infrastructure.

As shown in Figure 11-24, the idea is to enable database consumers such as application developers, testers, and architects and owners to provision databases easily and quickly using an on-demand, self-service platform.

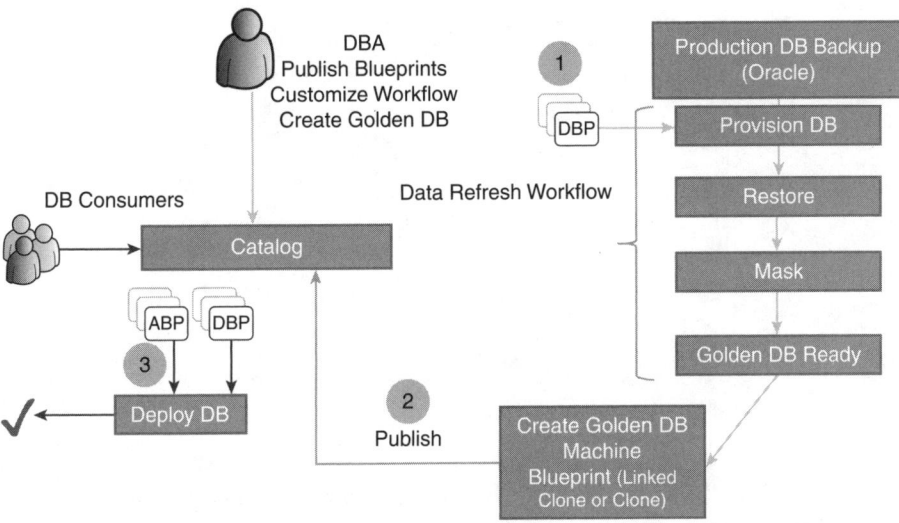

Figure 11-24 Building and publishing application and DB blueprints

Listing the Benefits of DBaaS

Although some of the benefits of self-service and automated provisioning are obvious, the utility of quantifying them is equally obvious:

- Reduce application time to market.

- DBaaS, as shown in Figure 11-25, enables the admin to rapidly develop, test, and deploy new applications at a fraction of the time that it previously took with legacy systems. New applications can be delivered to market much faster and gain an edge over competitors (and can also service customers more effectively).

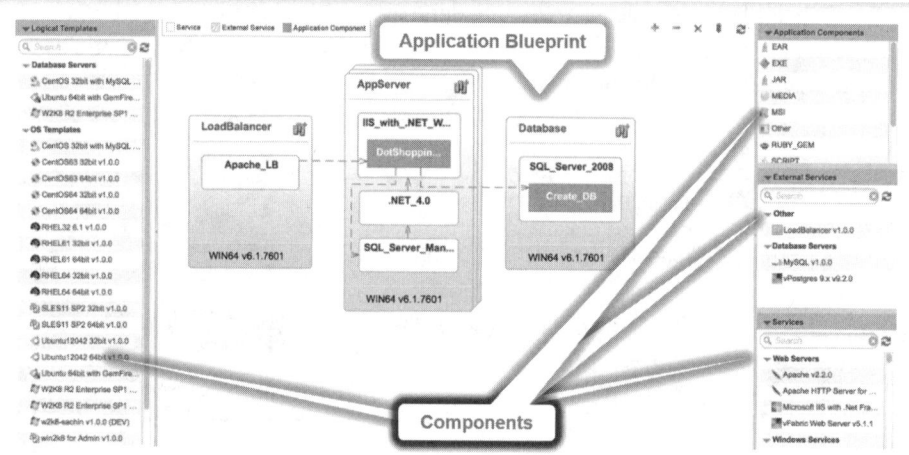

Figure 11-25 Accelerating database deployment

- Automate all database lifecycle management.

- Database sprawl can be addressed directly with consolidation and retirement. Many IT departments have difficulties keeping track of all the DB instances that are deployed. This has implications from a licensing, data governance, and security standpoint.

- A DBaaS approach will ensure that complete visibility exists to all database environments and that governance through policy-based management is enforced.

- Developers and DBAs will no longer need to go to public Cloud providers for their database/application infrastructure needs.

- Increase operational efficiency and resource utilization.

- DBaaS increases the efficiency of both database/application and infrastructure teams. The storage admin no longer has to spend time and effort on provisioning storage resources for databases. DBAs no longer have to wait for database resources to be allocated and provisioned. This frees up time for both teams to focus on more-strategic, higher-value activities (and reduces friction between the teams).

Allocating Storage as Part of the DBaaS Paradigm

Storage performance is often the limiting factor that holds back DBaaS projects. Traditional disk-based storage often cannot meet the performance needs for DBaaS and is inherently too complicated to manage. DBaaS requires the following:

- Highly performant storage infrastructure to ensure rapid provisioning of databases
- Efficient data reduction to ensure storage resources are not overwhelmed and exhausted
- A high degree of resiliency to ensure minimal to no downtime
- Ease of use/management

Many high-performing arrays can meet the low-intensity provisioning demands, but modern flash arrays such as those from Pure Storage and EMC prove especially effective when performing mass provisioning. Recent reference architectures produced as collaborative efforts between VMware and Pure Storage and VMware and EMC show that the flash arrays are especially suitable for the mass provisioning storms that frequent the DBaaS environments.

Flash arrays meet all of these requirements and allow administrators of all disciplines to deploy a DBaaS environment in the most cost-effective manner and avoid more-expensive, complex systems.

Choosing the Components of a DBaaS Architecture

You can optimize DBaaS with flash arrays in a number of ways, including the following:

Option 1

- **VMware vSphere/vCenter:** Virtualization platform.
- **VMware Cloud Automation Center:** Front-end self-service catalog and provisioning tool.

- **All flash array (Pure Storage, EMC ExtremeIO, Tintri, Violin, and so on):** Highly performant, resilient storage array.

- **Any x86-based server platform:** Server CPU and memory will vary based on the size of the environment.

Option 2

- **Oracle Enterprise Manager (OEM) 12C:** Management and self-service tool.

- **VMware vSphere/vCenter:** Virtualization platform.

- **Blue Medora plug-in:** Interface between OEM and vSphere.

- **All flash array (Pure, ExtremeIO, Tintri, Violin, and so on):** Highly performant, resilient storage array.

- **Any x86-based server platform:** Server CPU and memory will vary based on the size of the environment.

Summary

For years, DBAs have been provisioning databases in a number of manners, all of which are still in use today and all of which are just as effective as they were long in the past. However, when a DBA needs to provision dozens or hundreds of systems each day, this challenges the feasibility of the old methods. The modern approach to provisioning is innately linked with automation. The tools that both Oracle and VMware provide to both automate and provision allow the DBA or the vDBA to spend time on the more interesting facets of technology as opposed to the mundane acts of providing for the ever increasing number of user requests for more database resources. Essentially, those requests involve no more than an ever-increasing repetition of creating copies of old databases, which is why these sophisticated automation processes are so effective.

The ideas discussed in this chapter to include database-as-a-service are simply natural extensions of the use of modern technologies to automate the delivery process of IT services on an exponentially greater scale than was conceived of a few years ago. Combining that demand with the notion that it may be acceptable for the users, properly managed and accounted for, to provision those resources themselves has led to the idea of DBaaS and in a greater sense Clouds of all kinds.

The tools provided by VMware and described in this chapter such as vCloud Automation Center (vCAC)—which has been renamed vRealize Automation and part of the vRealize Suite—and vCenter Orchestrator (vCO) constitute the essential tool kit for the modern database architect who is interested in building out a modern self-service virtualized infrastructure. Refer to the VMware website for more details on the vRealize Suite.

http://www.vmware.com/products/vrealize-suite

It has been said that twenty-first century IT must move "at the speed of business," and it has also been noticed that most committed VMware customers view virtualized infrastructure as a true black box. Obviously, virtualized infrastructure is much more than a black box. The capabilities of vSphere immeasurably enhance the value of the physical infrastructure and the peripheral tools of the vCloud Suite allow the vDBA and the VM admin to create an environment that is secure, simple, and most importantly, effective. Although the boundaries of the virtualized infrastructure can seem unnecessarily impervious, those boundaries are simply the line that delineates the modern from the classic.

VMware software has been referred to as "magic pixie dust that is changing the world" by one rather prominent VMware executive a few years ago. Unfortunately, however, we all know that despite the rather convincing magical appearance of VMware software, the laws of physics still apply. We also know that the application of the features and capabilities that have been discussed in this chapter can be truly magical nonetheless.

Chapter 12

Case Studies

In this chapter, we approach the crescendo of the discussion of the previous 11 chapters and focus on the reality of the deployments and the implementations of Oracle software on vSphere. The software-defined datacenter is incomplete without each and every software application, especially the more common enterprise applications, being included within the virtualized infrastructure. The theme of the four V's comes to life only when the actual implementation is effective in a production environment. Hopefully by now, you understand the overall viability, accept the value, acknowledge the versatility, and embrace the vision of running high-workload or business-critical applications (BCAs) on vSphere. Appropriately, Figure 12-1 depicts and highlights each of the four V's. This chapter describes the customers who best commemorate the attributes described in this book. We truly hope that all of you who have read though the 11 chapters so far will aspire to emulate what they have accomplished.

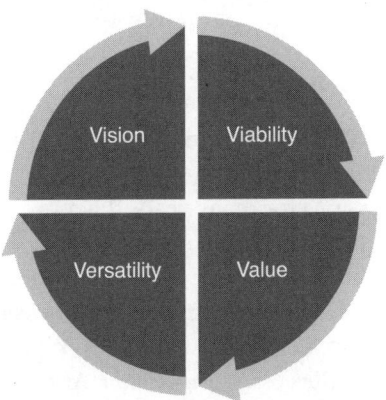

Figure 12-1 Four V's approach

It is imperative that future customers understand the success of past customers. More precisely, potential customers want to understand the lessons learned as well as the realities of those who blazed the trail toward comprehensive virtualization. In interest of that effort, this chapter describes a series of customers that have become publically referencable over the previous few years. In this chapter, you learn how they arrived at their decision to virtualize and how they actually completed their individual virtualization projects.

We recognize that the breath of solutions available to customers is inestimable and ever changing, so we make no claims as to having a cornerstone over all possible architectural solutions. In fact, certain popular products and well-known solutions in the market work extremely well under the right circumstances. We fully recognize that when those sets of conditions present themselves that solutions other than those presented in this book or those that have been adopted and described in these case studies may be supplanted. It is not our intention to make a claim of permanence of any particular architecture. It is equally not our intention to persuade the reader that the only solutions that will suffice to meet the challenges that we describe here are the solutions that were adopted at the time of the publication of the individual case studies. More important, our desire is to highlight the challenges that were overcome at the time of the implementation and proudly described in each case study.

These are publically available case studies, but we will further endeavor to succinctly describe the architectures and the usage models in this chapter. These trailblazing application owners, database administrators (DBAs), system admins, and virtualization champions have been publically acknowledged in a plethora of forums, including webinars, mini and mega conferences, white papers, and case studies. Others have completed the journey, but this group constitutes some of the most prominent individuals and entities that recognized and acted upon the incredibly compelling proposition of running Oracle on vSphere. There is no particular order to the grouping, but each of the stories provides a unique and valuable story that individually proves the wisdom of their decision.

Indiana University

The development of the case study with Indiana University (IU) goes back to before 2010. However, IU and their virtualization champion Dan Young have been participating in a wide variety of conferences and conventions delivering sessions for many years. They are also an omnipresent reference for many customers, particularly in the education space. Also, they have been staples on a variety of panel discussions well before 2010, and remain regular panelists up to the time of the writing of this book. Dan was a member of the select panel of Oracle customer success stories at VMworld 2014 in San Francisco. The specific panel is titled Applications on Oracle on vSphere Customer Success Stories Panel. At the same event, Dan also accepted the 2014 VMware Innovation Award on behalf of Indiana University.

Indiana University is a system of higher-education institutions with 8 campuses, nearly 20,000 employees, and more than 100,000 students scattered around Indiana. University Information Technology Services (UITS) manages all IT services for IU, and they are committed to a virtualization-first policy. The challenge was to migrate their Oracle based systems from expensive AIX pSeries servers to an x86-based system running vSphere, and with the help of VMware professional services and House of Brick (HOB), the objectives were quickly realized.

The driving consideration for this impressive migration project was increased flexibility. As described in the previous chapters of this book, a main pillar of the value of vSphere is the resource management capabilities, an aspect of which is the versatility of the virtualized infrastructure. IU wanted the ability to transition servers between physical hosts, reassign resources as needed, perform zero-downtime hardware maintenance, and execute comprehensive capacity planning at the datacenter level. All this was achieved on an amazing scale.

IU virtualized more than 1,000 servers, many of which ran Oracle software, including *PeopleSoft* and IU's largest transaction database supporting the *OnCourse* higher-education application with over 12,000 concurrent users. An application such as OnCourse has certain innate and major challenges, which include the variant workload. When students register for their year's classes in September and January, the short term but real load on the system can be an order of magnitude greater than the common experience. However, after the initial load testing and data-capture phase, the virtualized infrastructure was configured to handle these variations in load. After a short period of time, any uncertainty concerning the suitability of vSphere as the right infrastructure choice evaporated.

Dan, Indiana University's Manager of Database Administration, is a great champion of virtualization and often addresses technical audiences at conferences, such as VMworld, IOUG Collaborate, and others. At VMworld 2014 US in San Francisco, Dan accepted the VMware innovation award on behalf of Indiana University. Dan was also a panelist on the Oracle Applications on vSphere customer success stories panel. A favorite topic of his involves his pursuit toward the nirvana of the "Happy DBA," and through numerous public presentations on this subject, he has proved his prowess in the arena of educating and mentoring DBAs toward the bright lights of virtualization. Dan's immensely entertaining sessions highlight his own experiences in coaching and cajoling the always skeptical Oracle DBA to understand the value of vSphere to IU-IT, as well as the value of the vSphere experience, to each DBA's career. The official case study link is included in the here.

http://www.vmware.com/files/pdf/customers/
VMW_10Q1_CS_INDIANA_UNI_USLET_EN.pdf

American Tire Distributors

The quote at the start of the American Tire Distributors (ATD) case study from Tony Vaden, CIO of ATD, describes this success story as well as anyone could hope to do so:

> *VMware technology helps us, as a business, support business growth. It has helped us evolve our IT infrastructure so that we can provide more dynamic computing. It has also enabled us to truly "think outside the box" and find ways to deliver computing resources that drive the most value to our company's bottom line.*

HOB helped this early adaptor—which at the time in 2011 of the implementation of the solution was growing up to 20% annually—virtualize their infrastructure for Oracle Real Application Clusters (RAC). ATD also sought to achieve the levels of multidimensional scalability that are so critical in today's Internet-based retail markets. Therefore, scalability in every dimension was a focus of the comprehensive implementation plan. The goals were both vertical scalability by dynamic addition of processing power on a server level and horizontal scalability by addition of virtual machines (VMs) and hosts as increasing demand requires.

The answer was a solution which included vSphere for the Oracle RAC databases as well as the virtualization of the environment for the E-Business Suite (EBS) application. This implementation is the epitome of the versatility that has been referenced throughout this book. If you take the time to read through the entire case study, a point that stands out is that of the golden copies of application servers that can be then deployed within 30 minutes. It is also notable to point out the massive increase in server utilization reported in the actual case study. These are standalone achievements and individually warrant highlighting because they are effectively early elements of cloud computing. These capabilities are essential for an e-Commerce site that services over 80,000 customers daily in 37 states.

ATD, with the help of HOB, migrated between PA-RISC to HP ProLiant servers running the Red Hat operating system and successfully used the Oracle Real Application Testing suite as well as Swingbench to test and verify the performance capabilities and overall effectiveness of the virtualized infrastructure and the new system. The links to both the case study and the video interview are listed here.

Case Study—
http://www.emc.com/collateral/customer-profiles/h9654-amer-tire-dis-cp.pdf

Video—
http://www.emc.com/collateral/demos/microsites/mediaplayer-video/
american-tire-distributors.htm

EMC Information Technology

The Chief Architect of EMC IT, Darryl Smith, helped deliver the VMworld 2013 Oracle on vSphere Best Practices webinar. He did this on the great authority of the success of EMC IT in this space. EMC IT has been at the forefront of virtualization for all their BCAs for many years. The common perception when VMware field staff offer EMC IT as a reference to potential BCA-interested customers is that EMC as a substantial stockholder of VMWare stock would, of course, endorse vSphere. However, this perception is highly skewed because EMC IT has moved through successful virtualization efforts, which included both Oracle EBS and SAP software.

Darryl has played an enormous part in influencing the evolution of VMware publically distributed best practices, specifically in the Oracle space. For example, EMC IT successfully overcommits CPU resources by effectively utilizing hyperthreading and adhering to a policy that dictates each individual logical Oracle server remain under the 50% utilization threshold.

The case study describes the journey of EMC IT and how they successfully migrated their Oracle 11i CRM E-Business Suite database servers from a Sun E25K/Solaris infrastructure to Cisco's Unified Computing System (UCS) platform, as shown in Figure 12-2. More importantly, the paper highlights the methodology developed by EMC IT while migrating the Oracle relational database management system (RDBMS) and respective databases from RISC/SPARC to the target UCS (Intel and Linux) platform. The process created a starting point for EMC to transition from a legacy platform to a versatile platform of virtualized hardware that is innately open and enables the acceleration of many of their infrastructure objectives.

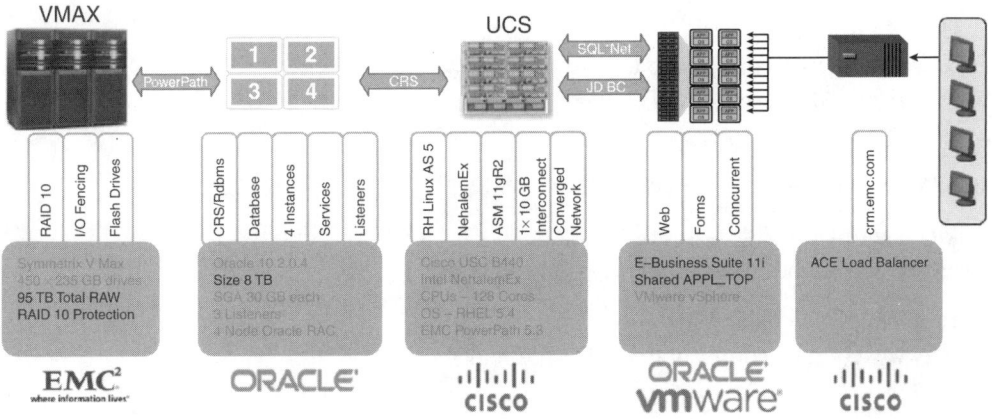

Figure 12-2 EMC IT high-level platform deployment

The aspirations were lofty:

- The ability to build to an open and scalable computing platform UCS (x86). This gives EMC IT a platform to commence its Journey to the Private Cloud.

- A working, documented EMC IT procedure to migrate EMC's 8 TB Oracle CRM E-Business Suite production database to an open platform (from Solaris/SPARC to Cisco's UCS/Linux/x86).

- CAPEX/OPEX savings of $5 million to $7 million in the following areas:

  - Datacenter environmental costs such as power, cooling, and floor space

  - Software licenses

  - Software and hardware maintenance

  - Support for the environment

Since the publication of the initial case study in 2011, EMC IT has moved in many directions to include the implementation of SAP as well as the inclusion of a futuristic software-as-a-service (SaaS) and database-as-a-service (DBaaS) set of service offerings internally. Darryl and EMC IT are leading the way in this space, showing unambiguously that the future is now. A sampling of the many papers, webcasts, and videos, including the Wikibon interview of Darryl Smith are easily found on both EMC and VMware's websites, but the links are included here as well.

Case Study—
http://www.vmware.com/files/pdf/customers/VMware-EMC-14Q1-En-CaseStudy.pdf?src=WWW_customers_VMware-EMC-14Q1-En-CaseStudy.pdf

Case Study Brief—
http://www.vmware.com/files/pdf/partners/intel/VMW-01996-AL-CaseStudy-Template-EMC.pdf

EMC Virtualizing Oracle Video—
http://www.youtube.com/watch?v=OPrlC9YgDyM

Wikibon Interview Video—
http://www.youtube.com/watch?v=ZrQxYIiQW5o

VMware/EMC Webinar Video—
http://www.youtube.com/watch?v=MXkIj3GbgkY

Green Mountain Power

In the hills of the state of Vermont lives a very forward-thinking power company, Green Mountain Power (GMP). In 2012, GMP decided to virtualize their most important infrastructure running their critical Oracle databases. The case study is particularly compelling because their decision paid immediate dividends in dramatic fashion. To learn exactly how Paula Fortin and Nayab Saiyad from GMP completed the implementation, refe rto the links included at the end of this section.

Serving more than 100,000 customers, GMP has a commitment to energy efficiency and customer service. GMP is dedicated to the inclusion of wind and solar energy as intrinsic aspects of its future energy-generation plans. And within the same mindset, the projects involving the notion of the "smart grid" as well as virtualization in aggregate, reveal a true commitment to modern technology.

You can see the details in the referenced case study linked below written by Bob Goldsand from VMware along with Steve Schuettinger from NetApp. Ultimately, with the help of VMware and NetApp, GMP successfully virtualized their Oracle infrastructure, which proved to be of tremendous value in August 2011 when Hurricane Irene slammed up the East Coast, cutting off power to 50,000 GMP customers. Prior to Irene moving into New England, GMP proactively used vMotion to maneuver the VMs running their most critical systems to ensure that those systems had adequate resources for the pending disaster. After the hurricane had dissipated, GMP continued to use vMotion to carefully negotiate the degradation in their physical systems and avoid information service outages. GMP customers were able to obtain critical information quickly. System repair details were readily available because GMP had the foresight to recognize the innate value and versatility of VMware vSphere. The videos which highlight various aspects of this implementation in the form of interviews with GMP and VMW personnel are listed here.

VMworld 2012—
http://www.youtube.com/watch?v=RB0dSxfSAWk

General interview—
http://www.youtube.com/watch?feature=player_embedded&v=ach6Qgc4aPs

Disaster recovery (DR)—
http://www.youtube.com/watch?v=xf9tuHEAyLg

Direct Network File System (dNFS)—
http://www.youtube.com/watch?v=TZWnu1nEZq4

Technical White Paper—
http://www.vmware.com/files/pdf/techpaper/Running-BCAs-Oracle-RAC-VMware-NetApp-Lessons-from-Green-Mountain-Power.pdf

The Idaho Supreme Court

In 2011, the Yucca Group, a small consulting company headquartered in Albuquerque, New Mexico, helped the Idaho Supreme Court (ISC) develop a platform of virtualized hardware for most of the major operations of the court, as shown in Figure 12-3. The value of VMware virtualization, particularly in their Oracle database and application space, had become obvious. The ISC is responsible for comprehensive court operations management throughout Idaho, which includes everything between the adjudication of traffic violations to criminal appeals. Forty-four separate locations stretch between Canada and Utah. The ISC systems provide general public access to statewide court information and services to include victim notification as well as parole and probation information. Legislation requires that certain information be available and updated in real time when possible. The ISC has an effort to streamline operations, reduce personnel requirements, and reduce downtime for application deployments and upgrades.

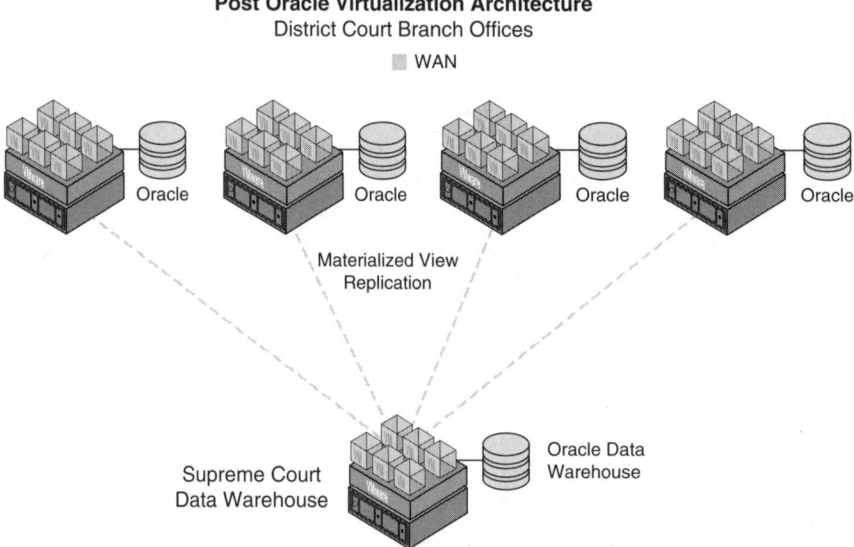

Figure 12-3 ISC Oracle virtualized architecture

The challenges facing the ISC were no different from most businesses in that they had limited personnel and resources. Scott Haverfield, the chief architect and champion of the virtualization project, realized that to meet the requirements of the ISC he would have to develop an efficient and flexible system that could effectively utilize all the resources he had available. From the case study, the following requirements were agreed upon:

1. Create an "all-purpose" (scalable) Oracle virtual appliance.

2. Design the virtual appliance to be completely scalable while maximizing performance and availability at the database and operating system (OS) level.

3. Use vSphere 5.x to optimize scalability and performance at the hypervisor level.

4. Rapidly deploy to multiple sites

    a. Distribute Oracle virtual appliance on a hard drive

    b. Requires minimal personnel resources

Other interesting requirements revolved around the single central data warehouse (DWH), which was in use for state agency reporting, public access, and victim notification. Prior to the virtualization effort, it was running on a dedicated physical server. Also, daily materialized view replication from branch offices was being used to update the DWH.

The intention was for the "virtualization of Oracle" effort to consolidate branch office servers, of which they initially had 85. The goal was to reduce the number to 48. To accomplish this massive effort, they allocated a staff of two. However, one of the two was Scott Haverfield, and Scott had Marlin McNeil and the Yucca Group to guide and aid him.

In 2013, Scott sat on the Oracle on vSphere Customer Success Stories panel at VMworld San Francisco and described the details of the deployment and the struggles that the ISC IT staff confronted during the migration effort and the subsequent management of the system.

In summary, the branch offices migrated to Dell PowerEdge T710 servers running ESXi 5.1 with four vCPU VMs. The main DWH has been virtualized on a single dedicated server with eight vCPUs optimized for licensing reasons. Interestingly, the team noticed that the DWH processing used only about 20% to 30% of the host's power and so decided to further consolidate. Ultimately, they were able to run 20 other VMs on that same physical host, achieving an 8:1 consolidation ratio. Despite the consolidation, the reports that were being generated by the DWH were being completed in amazingly fast time. In some cases, the reports that were taking up to 3 hours to generate were completing in less than 10 minutes. Consult the full white paper for the details of this triumphant accomplishment. The link is included here and you can find the white paper on both vmware.com as well as yuccagroup.com.

http://whitepapers.yuccagroup.com/published-whitepapers-2/
oracle-database-virtualization-with-vmware-vsphere-at-the-idaho-supreme-court-2/

The University of British Columbia

The University of British Columbia (UBC) is the second of the universities in this list of luminescent success stories. Clearly, there is a pattern here, and all institutions of higher learning should take note. Of all the well-defined verticals, institutions of higher education are at the top of the list in terms of being early adapters and industry trend setters. This is in no small measure due to the trailblazers that are highlighted in this list.

UBC has nearly 60,000 students from Canada as well as 140 other countries. The main campuses are in beautiful Vancouver and Okanagan. The case study describes the history of an earnest decade's old IT decentralization effort that grew into insurmountable disparate sprawl and the more recent effort to tame the sprawl and bring critical services back under the control of central IT. Virtualized infrastructure was at the heart of this successful effort. Initially, they elected to tackle only the problem of moving their applications servers, but with the help of HOB technologies, they eventually included their Oracle database servers in the all-encompassing virtualized infrastructure.

Using HP ProLiant servers and NetApp storage, UBC has been able to move applications, such as Microsoft Exchange as well as PeopleSoft, into their virtualized environment. Read the actual white paper to get the technical details. However, one specific quote deserves extra attention because it is truly one the most insightful quotes that we have seen. From Michael Thorson, Director of Infrastructure of the University of British Columbia and an excerpt from the white paper:

> When I talk to people about VMware virtualization, I tell them "don't believe everything you think." We're proving here at UBC that VMware is very viable. It works in production environments; it works for Oracle database servers, and everywhere in-between. VMware technology lets you architect a very reliable, very dynamic solution to your computing needs.

The beauty of this quote shines though the subtle but unmistakable challenge to all IT professionals to challenge the status quo and the premises on which you base your knowledge.

It is also worth pointing out that Michael believes (as do the authors of this book) in the first of the four V's, the *viability* of Oracle on vSphere. After all, less than a decade ago the viability of virtualized infrastructure was ridiculed as if it were science fiction. The very idea of trusting your production database on anything other than the most powerful big iron systems was a notion fraught with the danger of a career-limiting faux pas that was as unrecoverable as the databases that you might never manage again. That real uncertainty combined with the resistance of the RDBMS vendors had created a ubiquitous atmosphere of lifeless malaise, resulting in IT professional's inexhaustible paralysis. But the glowing effervescent message from Thorson, like a sermon from a great orator, charges his co-workers with dismissing their preconceived notions regarding infrastructure and to embrace the platform of the twenty-first century.

In 2013, Brent Dunington, Systems Architect of UBC IT, was an invited panelist on the Oracle Customer Success Stories panel at VMworld San Francisco and eloquently verbalized many aspects of the successes of UBC in this space, and we expect to see much more from him in the near future. The link to the full UBC case study is listed here.

http://www.vmware.com/files/pdf/customers/
11Q1_University_of_British_Columbia_Case_Study.pdf

VMware Information Technologies

VMware on VMware is a catchy phrase—so much so that we named the VMware IT case study exactly that. It is true that VMware is a top customer of VMware as well and that VMware has used VMware IT as both an internal and external reference. If you are tired of the clever word play, you had better tighten your seat belt because the double entendres have just begun.

Late in 2010, Oracle Corporation extended Metalink note 249212.1 (the Oracle on vSphere support statement) to Oracle RAC 11.2.0.2. About a month subsequent to that momentous event, VMware engineers, including Bob Goldsand along with Global Support Services and its manager Mike Matthies, completed the development of the recommended methodology for running RAC on vSphere. Shortly after that, Kannan Mani (author of this book) produced the first version of the *RAC Deployment Guide*. We described the details of the SCSI multi-writer-flag in previous chapters, so we do not delve into it now; suffice to say that from that point on, we had opened a new door to Oracle on vSphere deployments. This was a door that VMware itself had to boldly walk through with confidence and respective eagerness.

By 2012, VMware IT had completed its first production-level RAC on vSphere implementation. Rick Lindberg, VMW IT Lead Operations Architect, spoke at VMworld 2012 in both San Francisco and Barcelona as part of a collaborative effort to deliver the landmark RAC on vSphere session. Rick spoke about how VMW IT initially virtualized their Web-Logic servers and later included their E-Business Suite software virtualized environment on their HP ProLiant 620c blades. Figure 12-4 depicts that deployment.

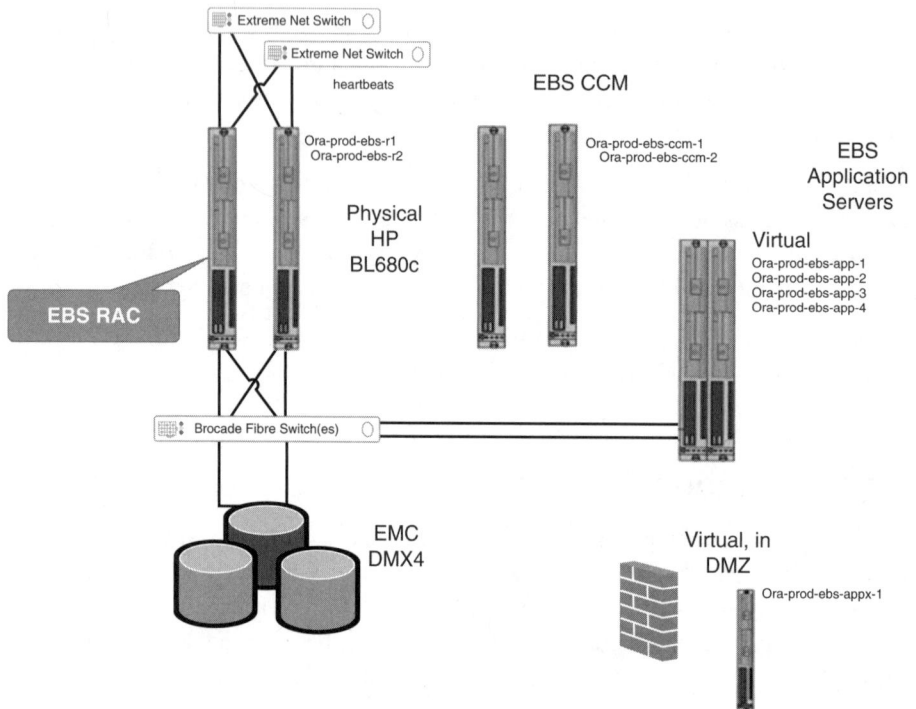

Figure 12-4 VMware's Oracle EBS environment logical overview

However, the case study we are referencing here describes a later set of implementations. Finally, we can proudly state that VMware IT has migrated all of its mission and business-critical RAC databases to vSphere. In support of this endeavor, having been clearly defined both publically and internally by VMware Global Support Services back in late 2010, VMware IT boldly transitioned to comprehensive virtualization with the same confidence and commitment as so many other customers. With aid from VMware Engineering, VMware Professional Services (PSO), and Global Support Services (GSS), 100% of the VMW IT RAC database clusters are now virtualized. The migration passed all QA functional, performance, endurance, and resiliency test criteria. All performance criteria defined by the baselines established in the nonvirtualized environment were satisfied.

According to the case study, the following aspirational goals were achieved.

The scope was to migrate each physical RAC clusters to virtual RAC clusters. The following RAC clusters were migrated to virtual RAC:

- **12TB EBS:** Five-node RAC database cluster

- **1TB service-oriented architecture (SOA):** Three-node RAC database cluster

- **500G Identity Management (IdM):** Three-node RAC database cluster

All this was accomplished using HP ProLiant blades and Oracle Enterprise Linux (OEL) 6.2. Figures 12-5 and 12-6, which also appear in the public case study, depict the actual implementations. The full story of this triumphant implementation was on display at VMworld 2014 in San Francisco and VMworld 2014 Europe in Barcelona. The full case study will be published in late 2014 and it will be available on VMware's website.

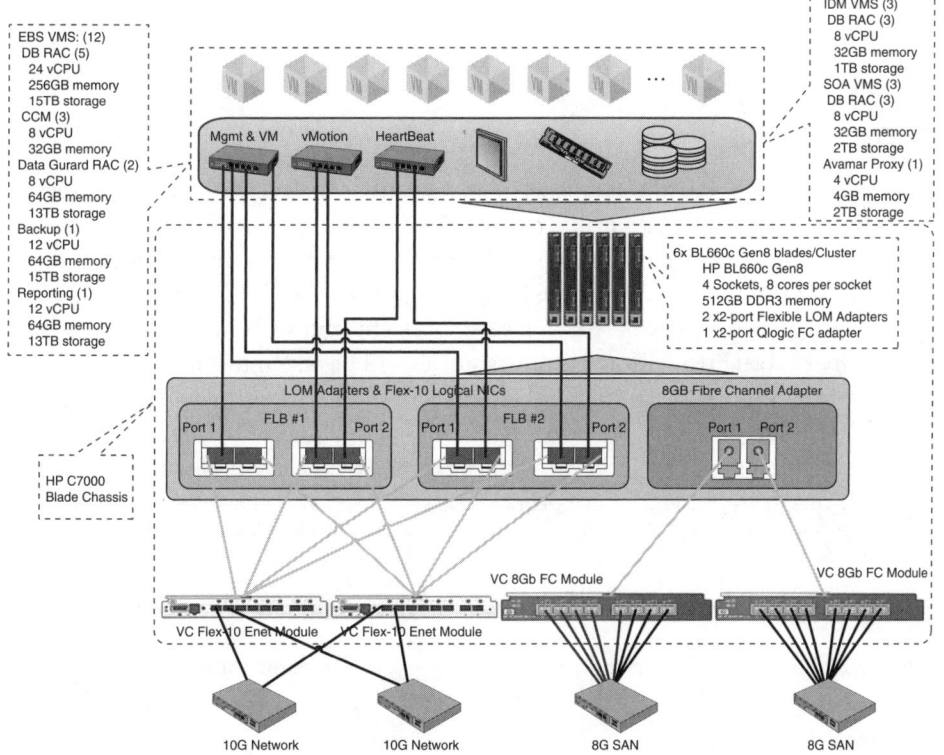

Figure 12-5 VMware IT high-level Oracle EBS and RAC environment

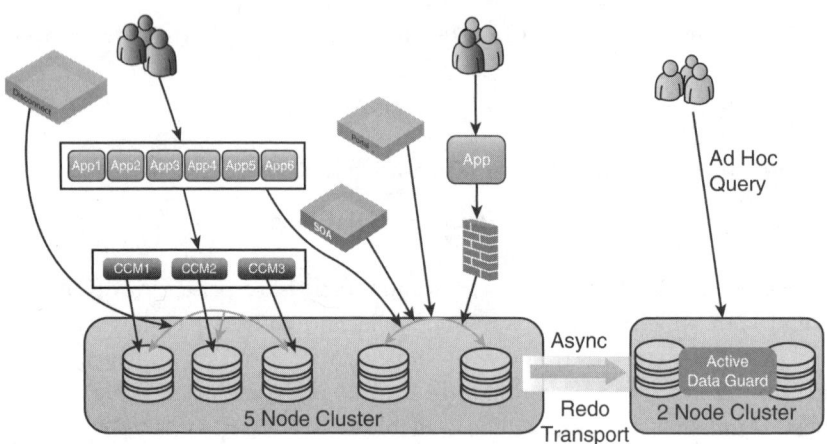

Figure 12-6 VMware IT Oracle RAC five-node monster VM cluster

So Many Others

VMware has more than 500,000 customers and many tens of thousands who have virtualized infrastructure for the database management systems, some of whom have been already described in this chapter. Any effort to comprehensively cover even a small sample of the broad customer base would be futile, so we have attempted to list and describe a set of prominent and highly visible customers with very successful and somewhat unique implementations. Other substantial customer success stories will be added to a later version of this work. However, it is important to highlight, in addition to the customer success stories already mentioned, certain events that are especially useful in understanding the theme of this book. The customers and the events together encompass the omnipresent four V's: viability, value, versatility, and visionary proposition.

Working with Events

Although you can find more information on VMworld panel sessions online at vmware.com and by watching the videos that are linked right here, this section briefly discusses those panels.

The subject of Oracle on vSphere has been a staple at many major IT conferences over the past decade, including include VMworld (both U.S. and Europe), VMware Partner Exchange (PEX), Oracle Open World (OOW), Independent Oracle User Groups (IOUG)

Collaborate, EMC World, NetApp Insight/Foresight as well as many other smaller events such as local OUG and VMware User Group (VMUG) events. The authors of this book are presenting at Oracle Open World 2014.

At the VMworld 2011 Las Vegas event, VMware elite partners gathered in the Venetian to espouse, advocate for, and embellish on their experiences in this space. The group included Dave Welch of HOB, Jeff Browning from EMC, Chris Williams, who was at the time with Cognizant but has since moved on to Dimension Data, Charles Kim of Viscosity, and Howard Ostrow, who is an original Oracle Certified Master. This group constituted a veritable "who's who" in the dataverse of Oracle on vSphere.

http://www.youtube.com/watch?v=rwEs9et26mI

At the VMworld 2013 San Francisco event, VMware had a group of highly successful Oracle customers gather to answer pertinent questions regarding both the uniqueness and communalities of their implementations. Brian Pearson from General Electric Appliance and Lighting discussed their incredible use of Site Recovery Manager for their Oracle environment, Eric Buono from Blue Cross Blue Shield of Michigan discussed their overall success, Scott Haverfield of the Idaho Supreme Court answered questions regarding the massive 47-site Idaho Supreme Court's implementation, and Brent Dunington from the University of British Columbia elaborated on the story told earlier in this chapter.

https://www.youtube.com/watch?v=KreFutmwGZs&feature=youtu.be

At the VMworld 2013 San Francisco event, the panel was focused on applications that run on Oracle running on vSphere. The panel consisted of Dan Young from Indiana University who was discussed in the case study earlier in this chapter. Mike Peters from Conagra represented his company and discussed their SAP on Oracle implementation, and Jon Tucker from First National Bank of Nebraska conversed about the success of their many application implementations. Wrapping up the 2014 panel was Kris Cook from SITA who contributed his input regarding their home grown applications. Each of these panelists, and the organizations represented by them, are included in the long list of successful House of Brick customers.

The members of this massive audience were treated to a broad range of success stories that traversed four distinct verticals with nearly a dozen well-known or proprietary critical applications. Everyone having attended this elite panel session should have left with clarity of understanding, centered on the idea that Oracle on vSphere was a compelling proposition because the stories that were told depicted some of the largest, most critical and most sophisticated implementations that anyone would encounter under any circumstances.

Summary

The types of implementations discussed in this chapter are examples of where versatility becomes true alacrity and where we actually start to delve into the facets and features of modern Cloud architectures. Clouds come in many shapes and sizes, but they all must possess certain fundamental attributes. The case studies we have studied in this chapter are customers of both Oracle and VMware, and they are the pioneers of running Oracle on vSphere.

We have taken great care in this chapter and this book to refer to the Oracle RDBMS when we intend to talk about the database. We have given equal deference when referring to a specific application that uses an Oracle database regardless of whether it is an Oracle application. It is for that reason that we have named this book *Virtualizing Oracle on vSphere*. The title is explicitly referring to all things Oracle, not only the database, and the case studies cited and described in this chapter illustrated that point much better than any chapter summary that we could write. Finally, it is important to emphasize in this, the final chapter summary, the four V's that are thematic to this book. Note that each of the four V's is highlighted in this chapter; after all, the ultimate reasoning behind any customer's decision to move their BCAs and respective databases to the platform of virtualized hardware known as vSphere is the reverberating combination of each of these seemingly separate categories. The four V's are simply components that lead to a decisive resonant conclusion: that running Oracle on vSphere results in running the world's most powerful software combination.

Book Conclusion

According to the National Institute of Standards and Technology (NIST), the most essential attributes of a Cloud, are on-demand self-service provisioning and rapid elasticity. It is reasonable that an intricate facet of this definition should be the attribute of 100% abstraction between the user resources and the hardware. However, many of the vendors that have products that are built on the "official" definition of the Cloud cannot make that claim. We have listed the link to the NIST Cloud definitions here.

http://www.nist.gov/itl/csd/cloud-102511.cfm

Throughout this book, we have journeyed through the sophisticated ideas of the Oracle RDBMS as well as the platform of virtualized hardware known as vSphere. More important, we have discussed how those two evolutionary software products both have individually permanently altered the history of IT but how they are also completely complementary. The thorough reader will recognize the undeniable fact that when combined, these individually marvelous technologies render each other more effective, and when used in concert, bring to their joint customers an unparalleled database management and infrastructure solution.

Chapter 1, "Introduction to Oracle Databases on Virtual Infrastructure," discussed the idea of the four V's of virtualization. First, technical personnel would never consider a platform, even a capable platform of virtualized hardware such as vSphere, without being completely convinced that it was a viable platform to run enterprise-class applications. Second, once the question of viability was settled, both technical and management personnel would need to be convinced that there was innate value in vSphere itself. Only a compelling argument that vSphere would bring substantial value to their BCAs and the respective databases that those applications ran on would be adequate for them to consider a platform transformation, especially one that led to a virtualized environment. Third, we considered how all personnel who have a stake in these important applications want to be ensured that they are not locked into any particular component of the physical stack, so it is imperative for them to understand the complete versatility at the heart of the fundamental VMware proposition. Finally, the fourth V is that of vision. The main question at the heart of the strategic concerns is "what will this all look like in a few years?" Throughout the book, we have endeavored to focus on each of the four V's that were central to this chapter's particular focus.

Chapter 2, "Virtualization and High-Performance Oracle Workloads," discussed high-performance workloads and introduced a number of application examples to elucidate those points. The examples are not actual case studies and do not contain real customer data. They do, however, serve the purpose of illustrating both the basic approach to virtualization as well as highlighting the key benefits of virtualization for business-critical environments. We also discussed other aspects of the initial phases of the adoption of a platform of virtualized hardware by presenting the long list of challenges that face modern IT professionals such as sprawl, ever-increasing support and licensing costs, and the fear of newly introduced technologies.

Architecture was the subject of Chapter 3, "Oracle Databases and Applications in Virtual Infrastructure: Architectural Concepts." We introduced the features of vSphere as well as the peripheral products as they relate to the application and database architects immediate and long-terms needs and aspirations. High availability was introduced as an important consideration, and therefore we started the discussion, which would persist throughout the book, about Oracle RAC. You learned about the various aspects of performance from the architectural perspective. We discussed the various factors that are significant when undergoing a consolidation effort. The most important concept (satisfying expected aggregate performance) centered on was the idea of *right-sizing*. This is the simple notion of allocating the exact amount, but only the exact amount, of resources needed to a VM that the applications that run within that VM actually use. The various approaches to the individual resources vary, but the idea of right-sizing remains consistent.

Best practices were the subject of Chapter 4, "Oracle on vSphere Best Practices." A central idea of this chapter is the main pillar of the Oracle on vSphere proposition, which is the axiom that very little changes about Oracle when run on vSphere. This is because ESXi is a nonparavirtualized hypervisor that does not change the kernel of any OS that is running as a guest operating system. The axiom implies that the basic ideas of classic Oracle database best practices to include database storage layout will remain the same in the virtual environment as the nonvirtual. DBAs and vDBAs are familiar with the fundamental ideas of Oracle best practices, making this subject little more than a review, with the emphasis on the fact that very little needs to be adjusted to run Oracle on vSphere as opposed to on a nonvirtualized system.

We also discussed the various different network protocols that you can use within the scope of network best practices as well as the ideas of network isolation and prioritization. The storage discussion in this chapter included a comparison of Virtual Machine File System (VMFS) and raw device mapping (RDM). You learned that very little performance exists difference between the two but that VMware highly recommends the use of VMFS absent compelling reasons to do otherwise.

There is little doubt that an intrinsic requirement of the great majority of production-level Oracle implementations is some degree of high availability, as discussed in Chapter 5, "Oracle Database High Availability: Planned and Unplanned Downtime." The degree of that high availability is a subject of the specifics of the negotiated service level agreement (SLA) between the application owners and the various operational administrators and ultimately dependent on how much the responsible party is willing to pay.

You learned that regardless of the amount of technological prowess innate within the Oracle software or the effort exerted by the Oracle DBA, the high availability outcome is made better when the Oracle software and database are run on vSphere. It is indisputable that Oracle RAC is the most powerful and sophisticated database management technology in human history, and it is equally indisputable that its high availability upshot is made more effective when run on vSphere. We discussed many examples, such as downtime for hardware maintenance being eliminated when running on vSphere and the how to properly utilize maintenance mode. If you take one succinct and powerful message from this book, it should be that vSphere and Oracle RAC are two completely complementary technologies. And if a DBA decides, after the requisite due diligence, to implement Oracle RAC, the same motives that led that courageous DBA to choose RAC should translate to the decision to run RAC on vSphere.

Chapter 5 also introduced some of the more impressive performance and functional stress tests that have been done to date. These tests highlighted the vSphere capability of vMotion when used in conjunction with Oracle RAC. We described how numerous tests proved the effectiveness of vMotion when moving an Oracle RAC node between physical hosts even when that RAC node was under high stress. The Principled Technologies report showed that RAC nodes could be transitioned between physical ESXi hosts simultaneously when under high stress without any disturbance to the functioning of the RAC nodes.

Performance workloads and functional stress tests were the subjects of Chapter 6, "Performance Workload and Functional Stress Test Studies." Here the reader learned about the stress tests introduced in Chapter 5, but in much more depth. The architectures used in those tests were elaborated on in great detail. The RAC workload characterization study was also described in detail.

We discussed at length the impressive concurrent vMotion tests run at Principled Technologies first introduced in Chapter 6, in which three separate RAC nodes under high stress were simultaneously transitioned via vMotion without any false ejections or fencing anomalies.

In Chapter 7, "Support and Licensing," we detoured from the technical to the political aspects of the proposition of running Oracle on vSphere and discussed the basic ideas of support and licensing. We have seen how both Oracle Corporation and VMware GSS provide unprecedented support for Oracle software running on vSphere to include the RDBMS as well as the peripheral application products. Most importantly, we discussed how VMware has its own set of Oracle support specialists who can and will address all Oracle-related issues and maintain focus on any Oracle-related concern under all circumstances until the issue is resolved. We discussed how this exceptional team will pursue a particular problem that presents with some degree of ambiguity as to its root cause through the provisions provided by the Technical Software Alliance Network (TSANet). The GSS Oracle Support team will use TSANet to collaborate with Oracle support until the customer problem is solved and the customer is satisfied.

Consolidating will always save resources and subsequently money. Chapter 7 covered the various positive outcomes of the different approaches to consolidation. The obvious conclusion of the licensing discussion is that when a joint Oracle and VMware customer understands the specifics of their respective license agreements, they will save money when they properly and comprehensively consolidate.

We broke performance down into its four requisite dimensions in Chapter 8, "Performance Management and Monitoring." These dimensions are compute, memory, networking, and the ever-important storage. The allocation of compute resources, for example, starts with a precise understanding of the actual CPU utilization rate of the application or database to be virtualized. Once the administrators understand both the peak and average workloads, they can then make an educated assessment of the compute resources to be allocated to the VM. If hyperthreading is available, the VMAdmin will make certain that it is enabled on the physical host but then decide, based on various criteria discussed in

Chapter 8, whether to leverage hyperthreading on the VM level. The administrators may also decide to overcommit on the physical host if appropriate for that particular environment. A plethora of options allow the VMAdmin and the DBA to create a completely customized environment for their Oracle databases and applications.

Memory allocation is a much simpler proposition than the apportionment of compute power. The more critical an application, the more important it is to guarantee that all the memory used by that application is mapped to physical memory. Memory reservations should be set to accommodate all the shared memory used by an Oracle database and/or application running in a VM. That is a simple statement, and it is a completely true statement. Although vSphere has quite sophisticated memory management techniques, such as ballooning, all of which were discussed at length in Chapter 8, the goal is to avoid using any of those capabilities. We provided formulations to estimate the amount of shared memory an Oracle database uses, and that total should be specified within the memory reservation. To finish this discussion, we will again reiterate that there is no recommendation that we give more seriously than to carefully set and use memory reservations for important Oracle databases.

Establishing adequate networking for Oracle implementations is a relatively straightforward exercise. We advised DBAs and VMAdmins to separate the VMkernel traffic from the vMotion traffic and from the public network traffic. We also advised administrators to consider using a Virtual Distributed Switch (VDS) as opposed to a set of vSwitchs if only for the ease of management. In addition, we highly recommended that special attention be paid to the guarantee of bandwidth and isolation of the network for the private interconnect between Oracle RAC nodes.

We discussed the necessity of using the paravirtualized network driver provided with vmtools, vmxnet3. We also deliberated on the value and the hazards of using jumbo frames, with the conclusion being that jumbo frames were worthwhile provided 10GigE bandwidth and jumbo frames were available at every network hop. We made it clear that the jumbo frames and 10GigE proposition was especially compelling when using IP storage, particularly Network File Storage (NFS). Finally, we noted that the future will bring significant changes in the philosophy of the approach to networking in the virtualized environment.

Our storage discussion revealed how storage allocation and management was mostly a matter of arduous and careful arithmetic. There are many different valid choices with regard to the storage component of the stack and many different philosophical approaches. The storage discussion truly spotlights the versatility perspective of the four V's theme of running Oracle on vSphere and so thematic to this book. VMware is truly agnostic with regard to storage, but given that unwavering commitment, the discussion becomes far-reaching. So, rather than run the risk of rehashing large parts of Chapter 8, we will summarize the main categories of storage as Internet Protocol (IP), Fibre Channel (FC), and direct attached.

We will also, however, again remind you of the most important points and warnings of the storage discussions. Size your storage appropriately for your expectations. In other words, do not expect vSphere to work magic, because the laws of physics will limit the outcome. If you run too many high-I/O VMs on the same storage access paths, the throughput will be inadequate, and your expectations will remain unsatisfied. This point seems axiomatic as the intrepid reader, the experienced IT administrator, or even the attentive civilian would agree. But as referenced a number of times throughout this text, 90% of the problems addressed by VMware support relate directly to badly configured storage.

Use the paravirtualized SCSI driver for the virtual controllers managing most high-work-load virtual disks, with the rare exception of those that are extremely highly latency sensitive, such as those that contain certain very highly latency-sensitive redo logs. Use classic Oracle best practices for disk layout when the array will allow. The classic best practices for storage layout are still worthwhile to consider to whatever extent possible, even when a modern storage array comes preconfigured from the factory.

VMware recommends the use of VMFS by default for two main reasons. First, all future features will be supported because the future direction of VMware is coincidental with VMFS. Second, very little performance difference exists between VMFS and its ancient virtual counterpart RDM. Although in certain cases RDMs do make sense to consider, as described in Chapter 8, there are very few remaining compelling reasons not to use VMFS.

If using NFS storage, consider using in-guest NFS with Oracle Direct-NFS (dNFS) for the database files; that approach has almost complete unanimity of support from most experts in the field, including the authors of this book.

There is a multidimensional angle to right-sizing that we discussed that involves all the dimensions of performance, but most importantly processing. Resource flexibility is a luxury not afforded to nonvirtualized systems, but it is a staple of those that are virtualized. The Hot Add capability, which is an innate feature of vSphere, allows the VMAdmin or the vDBA to add resources dynamically without even a reboot of the operating system in most cases. Oracle has been able to take advantage of newly introduced processors in the operating system for many years by simply reconfiguring many of its dynamically adjustable values to reflect the new CPU count. The number of latches is dynamically altered as well as the parallel process, which, of course, can present difficulties as well as benefits.

Chapter 9, "Business Continuity and Disaster Recovery," covered the always controversial, often misunderstood, and sometimes underrated subject of business continuity and disaster recovery. You learned that disaster recovery (DR) and high availability (HA) are two separate subjects and that the discussions should usually remain separate—the exception being the crossover technologies that allow HA to effectively become DR, such as vSphere Metro Storage Clusters (vMSC) certified solutions to include EMC vPlex and HP 3Par Peer-Persistence. Unfortunately, DR is often ignored because it is an intellectually challenging subject and considered to be a highly inconsequential problem, or it is deferred indefinitely because there are more "pressing" issues to solve. Of course, disasters never happen until they happen. But the experienced DBA, VMAdmin, or any IT professional understands that disasters are not about the dramatic events that capture the evening news. Disasters occur when mundane mistakes or everyday failures cause storages to fail, and if that storage is not redundant, a disaster has just occurred.

Site Recovery Manager (SRM) is a system that orchestrates workflows and facilitates coordination of failover of the VMs and the storage in the event of a disaster. SRM allows for controlled testing of those scenarios. Chapter 9 discussed the details of a variety of disaster scenarios and the various outcomes. We also discussed how SRM can be combined with the Oracle DR products and tools such as Data Guard and Golden Gate. The vDBA can develop a comprehensive DR system to protect against all types of failures, from the mundane storage failure to the random data block corruption to the catastrophic disaster that might dominate the breaking news. The experienced vDBA will take advantage of the variety of arrangements made possible by combining the capabilities of the VMware and Oracle toolsets to satisfy the requirements of the individual DR SLAs.

The always essential topic of backups is central to Chapter 10, "Backup and Recovery." That chapter covered the basic ideas of backups, both classic and modern, that are pertinent to Oracle and Oracle when run on vSphere. The chapter included advice and ideas specific to certain common hardware platforms. Most importantly, we emphasized the idea that the approaches to backing up databases, and in a greater sense BCA environments, does not fundamentally change when running on vSphere. Although backups become easier when running on virtualized infrastructure and leveraging the capabilities of vSphere, the need for backups does not change, and the requirements for recoverability are still based on the SLAs that must still be negotiated with the application owners.

Database-as-a-service (DBaaS) is the subject of Chapter 11, "Provisioning and Automation," so we discussed the future of databases and database provisioning and noted that the future is now. DBaaS comes in many different forms and flavors. Oracle uses the ideas of container and pluggable databases in 12c to attack the demand for DBaaS. VMware, EMC, and other storage partners of VMware address the issue from a number of different perspectives, including an actual public Cloud (vCloud Hybrid Service [vCHS]) service offering to a series of engineered solutions.

These solutions start with vCloud Automation Center (vCAC) as the DBaaS provisioning tool. Preexisting "blueprints" are customized to allow for sizing and specific template configurations prior to provisioning. The vDBA in collaboration with the VMAdmin will add their specific adjustments and then allow for access on whatever level the internal procedures and policies demand.

Flash storage arrays such as ExtremeIO and Pure Storage allow for extremely fast provisioning as well as storage-level features that integrate with vSphere through the VMware Advanced Array Integration (VAAI) interface. This allows for significant offloading of certain operations that can be more effectively handled by the storage. The arrays themselves have significant individualized capabilities that add significant value to the overall and individualized solutions.

Finally, Chapter 12, "Case Studies," allowed the authors of this book to highlight the greatest success stories that constitute the proof of the ideas described in this book. We described a number of powerful publically available case studies, and we described some aspects of their individual journeys resulting in their use of virtualized infrastructure for Oracle.

We want to add a final note. We are in the midst of an industry-wide transition to the ideas of the software-defined datacenter, and soon the world will be embracing the reality of complete stack virtualization as the changes that VMware brought to the server with virtualization are replicated on the network and storage layers.

The network discussion now includes the capabilities of VMware NSX, which is the network virtualization and security platform for the software-defined datacenter. Basically, rather than using the existing network software's capabilities and being subject to its limitations, VMware is extending the virtualization paradigm that has been so successful on the server level to both the network and the storage. The future looks bright in both these areas.

The storage arena includes the ideas of vFlash Cache, which is the capability of a host-level cache being used by the VM to store often read blocks, thus minimizing physical storage access for repetitive reads. Other new storage concepts, such as virtual storage-area network (vSAN), are now available and allow local storage on a cluster of physical hosts to be accessed as a virtual SAN. Virtual volumes, or vVols, will allow the DBA or the VMAdmin to take a snapshot of the VM at the storage level. These descriptions are only the proverbial "tip of the iceberg" of what these new features will provide in terms of functionality. The possible applications to Oracle are limited only by the imaginations of the vDBAs.

The precipitous uptick in the adoption rate of Oracle on vSphere over the past few years has been palpably obvious. A mere 3 years ago, we would deliver sessions at Oracle-related conferences on subjects connected to Oracle virtualization with sparse audiences, and our message, although not rejected, was received with a combination of confused stares and unenthusiastic hesitation. In 2014, however, when we ask the average audience for a show of hands regarding those who have virtualized or intend on virtualizing some part or all of their Oracle environments, we are commonly overwhelmed by the positive response; 50%, 60%, sometimes 75% percent of the audience raises their hands. Their questions are now of the advanced variety, which, of course, is the reason that the time has come for the writing of this book.

It is clear that the industry is accepting the idea that the platform of virtualized hardware known as vSphere is an ideal platform on which to run all Oracle software. We have every reason to believe that the adoption rate will continue to increase. We will allow the reader and the vDBAs of the world to decide, but we have tried in earnest to carefully develop and present a compelling picture of the viability, value, versatility, and vision behind the compelling idea of running Oracle on vSphere.

Index

A

access latency, NFS storage, 187-190
ACID (Atomic, Consistency, Integrity and Durability), 269
actions, application blueprints, 307
Adapter for Hyperic Oracle Plug-in, 229
adapters, paravirtualized SCSI, 78
affinity, 158
aligning file partitions, 77-78
alignment, partitions, 220-222
allocation, memory, 336
American Tire Distributors (ATD) case study, 320
AMM (Automatic Memory Management), 168-169
AppD (Applications Director), 26
application blueprints
    actions, 307
    adding application components, 304
    adding dependencies, 305-306
    adding multiple NICs, 308
    adding services, 303
    binding properties, 306-307
    configuring, vCAC, 302-310
    disk profiles, 308-309
    external services, 309-310
    rapid provisioning, 310

application vendor recommendations, databases, sizing, 32-34
application-based replication, 248
applications
    accelerating delivery, 41
    BCAs (business-critical applications), 15
    DHW (data warehouse), 15
    legacy rehosting, 50
    QoS, improving, 41
    RAC (Real Application Clusters), virtual machines, 89-98
    reducing costs, 41
Applications Director (AppD), 26
architectures
    databases, 11-12
    ESXi, 38
    Optimal Flexible Architecture (OFA), 73
    RAC VMs, 123-124
array-based replication, 258-264
ASM (Automatic Storage Management), 1, 55, 224
    disk groups, virtual provisioning, 255-256
    managing files, 73-74
    versus LVMs, 225-228
ATD (American Tire Distributors) case study, 320

Atomic, Consistency, Integrity and
    Durability (ACID), 269
Automatic Memory Management (AMM),
    168-169
Automatic Storage Management (ASM).
    See ASM (Automatic Storage
    Management)
automation, 289-291
availability, databases, enhancing, 19-21
Avamar, backup and recovery, 279-281
AWR (Automatic Workload Repository),
    reports, 155

B

back-end storage connectivity, 127
backup, 286, 338
    Avamar, 279-280
    cold/offline, 270
    data pump/export/import, 272
    databases, 10
        Database Backup strategy matrix, 287
    DG (Data Guard), 284-286
    essential components, 268
    Flashback, 272
    hot/online, 271
    in-guest software solutions, 270
    methods, 270-273
    NetApp, 274
        integrating with vSphere, 274
        Snap Creator, 276
        Snap Manager, 276
        Snapshot, 274-276
        storage, 277
    Netbackup, 273
    principles, 270-273
    RMAN, 271
    storage vendor solutions, 273-274
    VDPA (VMware Data Protection
        Advanced), 273, 282
ballooning, memory, 171-172
BCAs (business-critical applications), 15, 18
Benchmark Factory for Databases, 30
best practices, 55, 82, 334
    configuring storage-related, 68-76
    ESX, implementing host, 57-58
    implementing memory-related, 61-64

implementing vCPU-related, 65-68
    networking guidelines, 78-79
binding properties, application blueprints,
    306-307
BIOS settings, maximizing performance, 58
block alignment, 220-222
Blue Medora, 157
Browning, Jeff, 331
Buono, Eric, 331
business-critical applications (BCAs), 15, 18

C

capacity planning, databases, 8
case studies, 339
    ATD (American Tire Distributors), 320
    EMC IT, 321
    GMP (Green Mountain Power), 323
    Indiana University, 318-319
    ISC (Idaho Supreme Court), 324-325
    University of British Columbia, 326
certification, VMware environments,
    143-147
chief information officers (CIOs), 16
chief technology officers (CTOs), 16
CIOs (chief information officers), 16
clients, dNFS, configuring, 217-218
Closson, Kevin, 30
cloud
    CloudDBA, 290
    vCAC (vCloud Automation Center), 338
    vCloud Hybrid Service, 338
clusters, 157
    EMC VPLEX stretch clusters, 6-7
    isolated ESXi, 150-151
    RAC (Real Application Clusters), 55
        virtualizing, 51-52
        virtual machines, 89-98
    vMSC (vSphere Metro Storage Clusters),
        338
    VMware, 42
cold/offline backups, 270
Comparison of Storage Protocol
    Performance in VMware vSphere
    5.x, 72
compliance (IT)
    achieving, 24
    maintaining, 48

configuration
    vCenter SRM connections, 257
    vSwitches, 125
connections, vCenter SRM, breaking and
        configuring, 257
consolidating databases, 48-51
consolidating platforms, 17-19
controllers
    LSI, 222
    pvSCSI, 222-224
cost-effective disaster recovery, 19-21
costs, applications, reducing, 41
CPUs (central processing units)
    affinity, 158
    best practices, 65-68
    overhead, 157
    ready time, 160-164
    versus vCPUs, 159-164

D

dashboard, Oracle Database
    configuring metric graph widget, 235
    creating, 233-235
    finalizing, 236-238
database administrators (DBAs). See DBAs
        (database administrators)
Database Backup strategy matrix, 287
database-as-a-service (DBaaS). See DBaaS
        (database-as-a-service)
databases
    architectures, 11-12
    backup and recovery, 10
    backup methods, 270-273
    capacity planning, 8
    consolidating, 48, 51
    DBaaS (database-as-a-service), 22,
        311-314, 338
    DBAs (database administrators), 1, 8, 15
        general tasks, 9-10
        performance management role, 158-159
    design, 8
    designing on VMware, 41-42
        HA (high availability), 44-47
        scalability on demand, 42-44
    enhancing availability, 19-21
    HA (high availability), 10, 44-47, 84-86

HammerDB, 30
    meeting SLA demands, 27-30
    monitoring, 10
    Oracle Database
        virtualization, 291-302
        dashboard, 233-238
        server metrics, 230
    performance studies, 36
    performance tuning, 10
    protecting against downtime, 98-100
    protecting applications, Symantec
        AppHA, 86-87
    protecting virtualized environment,
        vSphere HA, 84-86
    provisioning rapid server environments,
        21-22
    recovery, cost-effective, 19-21
    security, 9
    sizing application vendor
        recommendations, 32-34
    sizing workloads, 30-31
    stress studies, 36
    troubleshooting, 10
Data Guard (DG). See DG (Data Guard)
data pump/export/import backups, 272
data warehouse (DWH) application, 15
datacenters
    consolidating platforms, 17-19
    implementing dynamic resource
        management, 26-27
    protecting, site recovery manager, 46-47
    SDDC (software-defined datacenter), 4
    virtualizing, 17
datastores
    adding extents to, 223
    growing, 224
DBaaS (database-as-a-service), 22, 311, 314,
        338
    allocating storage, 313
    benefits, 312-313
    choosing components, 313-314
DBAs (database administrators), 1, 8, 15
    general tasks, 9-10
    performance management role, 158-159
decision support system (DSS) kits, 30
dedicated RAC interconnect networks, 178
dependencies, application blueprints, adding
        to, 305-306

designing databases on VMware, 41
    HA (high availability), 44-47
    scalability on demand, 42-44
DG (Data Guard), 20, 248-249, 284-286
    combining with VR (vSphere
        Replication), 250-251
    repairing logical data block corruption,
        249
Direct-NFS (dNFS). *See* dNFS
    (Direct-NFS)
disaster recovery, cost-effective, 19-21
disaster recovery (DR) plan, 337
    configuring VMs in, 261
    creating, 257-261
    editing, 261
    exporting, 264
    removing, 261
    running, 263-264
    testing, 262
disk groups (ASM), virtual provisioning,
    255-256
disk profiles, application blueprints, 308-309
Distributed Resource Scheduler (DRS), 19,
    23, 43-44, 167
dNFS (Direct-NFS), 215-216, 270, 337
    client configuration, 217-218
    verification, 218-219
downtime, protecting databases against,
    98-100
DRD (Distributed Resource Scheduler), 19
DR (disaster recovery) plan, 337
    configuring VMs in, 261
    creating, 257-261
    editing, 261
    exporting, 264
    removing, 261
    running, 263-264
    testing, 262
dropped packets, monitoring, 177-181
DRS (Distributed Resource Scheduler), 23,
    43-44, 167
DSS (decision support system) kits, 30
Dunington, Brent, 331
DWH (data warehouse) application, 15
dynamic expansion, VMFS, 223
dynamic resource management, datacenter,
    26-27

E

eager-zeroed thick disks, 225-226
EMC IT (Information Technology) case
    study, 321
EMC VPLEX stretch clusters, 6-7
EMC World, 331
Enterprise Manager, vCOPS, 228-238
ESX
    hosts and VMs, SCSI queues, 191-219
    implementing host best practices, 57-58
    upgrading, 60-61
ESXi, 1
    architecture, 38
    hosts and VMs, SCSI queues, 191-219
    hypervisor, 38-41
    isolated cluster, 150-151
    upgrading, 60-61
    virtualization, 3
Esxtop, 109
events, 330-331
    key trigger, 24-25
exporting
    recovery history results, 264
    recovery plans, 264
extended page tables, 19
extents, adding to datastores, 223
external services, application blueprints,
    309-310

F

fast recovery area (FRA), 255
file systems
    dNFS (Direct-NFS), 270
    VMFS (Virtual Machine File System),
        282-284
files
    managing, ASM, 73-74
    partitions, aligning, 77-78
first write penalties, 225
Flashback, 272
flash storage arrays, 339
four Vfs, 1-2, 16, 37, 56, 83-84, 105, 142,
    242, 267, 317, 333
four V2s approach, 289

four Vss (viability, value, versatility, and vision), 155-156
FRA (fast recovery area), 255

G

Giles, Dominic, 107
GMP (Green Mountain Power) case study, 323
GOS (Guest Operating Systems), 270
Green Mountain Power (GMP) case study, 323
growing datastores, 224
Guest Operating Systems (GOS), 270

H

HA (high availability), 83, 104, 337
    databases, 10
        protecting against downtime, 98-100
        protecting virtualized environment, 84-86
    designing databases, 44-47
    enhancing databases, 19-21
    protecting applications, 86-87
    vMotion, 121-122
    VMware, 121-122
HammerDB, 30
hardware-assisted Memory Management Unit (MMU), 61
Haverfield, Scott, 331
Health Insurance Portability and Accountability Act of 1996 (HIPAA), 48
high availability. See HA (high availability)
high-performance scheduler, 19
HIPAA (Health Insurance Portability and Accountability Act), 48
hosts
    ESX, implementing best practices, 57-58
    RAC nodes, transitioning between, 100-103
    VMware, 42
hot-add feature (VMware), 42
hot/online backups, 271
HP Load Runner, 30

Huge Pages, 167-172
Huge Pages (Linux), 19
hypervisor (ESXi), 38-41

I

IBM SAN Volume Controller (SVC), 5-6
Idaho Supreme Court (ISC) case study, 324-325
IgniteVM, 156
Independent Oracle User Groups (IOUG) Collaborate, 331
Indiana University case study, 318-319
information technology (IT). See IT (information technology)
in-guest software solutions, backing up data, 270
installing
    OEM adapter, 232
    RAC, 130-132
Iometer (Windows Server 2008), 198-203
Iperf network testing tool, 176
ISC (Idaho Supreme Court) case study, 324-325
isolated ESXi cluster, 150-151
isolation, 158
IT (Information Technologies), 16
    achieving compliance, 24
    compliance, maintaining, 48
    organization hierarchy, 17
    VMware, 327-330

J-L

jumbo frame networks, 179-181

key trigger events, 24-25
Kim, Charles, 331

lab architecture, Oracle Database, 295-296
large pages, supporting, 64-65
large-scale order entry benchmark kit (Swingbench), 122-124
Large-Scale Order Entry Benchmark Kit with Swingbench, 106-108
latency, 157

layout, storage, 126-129
legacy application rehosting, 50
licensing, 335
    Oracle, 141-143
licensing Oracle, 147-154
    isolated ESXi cluster, 150-151
    subcapacity approach, 153
    subcluster approach, 151-152
Linux Huge Pages, 168
load testing networks, 176
logical data block corruption, repairing, DG
        (Data Guard), 249
logical volume manager, 224
LSI controllers, 222
LVMs (logical volume managers)
        versus ASM (Automatic Storage
        Management), 225-228

M

managing files ASM (Automatic Storage
        Management), 73-74
Mani, Kannan, 327
Maritz, Paul, 7
mega vMotion-RAC functional stress test,
        135-138
memory
    allocation, 336
    AMM (Automatic Memory
            Management), 168-169
    ballooning, 171-172
    oversubscription, 18
    performance management, 164-167
        Huge Pages, 167-172
        NUMA (non-uniform memory access),
            172-175
        TPS (Transparent Page Sharing), 172
    virtual, 4
    virtual machine memory reservation, 18
Memory Management Unit (MMU),
        hardware-assisted, 61
memory-related best practices,
        implementing, 61-64
metric graph widget, Oracle Database
        dashboard, configuring, 235
metric sampling, 155

migration
    Oracle Database, physical to virtual,
        296-302
    virtual machines, 117-119
minimizing server sprawl, 27
MMU (Memory Management Unit),
        hardware-assisted, 61
monitoring databases, 10
multinode RAC, implementing, 90-91
multipathing, 178

N

nested page tables, 19
nested/extended page tables, 19
NetApp
    integrating with vSphere, 274
    Snap Creator, 276
    Snap Manager, 276
    Snapshot, 274-275
        backing up virtualized databases,
            275-276
        restoring virtualized databases, 277-279
    storage, backing up virtualized
            databases, 277
NetApp Insight/Foresight, 331
Netbackup, 273
netstat, dNFS verification, 219
network bandwidth, vMotion, 177-178
Network File Storage (NFS), 336
Network Virtualization and Security
        platform (NSX), 4
networking guidelines, 78-79
networks
    dedicated RAC interconnect, 178
    jumbo frame, 179-181
    load testing, 176
    monitoring dropped packets, 177-181
    storage, 178
    VM, 178
NFS (Network File Storage), 336
    benchmark test, setup notes, 217
    datastores, backing up virtualized
            databases, 277
    dNFS (Direct-NFS), 215-216
        client configuration, 217-218
        verification, 218-219

mounting directly to ESXi hosts, 213
SCSI queues, 183
storage, 185-187
    access latency, 187-190
NICs (network Interface cards), application
    blueprints, adding multiple, 308
NIST Cloud definitions, 332
NSX (Network Virtualization and Security
    platform), 4
NUMA (non-uniform memory access),
    172-175

O

Occam's Razor, 268
OCFS (Oracle Clustered File System), 74
OCI (Oracle Call Interface), 103
OEM (Oracle Enterprise Manager) adapter,
    228
    installing, 232
OFA (Optimal Flexible Architecture), 73
offline/cold backups, 270
OLTP (online transaction processing)
    loads, 106-107, 157
One Node (RAC), implementing, 89-90
online/hot backups, 271
online transaction processing (OLTP)
    loads, 106-107, 157
ONS (Oracle Notification Services), 103
operating system processes, 59-60
Optimal Flexible Architecture (OFA), 73
Oracle
    adoption rate, 339
    licensing, 147-154
        isolated ESXi cluster, 150-151
        subcapacity approach, 153
        subcluster approach, 151-152
    obtaining support, 145
    software support and licensing, 141-143
    support
        negotiating terms of, 147
        obtaining, 146
Oracle Call Interface (OCI), 103
Oracle Clustered File System (OCFS), 74
Oracle Database
    virtualization, 291-306
        migration, 296-302

virtulization
    business scenario, 294-295
    facilitating deployments, 294
    lab architecture, 295-296
Oracle Database dashboard
    configuring metric graph widget, 235
    creating custom, 233-235
    finalizing, 236-238
Oracle Database server metrics, 230
Oracle Enterprise Manager (OEM)
    adapter, 228
    reports, 155
Oracle I/O Numbers (ORION). See
    ORION (Oracle I/O Numbers)
Oracle Notification Services (ONS), 103
Oracle Open World (OOW), 330
Oracle RAC node vMotion test, 132-135
Oracle server, creating workflow, 299
organization hierarchy, IT, 17
ORION (Oracle I/O Numbers), 203-208
    configuring disk shares, 209
    disk-to-disk, 204-206
    dNFS (Direct-NFS), 215-216
    RAID, 209-210
    RDM (raw device mapping), 211-219
    SIOC (Storage I/O Control), 206-208
    storage path selection, 210
Ostrow, Howard, 331
overhead, 157
oversubscription, memory, 18

P

packets, dropped, monitoring, 177-181
page tables, nested/extended, 19
paravirtualized SCSI adapters, 78
partitions, alignment, 220-222
Partner Exchange (PEX), 330
PCI (Payment Card Industry) standards, 48
Pearson, Brian, 331
Performance Analyzer, 156
performance management, 157, 239-240
    BIOS settings, 58
    DBA role, 158-159
    memory, 164-167
        AMM (Automatic Memory
            Management), 168-169

Huge Pages, 167-172
NUMA (non-uniform memory access), 172-175
TPS (Transparent Page Sharing), 172
networking, 175-176
dropped packets, 177-181
network load testing, 176
processing power, 159-164
storage, 181, 219-220
ASM (Automatic Storage Management), 225-228
block alignment, 220-222
LSI controllers, 222
LVMs (logical volume managers), 225-228
NFS (Network File System), 185-190
pvSCSI controllers, 222-224
SCSI queues, 182-185, 191-219
terminology, 157-158
vCOPS, 228-238
vSphere, 79-81
performance studies, 36
performance tuning, 10, 155
PGA (process global area), 165-167
platforms, consolidating, 17-19
process global area (PGA), 165-167
processes, operating systems, 59-60
protecting databases against downtime, 98-100
provisioning, 289-291
application blueprints, 310
pvSCSI controllers, 222-224

Q-R

QoS (quality of service), applications, improving, 41

RAC (Real Application Clusters), 1, 55, 103-104, 139, 333-335
architecture, 123-124
deploying on vSphere, 92-98
installation, 130-132
mega vMotion-RAC functional stress test, 135-138
multimode, implementing, 90-91
nodes, transitioning between hosts, 100-103

node vMotion test, 132-135
One Node, implementing, 89-90
virtual machines, 89-98
virtualizing, 51-52
workload characterization studies, 105, 121-129
RAC Deployment Guide, 327
RAID, ORION, 209-210
RAT (Real Application Testing), 30
raw device mapping (RDM). *See* RDM (raw device mapping)
RDBMS (relational database management system), 11, 37, 104, 243
RDM (raw device mapping), 282, 334
detriments, 211
ORION, 212-219
RDM-P, 211-212
RDM-V, 211-212
versus VMFS (Virtual Machine File System), 76-77, 282-284
ready time, CPUs, 160-164
Real Application Clusters (RAC). *See* RAC (Real Application Clusters)
Real Application Testing (RAT), 30
RecoverPoint, 256
RecoverPoint with vCenter SRM, 256
recovery, 286, 338
Avamar, 279-281
DR (disaster recovery) plan
configuring virtual machines in, 261
creating, 257-264
editing, 261
exporting, 264
removing, 261
running, 263-264
testing, 262
essential components, 268
FRA (fast recovery area), 255
NetApp, Snapshot, 277-279
principles, 270-274
Recovery Manager, 268
SRM (Site Recovery Manager), 241-245
breaking connections, 257
configure connections, 257
exporting system logs, 257
protecting new virtual machines, 258-259
removing virtual machines, 260

testing, 251-253
  unprotecting virtual machines, 260
Recovery Manager (RMAN), 10, 268
recovery point objective (RPO), 241
recovery time objective (RTO), 241
redo logs, 255
relapsed time, 157
relational database management system
    (RDBMS), 11, 37, 104, 243
replication
  application-based, 248
  array-based, 258-264
  combining DG and VR, 250-251
  DG (Data Guard), 248-249
    repairing logical data block corruption,
      249
  SRM (Site Recovery Manager), testing,
    251-253
  storage array-based, 247
    vSphere, 253-255
  VR (vSphere Replication), 245-246
reports
  AWR (Automatic Workload Repository),
    155
  Oracle Enterprise Manager, 155
reprovisioning, 26-27
resource pools, VMware, 42
restoring. See recovery
rEsxtop, display, 188
RMAN (Recovery Manager), 10, 271, 279
rolling view widget, Oracle Database
    dashboard, configuring, 235
RPO (recovery point objective), 241
RTO (recovery time objective), 241

S

SAN Volume Controller (SVC), 5-6
Sarbanes-Oxley (SOX) Act, 48
scalability, 157
  designing on demand, 42-44
scale-out charts, multiple virtual machines,
    116-117
SCSI controllers, virtual, 76
SCSI queues, 182-185
  ESX/ESXi hosts and VMs, 191-219
  Iometer, 198-203

NFS, 183
ORION (Oracle I/O Numbers), 203-208
  storage benchmarking VMDK, 193-196
  storage path throughput, 192-193
SDDC (software-defined datacenter), 4, 7
security, databases, 9
server architecture, databases, 11-12
server environments, databases,
    provisioning, 21-22
servers
  database, consolidating, 48-51
  sizing vendor guidelines, 35
  sprawl, minimizing, 27
service level agreements (SLAs), 7, 19
service-oriented architectures (SOAs), 26
SGA (system global area), 12, 165-166
SICO (Storage I/O Control), 206-208
Silly Little Oracle Benchmark (SLOB), 30
single-instance workload study, 106-121
Site Recovery Manager (SRM). See SRM
    (Site Recovery Manager)
SLAs (service level agreements), 7, 19
  meeting demands, 27-30
SLOB (Silly Little Oracle Benchmark), 30
Snap Creator (NetApp), 276
Snap Manager (NetApp), 276
Snapshot (NetApp), 274-275
  backing up virtualized databases, 275-276
  restoring virtualized databases, 277-279
snapshots, VMware, 228
SOAs (service-oriented architectures), 26
software support, VMware environments,
    143-147
software support and licensing, Oracle,
    141-143
software-defined datacenter (SDDC), 4, 7
source environment, Oracle database lab
    architecture, 296
spindle busy time, 190
SRAs (storage replication adapters), 21, 247
SRM (Site Recovery Manager), 21, 241-245,
    338
  breaking connections, 257
  configure connections, 257
  exporting system logs, 257
  protecting datacenters, 46-47
  protecting new virtual machines,
    258-259

removing virtual machines, 260
    testing, 251-253
    unprotecting virtual machines, 260
stakeholders, identifying key, 53-54
storage
    best practices, 68-76
    categorizing virtualization technologies,
        71
    benchmark tools, 31, 193-196
    DBaaS (database-as-a-service),
        allocating, 313
    layout, 114-115, 126-129
    networks, 178
    path throughput, SCSI queues, 192-193
    SRAs (storage replication adapters), 21,
        247
    vendor backup solutions, 273-274
    virtualization, 5
storage array-based replication, vSphere,
    253-255
Storage I/O Control (SIOC), 206-208
storage performance, 219-220
    ASM, 225-228
    block alignment, 220-222
    LSI controllers, 222
    LVMs, 225-228
    monitoring, 181
        NFS, 185-190
        SCSI queues, 182-185
    pvSCSI controllers, 222-224
    SCSI queues, 191-219
storage replication adapters (SRAs), 21, 247
stress tests, 36
    mega vMotion-RAC functional stress,
        135-138
stretch clusters, EMC VPLEX, 6-7
studies
    RAC workload characterization, 121-129
    single-instance workload, 106-121
subcapacity licensing, 153
subcluster licensing, 151-152
support, 335
    Oracle, 145-146
SVC (SAN Volume Controller), 5-6
Swingbench large-scale order entry
    benchmark kit, 30, 122-124

switches, VDS (Virtual Distributed
    Switch), 336
Symantec AppHA, protecting applications
    with, 86-87
system global area (SGA), 12, 165-166
system logs, vCenter SRM, exporting, 257

T

TAF (Transparent Application Failover),
    103
target environment, Oracle database lab
    architecture, 296
teaming, 178
Technical Software Alliance Network
    (TSAnet), 335
temp files, 255
testing
    recovery plans, 262
    SRM vSphere replication, 251-253
tests
    stress, 36
        mega vMotion-RAC functional stress,
            135-138
        Oracle RAC node vMotion, 132-135
        single-instance workload study, 106-121
        twenty-four hour workload, 131-132
thin provisioning, VMDKs, 225
throughput, 157
timekeeping, virtual machines, 81
TPS (Transparent Page Sharing), 172
Transparent Application Failover (TAF),
    103
Transparent Page Sharing (TPS), 172
troubleshooting databases, 10
TSAnet (Technical Software Alliance
    Network), 335
twenty-four hour workload test, 131-132

U-V

University of British Columbia (UBC) case
    study, 326
upgrading ESX/ESXi and vSphere, 60-61

VAAI (vSphere Storage APIs - Array
    Integration), 226-227
vCAC (vCloud Automation Center), 21-22,
    338
    configuring application blueprints,
        302-310
vCenter
    environment, Oracle database lab
        architecture, 296
    Operations Manager Suite (vCops), 25
    SRM (Site Recovery Manager), 241-245
        breaking connections, 257
        configure connections, 257
        exporting system logs, 257
        protecting new virtual machines,
            258-259
        removing virtual machines, 260
        testing, 251-253
        unprotecting virtual machines, 260
vCloud Automation Center (vCAC), 21-22,
    338
vCloud Hybrid Service, 338
vCOPS (vCenter Operations Manager), 25,
    156, 228-238
    Adapter for Hyperic Oracle Plug-in, 229
    Database server metrics, 230
    OEM (Oracle Enterprise Manager)
        adapter, 228
vCPUs (virtual CPUs), 4
    best practices, 65-68
    hot-add, 119-120
    ready time, 160-164
    versus CPUs, 159-164
vDBA (virtual DBA), 290
VDPA (VMware Data Protection
    Advanced), 273, 282
vDS (virtual distributed switch), 4, 336
verification, dNFS, 218-219
vFabric Application Director, 21
vFabric Data Director, 26
virtual CPUs (vCPUs). See vCPUs (virtual
    CPUs)
virtual DBA (vDBA), 290
virtual distributed switch (vDS), 4
virtual machine disks (VMDKs). See
    VMDKs (virtual machine disks)
Virtual Distributed Switch (VDS), 336

virtualization, 1, 12
    ESXi, 3
    Oracle Database, 291-302
        migration, 296-302
    Oracle Database
        business scenario, 294-295
        facilitating deployments, 294
        lab architecture, 295-296
    SDDC (software-defined datacenter),
        4, 7
    storage, 5
    vSphere, 3
virtualized databases
    backing up
        NetApp Snapshot, 275-276
        NetApp storage, 277
        NFS datastores, 277
    restoring, NetApp Snapshot, 277-279
virtualized environment, databases, vSphere
    HA, 84-86
Virtualizing SQL Server with VMware:
    Doing It Right, 173
virtual machine disks (VMDKs). See
    VMDKs (virtual machine disks)
Virtual Machine File System (VMFS).
    See VMFS (Virtual Machine File
    System)
virtual machines, 4
    live migration, 117-119
    memory reservation, 18
    protecting new, 259
    protecting new, 258-259
    RAC (Real Application Clusters), 89-98
        architecture, 123-124
    removing, 260
    scale-out chart, 116-117
    scale-out test, 113
    single-instance workload study, single
        scale-up results, 111-112
    storage layout, 114-115
    timekeeping, 81
    unprotecting, 260
virtual memory, 4
virtual network interface card (vNIC), 4
Virtual Networking Concepts and Best
    Practices, 79
virtual provisioning, ASM disk groups,
    255-256

virtual Real Application Clusters DBA
    (vRAC-DBA), 290
virtual storage-area network (vSAN), 339
VM networks, 178
VMDKs (virtual machine disk), 4, 71, 184
    thin provisioning, 225
    storage benchmarking, 193-196
VMFS (Virtual Machine File System), 43,
    71, 282-334, 337
    dynamic expansion, 223
    versus RDM (Raw Device Mappings),
        76-77, 282-284
vMotion (VMware), 23, 43, 103-104, 117
    HA (high availability), 121-122
    mega vMotion-RAC functional stress
        test, 135-138
    network bandwidth, 177-178
    RAC node vMotion test, 132-135
    transitioning RAC nodes between hosts,
        100-103
vMSC (vSphere Metro Storage Clusters),
    338
VMware
    advising customers of, 149
    clusters, 42
    designing databases on, 41-47
    DRS (Distributed Resource Scheduler),
        43-44
    HA (high availability), 121-122
    hosts, 42
    hot-add feature, 42
    IT (Information Technologies), 327-330
    obtaining VMware support, 146
    resource pools, 42
    snapshots, 228
    solving deployment and management
        issues, 25-26
    VAAI, 226
    vMotion, 23, 43, 103-104, 117
        HA (high availability), 121-122
        mega vMotion-RAC functional stress
            test, 135-138
        network bandwidth, 177-178
        RAC node vMotion test, 132-135
        transitioning RAC nodes between hosts,
            100-103

VMware Data Protection Advanced
    (VDPA), 273, 281-282
VMware on VMware, 327
VMware Partner Exchange (PEX), 330
VMworld, 330
vNIC (virtual network interface card), 4
VR (vSphere Replication), 245-246
    combining with DG (Data Guard),
        250-251
vRAC-DBA (virtual Real Application
    Clusters DBA), 290
vSAN (virtual storage-area network), 339
vSphere, 333
    best practices, 334
    certification, 144-145
    integrating with NetApp, 274
    maximizing HA capabilities, 45
    monitoring performance on, 79-81
    storage array-based replication, 253-255
    supporting large pages, 64-65
    upgrading, 60-61
    virtualization, 3
vSphere Metro Storage Clusters (vMSC),
    338
vSphere Replication (VR), 245-246
vSphere Storage APIs - Array Integration
    (VAAI), 226-227
vSwitches, configuring, 125

W-Z

Welch, Dave, 331
Williams, Chris, 331
workload, 333
    databases, sizing, 30-31
    OLTP (online transaction processing)
        loads, 106-107
    RAC workload characterization study,
        121-129
    single-instance workload study, 106-121